D1823187

IEE CONTROL ENGINEERING SERIES 43

Series Editors: Professor P. J. Antsaklis
Professor D. P. Atherton
Professor K. Warwick

TRENDS in INFORMATION TECHNOLOGY

Other volumes in this series:

TRENDS
in
INFORMATION
TECHNOLOGY

Edited by

D.A. LINKENS
&
R.I. NICOLSON

Peter Peregrinus Ltd. on behalf of the Institution of Electrical Engineers

Published by: Peter Peregrinus Ltd., London, United Kingdom

© 1990: Peter Peregrinus Ltd.

Peter Peregrinus Ltd.,
Michael Faraday House,
Six Hills Way, Stevenage,
Herts. SG1 2AY, United Kingdom

**A CIP catalogue record for this book
is available from the British Library**

ISBN 0 86341 231 9

Printed in England by Short Run Press Ltd., Exeter

Contents

Preface

This book is based on the lectures given at a SERC-sponsored Vacation School entitled 'Trends in IT' in July 1990 at Sheffield University. For many years the Information Technology Directorate of the Science and Engineering Research Council have sponsored Vacation Schools in the area of Systems and Control Engineering. This particular course was initiated two years ago as a collaborative venture with the Computing Section of SERC. On that occasion there was no formal publication of the lecture material. The success of the course and the timeliness of the material has encouraged us to produce the lectures this time in book form.

The students on the course come from a wide background in engineering and computer science. As a result, the lectures are intended to give a broad exposure to many aspects of IT relevant to the applied sciences. Because of the vast nature of the subject, it has been necessary to be partially selective in the material covered. Thus, the important aspect of office automation has been omitted, although research concepts in databases and information processing are included.

The book has been organised loosely into five parts. After an introductory chapter on expert systems, the first section on *Computing* deals with developments in the enabling technologies of software and hardware for computers. Part 2 is concerned with *Systems*, meaning the incorporation of modern IT concepts into industrially-related environments. The emphasis is primarily on software engineering and AI methodologies. Part 3 deals with *Robotics*, both from a control perspective and an application-driven viewpoint. Advanced concepts in 3D vision are included in this section. Part 4 covers a range of topics loosely gathered under the heading of *Cognitive science*. This includes contributions on Prolog programming related to this particular subject, neural networks, and the problems of speech recognition. The final section is on the important subject of *Human-computer interaction* (HCI). This importance is illustrated via a number of wide-ranging research areas of current interest.

We are grateful for the support given by the Departments of Control Engineering and Psychology, University of Sheffield, in running the course. Also, we acknowledge gratefully the financial support of the Science and Engineering Research Council which made it possible to run the course.

Professor D. A. Linkens
Dr R. I. Nicolson
University of Sheffield

List of contributors

Dr R. I. Nicolson
Dr P. J. Scott
Mr P. Tomlinson
Department of Psychology
University of Sheffield
Western Bank
Sheffield S10 2TN
UK

Dr M. Crawford
Dr P. D. Green
Professor M. J. Holcombe
Dr J. M. Kerridge
Mr A. J. H. Simons
Department of Computer Science
University of Sheffield
Portobello Centre, Pitt Street
Sheffield S1 4DD
UK

Professor J. P. Frisby
Dr J. E. W. Mayhew
Dr S. B. Pollard
Dr J. Porrill
AI Vision Research Unit
University of Sheffield
Western Bank
Sheffield S10 2TN
UK

Dr S. Bennett
Dr R. F. Harrison
Professor D. A. Linkens
Dr A. S. Morris
Department of Control Engineering
University of Sheffield
Mappin Street
Sheffield S1 3JD
UK

Professor M. F. Lynch
Department of Information Studies
University of Sheffield
16 Claremont Crescent
Sheffield S10
UK

Professor R. Leitch
Intelligent Automation Laboratory
Department of Electrical Engineering
Heriot-Watt University
31-35 Grassmarket
Edinburgh EH1 2HT
UK

Professor E. A. Edmonds
LUTCHI
Department of Computer Science
Loughborough University
Loughborough LE11 3TU
UK

Professor P. Taylor
Department of Electrical Engineering
University of Hull
Hull HU6 7RS
UK

Chapter 1

Introduction to research issues in expert systems

John P. Frisby

1 OVERVIEW

The goal of this chapter is to provide a tutorial overview of current research issues in the field of Expert Systems (ES) as a prelude to subsequent chapters which deal in detail with case studies and various Intelligent Knowledge Based Systems (IKBS) techniques. The chapter will therefore concentrate on introducing basic concepts and terminology[1] and will presume little or no prior knowledge. The literature on ES and IKBS[2] is vast and can be only touched on here, with the reference list offering pointers to ways of entering that literature.

The chapter will begin with a description of the classic Expert System architecture. This is followed by short notes on various research themes running through the ES literature.

2 THE CLASSIC EXPERT SYSTEMS ARCHITECTURE

An ES is commonly described as a program which incorporates a wide base of knowledge in a restricted domain and which uses complex inferential reasoning to perform tasks that if a human expert did them would be said to require intelligence. One point immediately worthy of note here is that it should not be presumed from use of the terms *knowledge, reasoning* and *intelligence* in this description that the program can be said to understand the task in the sense that the human expert does. To go beyond a statement that an ES program simulates some limited species of human expertise to a claim that it possesses 'human-level understanding' would be foolhardy indeed for present-day ES. It would also raise deep problems in the philosophy of computational models of mind which will not be tackled here (see Churchland, 1988, for a good introductory review), although the major short-comings of present-day ES to be reviewed later provide a background to some of the complexities involved.

The expert knowledge in an ES is typically represented *explicitly* and *declaratively* in a *long-term memory (LTM)* or *knowledge base* of *production rules* (figure 1). The explicit and declarative character of the rules consists in them being written as *If/Then* statements comprising a *Left Hand Side* specifying the *Condition(s)* that must be met for the *Right Hand Side* to execute some *Action(s)*. Hence these rules are sometimes called Condition/Action pairs. An example of a production rule taken from a classic ES called MYCIN that was written to assist a physician who is not an expert in the field of antibiotics with the diagnosis and treatment of blood infections is as follows:

---

[1] All technical terms will be italicised but for brevity often only the context in which they are used will provide an (implicit) definition.

[2] Note that the labels ES and IKBS are frequently used interchangeably.

Figure 1 Classic Expert Systems Architecture

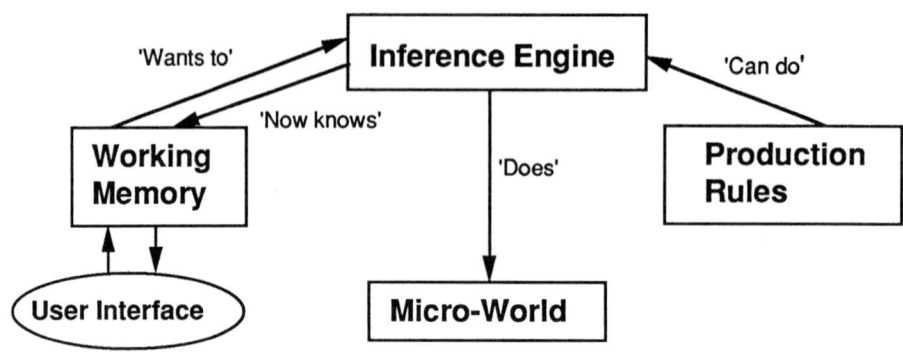

Figure 2 Overview of AI Systems (based on Nillson, 1982)

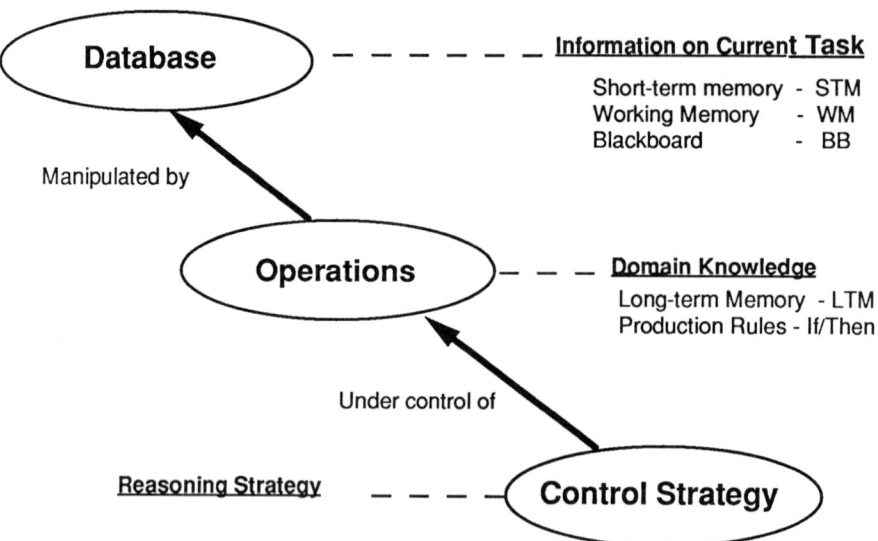

If   (1)   The Stain of the organism is gramneg, and
     (2)   The morphology of the organism is rod, and
     (3)   The aerobicity of the organism is aerobic

Then   There is strongly suggestive evidence (0.8) that the class of the organism is enterobacteriaceae.

Information about the current task is stored in a *working memory*, also variously called a *blackboard, short-term memory [STM]*, or simply the *database* (figure 2). Information in the working memory can arise either from *input* data delivered via a *user interface*, or it can appear as the consequence of production rules in the LTM being *fired*. Hence if the above rule were to be *triggered*, the 'suggestive evidence' that enterobacteriaceae is the organism in question would be held in the working memory where it might well contribute to other rules being fired on the next processing cycle.

It is frequently the case that several rules can be activated by the information in the working memory at any one time, leading to the *conflict resolution problem*. This is solved by an *inference engine* whose job it is to control the reasoning undertaken by the system from moment to moment. *Exhaustive search* of all possible sequences for applying the rules in the knowledge base is usually out of the question for realistic large-scale problems. Hence the inference engine often has embedded in it *heuristic* control strategies such as: *recency* (choose the most recent rule), *specificity* (choose the most specific rule), *refractoriness* (don't choose the rule that has just fired; this helps stop the program getting hung up in processing loops), and *order* (choose rules in a sequence laid down in advance by the programmer that reflect some notion of the task structure).

The inference engine can utilise *forward* or *backward chaining* of the rules. As an example of the former, suppose data item A was presented to a system as an input. This could lead to firing of the rule *If A then B*; which in turn leads to the firing of the rule *If B then C*; this leads to firing of the rule *If C then D*; allowing the system to conclude D. This type of chaining is used in the classic ES called *R1* (now called *XCON*) that configures Vax computers. The alternative backward chaining method is used in the even more classic ES called MYCIN and works as follows. Again suppose A has been given as input but now also suppose that the system is trying to answer the question "Can I conclude D?". A search of the knowledge base discovers the answer is "Yes if C is true" because of the rule *If C then D*. This leads to the next enquiry which is "Can I conclude C?". This time the answer is "Yes if B" because of the rule *If B then C*. This leads to the query "Can I conclude B?", to which the answer is "Yes" because of the rule *If A then B*. At last the sequence terminates because A is true, hence the ES asserts that "D is true".

It can be helpful (but it seems rarely done) to distinguish forward/backward chaining from *forward/backward reasoning* (Jackson, 1986). Forward /backward chaining refers only to the way rules are activated, i.ei whether Working Memory elements are matched against the left hand or right hand side of the rule, with processing then flowing from the other side.   Forward/backward reasoning refers to the problem solving strategy underlying how the program as a whole is organised. For example, it turns out that R1, at a certain level of abstraction, can be described as reasoning backwards from its main goal via subgoals even though the program, when running, is forward chaining on its production rules!

To summarise, the classic production rule ES architecture has a clean separation of three major components: a *database* which is manipulated by set of *operations* that change its contents under the influence of a *control strategy* (Nilsson, 1982; figure 2).

How does this architecture differ from conventional programming? The latter has a more rigidly organised style, in which step-by-step algorithms are followed through in a sequence that is completely predetermined by the programmer (absence of bugs permitting), even when complex branching is involved. The exhaustive search of that style is sufficient for problems with rather few potential solutions. Yet many problems that human experts readily cope with are ill-defined and open-ended, with the search space for solutions rendered so large by the combinatorial explosion of possibilities (think of playing a game such as chess) that a different approach is required. Hence the emergence of the ES way of programming in which heuristic search methods are used under the control of an inference engine. It is worth noting here, however, Hayward's (1984) critique in which he claims that many ES, including MYCIN, do not in fact solve significantly large search problems (see later comments on this theme).

It is sometimes claimed that the rule-based ES architecture has the virtues of:-
(a) *simplicity*;
(b) *modifiability*: it is easy to change a rule or add a new one;
(c) *expressiveness* : it is (allegedly) easy to read the rules and hence appreciate the information in the knowledge base; and,
(d) *modularity*: each rule, which can in principle have a long list of conditions comprising the *If* side of the rule, can be thought of as a small module; or more realistically, groups of rules can be arranged to operate as a unit, sometimes called a *knowledge source*. One simple if clumsy way to do this is to label rules as members of a functional grouping by inclusion of a suitable statement in the *If* list of each one, eg *If* The current goal is X, and A, and B, *Then* ...., where the label X is effectively the module identifer. Some ES shells offer *frame-based* facilities that can be used for a similar purpose (see subsequent chapter by Linkens).

However, whether these alleged virtues of the ES architecture apply to even modestly sized systems (of eg 50 - 100 rules) is debatable. It easy enough to write down a few rules, or to change existing ones, but not so easy to predict the resulting performance, and this problem usually scales horribly with size. Surprises are commonplace and can lead to debugging problems as great as in any other form of programming. Problems regarding the suitability or otherwise of the conflict resolution strategy are frequent; this is one reason why commercially available *expert system shells* with built-in unchangeable control strategies are often found too restrictive by their purchasers who thus find it necessary to write their own ES architecture from scratch (the large expensive IKBS environments such as KEE and ART are another story: they permit great scope for configuring an ES architecture suitable to the particular problem being tackled).

Also, representation of task knowledge as unstructured lists of rules firing away 'short-sightedly on local knowledge' under some rather general conflict resolution strategy can make it difficult for the user to appreciate what is going on, though this problem is alleviated in frame-based systems that bring semantically-related clusters of rules together. In short, the rule-based code is not always that 'expressive', either for the creator or for a new user perusing the code. Worse still, the ES style of programming can lead the creator to neglect proper study of the nature of the problem being solved because it presents a highly seductive temptation to rush in with a host of seemingly sensible rules. All too often, these proceed to flail around wildly, needing ever more ad hoc patching if they are to 'work' at all reasonably, if indeed they ever do when exposed to real data beyond that used for their original development. It is difficult to over-emphasise the point that utilisation of an ES architecture is no substitute for careful thought about *the structure of the problem* being solved (Marr, 1982; see later).

3 RESEARCH THEMES IN THE ES LITERATURE

Amongst the many important research issues raised by the classic ES architecture are the following:

3. 1 Knowledge Acquisition

An ES credo is *"In domain-specific knowledge lies the power"*. Early work in AI on problem solving tried to build highly general purpose reasoning architectures, the classic being Newell and Simon's *General Problem Solver, GPS*. Lenat (1978) provides a good introductory review of that work, explaining how general methods proved weak and how this realisation led to emphasis on exploiting task-specific knowledge. But getting such knowledge from an expert is difficult. Indeed, this problem is often regarded as *the* bottleneck in creating an ES. The various contributions in Kidd (1988) provide a good review of current research in *knowledge acquisition* and Hart (1986) provides an excellent introductory text at the undergraduate level.

Experts are usually unable to articulate their knowledge at all well. Moreover, textbooks are often imprecise, inaccurate, incomplete, or out of date. The usual knowledge acquisition method is therefore intensive discussion between the ES *knowledge engineer* and the subject expert(s), with iterative refinement of knowledge in the evolving ES as its performance on test data is found wanting. Refinement is assisted in many ES by a *rule trace* facility which allows a user to 'walk through' the sequence of rules that fired in generating an answer to some enquiry. This can be useful in identifying the source of a disagreement between ES and expert, and hence to modification of an existing rule or insertion of a new one.

More structured techniques for knowledge acquisition than simply intensive interviewing have been explored, such as the use of *repertory grids*. This is a psychological procedure devised by Kelly for eliciting the *personal constructs* used by individuals in trying to understand their lives and the people in it: the usual methodology involves asking a person which two members of a set of three people are alike in some way and different from the third, a procedure that generates constructs such as friendly/unfriendly, happy/sad, tall/short, etc etc. This technique can elicit constructs from experts regarding their domain of expertise (see Hart, 1986, and Kidd, 1988, for details of how it can be used in the ES context).

Experts are usually busy people who cannot give unlimited time to interviews with the knowledge engineer. Hence methods have been devised for *machine induction* of rules from test data sets. Commercially available packages are now available (based for example on Quinlan's inductive algorithm ID3 - *Inductive Dichotimizer 3*) but although they can be useful they are no panacea (see Hart, in Kidd, 1988). Genetic algorithms have also been used to good effect for automatically generating rules. The key idea on which they rely is breeding new rules by a random reassortment of parts of the lists of conditions and actions in existing rules. The effectiveness of the new rules is then assessed, and the better ones are allowed to enter a further generation of breeding and testing. This proceeds until the required goal is achieved, the whole learning sequence being modelled roughly on Darwinian evolution. Goldberg (1989) provides a superb introductory text on genetic algorithms.

The knowledge acquisition problem should not be under-estimated. Because it is so time-consuming, the knowledge engineer should be careful to ensure adequate access to the expert(s).This is the major reason why it is so important to secure the full support of senior management as a first step for anyone considering developing an ES in a business setting (d'Agapeyeff and Hawkins,1983). But failing to do that is only one of a wide number of mistakes that can be made in managing an ES project, the principal ones being choice of an inappropriate problem (too hard, too easy) and lack of clarity about project aims and objectives. Table 1 provides the long list of potential stumbling blocks for budding knowledge engineers set out by Hayes-Roth et al (1983). Many of these are characteristic of any large-scale software engineering enterprise, not just building an ES.

Table 1 Problems in Building an Expert System (Based on Hayes-Roth et al, 1983).

(a) Typical mistakes in managing an expert systems project
bad evaluation of project aims and objectives,
bad planning of time and resources,
inappropriate choice of knowledge domain,
imprecise objectives,
insufficient involvement of management,
failure to get agreement of schedule and objectives,
change of key staff during the project,
change of objectives without reassessment of feasibility,
inadequate documentation,
purpose not clear to management or users,
no targets or checkpoints.

(b) Before setting out to build an expert system ...
How important is this problem?
What would be the advantages of an expert system?
How common is the problem?
How important will it be in a few years' time?
Can the problem be easily defined?
Would it be practical to use a computer?
Has anyone tried a similar project elsewhere?
Who would use the expert system? Why?
Is there a shell we could use?
Is there any documentation?
How do the experts learn their expertise?
Can we spare an expert's time?
What resources do we need?
What might make this project difficult to develop?
Do the experts disagree?
How long does it take to become an expert?
How much can be invested in this project?
Are there any times when the experts are not available for consultation?
Is the knowledge complex, needing several inferences mechanisms and knowledge representations?
Will the expert system need up0dating frequently?
Can we tolerate imperfect output?
Will the development of the interface require great effort?

3.2 User Interface

It hardly needs to be emphasised that an ES lacking a good user interface, defined as the sum of all communication routes between the ES and its user, is likely to be rejected. The exact form of the user interface will clearly depend on the domain and scope of the ES but the question of *user modelling* is central: what can and cannot be assumed about the user's capacities, and how can that knowledge be exploited to create fluent interactions? Indeed, emphasis on a non-naive model of the end-user is one of the characteristics that distinguishes ES from conventional programming.

The general principles that Apple (1987) claim as the basis for the success of the widely-admired Macintosh user interface are helpful to bear in mind:

User centred: the guiding theme throughout is that users are instinctively curious; users desire control; people are skilled at manipulating symbols; people are productive and imaginative in challenging enjoyable environments.

Use real-world metaphors: eg files displayed as meaningful icons on the 'desktop'; they are quickly understood; they take advantage of people's direct experiences with their immediate world; concrete metaphors allow users to apply set expectations to computer environments.

Direct manipulation: eg dragging icons with the mouse; users want to feel in charge of the computer's activities; people expect their physical actions to have physical results.

User control: the user initiates and controls all activities; the user 'acts', the computer 'reacts'; in risky situations the computer provides warnings, but the user ultimately decides.

See-and-point: eg selection of icons with the cursor; recognition is better than recall; users select actions from alternatives presented on the screen; average users are not programmers and are not familiar with command-line interfaces.

Consistency: all applications disciplined to same style; hence no need to reinvent the interface with each application; users can transfer their knowledge from one part of the system to another with less likelihood of mistakes.

WYSIWYG: what you see is what you get; no secrets from the user; no abstract commands without immediate feedback.

Feedback and dialogue: keep the user informed of what's going on; provide immediate feedback; use visual effects, sounds and/or brief messages expressed in a user's vocabulary, not a programmer's; turn complex activities into small simple steps.

Forgiveness: users learn best through exploration; users make mistakes when they explore - forgive them by allowing them to reverse their actions - inform them in advance whenever they won't be able to.

Perceived stability: users are most comfortable in an environment that appears to stay the same; use consistent graphical elements, visual landmarks.

Aesthetic integrity: stress attractive visual displays, visual clarity, simplicity, consistency; visual confusion detracts from effectiveness; different 'things' should look distinct; use the skills of a graphic designer to take advantage of the visually rich possibilities.

General Design Suggestions: use both text and graphics but use icons wherever possible; use graphics to communicate, make the user's context clear; integrate graphics early in the design; keep graphics simple; avoid using too much text; break up large areas of text.

Testing an Interface Design: try rough ideas on users early in the design process - before a full prototype; test users regularly; iterate the design; use 'naive experts'; rigorous testing is not always essential; ask users to talk as they work; videotape users as they work.

Would that Unix designers had read the above list! Note that most but not all items apply mainly to visual interfaces, and they extend well beyond the field of ES interface design.

It is also worth noting that it is now feasible to contemplate ES interfaces incorporating quite sophisticated *natural language understanding* systems tuned to interpret typed messages relating to the particular domain of the ES. In considering the *dialogue structures* which either type of interface might support, a key issue that recurs again and again is the question of explanation, to which we turn next.

3.3 Explanation

This is the problem of how to answer the queries of a user as to *why* a particular conclusion has been reached. This is widely regarded as the crucial area in ES research on which progress is essential if ES are ever to lodge serious claims to incorporate a 'human-level understanding' of their domain.

The explanation problem is sometimes referred to as giving the user *a human window* (a phrase due to Michie) into the workings of the ES. Without this, the advice offered by the ES is likely to be ignored, particularly (and properly!) if that advice appears surprising and of high short-term cost to the user (..."launch the nuclear missiles immediately ..."). Regrettably, explanation facilities in current ES are most often limited to providing a trace of the rules that fired in reaching a given conclusion, or to a display of pre-canned explanantory notes. Either of these is better than nothing but neither is to be regarded as providing an adequate substitute for what an expert would say if called upon to justify a selected course of action. This area is closely related to the next research issue.

3.4 Deep vs Shallow Reasoning

Shallow reasoning is what most ES currently deliver: *if/then* rules firing away in a 'short-sighted' maner on local knowledge. The MYCIN rule illustrated above provides a typical example.

'Deepness' is a more difficult concept to pin down, definitions variously referring to notions such as causality, temporal reasoning, qualitative reasoning, reasoning from first principles, or reasoning from structure and function. Advocates of deep reasoning claim that richer explanations, more adequate dialogue structures, and higher flexibility in problem solving will all flow from its pursuit.

Interestingly, Keravnou & Washbrook (1988) report that CASNET, a medical ES that incorporates causal reasoning, is less well accepted by users than NEOMYCIN which does not but which scores more highly because at all times the user is made aware of what it is doing. They conclude that deepness may mean different things to the knowledge engineer and the user and that causal reasoning alone is insufficient.

The minimal requirement is that the user needs to be able to find out easily what factual and strategic knowledge is being used, and to be able to gain this information not just at the end of a consultation but at intermediate points. All too often, the rules logged in the database of productions blur factual knowledge about a domain with a particular reasoning strategy being used (such as top-down refinement). Also, the real reason why certain clauses are present in an *if* list of conditions is frequently far removed from the surface structure. For example, a rule in MYCIN that *inter alia* requires a patient to be at least 17 years old turns out to use age as a simple screening device for alcoholism - as children are unlikely to be alcoholics! A simple trace of the rules used to reach a given conclusion will not reveal such information.

A better term than deepness may be 'model based reasoning'. Figure 3 sets out the various levels for modelling expertise identified by Wielinga and Breuker (1986). Models of expertise can be made manifest using good visual displays (see e.g. the GUIDON-WATCH system of Richer & Clancy, 1987).

Figure 3 Layers of description of expert knowledge (based on Wielenga and Breuker, 1986)

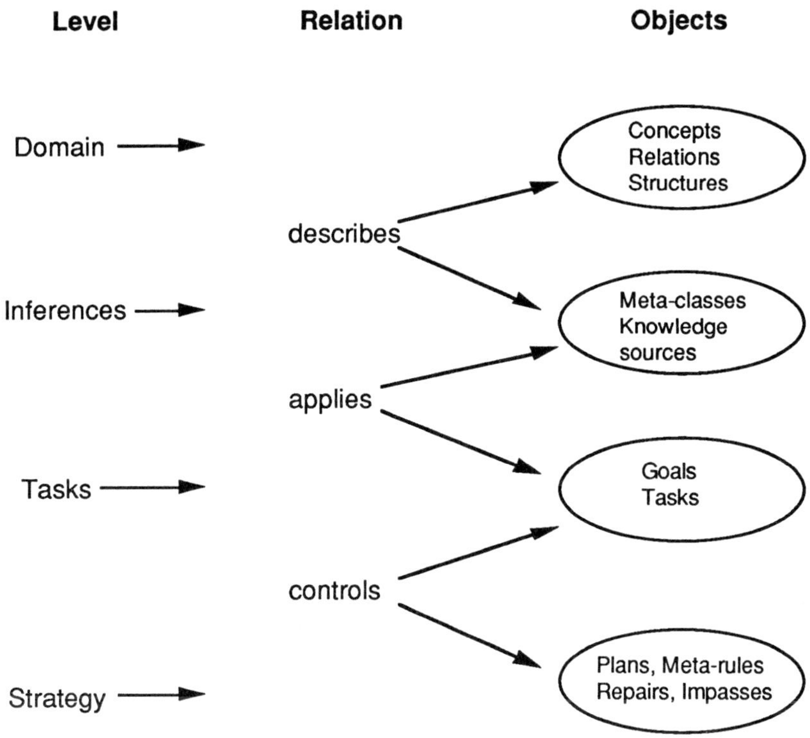

Level	Relation	Objects

Domain ⟶

describes

Concepts
Relations
Structures

Inferences ⟶

applies

Meta-classes
Knowledge
sources

Tasks ⟶

controls

Goals
Tasks

Strategy ⟶

Plans, Meta-rules
Repairs, Impasses

3.5 Handling Uncertainty

Experts frequently like to express their knowledge using terms such as 'frequently', 'usually', 'most often', etc. Many ES allow assertions to be added to the database with confidence ratings attached to them, as in the MYCIN rule cited above which when firedleads to the conclusion that the evidence is 'strongly suggestive' of enterobacteriaceae at a level of 0.8 on a scale up to 1. This approach has been strongly criticised for wildly inappropriate use of statistics, neglect of Bayes' Theorem, etc (White, 1984). The use of *fuzzy logics* is a principled solution to some uncertainty problems but not all (Hart, 1986, provides an elementary iintroduction to fuzzy reasoning; Graham and Jones, 1988, give an extended textbook account of the problems of uncertainty in ES).

3.6 Blackboard Architectures

The blackboard metaphor is due to Newell (see Craig, 1988): "Metaphorically, we can think of a set of workers, all looking at the same blackboard: each is able to read everything that is on it and to judge when he has something worthwhile to add to it." The claimed virtue in this scheme is that it breaks away from the need for an algorithmic style of programming in which one process follows another in a sequence pre-determined by the programmer according to the various eventualities foreseen.

The blackboard concept has not received a precise definition. The term is often used interchangeably with working memory, short term memory, or simply database. The first major blackboard system was the speech understanding system *HEARSAY* (Erman & Lesser, 1975; Erman, Hayes-Roth, Lesser & Reddy, 1980). This brought to the fore the non-trivial problems of controlling the integrity of a potentially massive blackboard memory structure that is read and written to by many processes. One current approach to this problem is to use a *control blackboard* to manage sophisticated control strategies for updating and maintaining the main blackboard (reviewed in Craig, 1988). Whether this approach is likely to pay dividends or simply lead to yet another set of integrity of memory management problems is a current research issue. The overall research goal can be described as 'autonomous asynchronous variable-grain competences communicating smoothly!' (Mayhew, personal communication). How to achieve that effective communication between knowledge sources is unknown.

3.7 Truth Maintenance Systems

It commonly happens that triggered rules add assertions to the working memory which are contradictory. It is thus necessary to detect such contradictory information and do something about it, i.e. to develop what are variously termed *belief revision systems, truth maintenance systems, consistency maintenance systems*. The conventional approach consists of blaming the contradiction on the most recent decision and changing it, termed *chronological backtracking*. An alternative proposed by Stallman & Sussman that started a great deal of AI research in belief revision is termed *dependency-directed backtracking*. This consists of changing not the last choice but the choice that caused the unexpected condition to occur. Martins & Shapiro (1988) provide a recent review and a source of references. Problems confronted in this field include: the *inference problem* (how do new beliefs follow from old ones?); the *nonmonotonicity problem* (what methods are suitable for recording that one belief depends on the absence of another?); *dependency recording* (what methods are suitable for recording that one belief depends upon another?); *disbelief propagation* (how should one ensure disbelief in all the conseqences of a proposition that is disbelieved?); and *revision of beliefs* (how best to change beliefs in order to get rid of a contradiction?).

3.8 Connectionism

The classic ES architecture incorporates so-called *explicit* representations of knowledge - the *If/Then* rules. Some problems addressed using that architecture, particularly classification or diagnosis tasks, are now being tackled with *neural networks* that rely on *implicit* knowledge, the latter being encoded in a distributed manner as the weights on the connections between massively interconnected 'neurone-like' computing elements - hence the term *connectionism*. Numerous algorithms have been proposed for training neural nets to recognise patterns of various types. Rumelhart & McClelland (1986, two volumes) give an overview of the field; Lippmann (1987) and Carpenter (1989) provide useful and brief tutorial reviews, as does the chapter here by Harrison. Sharkey (1989) provides a helpful introduction to some of the basic mathematics underlying network models to those unfamiliar with matrix algebra.

The neural nets field is currently a research hotspot and the rapid emergence of commercially viable systems are rumoured. Their potential includes the fact although it may take a large fast computer a long while to train a net on sample data, once trained the net then operates essentially instantaneously, especially if the weights learnt for the connections between the computing elements are laid down in silicon.

Neural net systems offer little or no prospect of providing helpful explanations as to why a particular decision has been made: the knowledge is 'in' the weights. But that may not matter for certain pattern classification applications; after all, we have little or no ability to introspect usefully into the processes mediating human visual object recognition and yet our abilities in that domain are exquisite. Also, it could well be that the reason human experts find it so difficult in general to reveal their expertise to knowledge engineers is that much of that expertise is 'compiled' into (real) neural net classifiers. Perhaps the medical expert that MYCIN struggles to duplicate, for example, is *inter alia* good at recognising patterns of symptoms and signs they have encountered rather than good at reasoning from first principles using rules.

There is a strong echo here of the arguments raised by Dreyfus and Dreyfus (1987) as to why skills cannot be represented by rules. They regard Socrates as the first known knowledge acquisition engineer to attempt (also without success, like his present-day counterparts) to extract expertise from experts in the form of rules. In Socrates' case, Euthyphro was the hapless expert who was unable to state the rules for what counted as pious behaviour, even though Euthyphro claimed to be able to recognise pious acts from impious ones. Dreyfus and Dreyfus go on to suggest that rather than the expertise of experts being the result of abstracting rules from many specific cases, it is only the *novice* who is reliant on rules. The expert does things differently, by developing the capacity to be a pattern recogniser of huge numbers of 'typical' cases (it has been estimated, they note, that a master chess player can distinguish roughly 50,000 types of positions). They say: "It seems that a beginner makes inferences using rules and facts just like an heuristically programmed computer, but that in most domains with talent and a great deal of involved experience the beginner develops into an expert who intuitively sees what to do without applying rules (p.326)." They go on to suggest that perhaps neural nets are the machinery for the ability to recognise fluently and without apparent effort thousands of special cases, knowledge of which, they maintain, underlies high-class human expertise in a given domain. For a review of attempts to compare the performance of neural net and rule-based representations of expert knowledge in present-day ES, see Hunt (1989).

3.9 The Final Commandment: Beware of Neglecting the Ever Present Need to Distinguish Different Levels of Understanding of Complex Information Processing Systems

Marr (1982) has made much of the claim that it is necessary to understand complex information processing systems, such as biological brains or man-made computers undertaking a given task, at three different levels, each complementary but each concerned with different issues:

1 *Computational Theory:* The questions raised here are two-fold. First, what exactly is the goal of the computation? And secondly, what method(s) can be devised for achieving the required goal? In short, what is the structure of the task to be solved, and what constraints does that structure provide as a foundation for a principled method for solving the task?

2 *Algorithm:* Exploiting the computational theory in a practical system requires attention to a second level of analysis, called by Marr the algorithm level. Here the issues are to do with achieving a workable implementation of the abstractly defined method(s) specified in the computational theory. This forces choices about the particular input and output representations to be used and the detailed sequence of processing steps needed to achieve the required input-to-output transformation. Marr (1982, p.20) defines a representation as a formal system for making explicit certain entities or types of information, together with a specification for how the system does this. He calls the result of using a representation a *description* of an entity in that representation. By an *explicit* description is meant one which makes the information required available for immediate use, that is, without any need for further work by subsequant processers using the description.

3 *Hardware:* Marr's third level of analysis concerns the question: how can the algorithm be realized physically? Often the same algorithm can be implemented in quite different technologies.   The choice will usually have much to do with practicalities such as availability and cost. For example, Marr (1980, p.24) observes that "wires [i.e. nerve fibres] are rather cheap in biological architectures, because they can grow individually and in three dimensions. In conventional [computer] technology, wire laying is more or less restricted to two dimensions, which severely restricts the scope for using parallel techniques and algorithms; the same operations are often better carried out serially."

Marr claimed that : "These three levels of analysis [computational theory, algorithm, hardware] are coupled but only loosely: The choice of algorithm is influenced for example, by what it has to do and the hardware in which it must run. But there is a wide choice available at each level, and the explication of each level involves issues that are rather independent of the other two (1982, p.25)".

Marr's (1982) book provides an excellent introduction to his general approach applied to vision: it has the merit of being written for a reader unfamiliar with the background literature. A tutorial review of Marr's approach is given by Frisby (1990).   Boden (1988) provides an excellent and broadly-based review of computational attempts to model mind, frequently using as a touchstone Marr's levels distinction to evaluate the worth of any given piece of research.

The need to distinguish different levels of discourse is accepted without question in computer science in the design and analysis of man-made complex information processing systems. Many technical concerns at the level of digital hardware are quite irrelevant to the business of devising good algorithms to run on that hardware. This is reflected in the important notion of a *virtual machine* in computer science, defined as a set of information-processing operations: "A physical mechanism (a calculator, a computer, or brain, perhaps) may instantiate a particular virtual machine which can be used as a basis for implementing other virtual machines (using programs which define operating systems, compilers, interpreters, and so on) (Sloman, 1980, p.403)."

Indeed, although Marr's particular prescription for the kind of analysis required at the computational theory level is distinctive, insistence on the general importance of this separate explanatory level does not originate with him. The whole enterprise of AI rests on Newell and Simon's assumption that "A physical symbol system has the necessary and sufficient means for general intelligent action (Newell, 1976, p.116)", which itself can be traced to Turing's analysis on the notion of 'computability' (see Johnson-Laird, 1988, for an introductory review). In other words, many different 'physical symbol systems' can support intelligence, not just biological ones. This is also the central, though not unchallenged, claim of the functionalist approach to the philosophy of mind (see Churchland, 1988). Marr's achievement was not therefore a new insight that different levels of analysis are required for understanding complex information processing systems, but a specification for what those levels are and what each should be concerned with.

In an entertaining and provocative epilogue with an imaginary interlocutor, Marr (1982) expresses in trenchant terms his view that analysis at the computational theory level has been neglected in much cognitive psychology and also in much artificial intelligence. For example: "As a computing mechanism, a production system [i.e. a rule-based IKBS] exhibits several interesting ideas - the absence of explicit subroutine calls, a blackboard-like communication channel, and some notion of a short-term memory. However, just because production systems display these side effects does not mean that they have anything to do with what is really going on [in human cognition]. For example, I would guess that the fact that short-term memory can act as a storage register is probably the least important of its functions. I expect that there are several 'intellectual reflexes' that operate on items held there about which nothing is yet known and which will eventually be held to be the crucial things about short-term memory. Studying our performance in close relation to production systems seems to me a waste of time, because it amounts to studying a mechanism, not a problem. Once again, the mechanisms that such research is trying to penetrate will be unravelled by studying the problems that need solving, just as vision research is progressing because it is the problem of vision that is being attacked, not neural visual mechanisms (p.348)."

ES are production systems *par excellence* and Marr's structures clearly throw down a challenge as to why progress has not been as rapid as was hoped in the early days of their development which is: their begetters have typically neglected a rigorous analysis of the theory of the task that the ES is to solve, and instead rushed in prematurely with a lot of programming hacks.

As might be expected, this criticism has itself not gone unchallenged. For example, Sloman (1980) believes Marr's three levels assumption is "confused" because it rests on the mistaken belief that the topmost computational level of theorising can in general be separated from the level of algorithms and the study of representations. The point at issue here may prove to be a deep one or it may be no more than a matter of terminology. Marr used the term representation in the context of (level two) discussions of practical design questions about how to devise an effective set of procedures for implementing a set of constraints. Others might wish to use the term 'representation' in different (more abstract?) senses in (level one) debates about what constraints are available and what mathematical proofs can be demonstrated regarding the implications of those constraints.

This raises a further complaint from Sloman (1980): pursuing Marr's set of levels is likely to divert attention from difficult and messy problems in cognition to relatively simple mathematical problems: "Many of the most important issues in AI have been concerned with the study of trade-offs between ..... space and time, efficiency and flexibility, completeness and speed, clarity and robustness. It is possible that such trade-offs are the key to much of the complexity of human and animal psychology, and ultimately neurophysiology. If so, it may be a serious impediment to scientific progress to advocate an oversimple methodological stance. ... The rigidity of function of a typical calculator makes it unnecessary for our understanding of it to involve consideration of many layers of implementation or the kinds of trade-offs and mixtures of levels found in human psychology. By contrast, when we study *human* arithmetical expertise (acquired after many years of individual learning), most of the mathematical theory of numbers is an irrelevant digression. Instead we have to consider issues of storing many 'partial results', indexing them, linking them to methods of recognising situations where they are applicable, associating them with monitoring processes for detecting slips and mistakes, and so on (Sloman, 1980, p.403)."

Marr's answer to this would probably be Yes and No! (One can say only probably, because Marr died from leukaemia at the age of 35.) Sloman's list of trade-offs is important and they are exactly the kinds of things that need to be understood at the algorithm and hardware levels. But it is premature to consider their significance via tasks such as mental arithmetic (or chess) which are: "...problems for which human skills are of doubtful quality and in which good performance seems to rest on a huge base of knowledge and expertise. I would argue that these are exceptionally good grounds for *not* yet studying how we carry out such tasks. I have no doubt that when we do mental arithmetic we are doing something well, but it is not arithmetic, and we seem far from understanding even one component of what that something is. I therefore feel we should concentrate on the simpler problems first, for here we have some hope of genuine advancement (Marr, 1982, p.348)."

The academic controversy continues. And yet, when viewed as commercial systems, ES have proved to be big business (estimated at $400m in the USA in 1988). The reason for this success may be that their practical use has been for simpler problems than those envisaged at the outset of their development. For problems of modest scale (requiring say 100 rules or so), the ES environment may be an attractive one for those with little education or skill in programming (see the discussion in Appendix B of d'Agapeyeff and Hawkins, 1987). For such small-scale problems, the deployment of heuristic search to cope with a combinatorial explosion of possible reasoning steps may be less of a reality than a hollow boast. Indeed, as Steels (1987) points out, when used for simpler domains requiring less knowledge acquisition, and needing only an algorithmic sequence of rule calls with no model for explanation, the ES becomes trivialised to just another computer program and to superficiality of results (see also Hayward, 1984). Steels goes on to speculate that this is why there has been a stagnation of interest in ES on the part of the AI community since the mid-70's. His suggested remedy is not unlike Marr's: there should be less emphasis on implementation and more on the task level. This recommendation still often goes unheeded in ES development. Meanwhile, the neural net bandwagon rushes noisily onward - but perhaps to the same realisation?

REFERENCES

Apple (1987) *The Apple Human Interface Guidelines: The Apple Desktop Interface.* Apple Computer Publisher: Addison Wesley.

Boden, M. A. (1988) *Computer Models of Mind.* Cambridge: Cambridge University Press.

Carpenter, G. (1989) Neural Network Models for Pattern Recognition and Associative Memory. *Neural Networks, 2,* 243-257.

Churchland, P.M. (1988). *Matter and Consciousness* (rev. edn). Cambridge, MA: The MIT Press.

Craig, I.D. (1988) Blackboard Systems. *Artificial Intelligence Review, 2,* 103-118.

d'Agapeyeff, A. and Hawkins, C.J.B. (1987) Report to the Alvey Directorate on the Second Short Survey of Expert Systems in UK Business. Published by the IEE on behalf of the Alvey Directorate, 66-74 Victoria Street, London SW1E 6SW

Dreyfus, H.E. and Dreyfus, S.E. (1987) Why skills cannot be represented by rules. In Sharkey, N.E. (Ed.) *Artificial Intelligence: A Cognitive Science Perspective.* Ellis Horwood

Erman, L.D., Hayes-Roth, F., Lesser, V.R. and Reddy, D.R. (1980) The Hearsay-II speech-understanding systems: Integrating knowledge to resolve uncertainty. *Computing Surveys, 12,* 213-253.

Frisby, J.P. (1990). The computational approach to visual perception. In Eysenck, M. W (Ed.) *The Blackwell Dictionary of Cognitive Psychology.* Basil Blackwell: Oxford. (In press.)

Goldberg, D.E. (1989) *Genetic Algorithms: In Search, Optimization & Machine Learning.* Addison-Wesley.

Graham, I. and Jones, P.L.(1988). *Expert Systems Knowledge, Uncertainty and Decision.* Lomdon: Chapmand and Hall.

Hart, A. (1986) *Knowledge Acquisition for Expert Systems.* Kogan Page.

Hayes-Roth, F., Waterman, D.A. and Lenat, D.B. (1983) *Building Expert Systems,* Addison-Wesley.

Hayward, S.A. (1984) Is a decision tree an expert system?   In Bramer, M.A. (Ed.) *Research and Development in Expert Systems: Proceedings of the fourth Technical Conference of the Britsih Computer Society Specialist Group on Expert Systems,* University of Warwick December 1984. Pp. 41-50.   Cambridge University Press: Cambridge.

Hunt, E. (1989) Connectionist and rule-based representations of expert knowledge. *Behaviour Research Methods, Instruments, & Computers,* **21** (2) 88-95.

Jackson, P. (1986) *Introduction to Expert Systems.* Addison-Wesley.

Johnson-Laird, P.N. (1988) *The Computer and the Mind - An Introduction Cognitive Science.* London: Fontana Press.

Keravnou E.T. and Washbrook, J. (1988) Deep and Shallow Models in Medical Expert Systems, *Expert Systems in Medicine Fifth Annual Meeting,* Programme and Abstracts, British Medical Informatics Society, Royal Free Hospital School of Medicine, London.

Kidd, A.(Ed) (1987) *Knowledge Acquisition for Expert Systems,* Plenun Press.

Lenat, D.B. (1978) The Ubiquity of Discovery. *Artificial Intelligence* **9** 237-285

Lippman, R.P. (1987) An Introduction to Computing with Neural Nets. *IEEE ASSP Magazine* 4-22.

Marr, D. (1982) *Vision: A computational investigation into the human representation and processing of visual information,* San Fransicso: W. H. Freeman & Co.

Martins, J.P. and Shapiro, S.C. (1988) A Model of Belief Revision. *Artificial Intelligence* **35** 25-79.

Newell, H. (1980) Physical Symbol Systems. *Cognitive Science* **4** 135-183

Nilsson, N.J. (1982) *Principles of Artificial Intelligence.* Springer-Verlag.

Richer, M.H. and Clancey, W.J. (1987) GUIDON-WATCH: A graphic interface for viewing a knowledge-based system. *In* R.W. Lawler and M. Yazdani (Eds) *Artificial Intelligence and Education, Volume 1: Learning Environments and Tutoring Systems.* Ablex, Norwood NJ, USA.

Rumelhart, D.E. and McClelland, J.L. (1986) *Parallel Distributed Processing* Vols I & II. MIT Press.

Sharkey, N.E. (1989) Fast connectionist learning: words and case. *Artificial Intelligence Review,* **3,** 33-47.

Sloman, A. (1980). What kind of indirect process is visual perception? *The Behavioural & Brain Sciences, 3(*3), 401--404.

Steels, L. (1987) The deepening of expert systems. *AI Communications* **0** (1) 9-16.

White, A.P. (1984) Inference deficiencies in rule-based expert systems. In Bramer, M.A. (Ed.) *Research and Development in Expert Systems: Proceedings of the fourth Technical Conference of the Britsih Computer Society Specialist Group on Expert Systems,* University of Warwick December 1984. Pp. 41-50. Cambridge University Press: Cambridge.

Wielinga, B.J. and Breuker, J.A. (1986) Models of Expertise. *Proceedings of the 7th European Conference on Artficial Intelligence*, July 1986, Brighton, U.K.: Volume 1.

Chapter 2

Software engineering

Mike J. Holcombe

Introduction

The aim of this chapter is to introduce some of the main
current themes and preoccupations of Software Engineering -
with some discussion on possible future directions.   The
subject could extend to many complete volumes and so we
have to be very selective and inevitably we can only sketch
ideas in a rather brief way.

   The design of software systems has never been easy - and
the growth in the power and speed of computers has ensured
that the types of software systems being constructed are
also developing at a tremendous pace.   The highly dynamic
nature of the subject brings with it many problems - and it
is impossible to contemplate a very precise definition of
what Software Engineering actually is.   As a working
definition we might consider it as 'an attempt to construct
software systems according to sets of engineering
principles'.   This implies, of course, that in the past
software was not based on 'principles' which is perhaps
overstating the case.   Nevertheless the evolution of
Software Engineering as an engineering discipline did
involve the transformation from a 'craft-based' activity to
one based on a stronger theoretical foundation and
organised around accepted engineering design procedures
assimilated from the more traditional engineering subjects
such as mechanical and electrical engineering.

§1.   CAUSE FOR CONCERN

During the last decade the problems besetting the software
industry have intensified dramatically.   We can summarize
the most dramatic of these as follows:-

(i) *failure to deliver any system at all*

   There have been a number of spectacular cases of complex,
high profile software projects that have collapsed at a
cost of many millions.   In many cases the publicity
attached to these failures has been of considerable
embarrassment to companies, governments, politicians etc.

There have been surveys of some market sectors that uncovered a failure rate of up to 50%. That is, around half of the contracted systems were not delivered at all.

(ii) *system delivered is inappropriate*

Many systems that are delivered are not what was wanted. This has been the case even when the system was specifically commissioned from a software house.

(iii) *system delivered is unusable*

This is such a widespread problem that comment is almost superfluous. We now often *assume* that a new system is going to be difficult to use before we even switch it on for the first time. The computerization of large companies - such as banks etc., - has been abandoned in some cases because the users could not understand how to use it.

(iv) *system delivered is unreliable*

We all know about the problems of 'software bugs' - unfortunately they are such a problem that some systems need almost continual repair - 'maintenance' just to keep them running.

(v) *system delivered is unsafe*

Many applications of computers involve the control of some safety-related system - fly-by-wire airliners, nuclear reactors, transport systems, washing machines etc. A number of serious failures have been caused by software errors - hardware flaws are also known to have been responsible for accidents. Since lives and the environment can be endangered it is a serious *cause for concern*.

§2 SOME OF THE MAIN THEMES OF MODERN SOFTWARE ENGINEERING

The problems discussed above have forced the industry to investigate new and better ways of designing software systems - especially large systems and this is the content of the emerging discipline of Software Engineering.

2.1 MANAGEMENT OF THE SYSTEM DEVELOPMENT PROCESS

The sheer scale of some of the systems creates serious management problems and some of these are at the heart of the difficulties outlined in §1. Imagine a large system involving many hundreds of designers, several millions of lines of code and you can immediately get an impression of the difficulty of managing such a project. There could be several teams working on related aspects of the system, sharing resources and possibly using the products of each others labours. In some situations one team may be wishing to use software modules developed by another team. This latter team may then wish to change some of their earlier modules in the light of new difficulties with their current work. This will affect the work of the other team. The problem of <u>change management</u>, as it is called, is a serious one. Different versions of part of the system are both being used by other teams and changed by the originating team at the same time. Problems like this highlight the need for accurate up-to-date 'documentation' of the state of the design and efficient communication processes between all parts of the design workforce.

An interesting paper by C.A.R. Hoare (Hoare [1981]) describes his early career leading a design team in industry. The comments he makes about these experiences are as valid now as they were then (the early 60's). An important comment he makes is that project managers should be able to understand what their project teams are doing, and presumably this implies that the members of the team must be able to explain what they are doing to other teams and to their managers. In many ways communication problems lie at the heart of the software development crisis - communication between designers and clients/users - communication between designers; communication between managers and designers etc.

There is an increasing literature devoted to software project management, drawn on the analysis of many case studies. Like much of engineering, progress is as much based on an analysis of disasters as on an analysis of the theoretical foundations of the subject. Perhaps more emphasis is placed on the former in software engineering because of the lack of understanding of the latter within the software industry.

Considerable effort is given to estimating the resources a proposed project might require. These resources could be manpower, time, equipment, money etc. We are still very bad at this because of the rapid change in the technology which has occurred over such a short time scale. The industry is not in a 'steady state' and previous experiences are not always valid. Some approaches to this problem involve the definition of <u>metrics</u> that attempt to quantify some of the variables involved in the management of a project.

Much of this is based on empirical evidence - for example Walston & Felix [1977] analysed some case studies to arrive at the formula

$$\text{Effort in man-months} = 5.2 \text{ (thousands of lines of delivered code)}^{0.91}$$

as a basis for determining, from an estimate of the size of the final program, what the human resource needed was.

More sophisticated formulae are now used in many projects,they are almost always very unreliable and can have an error capability of many orders of magnitude!

As well as metrics used for predicting the resources needed for a project there are also metrics which help managers to monitor the development process, to identify quality characterization and error tracking. Attempts are now being made to construct mathematical models of project management (like Liu & Horowitz [1989]) in an attempt to try and understand the processes involved more thoroughly. It will be interesting to see if useful insights and techniques emerge from this work.

2.2   THE SEARCH FOR QUALITY

The simple definition of a quality software system is that it works properly, has no 'bugs' and does what the user wants it to.   ISO 8402 - "The totality of features and characteristics of a product or service that bear on its ability to satisfy stated or implied needs".   However, to understand what is involved we must look a little deeper at the various facets of quality.

Reliability: the system should perform according to the agreed specification.   This is not as simple as it seems since the specification of software systems is often abstract and complex.

If the specification is written in a natural language (perhaps some form of structured English) it is prone to ambiguity.   There are many cases of clients and designers interpreting the same sentence in different ways.   There are examples of different designers interpreting the same specification differently, which is why there are many incompatible ALGOL compilers.   Even Modula-2 compilers have been built that behave differently because of ambiguities in the language definition - and this is supposed to be a modern language!   Having set this as an aim how do you establish that a given system is reliable? This is where validation and verification come in.   We will discuss this later.

Safety: is the system safe?   Many software systems control processes of various types within a dynamic environment - chemical plants, airliners, domestic appliances.   Often the models we have of the system interacting with this environment are incomplete and there is a need to guarantee that the system does not fail in such a way that life and surroundings are endangered.   The designers must carry out detailed hazard analyses of the total system (including operators) and attempt to ensure that the system never gets into an unsafe state, no matter what eventuality. The concepts of fail-safe and fault-tolerant systems are important here. Note that safety is not synonymous with reliability. In many cases the specification could be unsafe itself - perhaps due to an incomplete understanding of the environment. Despite this the system must still be able to remain in a safe condition.

Usability: is the system usable? The problems arising from badly designed user interfaces are legion. We have all met systems like this. Yet we don't seem to be getting much better at designing the interface - despite all the research carried out recently. Some of the problems obviously arise because we are all individuals with different needs and aspirations. It is also very difficult to identify what these are. Research into the 'capture' of these needs for use in the design of systems is usually carried out in a rather informal manner with the consequent problem of translating this into a precise requirement that can be the basis for a formal design problem. There is the further problem that these needs change with time - users become familiar with a system and wish to interact with it in a different way. The conceptual model the user has of the system changes with experience and understanding - how do we reflect this in designing an 'evolving' interface. These and many other issues are of great importance and progress in dealing with them is slow. How do we actually evaluate the usability of a system? Techniques involve software sampling of user actions, video filming of interaction sessions and questionnaires. But are we always asking the right questions when we carry these investigations out?

Adaptability: can the system be altered easily with changing needs? We don't want to have to buy a completely new system every time our needs change. Can we design systems so that they can evolve and reuse old components? Some progress is being made in this area but we have a lot to do. It is clear that a prerequisite for this is that we actually know what the current system does. Is it documented adequately? Is the structure of the system modular and is this decomposition sensible? These and many other questions need to be addressed.

Maintainability: can we repair the system easily if faults are uncovered? This problem also relates to adaptability and the need to extend or upgrade systems from time to time. Inevitably systems are delivered with errors in them. Many commercial companies will release their products when the number of predicted errors has fallen to a level which makes it more economic to 'fix' problems on the customer's site (or more likely send garbled instructions for the customers to use themselves) than to continue to redesign the system. A problem faced by software developers is that the location and correction of errors usually leads to the creation of new errors and because of this there is a danger that the system will never be fully designed!

Efficiency: does it consume a reasonable amount of resource?   In the past *resource* has been measured in CPU time, memory etc., - hardware based considerations.   This has resulted in a somewhat perverse philosophy whereby speed of transaction etc., is more important than the total cost of running the system - be it in expensive support staff, cost to the company of system failures (both know and unknown failures) etc.   With the increasing speed of microprocessors   and   the   introduction   of   parallel architectures   some   of   these   'run-time'   considerations should recede - but naturally we want 60 do more and more sophisticated   processing   so   we   will   always   be   worrying about the speed of the operation.   The point here is that buying fast processing at the cost of an unreliable system is a false investment.

Suitability: do we need a computer solution?   A somewhat controversial question but one that should be asked more often.   Using computers to solve a problem may, in the long run, be no better than solving it in some other way. Don't be blinded by technology!

2.3   STANDARDS

The growing development of international standards as a mechanism for ensuring quality is generally having a good effect   on   the   industry.   Like   other   engineering activities, however, standards can inhibit developments and the quality of the committees defining the standards is often a limiting factor on their value (see Hoare [1981] again).

A major preoccupation is with standards for safety-critical systems.   Several organisations are involved, international bodies (IEC), national organisations (HSE) and specific industry-based bodies (MOD, Nuclear Industry etc.).   Some   of   these   standards   define   levels   of criticality and integrity (IEC [1989]) as an important first   step   to   the   understanding   of   what   standard   is appropriate to the system in question.   (Johnston & Wood [1989]).

The MOD Draft Interim Defence Standards 00-55 and 00-56 [1989] have created much interest in the community.   For systems with an identified safety critical aspect the standards lay down various procedures and methods that must be used.   Generally the emphasis is on the use of certain formal methods (that is mathematical methods) for the specification and analysis of systems together with strict analysis of hazards and a rigourous programme of testing and validation procedures.   This is all integrated into a precise   management   structure   which   involves   full certification of the various stages of the development.

One interesting section concerns what are identified as unacceptable practices.

" *21.   Unacceptable Practices*

21.1 This Standard prohibits the use of practices which are unsafe, or difficult to analyse such as:

1. *floating point arithmetic;*
2. *recursion, whether simple or mutual;*
3. *interrupts, except for a timer interrupt at fixed intervals;*
4. *assembly level programming languages;*
5. *dependence on separate elements being executed on parallel asynchronous processors. The complete set of Safety Critical Software modules should run in a single processor;*
6. *multi-processing on a single processor;*
7. *object code patching;*
8. *software architectures that are re-configurable under application program control;*
9. *dynamic memory management."*

[MOD Defence Standard 00-55 (1989)]

Other standards are concerned with defining specific languages and methods. We will look at some of the latter in the next section.

2.4 METHODS AND TOOLS

Engineering, as it develops, becomes more and more dependent on the use of standard methods and tools to support these methods, whether they be physical or intellectual. Software Engineering is no different and increasingly the development of software systems involves the use of methods and tools to support the various stages and processes of the design effort.

The reasons are clear, greater standardisation, improved quality and productivity all follow from the use of good tools and methods. However, with the subject being so new, it is not always clear whether a given tool or method is good. The continued introduction of 'better' methods and tools is a noted feature of the subject and only time will tell which are the best - although these may not be the most popular!

Most methods support one or more aspect of the software life cycle and a few claim to support all of it. Some methods allow the user to design, others to analyse and the main problem is the integration of these into a coherent whole, an environment which enables designers to explore, synthysize, analyze, and redesign to a high level of quality and to manage all these processes in a efficient and effective way.

2.4.1 <u>Formal methods</u>. Some methods are based on mathematical abstractions of systems and allow for the specification, analysis or simulation of aspects of systems. These are called *formal methods* and they are becoming extremely important in the drive for high quality, reliable and safe systems. A useful introductory text is Woodcock & Loomes [1988]. The basis for these methods lies in Logic and Abstract Algebra and tools such as specification editors, theorem provers and test generators are becoming available. From the mathematical description of a system it is possible to logically derive mathematical statements about the behaviour of the system. Thus, if the specification gives us a detailed description of the behavioural characteristics of the system and we have a mathematical representation of the design of the system then we can use theorem provers and theorem checkers to formally prove that the design meets it's specification. The main problem with this approach is the sheer scale of the systems now being designed and the inability of the theorem provers to handle large systems satisfactorily. However it is now clear that the use of formal methods to specify precisely what the system is supposed to do is feasible, and even necessary, in many cases. (The MOD standards 00-55 & 00-56 require this.) From this information it is now becoming possible to generate automatically the code for the system and also suitable testing strategies. Many of the formal methods are intensely symbolic and this abstraction seems to be an obstruction to their widespread take-up in industry - unless it is essential. Some formal methods are a combination of symbolic and graphical techniques, for examples Petri nets and those based on the idea of a state machine. Examples of the latter will arise soon.

2.4.2 <u>Graphical techniques.</u> There are a group of methods that are based on the use of diagrams and which are linked into an overall management and documentation structure. These are widely used in industry, they are called structured analysis and design methods and there are many slight variations on the theme.

Essentially the methods proceed in a 'top down' manner by modelling the proposed system from a variety of different 'angles'. The initial diagrams try to identify the broad components of the system and the relationships between them. They may address the way in which data flows through the system, the way in which different processes control other aspects of the system, the way that data changes during the course of operation of the system and so on. At each level each major process is then broken down into subprocesses and the same procedure is carried out, down and down into the system until we get to a level detailed enough to enable the code to be constructed or generated automatically. The results of each of these investigations is recorded in special diagrams with appropriate documentation and the hierarchy of this documentation is carefully numbered in a consistent way.

The result will be a very detailed series of interrelating models of the system which should be understandable to anyone trained in the method. This is a very significant improvement over traditional approaches which often resulted in thousands of lines of obscure, uncommented code that could be understood by the author and noone else. So when the author left there were bound to be problems!

The integration of the tools to support these methods has now produced the various CASE tools that not only provide the graphical editors for the construction of the diagrams but also help in :

resolving conflicts, a process in one diagram may be related to different data or processes in another and this will cause a conflict in the model which must be sorted out,

completing the model, a process may feature in one model and fail to appear in a related one,

generate outline code under certain circumstances,

contain a reference collection of standard components which can be used over and over again.

There are several other features that appear in some CASE packages, analysis tools and tools for the reengineering and maintenance of existing systems. Clearly these will become more and more important as the subject develops and the main worry is over the quality of the tools themselves because, as in most things, bad tools and methods will generally produce bad artifacts.

We will briefly look at a CASE tool later.

$3 SOFTWARE LIFE CYCLES

In this section we look at some of the ways that the complete design and build process for software systems has begun to change.

3.1 TRADITIONAL 'WATERFALL' APPROACH

In this model of the lifecycle of a software system the process are divided up as follows :

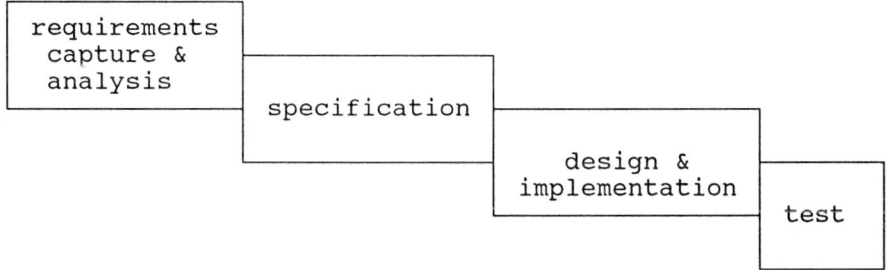

followed by a delivery and maintenance phase. In many cases the main emphasis was placed on the design and implementation phase with the next most importanat part being the testing phase but this was often curtailed when the number of errors thought to remain became acceptable to the company designing the software (after a certain point it is cheaper to send out maintenance engineers to fix bugs than to keep rewriting the software prior to release, at least that way the company gets some money in!). The main effects of this approach is that the delivered software is often not what the purchaser really wants, the quality is usually poor, the costs of maintenance and introducing changes to the system become collosal.

3.2 SOME MODERN LIFE CYCLE MODELS

Almost every author has his/her own lifecycle model differing, perhaps, in detail or emphasis, and so it is difficult to generalise about the current situation. We will select a few interesting developments that seem to be proving useful. There is some empirical research on the benefits of different life cycle approaches. Many of these are based on fairly small scale experiments, usually by competing teams of students building the same system using different approaches. However there are various databases associated with large software projects (eg NASA) that can be analysed and some conclusions drawn.

(i) *modular design techniques* Traditionally engineering has taken advantage of the opportunities for the use of standard components in the design of artifacts, be they buildings or electronic systems. It is clear that such an approach would pay dividends in software engineering. The problems are that there are no standard methods for specifying software modules, their behaviour, functionality and performance. There are no quality standards and so many software designers would prefer to design everything from scratch rather than rely on someone else's work. The introduction of module based languages such as Modula-2 and Hope provide a sensible way to define modules and interface them together and this could be helpful. The introduction of a modular approach to design is beginning to influence the software life cycle but there is a long way to go. It is a step away from the monolithic approach to design represented by the 'waterfall' model. (Parnas. [1972])

(ii) <u>rapid prototyping</u> This method concentrates much more on the satifaction of the user's needs by delivering at an early stage a working model of the user interface for evaluation. The prototype interface may contain much of the input/ouput structure of the proposed system but there is nothing behind it in the sense that little real processing is done. It helps to identify the sort of system that the user wants at an early stage before the designers have committed themselves to decisions about the implementation of data and algorithms that will be expensive to change later. On the basis of an extensive evaluation with the user a clear understanding of the required system will hopefully emerge. (Gomaa & Scott, [1981])

(iii) the clean room This approach to designing the system has been pioneered by IBM. One of the more negative aspects of the improvement of technology is the introduction of interactive compilers. When everything was based on batch processing the programmer took much greater care over his/her work because simple errors would not become known for a day or so. Now we can compile instantly and we put less mental effort into our work. In the clean room system the design team writing the software have no access to general compilers, although they can use syntax checkers, but they cannot run their programs and therefore test them. After they have finished their system they hand it over to an independent team who then carry out carefully designed testing on the system. The resulting increase in productivity has been remarkable as evidenced by empirical results from experiments involving this approach compared to traditional approaches. (Selby & Basili, [1987]).

$4 SOME NEW AREAS OF RESEARCH

The emphasis on improving quality and productivity has lead, as we have seen, to revisions to the traditional life cycle, to improved project management and to the use of methods and tools based on scientific principles rather than on folklore and a craft ethic. However there are still many ways in which current 'state-of-the-art' practice can be improved.
   We will briefly discuss three new areas that are becoming of interest and which relate to the desire for better methods and tools for software engineering. A further area, that of object-oriented design is the subject of another paper. The three basic areas are concerned with improving the usability and the reliability of systems. We could have highlighted several other aspects, such as safety, maintenance etc. but we lack time here.

4.1 USER CENTRED DESIGN
The greater emphasis on the user, the introduction of a 'user centered design philosophy' through the use of rapid prototyping and the definition of the user's needs are a major research theme at present. The combination of talents from software engineering, psychology, cognitive science etc. will, hopefully, generate practical methods for the construction of highly usable systems.
   One problem with some of the recent research is that it concentrates to a certain extent on the more 'superficial' aspects of the system interface - screen layout, colour, menus and icons, ie. the ergonomic aspects of the interface. It is much more difficult to describe the goals and the reasoning processes undergone by users interacting with systems at a higher level. People are individuals, they may act very differently from one another. People also learn so their needs on one occasion may differ from their needs on another.

With the increasing use of formal mathematical models of the processing and data aspects systems it is becoming necessary to consider how we can build models of users interacting with these systems so that some predictions can be made and designs improved accordingly. At the moment the formalising of user's conceptual models seems to be difficult task. It is an important one because of the use of computers in the control of dangerous processes. Many industrial disasters, such as Three Mile Island, can be attributed partly to an inadequate understanding of the system by a user. There has been some work on this area as applied to industrial processes but the techniques are not always sophisticated enough to handle the highly abstract needs of software systems.

The use of unusual logics, such as belief logics, to try and provide a framework for modelling human reasoning is an interesting area. (Fagin & Halpern. [1988])

4.2   DESIGN FOR TEST

One of the major thrusts of formal methods has been in the verification of systems. This involves the formal mathematical proof of algorithms and processes using logic and algebraic techniques. Serious problems of scale have arisen and it is not obvious that the methods are scalable to the size required by modern software developments. There is also the unfortunate weakness that the platform on which any software system is situated, compilers, operating systems and ultimately the hardware itself, are unlikely to be perfect. The original specification of the system may also be based on assumptions, often unconscious, made about the operating environment. Thus a formal prooof of the correctness of the system does not usually imply that the system will run perfectly and according to requirements. Thus testing is, and will remain, a crucial area of the design process. The testing of individual modules, the testing of the integrated system and the testing of the installed system have to be done with great care. Subsequent testing during operation is also important because operating conditions change - environmental changes, unpredicted user behaviour, intermittent hardware faults etc. can cause serious problems.

The problem here is that consideration of the method of testing is often left to the end of the design and implementation process. By then design decisions have been taken that may make the testing of parts of the system difficult or even impossible. The lack of an adequate theoretical foundation for functional software testing also prevents the full use of statistical techniques for the measurement of quality. The main design methods, both formal and graphical (or structured) do not insist on the development of testing strategies in an integrated way. Like the user interface, the testing strategy is usually an afterthought and this can only exascerbate the problems of designing quality software systems.

We are proposing the development of a testing strategy in tandem with the specification of the system and as this specification is refined to more detailed levels, the testing methods should similarly be refined. Extra testing functions can be introduced where appropriate to enable the easier and more thorough testing of the system. The whole testing process must be documented precisely. The philosophy of 'Design for Test' found in VLSI circles, although motivated by a slightly different testing need, is still a valuable one to learn from.

4.3 EXPERT SYSTEMS FOR SOFTWARE ENGINEERING

The use of expert systems to support software engineers is another modern approach. The major problem is that our understanding of the software engineering process is not sufficiently great to enable us to develop a robust and practical 'knowledge base' of information to guide such a system. Nevertheless, there has been some research into the relative merits of different approaches to the design of such expert systems. The work of Ramsey & Basili [1989] has shown that rule-based systems seem slightly better than frame-based systems and knowledge organised in a 'bottom-up' manner is better than 'top-down' approaches. However, great care must be taken with these results at this stage because of our ignorance on how to manage large software projects properly.

$5 A SIMPLE CASE STUDY

In this section we will look at the early stages in the design of a simple information system in order to explore some of the preceeding ideas. The main emphasis will be on using CASE tools, formal methods and approaching the problem from a user-centred point of view. Space does not allow us to address all of the issues but it will allow us to introduce some of the notations and diagrams now used in the subject.

The system is an information system that will contain basic information about journal articles of interest to the owner. The user will wish to *enter* the details of new journals, *show* the details of articles already described in the system, *delete* the details of articles which are no longer relevant and to *list* all articles by a given author or authors.

We will first examine the way data might flow around the system by use of a data flow diagram - or context diagram - of the top level system. The tool we are using is the *Software through Pictures (StP)* CASE tool produced by IDE. It supports several methods, the syntax we are using is based on the Hatley & Pirbhai method (which is really aimed at real-time systems).

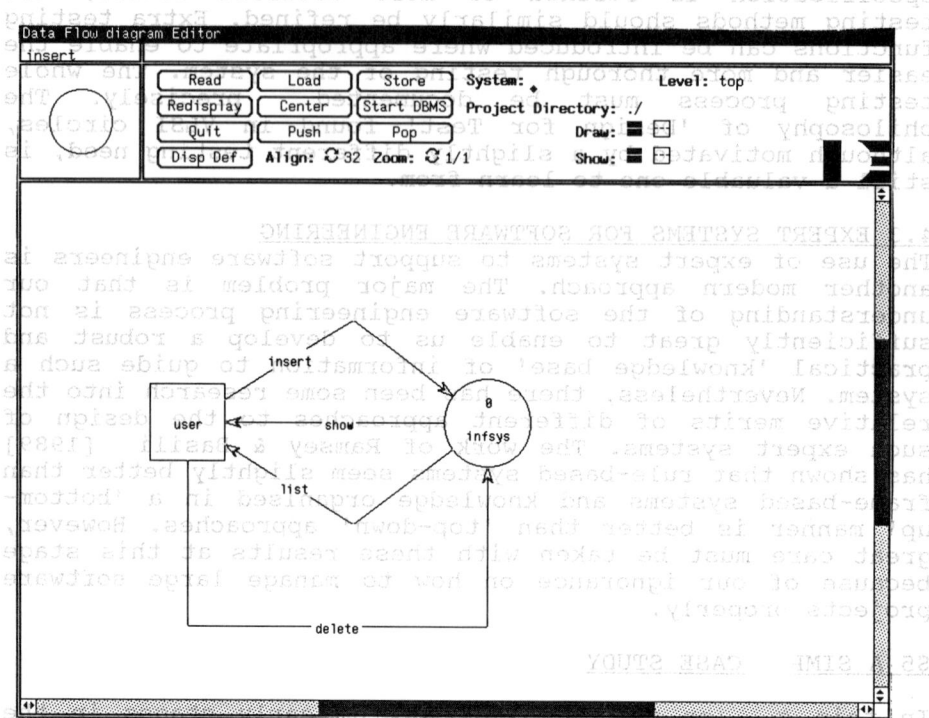

Top level context diagram.

The process in the circle represents the complete system and the box represents the user in this example.

The user wishes to control the system by virtue of specific command inputs which are described using a state machine diagram that defines the system as four basic modal components, one for each main function. The system could be a menu based one, driven either from the keyboard by pressing, for example e to select the *enter* function etc. or using icons and a mouse input device. The structure of the system would be basically the same. The diagram describes the top level control model of the system.

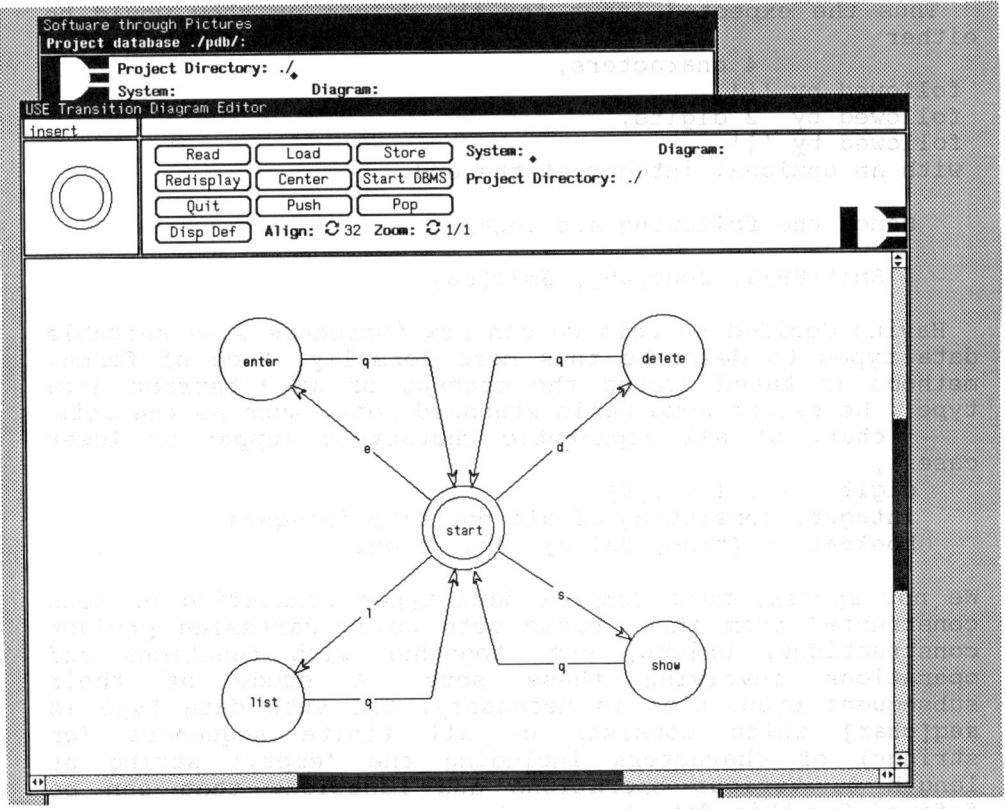

Top level control model.

After this we need to consider in more detail the user's conceptual image of the data in the system and how this will be reflected in a natural input/output dialogue.

In many articles the references that are referred to in the text appear in abbreviated form there. Thus 'Smit[89]' might be used in the article to refer to the paper:

Smith, A.B. 'Generalised discussions on specific issues.'
International Journal of Woffle. 24, 1989, 347-782.

With the user's agreement it might be resolved that the use of Smit[89] is a natural way to attempt to retrieve such a paper. There is a problem with a prolific author such as Smith - there might be several papers in a single year. So we could add an extra, optional, parameter, namely a number indicating which of the author's papers that appeared that year was meant.

Thus the expected input for the *delete* or *show* would be either

     4 characters,
followed by '[',
followed by 2 digits,
followed by ']',
with an optional integer at the end.

   Hence the following are legal :

   Smit[89]3, Jone[45], SmJo[86]

   Having decided on this we can now introduce some suitable data types to describe this more formally. Much of formal methods is based around the concept of an 'abstract data type'. We select some basic standard sets, such as the sets
     char, of all alphabetic characters (upper or lower cases),
   digit = { 0,1,...,9}
   integer, consisting of all positive integers
   boolean = {true, false} and so on.

We now specify more complex data types consisting of sets constructed from these basic sets using cartesian product constructions, unions, etc. together with functions and operations involving these sets. A study of their subsequent properties is necessary. One such data type is **seq[char]** which consists of all finite sequences (or strings) of characters including the 'empty' string of length 0. Various operations and functions that can be defined for this data type include :
     concatenation - sticking one string alongside another,
     head - extracting the leftmost character form a string
     length - which counts the number of characters in the string etc.

   Now we can define the principle data types and functions for the system in question.

   The basic ingredients will be a data type called **key** which is the mechanism for identifying the paper needed in the database and **record** which contains the information stored.
   Thus
               Smit[89]

is an example of an element of the data type **key** and

     Smith, A.B. 'Generalised discussions on specific issues.'
          International Journal of Woffle. 24, 1989, 347-782.

is an example of an element of the data type **record**

Thus we can define

key ≡ **seq[char]** x **digit** x **digit** x **seq[digit]**

subject to the condition that the sequence of characters is of length 4.

Formally

> **key**
>
> **seq[char]** x **digit** x **digit** x **seq[digit]**
>
> ---
>
> for all (a,b,c,d) ∈ **key** ;
> length(a) = 4

This notation consists of a 'declaration' in the upper box and the 'semantics' in the lower box. It is written in a mathematical specification language called *Z*.

Define   **name** ≡ **seq[char]**,
           title ≡ **seq[char]**,
      volume ≡ **integer**,
         year ≡ **integer**,
  start_page ≡ **integer**,
    end_page ≡ **integer**.

Then

> **record**
>
> **name** x **title** x **volume** x **year** x **start_page** x **end_page**
>
> ---
>
> for all (a,b,c,d,e,f) ∈ **record** ;
> d ≤ 1999
>
> e ≤ f

The next thing is to define a data type that describes the state of the data in the system.

system ≡ **key** --+--> **record**

This describes the system as a partial function that relates the keys to the information that they point to. Initially the state of the system is empty and we then enter information in such away that each **key** element relates to a unique **record** element. It is unlikely that **system** becomes a complete function because that implies that every possible **key** value is in use.

We now describe how to define two of the basic functions.

---

enter : **system** x **key** x **record** --+--> **system**

enter (s,k,r) = s ⊕ { k --> r }

This describes the function *enter* in terms of the input data - namely the current state of the **system**, s and the input **key** value, k and the input **record** value, r. The result is the new partial function overwritten with the correspondence { k --> r }.

---

delete : **system** x **key** --+--> **system**

delete (s,k) = {k} ◄ s

---

which describes the partial function with all reference to the domain element 'k' removed.

Finally we will discuss how to set up a model of the interface for the *delete* mode. The state machine describing the top level model can now be refined with respect to the *delete* operation to produce a model using a similar theoretical concept to a state machine. This model is not supported by any existing CASE tools but it represents a very general approach to the formal specification of dynamic systems which allows us to refine specifications in a systematic way, Holcombe [1988].

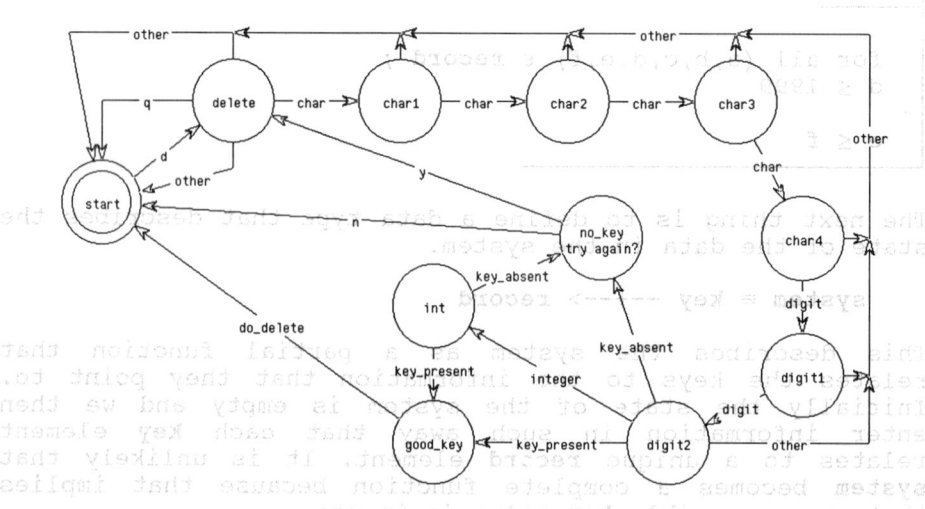

A machine diagram for *delete*

In this diagram we have tried to account for possible user input errors in a sensible way. Further refinement and analysis as well as the automatic generation of code and the generation of test sets should be possible with this type of method. The further functions found in the diagram, such as the function that checks to see if the **key** value is present in the current **system** state, need to be formally specified and refined to an appropriate implementation.

This has been a rapid tour around some interesting aspects of software engineering. There are many books on the subject of varying quality and the interested reader wishing to design software systems is encouraged to read further and to try and put some of these ideas into practice. The result will be better systems built more efficiently.

REFERENCES

H. Gomaa &
D. Scott,
'Prototyping as a tool in the specification of user requirements' 5th. IEEE Conf. Software Engineering 1981

C.A.R. Hoare,
'The Emperor's Old Clothes'. Comn. ACM. 1981

M.Holcombe,
'X-machines as a basis for dynamic system specification'. Software Engineering Journal, 1, 1988.

IEC [1989],
'Software for Computers in the application of Industry Safety-Related Systems'. Proposals I.E.C. Sub-Committee 65A.WG9.

I.H.A. Johnston &
A.P. Wood,
'Integrity levels and assessment levels in practice'. Proc.

R.Fagin &
J.Y.Halpern,
'Belief, awareness and limited reasoning' A.I. 34, 1988.

L-C Liu &
E. Horowitz,
'A Formal Model for Software Project Management'. IEEE Trans. Soft. Eng. 1989.

D.Parnas,
'On criteria to be used in decomposing systems into modules' Comm. ACM, 15, 1972.

C.L.Ramsey &
V. Basili
'An evaluation of expert systems for software engineering management' IEEE Trans. Soft. Eng. 15, 1989.

R.W.Selby &
V.R.Basili,
'Cleanroom software development approach - an empirical evaluation' IEEE Trans. Soft. Eng. 13, 1987.

C.E. Walston &
C.P. Felix,
'A method of programming measurement & estimation'. IBM Systems Jour. 1977.

J.Woodcock &
M.Loomes,
'Software Engineering Mathematics' Pitman, 1988.

Chapter 3

Trends in object-oriented programming

A. J. H. Simons

Object-Oriented Programming (OOP) is a style of programming whose popularity is rapidly growing in Computer Science and Software Engineering. Its basic philosophy is that of 'turning programs on their heads', in other words, instead of designing structured routines to process some data objects, you design structured data objects and give them the power to interact with each other in clearly prescribed ways. This is all that is essential in an object-oriented view of some computational task; however there are a large number of additional features and facilities that come with any OOP language and working environment which merit discussion in their own right. First, we shall investigate where OOP is coming from. Later we shall introduce common features in the design of several OOP languages. Finally, we shall discuss some current issues and look ahead to the future of OOP in mainstream programming.

1   THEMES IN OBJECT-ORIENTED PROGRAMMING

It is helpful to analyse the aims and goals of the research which has given rise to various OOP languages and systems. There is no single homogenous view as to what objects and their relationships should be; this is in part a consequence of different views on what object-oriented systems are designed to achieve. Three main schools of thought have influenced the development of OOP over the last 25 years:

1.1   The Human Computer Interaction Viewpoint

OOP was originally developed in laboratories investigating Human-Computer Interaction. Researchers observed that programmers' errors and frustrations with computers were due in large part to the mismatch between the way they naturally thought about problems and the way they were forced to represent the same problems for a computer to tackle. The HCI school makes a strong claim that people *think in terms of objects*, rather than abstract processes, so a programming language should support this intuition explicitly. Various advantages are cited, the most usual being that the programmer deals more directly with the real-world objects he is trying to model; and that these objects change very little throughout the development of programs, compared with the volatile nature of the processes used in different programs. Early experiments in *Simula* (1), a simulation language for modelling real-world objects and their interactions (such as machine shops, factory installations), demonstrated the usefulness of objects as abstractions when sequencing complicated co-routines. This philosophy eventually led to the development of *Smalltalk-80* (2,3), the world's first and still the only *completely uniform* OOP language and software support environment in which absolutely everything is done with objects.

Smalltalk grew out of Alan Kay's vision for the *DynaBook*, a portable graphics-based workstation that even non-computer people would find easy to use. Smalltalk is famous for its user-interface in which windows, mouse-pointer and icons were originally introduced, allowing you, the programmer, simply to point at the thing you want to do. You can edit, run, debug and file objects away without leaving the same working environment; you are never *locked into a mode* since all resources are constantly available. Smalltalk supports a style of programming known as *rapid prototyping* - developing new ideas by assembling existing objects and extending some of their capabilities incrementally in a new application. This profits from the idea that programs are never totally new and saves having to 're-invent the wheel' each time. Although the *DynaBook* was never fully realised, implementations of Smalltalk now exist for a variety of hardware platforms, including the PC. A whole host of software toolkits now use the industry standard window-and-menu based style of interface.

1.2   The Artificial Intelligence Viewpoint

Independently, researchers in Artificial Intelligence had been investigating the nature of the organisation of human knowledge. Partly, this was to attempt to validate working models of human memory, as in Quillian's *Semantic Nets* (4); partly this was to find more effective ways of representing 'untidy' real-world knowledge for a computer to use, as in Minsky's *Frames* (5). Both strands eventually incorporated the idea of inheritance, which has posed many interesting problems for researchers (6).

The AI school of thought makes a strong claim that human knowledge about the real world can be arranged as *structured concepts*. This usually means a representation in terms of a hierarchy of *typical cases* with *exceptions*. The advantage cited here is that an explicit model of a *domain* (an area of human knowledge or expertise) may be constructed. This has two benefits, the first being that all knowledge common to several concepts may be factored out in an inheritance hierarchy. This is referred to as *the principle of cognitive economy*. The second advantage is that a structured model of the problem domain directs inference about the concepts it represents, which compares favourably against rule-based models of human knowledge whose only mechanism is to match patterns against evidence repeatedly. Aikens demonstrated (7) that CENTAUR, a frame-based medical expert system for the diagnosis of respiratory diseases, asked more pertinent questions than other rule-based systems given the same task. It diagnosed cases in shorter times, using strategies that were transparent to medical experts. The system had a high acceptance amongst doctors.

Inference mechanisms which use an object-oriented representation are often substantially different from rule-based systems (eg OPS5; or the straightforward use of Prolog), which implicitly construct and destroy, in *working memory*, chains of data (representing chains of reasoning) from the rules known to the system. In OOP, the objects themselves are the data, the equivalent of the rule is *sending a message* to some object to develop or extend some relationship with other objects.

Many OOP systems have been built on top of existing AI languages (Lisp, Prolog) to facilitate this kind of knowledge representation. *Flavors* (8) and *LOOPS* (9) were two early examples incorporating multiple inheritance for the first time. The MIT system *Flavors*, which implemented objects as an additional kind of datatype in Lisp, was followed in Europe by many research systems (such as *ObjVLisp* and *Lore*) which tried to integrate objects (in the OOP sense) with basic datatypes in Lisp in a more coherent way. The Xerox PARC system *LOOPS* provided a rich mixture of objects, rules, 'active values' (daemons) and Lisp; this kind of mixture was later marketed, at the height of the Expert Systems boom, in industrial quality prototyping toolkits such as *KEE, ART,* and *KnowledgeCraft.* Although not fully uniform OOP languages in the Smalltalk sense, these toolkits provide *object-oriented extensions for knowledge representation* on top of a *host language* (usually Lisp).

A more recent attempt to integrate Lisp with OOP at a low level is the Common Lisp Object System, *CLOS* (10). This is essentially a fusion of the best ideas from the East- and West-Coast research laboratories, with some new additions. It aims to become the standard extension for Common Lisp. It synthesises the object-centred and function-centred views in a balanced manner.

1.3 The Software Engineering Viewpoint

The most recent interest in OOP has been shown by language designers with Software Engineering goals clearly in sight. They see in the Object-Oriented paradigm a natural extension, or alternative to, existing modular paradigms such as those offered by *Modula 2* and *Ada.* These already bring the benefits of *data abstraction, encapsulation* and *information hiding.* The SE school makes a strong case that software should be, in addition, as *reusable and interchangeable* as common items of hardware such as integrated circuits and chips. Part of reusability should be the *extensibility* of existing software systems without the need for a total re-design and re-implementation.

Software components should be modular, with well-defined interfaces to the outside world, explaining how client programs may make use of the facilities they offer. Each modular component describes the (concrete) form of an *abstract data type* and all the permissible operations defined over it (eg a stack, with push and pop operations). The module is a text-description of one or more objects (software components) which may be created from the description by a program. Each object has a secure *private state* which cannot be corrupted by some other part of the program, since its state may only be changed through one of its own procedures. New datatypes may be designed as extensions or restrictions of previous ones (by inheritance). An alternative to *reuse by inheritance* is *reuse by composition* (including objects as components of a new composite object).

OOP languages fulfilling these goals include *Objective C* (11), *Object Pascal* (12), *C++* (13) and most recently *Eiffel* (14), which introduces some of the techniques from formal methods in Computer Science (15,16) into a real programming language. These languages fall into two groups. *C++* and *Object Pascal* provide *object-oriented extensions* on top of their *host language* (C and Pascal, respectively) giving the programmer a choice of styles ranging over traditional *imperative programming*, modular *data abstraction* and full *object-orientation.* *Objective C* and *Eiffel* are *independent languages supporting object-oriented design* (with compilers that happen to use C as an intermediate language). Crucial to this last distinction is the difference between what programming styles a language *merely enables* and programming styles that a language *explicitly supports* (and usually enforces). Advocates of the strong Object-Oriented view argue that compromises with traditional languages invalidate the purity of the approach. On the other hand, a disciplined use of a language like *C* that allows the direct addressing of hardware can be an easier way to extend a filing system, or display system without having to learn the machine code for the platform upon which your 'pure' OOP language runs.

2 STANDARD FEATURES OF OBJECT-ORIENTED PROGRAMMING LANGUAGES AND SUPPORT ENVIRONMENTS

We now turn to a discussion of the features usually supplied with OOP languages. These include a working environment, classes, inheritance and polymorphism. We shall present these in a fairly introductory way and go on to discuss arguments for and against particular features in a later section.

2.1   Modeless and Traditional Working Environments

The environment is an important feature which enables the higher productivity possible in OOP systems. If the programmer is to adapt existing objects to create new applications, he requires a set of powerful tools for *browsing* over the objects available in the system already. This is often provided in the form of a graphical interface with an *object inspector* and source-code editor. The environment is said to be *modeless* if it does not require the user to press some sequence of escape codes to alternate between different modes for editing, compiling, running or debugging software.

The *Smalltalk* model provides total access to the sources of *Smalltalk* itself; fully interactive browsing features in the *LOOPS* model and its descendents. It works extremely well in rapid prototyping environments, where the envisaged use is single-user workstations (or, few users per workstation; a single application development on one machine). For very large software projects developed on many machines, the problems of code-sharing and version management arise. The possibility of unconstrained hacking at system definitions could give a software manager a nightmare to resolve. Cox talks in terms of *specification sheets* that should be circulated with each new update of a software component (ie just like hardware); Meyer talks in terms of *abstraction tools* which create specifications from the source code itself: this is more immediate and guaranteed to be up to date. The SE-oriented languages nonetheless have a lot to learn from earlier OOP systems: most of them still rely on the traditional edit-compile-load-run-debug cycle. Work is in progress on the creation of browsing tools for *Eiffel* and *C++*; these will allow inspection, but not unconstrained modification.

Another feature of original OOP systems is that they permit (and actively encourage) the creation, dynamically, of many objects based on typical descriptions. These objects are *persistent*, that is, they remain in the environment until the system detects that they are no longer required by any other objects. A *garbage collector* takes care of reclaiming memory when these objects are finished with. Many other aspects of the environment, including *threaded processes* (simultaneous activities that may be suspended or resumed at will) and *implicit file handling* help to create a *virtual image* - a whole system of objects with which the programmer may interact without needing to know whether they are stored in memory, on file or whether they are running under a different process.

This degree of support for dynamic object creation is present to differing degrees in the SE-oriented languages. *C++* requires the programmer to define his own garbage collection strategy, whereas *Eiffel* sees automatic garbage collection as an essential element in a language based around dynamic objects. Both languages treat the runtime system as separate from the development system, which means that objects are not naturally persistent (although *Eiffel* has a class *Storable* giving objects a basic ability to file themselves away). There is no notion of a *virtual image* in these systems. *Persistency* is therefore a major research area; this is fuelled by the additional prospect of maintaining seriously large databases of objects, something which even the *Smalltalk* model does not address.

2.2   Objects, Classes and Instances: Basic Building Blocks

An object may be defined as some coherently organised piece of data that has an *identity* and a *state* (17). Its state is the private memory of the object. Its identity is the unique handle which distinguishes it from all other objects. An Object-Oriented

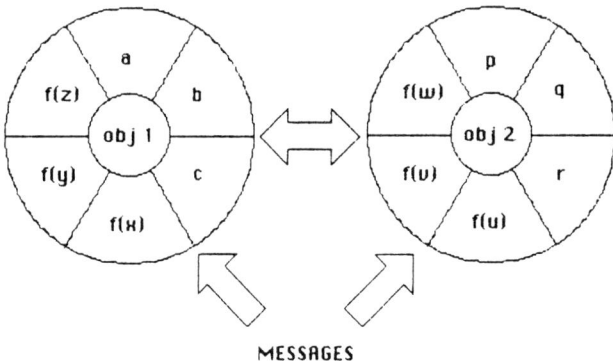

MESSAGES

Figure 1 · The Object-Oriented Viewpoint

Program is one conceived at the highest level in terms of objects and their interactions (Figure 1). Here, both data and procedures are considered part of the object's state.

Classes are typical descriptions of some object required in a program; they are somewhat analogous to prototypes (in AI), to sets (in formal theory), to records (in conventional DP) and fuse the notions of *module* and *datatype* in one computational entity (the view of *Eiffel*). Most programming effort in OOP goes into designing a useful set of classes which will be used over again in different applications. A program will generate possibly many objects from a class template; these are called *instances of* the class.

Each class specifies what attributes its instances may have. Some of these attributes take individual values in each instance: these are often known as *instance variables*. Other attributes are shared by all instances of the class: these are often known as *class variables*. Both kinds of attribute are stores for the data an object holds; a perspective sometimes emphasised by referring to an object's *slots* and *fillers* (from Minsky's *Frames*). In OOP, individual procedures or functions are viewed in the same way as attributes of an object: they belong to a particular class, eg a class *Vehicle* might have its own *methods* (personal procedures or functions, the *Smalltalk* terminology) for starting, stopping, turning, re-fuelling etc. which differ from the *methods* a class *JetAircraft* might use to achieve the same result.

2.3   Inheritance of Storage and Procedures

Inheritance is the mechanism whereby a class may acquire much of its description from other classes already described. Both *variables* (storage space) and *methods* (personal procedures) may be inherited. What this basically means (see Figure 2) is that *methods* defined in a superclass are applicable to all instances of its subclasses (a sort of type compatibility relation); *class variables* defined in a superclass are 'seen' and shared by all instances of its subclasses (a sort of scoping rule for shared data); and *instance variables* defined in a superclass are automatically added onto the space to be allocated to all instances of its subclasses (a sort of shorthand for creating records by extension).

Various inheritance schemes exist, including *single inheritance* (*Smalltalk*, *C++*, *Object Pascal*, *Objective C*), where every class has only one superclass, therefore only one possible inheritance path; and many kinds of *multiple inheritance* (*Flavors*,

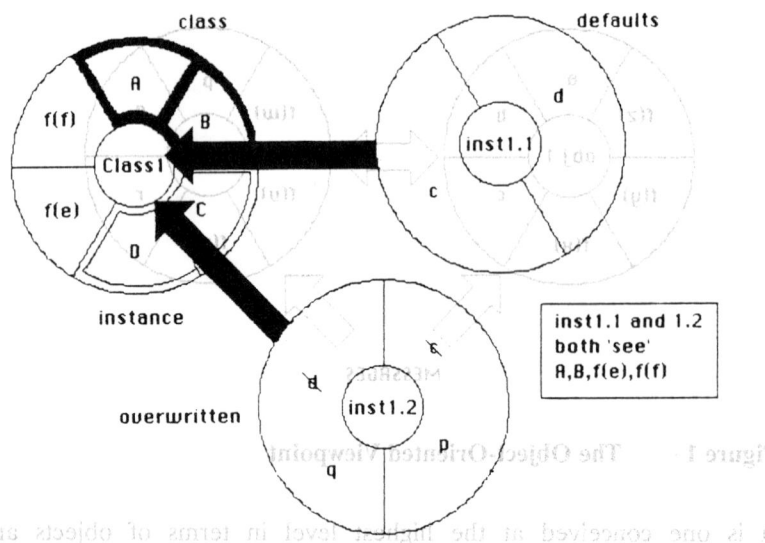

Figure 2   Copying of Instance Structure

LOOPS, Eiffel, CLOS, new C++), where every class has one or more superclasses, so potentially many inheritance paths. A new class may be defined as an *extension* or *restriction* of a previous class (classes). This is referred to as a process of *specialisation*. New variables or methods may simply be *additive* or they may *override* previous variables and methods of the same name (Figure 3).

Inheritance is a much-debated topic. Researchers with a philosophical interest try to determine what it means to inherit two incompatible values for one attribute (18,19). Others simply wish to determine formally what the lookup algorithm should be: the *CLOS* specification is a good example (20). *Eiffel* forbids *implicit* overriding: the compiler checks for repeated inheritance of the same named attribute and forces the programmer to redefine or rename one. Certain OOP languages based on prototypes rather than classes (21) use a more general mechanism called *delegation*, whereby an object may specify which other object(s) field a request which it does not understand. Inheritance can be seen as a 'hard-wired' special case of delegation.

2.4   Polymorphism: or Generic Access and Invocation

Polymorphism is a feature of interest to researchers working on formal theories of types. Strictly, a *polymorphic* function or procedure is one that can be applied to arguments of more than one type, such as the list constructors and deconstructors in typed functional languages like *Hope* and *Standard ML* (*ad hoc* polymorphism). The term *polymorphism* also refers to the existence of more than one function or procedure of the same name, designed to do similar operations on different datatypes (*parameterised* polymorphism), such as the integer- and real-arithmetic addition operations which are both named '+' in most languages.

In OOP, polymorphism results from the names of variables or methods being local to a class. This means that the same name may refer to (actually) different data (or procedures) in different objects, although conceptually they may be the same kinds of thing; eg the *steering-system* variable of class *Vehicle* might refer to the steering wheel and its linkage to the front wheels, whereas the *steering-system* of class

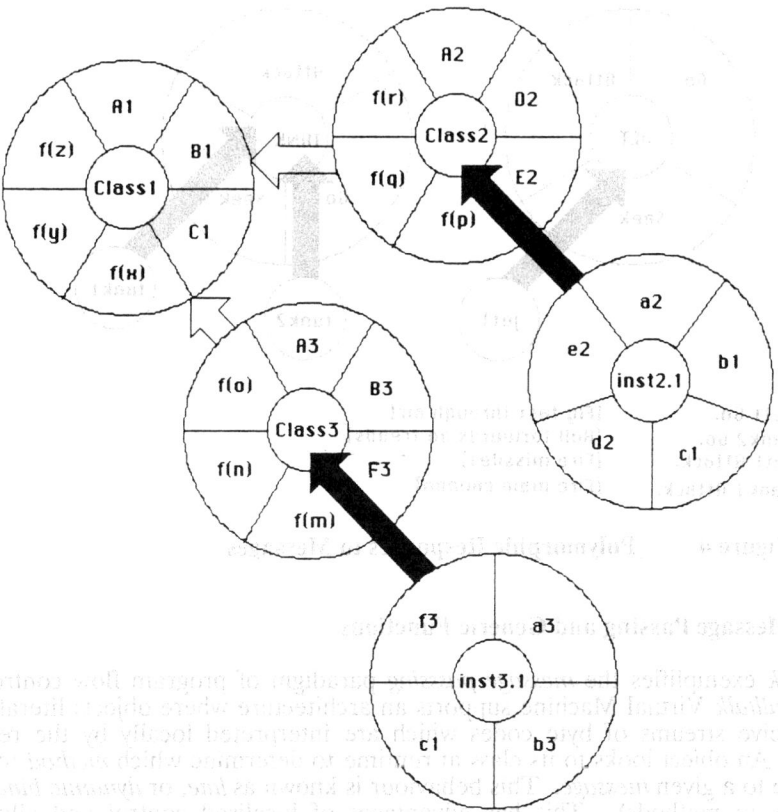

Figure 3   Inheritance and Overriding of Values

*Class1 defines instance variables A, B and C.   Class2 overrides A and
adds D and E.   Class3 overrides A and B but adds F.   The instances
inherit the latest definitions of each variable.*

JetAircraft would refer to the joystick and its linkages to the ailerons and tail fin. The
Attack-method of class *Tank* might involve firing the main cannon, whereas the
Attack-method of class *JetAircraft* would involve firing missiles (Figure 4). In terms of
the definitions above, this constitutes a kind of *parameterised polymorphism* (typed by
the owning class). However, since the methods of a given class are applicable to
instances of arbitrary subclasses (unless overridden), this also provides a kind of *ad-
hoc polymorphism* bounded by the inheritance hierarchy.

Polymorphism permits a high degree of abstraction in the parts of a program which
use these facilities of objects: other objects communicate with instances of *Tank* or
JetAircraft simply by sending them a request to perform one of their actions, without
needing to know how those actions are implemented and without having to worry
whether the message recipient is going to be *Centurion-5* or *Tornado-3*.

Placing polymorphism under the programmer's control allows you to extend the
meaning of an existing operation: eg '+' could be defined, further to its arithmetical
meanings, as the string concatenation operator, or the set union operator. This
facility is referred to as *operator overloading* (qv *function overloading*).

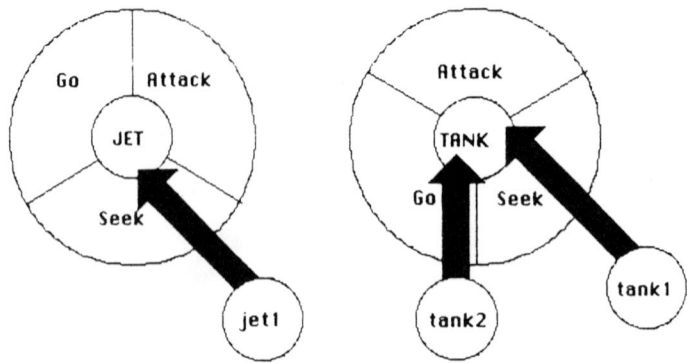

jet1 Go.   [Fly fast through air]
tank2 Go.   [Roll forwards on treads]
jet1 Attack.   [Fire missiles]
tank1 Attack.   [Fire main cannon]

Figure 4   Polymorphic Responses to Messages

2.5   Message Passing and Generic Functions

Smalltalk exemplifies the *message passsing* paradigm of program flow control (22). The *Smalltalk* Virtual Machine supports an architecture where objects literally send and receive streams of byte codes which are interpreted locally by the receiving objects. An object looks to its class at runtime to determine which *method* to use in response to a given *message*. This behaviour is known as *late*, or *dynamic binding* (of receivers to methods). This has advantages of localised control and allows the system itself to be modified or extended easily. On the other hand, the overhead of lookup leads to inefficiencies.

The message passing approach has uses in Artificial Intelligence, where objects model separate processes, each armed with their own procedures and data. In *Simula*, objects can 'suspend' and 'resume' activity according to a sequential implementation of co-routines. Similar OOP languages and systems are usually called *Actor*-based languages, since they deal in explicit simulations of communicating agents. Concurrent models of OOP literally use asynchronous messages as semaphores on parallel hardware.

Statically scoped languages such as *Eiffel* or *C++* like to view procedure and function calls in the traditional way; the syntax of the languages reflect this. However, any one procedure name may refer to different implementations of that procedure for different classes. Such procedures and functions are sometimes called *generic*. Compilers for these languages attempt to replace the (potentially generic) call to a procedure by the most specific implementation. This is referred to as *early*, or *static binding*. There are basically three compilation possibilities: *inline function substitution* (eg *C++*) for cases where a unique method can be found, *generic functions with runtime type discrimination* (eg *CLOS*) for cases where a small subset of methods are found and *full dynamic binding* for cases where runtime tables of all methods are required (eg *Objective C*).

CLOS takes the view that no one argument to a generic function should take pride of place as the receiver-object. Method discrimination is done on the basis of the class of *all arguments* to generic functions. This provides an elegant solution to bivalent operations (eg 2 + 2.0) which, in a language with receivers, would otherwise require extra runtime type checking of the second argument. Critics of this approach say that it detracts from the object-centredness of the paradigm. *CLOS* allows your viewpoint to shift between an object-centred and function-centred view fairly seamlessly.

3   CURRENT ISSUES AND FUTURE DIRECTIONS IN OBJECT-ORIENTED PROGRAMMING

Here we shall expand on some of the themes introduced above in a second iteration round the spiral of object-oriented concepts introduced above. We shall seek to determine what we mean by *object-oriented* and whether given languages fulfil the criteria for being fully object-oriented. We shall ask whether classes are themselves objects and introduce the idea of *metaclasses*. We shall pay a second visit to inheritance schemes and method-combination. Finally, we shall look forward to developments in *Object-Oriented Analysis and Design*, the formal semantics of objects, persistency and databases, and concurrency.

3.1   What is Object-Oriented Programming?

Object-Oriented is the latest buzzword to hit the software headlines; it follows on in the tradition of *block-structured* in the 60s and *modular* in the 70s and 80s as being the latest epithet meaning 'good' or 'desirable'! We should be wary of false claims to the title (23). In real OOP the principal contrast is between *Object-Oriented* and *Procedure-Oriented* styles:

3.1.1   Procedure Oriented Style: program development is by top-down design of procedures (starting from abstract specifications) to produce a self-contained application.

3.1.2   Object-Oriented Style: program development is by modifying existing object descriptions from a permanently available 'toolbox' to produce integrated applications based on extensions of old applications.

The Object-Oriented style:-

*   lays emphasis on the entities used by the program, rather than on the processes used to manipulate them;

*   lays emphasis on the behaviours of software components, rather than on values passed to and from routines;

*   lays emphasis on the generalisation of typical operations (eg on stack, array, linked list);

*   lays emphasis on the design of clear interfaces, with foresight, anticipating use by client objects.

This means that languages like *APL*, *Ada* and *CLU* are not object-oriented (whatever their other merits).

There is also a second confusion between *Modular Design with Data Abstraction* and *Object-Oriented Design with Classes:*

3.1.3   Modular Design with Data Abstraction: the   language   supports   the definition of *abstract data types* with facilities for *encapsulation* (protection from unauthorised access or modification); a *module* is a *syntactic convenience* for

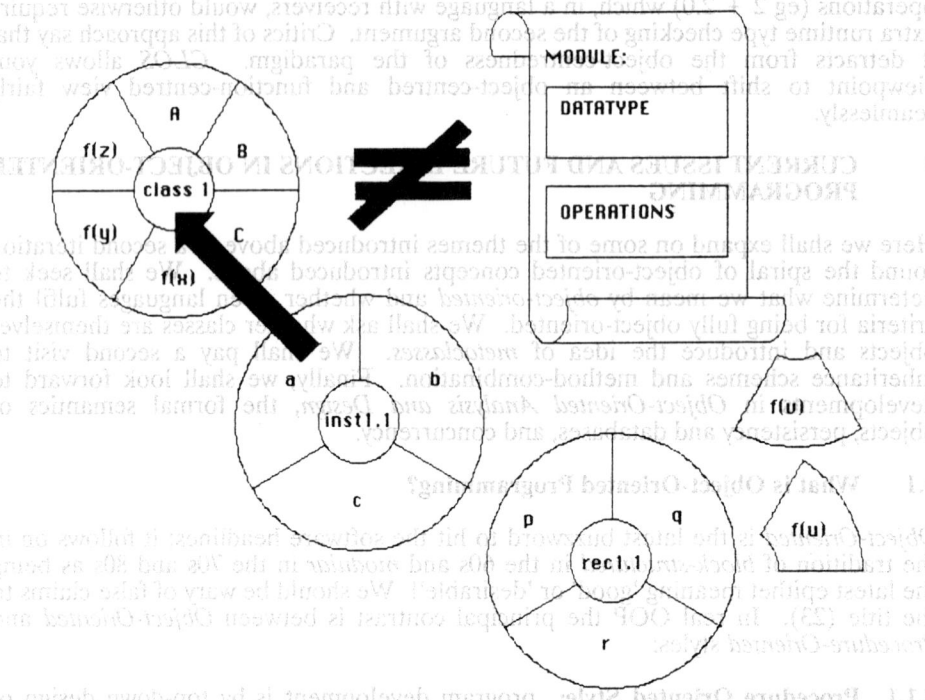

Figure 5   Contrasting a Tightly Coupled Class and Instance with Software Elements Generated from a Text Module

and all its associated operations (on file); a *main program* exists which uses facilities of modules.

3.1.4   Object-Oriented Design with Classes: the   language   supports   the specification of *complete communication protocols* (via inheritance and the external interface provided by methods) for classes;   module and datatype are actually indivisible notions; design is based solely on the assembly of tested components - *the assembly is the program*.

This contrast is illustrated in (Figure 5).

Following our earlier remarks on whether features are *enabled* or *supported* by given languages, we can say that:-

Pascal supports block-structured design; *Fortran* and *Cobol* merely enable block-structured design;

Modula-2 and *Ada* support modular design; *C* enables modular design; *C++* provides limited support for both data abstraction and object-oriented design independently;

Smalltalk and *Eiffel* support object-oriented design.

The following criteria for genuine object-orientation have been adapted from Meyer:

Table 1   Criteria for Object-Orientation

Object-centred rather than process-centred;
Class abstraction fusing module and type;
Definition by extension and restriction (inheritance);
Polymorphic behavioural responses;
Support for the management of dynamic objects.

The above would tend to rule out some languages on the fringes! Some authors prefer to draw on a richer set of taxonomic categories: object-based, class-based, inheritance-based, object-oriented and so on.

3.2   Are Classes First-Class Objects?

The answer to this is equivocal. *Smalltalk* and *CLOS* would say an unabashed *yes*. *Eiffel* says *no*, maintaining that classes are not part of the runtime object system, but are textual specifications only. *C++* and *Objective C* give a definite *maybe,* allowing some operations to address a common pool of data that would pass for class variables by any other name, without admitting whether class objects actually exist.

Eiffel's view is made possible only because the types of objects are known before they are created: in this way, the appropriate *Create* routine can be used to allocate and initialise instances.   In *Smalltalk* and *CLOS*, instance creation is dynamically controlled by the class-object which receives the message to instantiate itself. Classes are viewed, therefore, as first-class objects (as indeed are methods). This leads to the interesting and curious possibility of the object system defining itself recursively.

Recall that instances are gathered together under a class which specifies all the responses for its member instances. For a class to be a fully-fledged runtime object, it too must know how to respond to messages (principally to instantiate itself; but also to display itself in a hierarchical graph, for example). This means that classes, in systems which take this view, are themselves instances of some *metaclass* which specifics class like responses. In like manner, metaclasses are instances of some ultimate *meta-metaclass* which bootstraps the instantiation process. This meta-hierarchy is orthogonal to the class-subclass hierarchy which is the usual focus of program design.

Apart from the convenience of being able to send messages to classes at runtime, having a library of meta-objects at your disposal allows the customisation of the language itself. The forthcoming *CLOS meta-object protocol* document contains examples of how to specialise existing metaclasses in *CLOS* to obtain the behaviour of your own favourite OOP system. You can build *LOOPS*-style browsers, or create a new type of class that implements its instances in a different way. The meta-level, which controls the implementation of the object-system itself, is neatly decoupled from the domain-layer.

In *Smalltalk*, all classes are deemed to have a unique metaclass of the same name; in practice this means that each Smalltalk class is partitioned into its class-managing meta-part and its instance-managing domain-part. *Class methods* specify the class's own responses, whereas *instance methods* specify the responses of the class's instances.

3.3   Inheritance and Method Combination

Multiple inheritance presents interesting problems to the implementor: are classes most like their forbears in direct line, or like the classes closest to them in the

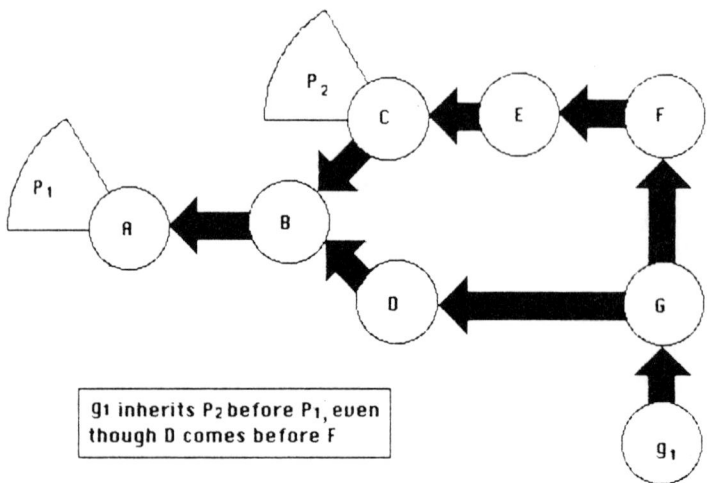

Figure 6   Up-To-The-Joins Inheritance

hierarchy? What happens when two inheritance paths join again at a higher node in the graph?

The problem can be posed as the kind of search-algorithm necessary to traverse the graph:-

3.3.1   Depth-First Inheritance: ensures that each class is most like its forbears in direct line (ie like the first class in its immediate superclasses list, recursively). This was the model used by an early version of *Flavors*.

3.3.2   Breadth-First Inheritance: ensures that each class is most like classes closest to them in the hierarchy (ie each class in the immediate superclasses list is searched before any of their parents). This model was used in experimental systems.

3.3.3   Up-to-the-Joins Inheritance: ensures that all paths leading to a join node are searched before the join node itself and classes beyond it are searched. This was the model adopted by *LOOPS* (in combination with a depth-first strategy).

The latter refinement is to tackle the problem posed by graphs of unbalanced growth (Figure 6) where it would otherwise be possible using just a plain searching algorithm to return a more general value for a property without having searched first for all the more specific values. (Both depth- and breadth-first searches fail in the example illustrated).

In practice, modern systems like *CLOS* precompute a *class precedence list* whenever a new class is defined. This is because the searching and sorting algorithm is often quite involved. Up-to-the-joins strategies require two passes, once to order the hierarchy and once to search this ordered list linearly. *CLOS* actually computes its class precedence list (CPL) using a sorting algorithm based on ordered pairs; but the algorithm may also be viewed as embodying a set of constraints, illustrated in (Table 2).

Table 2   CLOS Rules for Class Precedence

Classes only ever appear once in the CPL;
A subclass precedes all its direct superclasses;
The ordering of direct superclasses is preserved;
Tie breaking rule: add to the CPL the class with the most recently added direct subclass (to keep subtrees together in the CPL).

We have been assuming so far that we are only interested in returning the first inherited value for an attribute or procedure. A further aspect of software reuse is the ability to *add functionality* to existing methods (rather than redefine them by overriding). This is known as *method combination*.

Smalltalk devised the *send-super* mechanism adopted by many systems (so called because a message was sent to a pseudo-object called *super*). It essentially allows the inheritance mechanism to leapfrog the current implementation of a given method and to search for a more general version. *Super* is a variable referring back to the current receiver object (like *self* in Smalltalk), but in the context of the current method having already been bypassed. A previously defined method can be invoked, using *send-super*, within the body of a more specific method of the same name (Figure 7). Here, the instance of class *Metro* uses a specific *Drive-method*, which incorporates the more general *Drive-method* of *Car* by the *send-super* mechanism.

Flavors introduced a rich scheme for combining methods according to a complex ordering of *before* and *after* components. This was seen necessary to overcome problems such as that in (Figure 8). Here, a *TitledBorderedWindow* inherits from both *TitledWindow* and *BorderedWindow*. These in turn inherit from *Window*. When told to *Refresh* itself, an instance of *TitledBorderedWindow* would normally inherit just one of the *Refresh-methods* along one branch; it would fail either to draw the border or the title. If it could somehow be forced to inherit along both branches, *send-super* would cause the method *Refresh* in *Window* to be called twice, which is also unsatisfactory. The solution is to have one *primary* method, *Refresh*, defined in class *Window* and a set of *Refresh:after* components defined in its subclasses. The method combination rule then states that all *after* components will be executed after the *primary* method.

CLOS provides the function *call-next-method* to do the job of *send-super*; and also provides many of *Flavors'* combination types including *before, primary, after* and *around* method types. The SE-oriented languages have very rudimentary facilities for method combination, since they have not developed their ideas about inheritance to this extent. *Eiffel* does emphasise multiple inheritance; but you are required to redefine or rename any class feature (data or procedure) which gives rise to a name clash.

3.4   Future Directions in Object-Oriented Programming

The following areas are some of the currently active research topics in OOP. The best source of information on these is to be found in the conference proceedings of ECOOP (since 1987) and OOPSLA/SIGPLAN Special Notices (since about 1986). A new Journal of Object-Oriented Programming has recently started. Occasionally, BYTE and the BCS Computer Journal have special editions on OOP. The AT&T/Bell Telephone Journal gives regular updates on *C++*.

3.4.1   Object-Oriented Semantics: Work by Yelland (24), building on Wolczko and Reddy, seeks to create a fully abstract *denotational semantics* for Object-Oriented languages. This is an attempt to describe the formal properties of classes and objects in terms of sets, functions and relations that can be manipulated using mathematical

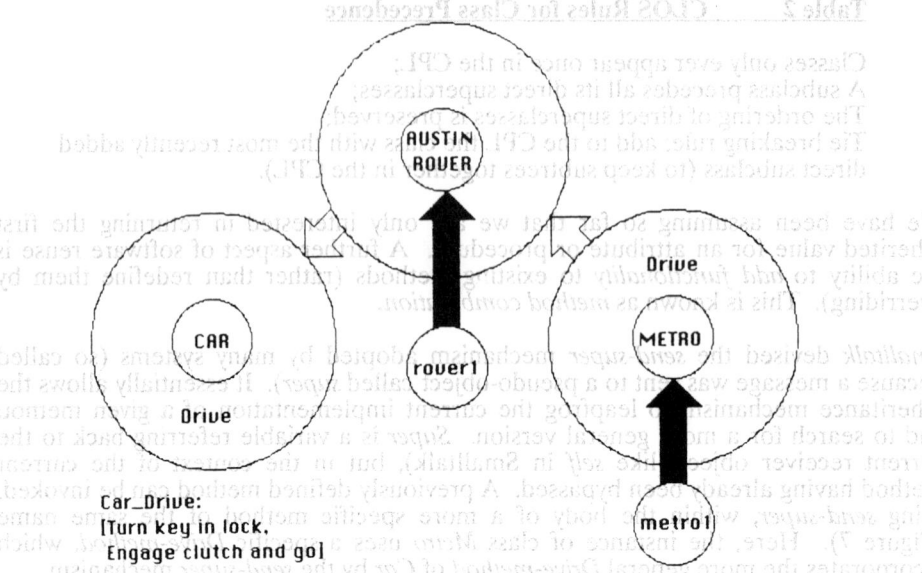

Figure 7   Invoking Super Methods Reuses Old Code

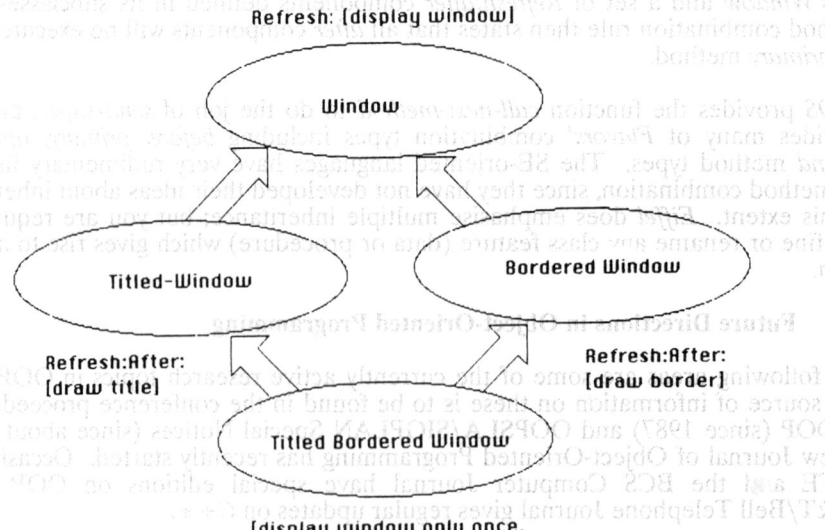

Figure 8   Method Combination Mixes in Different Flavors

logic. Some interesting anomalies in *Smalltalk* and *Eiffel* have been discovered. Other workers take a more *descriptive* approach, exploring the relationships between classes, types, hypothesis refinement and prototypes.

3.4.2 Object-Oriented Analysis and Design: Analysis is an extension of relational data analysis, to include the possibility of inheritance. Generally, the stages are the same up to a point (isolate the base objects in your application; determine which features are properties and which are relationships; choose your key identifiers), but then you factor out common elements to a superclass. Design is centred around the engineering of low-level software components (cf house bricks); it is viewed as a bottom-up process. It is becoming clear that some high-level constraining model (cf an architect's plan) is also necessary. Meyer has proposed a supplier-client model for reliability which rings true.

3.4.3 Persistency and Databases: SE-oriented language users now require the facility to store away large quantities of instances and recreate them from file at a later stage. This is trivially tricky, due to the mutually recursive nature of some objects (but Smalltalk manages this easily enough). However, trivial issues are made more complex by the need for seriously large object-storage and version management. Database people see potential benefits in switching between a relational view and an object-centred view of the same data. This would seem to point forward to the development of Object-Oriented front-ends to traditional database query languages (much in the spirit of the *external query* or *evaluable predicates* of some Prolog implementations).

3.4.4 Concurrent Systems and Custom Hardware: Work in Vulcan, Concurrent Smalltalk and a host of other experimental parallel systems is in progress. The main problem in concurrency is the difficulty in predicting the time of arrival of messages on different processors. The side-effect rich nature of OOP means that the migration of objects from processor to processor must be strictly controlled to avoid corruption through multiple versions. The notion of one object per processor is unrealistic in that it leads to message deadlock. Linn Smart Computing have recently developed a custom board for OOP called *Hades*, which uses the *Rekursiv* chip to manage objects in hardware at the speed of a C-machine. Massive hardware resources are devoted to managing the object store and performing arithmetical and logical operations on separate processors.

4 REFERENCES

1   G Birtwistle, O-J Dahl, B Myrhaug and K Nygaard (1973), Simula Begin, Studentliteratur Lund and Auerbach NY.

2   A Goldberg and D Robson (1983), Smalltalk-80: the language and its implementation, Addison Wesley.

3   A Goldberg (1985), Smalltalk-80: the interactive programming environment, Addison Wesley.

4   M R Quillian (1968), 'Semantic Memory', in: Semantic Information Processing, ed. M Minsky, MIT Press.

5   M Minsky (1975), 'A framework for representing knowledge', in: The Psychology of Computer Vision, ed. P H Winston, McGraw Hill.

6   D S Touretzky (1986), The Mathematics of Inheritance Systems, Research Notes in Artificial Inheritance, Pitmans London.

7   J Aikens (1983), 'Prototypical knowledge for expert systems', Artificial Intelligence, 20, 163-210.

8   H Cannon (1980), 'Flavors', Technical Report, MIT Artificial Intelligence Laboratory, Cambridge MA.

9   D Bobrow and M Stefik (1983), 'The LOOPS manual', Xerox PARC.

10   S Keene (1989), <u>Object-Oriented Programming in Common Lisp</u>, Addison Wesley and Symbolics Press.

11   B J Cox (1986), <u>Object-Oriented Programming: an Evolutionary Approach</u>, Addison Wesley.

12   L Tesler (1985), 'Object Pascal Report', Structured Language World 9 (3).

13   B Stroustrup (1986), <u>The C++ Programming Language</u>, Addison Wesley.

14   B Meyer (1988), <u>Object-Oriented Software Construction</u>, Prentice Hall.

15   C A R Hoare (1972), 'Proof of correctness of data representations', Acta Informatica, Vol. 1, 271-281.

16   C B Jones (1986), Systematic Software Development Using VDM, Prentice-Hall.

17   M I Wolczko (1988), <u>Semantics of Object-Oriented Languages</u>, PhD Thesis; Technical Report UMCS-88-6-1, University of Manchester.

18   W Wobcke (1988), 'A global theory of inheritance', Proc. European Conf. on Artificial Intelligence (ECAI-88), Munich, August, 214-219, Pitmans.

19   E Chouraqui and P Dugerdil (1988), 'Conflict solving in a frame-like multiple inheritance system', Proc. European Conf. on Artificial Intelligence (ECAI-88), Munich, August, 226-231, Pitmans.

20   D Bobrow, L DeMichiel, R Gabriel, S Keene, G Kiczales and D Moon (1987), 'Common Lisp Object System Specification', draft specification of ANSI X3J13 standards CLOS subcommittee, revision A, XEROX PARC. E-Mail contact: CommonLoops-Coordinator.pa@Xerox.com.

21   D Ungar and R B Smith (1987), 'SELF: the power of simplicity', Proc. OOPSLA 87, Orlando, publ. SIGPLAN Notices 22 (12), 227-241.

22   C Hewitt (1977), 'Viewing control structures as patterns of passing messages', Artificial Intelligence, 8, 323-364.

23   B Stroustrup (1987), 'What is Object-Oriented Programming?', Proc. ECOOP 87, Paris, publ. BIGRE 84, June 1987, 51-70.

24   P M Yelland (1989), 'First steps towards fully abstract semantics for Object-Oriented languages', Proc. European Conf. on Object-Oriented Programming (ECOOP-89), ed. S Cook, CUP, 347-364.

Chapter 4

Parallel processing and the transputer

Jon M. Kerridge

1   Introduction

The world in which we live is a highly complex parallel
system in which many activities interact with each other in
an apparently random manner. If we look at any system in the
large it is very difficult to build a single model that
captures all the interactions of which the system is
capable. As an example consider a model of the earth's
weather system.

A different way of building a model is to break the system
down into a number of different components some of which
provide the external interface to the real world and others
of which are there only to simplify the modelling process.
If the model is sufficiently refined into basic components
we arrive at the fundamental processes which make up the
complete system. At the lowest level these processes are
fundamentally easy to understand. These processes operate at
the same time (in parallel) and every so often communicate
with neighbouring processes. The communication may just be a
message to indicate some unit of work has been completed or
data values are passed from one process to the other. Thus
provided we can identify the basic processes of a system we
can construct other processes from these processes and so on
until we build the required model of the desired system.
This provides a very natural way of thinking for a human
being. The limitations of existing computer architectures
have forced humans to program in a sequential manner rather
than the parallel way in which they design.

Obviously, the inter-process communication cannot proceed
in a disorderly manner, for if it were so to do, one process
could send messages to another process in such a way that
messages could be lost or non-existent messages processed.
Consider a producer process P and a consumer process C. P is
to send a message to C. If P sends a message to C before C
has finished processing the previous message then data could
be lost if P is allowed to continue processing regardless of
the state of C. Similarly, if C tries to consume a message

before P has produced the message then C will consume a non-existent message generally with disastrous results.

The simplest way to overcome this problem is to ensure that the processes P and C synchronise with one another when they wish to communicate. This can be easily achieved by whichever process is ready to communicate first waiting until the second process is ready to communicate. The communication can then take place after which both processes can continue in parallel. Using this simple mechanism we can construct systems of processes which model as complex a system as required. This model of communication is known as Communicating Sequential Processes (CSP) [Hoare 78] [Hoare 85]. The model provides a system design environment which is the basis of a practical programming language, occam [INMOS 88].

CSP also provides a formal basis for reasoning about the behaviour of parallel systems. Much work has been carried out to develop a set of laws [Roscoe 86] that enable CSP based systems to be transformed. Such transformations maintain the logical correctness of a system but alter its physical attributes. These physical attributes are especially critical when a design is implemented on a multi-processor computer system.

CSP provided one of the major inputs to the development by Inmos Ltd of the transputer. The transputer is a processor that has been designed to explicitly exploit process parallelism. A transputer based system is intended to have more than one transputer in the physical realisation of a design. The transputer can be viewed as a hardware implementation of CSP concepts. The transputer is best programmed in the parallel language occam which was designed to exploit process parallelism at the logical design phase. The advantage of the transputer/occam combination is that a logical design expressed in occam can be mapped onto different transputer topologies. These topologies will yield different performance thereby enabling the solution to be optimised for a given performance requirement. Perhaps, more importantly, once a system has been implemented and the performance requirements change the transputer topology can be altered to match the change without re-designing the logic of the system. All that changes is the specification of the configuration of processes to transputers.

1.1   The Transputer

The transputer is a Very Large Scale Integration (VLSI) device comprising, processor, memory and communications on the same piece of silicon. Because the transputer was designed to implement the CSP paradigm it contains explicit provision to support parallel operation. As such it is the only currently available microprocessor that had as one of its design goals scalable parallel operation. To achieve parallelism the transputer employs synchronised point-to-

point communication rather than a shared resource such as
memory or a single communications bus. Thus each time a
transputer is added to a design not only does the processing
capability of the complete system increase but also the
total communications bandwidth. If a shared resource is used
then there will come a point when the bandwidth of the
shared resource is saturated and the addition of further
processors has no appreciable benefit.

The integration of memory and communications onto the same
piece of silicon as the processor also enable an increase in
functionality due to the closeness of the components. The
transputer has been organised so that processing and
communications can be overlapped. This is achieved by making
the communications links Direct Memory Access (DMA) devices.
The internal memory can be augmented by external memory as
required by an application.

The transputer is not just one processor but a family of
processors each with the same basic architecture. The basic
architecture is shown in figure 1.

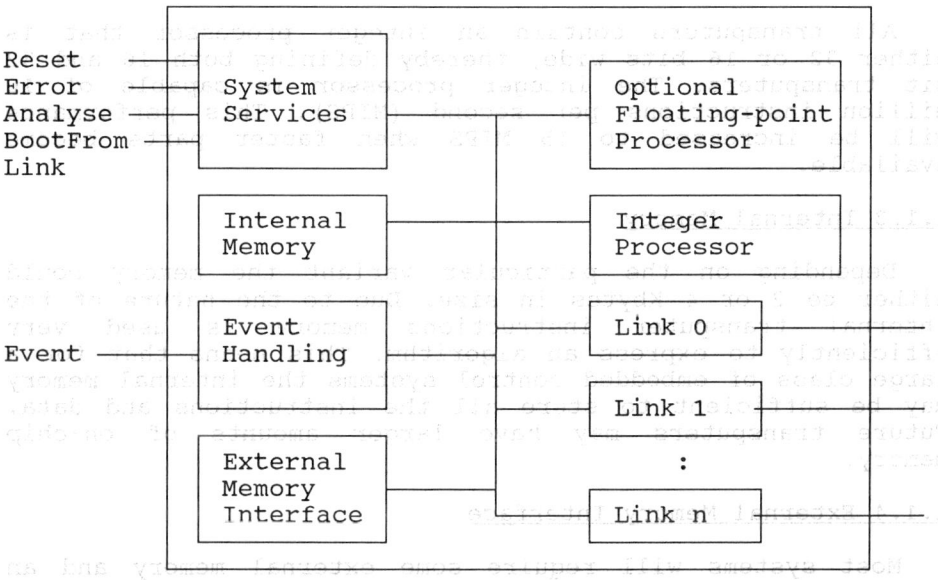

Figure 1 Generic Transputer Architecture

1.1.1 System Services

Systems services provides the basic housekeeping signals
for the transputer. Reset sets the transputer to a predefined state. Error indicates when an illegal state has
occurred within the transputer. Analyse can be asserted
after an error has occurred so that the state of the
transputer can be examined. BootFromLink is a signal that
indicates that the program to be loaded into the transputer

will be down loaded through one of the links. If this signal
is not asserted then the program to be loaded in the
transputer will be saved in some form of read only memory.
In a large system it would be invidious to have read only
memory located with each transputer. Thus all that is
required is a single root transputer which can access the
program to be loaded into each transputer which it then
communicates to all the connected transputers.

The transputer also contains a clock mechanism which
enables processes to determine a time value relative to the
transputer upon which it is executing. The time is
implemented as a free running counter which any process can
access by means of a communication. Any number of timers can
be declared. The granularity of a timer is either 1
microsecond or 64 microseconds. A process accesses a timer
by means of the same communication primitive that is used
for inter-process communication. A timer is always ready to
communicate so that a process accessing a timer channel
never has to wait.

1.1.2 Integer Processor

All transputers contain an integer processor that is
either 32 or 16 bits wide, thereby defining both 16 and 32
bit transputers. The integer processor is capable of 10
million instructions per second (MIPS). This performance
will be increased to 15 MIPS when faster parts become
available.

1.1.3 Internal Memory

Depending on the particular variant the memory could
either be 2 or 4 Kbytes in size. Due to the nature of the
internal transputer instructions memory is used very
efficiently to express an algorithm. This means that for a
large class of embedded control systems the internal memory
may be sufficient to store all the instructions and data.
Future transputers may have larger amounts of on-chip
memory.

1.1.4 External Memory Interface

Most systems will require some external memory and an
interface is provided that enables external memory to be
easily interfaced. For 16 bit transputers the total memory
that can addressed is 64 kbytes and for 32 bit transputers 4
Gbytes. The external memory interface has been designed so
that it can be configured to enable different memory types
to be placed at different places in the memory map. This
reduces the number of chips that are required to implement
the hardware of a system.

Peripherals and devices are memory mapped into the
external memory interface. Such devices are accessed using
the same communication primitives that are used to

communicate between processes. The only difference is that a device is always ready to communicate and thus a process never has to wait to communicate with a device.

1.1.5 Link Engines

A transputer can have either 2 or 4 links each of which is capable at communicating in both directions at the same time. That is, each link engine comprises two DMA devices, one for input the other for output. However, each link has to be connected to a single link connection on another transputer because the reverse direction is used to acknowledge messages. Data is transferred at either 10 or 20 Mbits per second (0.8 or 1.6 Mbytes per second). Data is communicated using a serial connection. It does not matter whether the communication is directed to internal or external memory.

1.1.6 Event Handling

A transputer will accept a signal from a peripheral device to indicate that the device has completed an operation. This is equivalent to an interrupt on a traditional processor design. The event handler achieves the same effect but in a manner that is consistent with the communication mechanism rather than something that causes the processor to halt what it is doing and deal with the interrupt and then return to where it was before the interrupt occurred. The event signal is effectively an output communication from a hardware process which is then input to a process executing on the transputer. A process can be made to wait until an event occurs when it completes the communication by inputting the event message.

1.1.7 Optional Floating Point Processor

Some versions of the transputer (T8's) have a 64 bit floating point processor that can operate in parallel with the integer processor. Thus floating point operation can be overlapped with address calculation. The floating point processor is capable of 1.5 million floating point operations per second (MFLOPS).

1.1.8 Process Scheduling

The transputer has a process scheduler implemented in the microcode. This avoids the necessity for a real-time executive or operating system. The process scheduler provides a two level priority scheme. It is relatively easy to construct a system that implements multi-level priority if that is required. High priority processes execute until they attempt a communication for which the other process is not yet ready. They are also descheduled when they delay themselves until a particular time has occurred. In addition, low priority process can also be descheduled when they obey a conditional jump instruction, at which point any waiting high priority process will be scheduled. It takes less than one microsecond to switch from one process to another.

In general communication bound processes execute at high priority and compute bound processes execute at low priority. This means that a system can be constructed in which data is received by a high priority process, which does not require processor intervention as communication is controlled by a link engine. Meanwhile, the processor can be processing, at low priority, the previous data set that was transferred to the processor. In a similar manner, results of the processing can be output by another high priority process. It is therefore easy to design a double buffered system which overlaps processing with input and output communication.

1.1.9 Communication Control

It does not matter whether a communication is between processes on the same transputer or between processes running on different transputers. The semantics are identical. The process which attempts to communicate first is made to wait until the second process is ready to communicate. The communication then takes place and the first process is added to the list of processes ready to execute. The second process just continues processing without waiting.

1.2   occam

Inmos developed occam [Inmos 88] so that parallel systems could be designed using a programming language that contained explicit parallelism. At the same time the designers of the language included features, based on the formal principles of CSP, that promote the design of rigorous systems. The language also contains features that support the best principles of software engineering.

The name occam is derived form the 14th century Oxford mathematician who developed a principle known as Occam's Razor. This principle states that "concepts should not be multiplied beyond that which is required" or perhaps more strongly "keep things simple". Therefore occam is a very simple language with a minimum of constructs and fundamental principles.

The basic concept of occam is that of the process and at the lowest level these processes are implemented by; an input primitive (?), an output primitive (!) and assignment (:=). Communication is achieved by means of a CHANnel that connects two processes in one direction only. One end of the channel undertakes an output operation and the other end undertakes an input operation. Whichever process undertakes the operation first waits until the second process is ready to communicate. The communication takes place and both processes can then proceed in parallel. The data that is communicated is typed to ensure that data in the correct format is passed between processes. In fact occam is a very strongly typed language and automatic coercion of data types is not permitted. Coercions have to be explicitly stated. Many errors occur in traditional programming languages due to automatic type coercion, many of which are not detected until some time after the system has been installed.

In order to construct large systems it is necessary to have constructors in the language that allow larger components to be defined. These constructors are SEQuence, PARallel, non-deterministic ALTernative, deterministic IF and a loop structure WHILE. Processes and procedures can be defined as parameterised PROCs. Functions can also be defined which are guaranteed to have no side-effects because they return a single value, only value parameters are permitted and they are not allowed to undertake a communication within the function body. In fact the whole language is side effect free in that assignment is not an operator as it is in C for example.

1.2.1 SEQ

The SEQ constructor introduces a sequence of processes that are to be executed in sequence.

```
CHAN OF INT p,q:
INT a,b,c:
SEQ
   b := 2
   p ? c
   a := b * c
   q ! a
```

Indentation is significant in occam programs in that the indentation delimits the effect of a constructor. In the above example the four processes (statements) will be executed one after the other. The complete structure is considered to be a process.

1.2.2 PAR

Processes that are to be executed in parallel are introduced by the constructor PAR. Thus the following example will transfer the value of y from the first component of the PAR to the second component. Note that variables are declared local to the individual processes. Global variables cannot shared between parallel processes. Only channels can be shared between processes.

```
CHAN comms:
PAR
  INT y:
  SEQ
    y := 0
    comms ! y
  INT x:
  SEQ
    comms ? x
    x := x + x
```

1.2.3 ALT

If a process accepts inputs from more than one process then in general it is not determined the order in which these inputs will arrive and therefore it is necessary to provide a construct that will wait until one of the channels is ready to communicate and then accept that communication. If more than one channel is ready to communicate when the ALT is obeyed then either one of the channels will be selected randomly or, in the case of a PRI ALT, the first channel that is ready in textual sequence will be selected to complete its communication. The following example describes the operation of an amplifier that is controlled remotely as occurs in a television controller. The process is organised so that the amplifier only receives only values between 0 and 10 inclusive.

```
PROTOCOL SIGNAL IS INT:
CHAN OF SIGNAL louder, softer, amplifier:
INT volume, signal:
SEQ
  volume := 5          -- initialise to half volume
  amplifier ! volume
  WHILE TRUE
    ALT
      (volume > 0) & softer ? signal
        SEQ
          volume := volume - 1
          amplifier ! volume
      (volume < 10) & louder ? signal
        SEQ
          volume := volume + 1
          amplifier ! volume
```

In this example we also see how the usual WHILE looping construct is organised. It is typical of occam based systems that they are used in embedded systems which run forever or until the power is switched off. Therefore the use of WHILE TRUE to loop forever is perfectly reasonable.

1.2.4 IF

The deterministic IF statement has similar semantics to that found in many high level languages. There are some important differences though which have been introduced to promote sound software engineering practice. There is no ELSE component as this leads to the 'dangling else' found in Pascal. Instead IF is a sequence of boolean expressions which are evaluated in sequence until one is found that evaluates to true. The process corresponding to that condition is then executed. If non of the boolean expressions evaluates to true then the process is made to stop execution. That is the process does not just carry on as in many other languages because this behaviour is known to be a source of many errors that are extremely difficult to detect. The programmer has to explicitly program the desired behaviour.

2   Handling Devices

An example is presented [Welch 87] that shows how devices can be handled using event in a style which is similar to that commonly used in interrupt driven systems. The great advantage of the occam description is that we can reason about the behaviour of the system and are not reliant upon any underlying real-time executive, commonly used in interrupt driven systems. We shall assume that events are going to be accepted from only one device, it is not difficult to generalise the solution to several devices.

2.1 Catching Events

First, a process is required which will wait for an event to occur and then wake up a process that will access the device. If interrupts are not to be missed it is vital that this process is short and has a behaviour that guarantees that it is always waiting for an event to occur.

```
PROC event.handler ( CHAN OF INT s.wake.up )
  CHAN OF INT hardware.event:
  PLACE hardware.event AT 8:
  VAL INT signal IS 1:
  WHILE TRUE
    INT interrupt:
    SEQ
      hardware.event ? interrupt
      s.wake.up ! signal
:
```

This process will wait until the channel *hardware.event* is ready to communicate. If this process is not to be blocked then the output on *s.wake.up* has to take place immediately. This can be guaranteed if there is a process waiting to communicate on the same channel. Assuming this is the case then *event.handler* will then loop round and therefore be waiting for then next input on *hardware.event*.

2.2 Accessing the device

A process is now required which is waiting to be woken up
and which can then access the device registers. It should
return to this state as quickly as possible so that the
event.handler process is not waiting to output on the
channel *wake.up*. For the sake of clarity we shall assume the
device is one from which a single integer is read.

```
PROC read.device ( CHAN OF INT d.wake.up,
                                s.data.value )
    INT data, signal:
    PORT OF INT data.register:
    PLACE data.register AT #0400 :
    WHILE TRUE
      SEQ
        d.wake.up ? signal
        data.register ? data   -- read from device
        s.data.value ! data
  :
```

This process is normally waiting for an input on *d.wake.up*
which is the state required by *event.handler*. Once it has
been woken up it reads a data value from the device which
cannot cause a delay as a device channel is always ready to
communicate. The process then outputs the data value before
it loops round to wait for the next signal on *d.wake.up*.
Thus this process cannot block *event.handler* provided we can
guarantee that the communication on *s.data.value* will not be
delayed.

2.3 Buffering the data

A process is required that can hold a data value in a
buffer in such a way that if the control logic is too slow
then data is overwritten with the latest value. It has to be
guaranteed that the buffer process will not cause a delay to
the *read.device* process. This process will also indicate how
many data values were missed by the control logic.

A PROTOCOL, called *DATA*, is specified that specifies the
format of the data   to be transferred from the *buffer*
process. This protocol is then used to specify the type of
the channel.

```
PROTOCOL DATA IS INT; INT:
```

```
PROC buffer ( CHAN OF INT d.data.value,
                          d.request.data,
              CHAN OF DATA s.send.data )
  BOOL loaded:
  INT data, missed, request:
  SEQ
    missed := 0
    loaded := FALSE
    WHILE TRUE
      PRI ALT
        d.data.value ? data
          IF
            loaded
              missed := missed + 1
            NOT loaded
              loaded := TRUE
        loaded & d.request.data ? request
          SEQ
            s.send.data ! missed; data
            loaded := FALSE
            missed := 0
:
```

The *buffer* process gives priority to communications coming from the *read.device* process as is required to prevent blocking of that process. The data value is read in and depending on the value of *loaded* either *missed* is incremented or *loaded* is set to TRUE at which point the process is ready to accept another input from *read.device*. This branch of the ALT has no communication and we can therefore guarantee this behaviour.

The other branch of the ALT can only be entered once data has been input from *read.device* because *loaded* has to be TRUE before the communication can take place. A process is therefore required which can request the data value from the *buffer* and which will then guarantee to input that value without any delay. A process is needed which prompts for the data.

2.4 Prompting for the data

The *prompt* process requests data from the *buffer* process and guarantees that it will not delay the *buffer* process. This ensures that non of the other processes will be blocked and that the system will be able to field events rapidly. The worst case scenario occurs when the *buffer* process has just accepted an input on *d.request.data* and that body of code has to be processed including the communication to the prompt process on *s.send.data*.

```
PROC prompt ( CHAN OF INT s.request.data,
              CHAN OF DATA d.send.data,
                           s.output.data )
    INT missed, data:
    VAL INT request IS 1:
    WHILE TRUE
      SEQ
        s.request.data ! request
        d.send.data ? missed;  data
        s.output.data ! missed; data
  :
```

The *prompt* process outputs a request for data on channel *s.request.data* which will only be completed when the *buffer* process is *loaded*. At which point the *prompt* process is ready to accept the data values (*missed* and *data*) from the *prompt* process causing no delay. The *prompt* process then outputs the data values on the channel *s.output.data*. It does not matter if there is a subsequent delay when the data values are output on channel *s.output.data* because the *buffer* process will have already looped round ready to accept an input from *read.device*. The worst that can happen is that all values that arrived at event will not be passed to the main logic of the controller but then this would be indicated by a non-zero *missed* value.

2.5 Main Controller Logic

The processes defined so far have been constructed with the sole intention of passing data to the main controller process in such a way that the event handler process has a guaranteed latency between events. The main control process requires a process heading of the following form.

```
PROC main.logic ( CHAN OF DATA d.output.data )
    INT missed, data:
    WHILE TRUE
      SEQ
        d.output.data ? missed; data
        -- process missed and data
  :
```

2.6 Instantiation of the System

The system is instantiated in the following manner, showing that at the outer level only channels are accessible as global objects. The processes that comprise the event handling part are executed at high priority and the main control logic is executed at low priority.

```
CHAN OF INT wake.up, data.value, request.data:
CHAN OF DATA send.data, output.data:
PRI PAR
  PAR
    event.handler ( wake.up )
    read.device ( wake.up, data.value )
    buffer ( data.value, request.data, send.data )
    prompt ( request.data, send.data, output.data)
  main.logic ( output.data )
```

3   Safety Critical Systems, occam and the Transputer

The transputer, together with occam, provide, possibly,
the only commercial system construction environment where it
is feasible to reason about the behaviour of the designed
system.   Further, because occam conforms to a number of
laws concerning its communication and process construction
mechanisms it is possible to transform occam programs.
These transformations can be undertaken for performance
reasons.   However, once a program is shown to be logically
correct under these transformations it is known that the
transformed program will also be correct.   The transformed
programme will have different physical properties which can
be utilised for performance, cost or flexibility reasons.

The major emphasis when designing an occam based system is
to identify and incorporate the maximum parallelism into the
solution as is possible.   This could well be more than is
realistically feasible.   Subsequently, the solution can be
transformed to introduce more sequential operations, for
performance and cost reasons.   It is much easier to remove
parallelism from a design than it is to add parallelism to
an inherently sequential design.   It is also easier to
reason about the behaviour of a highly parallel system.

4   An Application : Automotive Systems

Increasingly, automotive systems are becoming more complex
and are providing increased requirements for electronic
control functionality.   This is exhibited by the use of
electronic systems in areas other than engine control
management which provided the initial stimulus.   In safety
critical terms engine management is not as critical as, say,
a steering or brake control system.   Yet it is this latter
area that will see the major need for electronic control
systems with the concomitant requirement for safety critical
design and implementation.

The main areas in which there is likely to be increasing
use of electronic control systems are in;

    complex engine management,
    chassis,
    information,
and convenience macrosystems.

Where the chassis macrosystem could be subdivided into suspension and braking sub-systems.   Thus we could propose a basic parallel architecture shown in the diagram, where each square box represents one or more transputers depending on processing requirements.

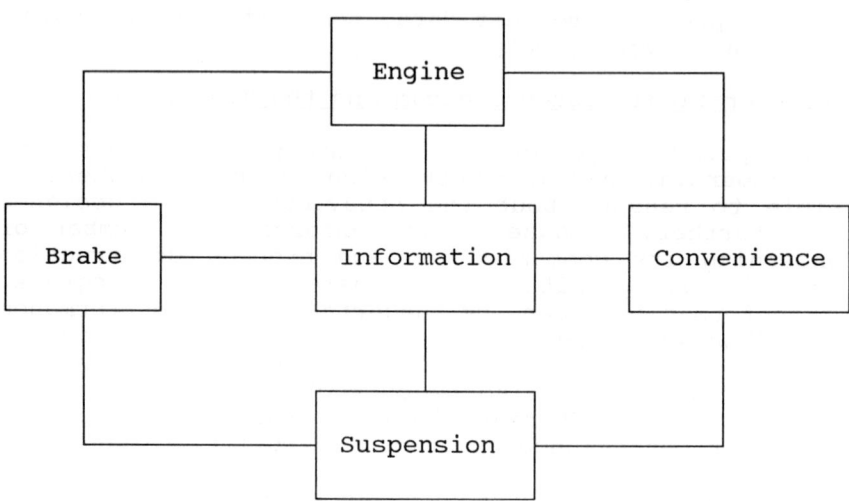

A single transputer can always be replaced by a 'super' transputer comprising four transputers as follows:-

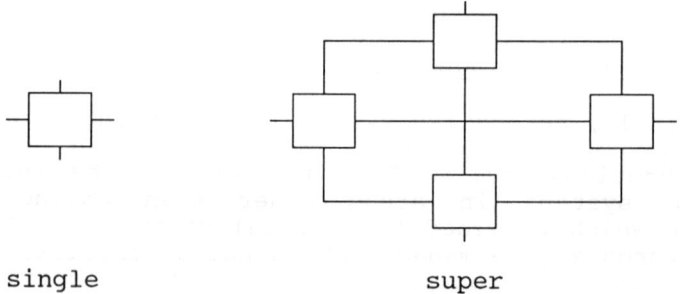

single   super

In general, however, this is not the approach that is adopted, but the processes that comprise the subcomponent are mapped onto a transputer topology that more closely reflects the inter-process communication structure.   The main benefit of the transputer based approach is that each part of the complete system can be augmented to reflect extra processing requirements imposed by facility enhancement.

This is achieved because there is no shared resource in a transputer based system. Thus, it is not possible to hit a performance bottleneck that occurs with other microprocessors when the limit of the shared resource is reached. It is unlikely that any single processor will be able to provide sufficient performance capability to satisfy the needs of a complete automotive control system. It would therefore appear more realistic to use a multi-processor design from the outset and further to incorporate parallelism as an important component of the initial design. A transputer system provides a linearly scalable environment for new features and retro-fitting facilities to existing installed systems.

5   Testing, Verification and Calibration of Control Systems

An important aspect of the design process is verification and calibration of a control system. It also has to be tested in an environment that is both controlled and realistic. This requires that the design engineer is able to modify parameters of the control system in a 'test rig' environment confident that the measured variations exhibited will occur in the production environment.

The use of transputers and occam provides such an environment because the control system can be connected to test rig data in such a way, that apart from the actual sensor/actuator processes the data fed into the control system will be identical. This arises because the data protocol between the sensor and actuator processes and the control system can be precisely defined. The behaviour of the interface processes will be precisely defined. Thus the designer will be able to experiment with different calibrations and parameter settings knowing that the effect in the test environment will be mapped directly onto the production environment.

It is therefore feasible to undertake large experiments in control algorithms prior to production. More importantly, once the design is finalised the time to installation of production versions can be reduced because the system can be formally verified. The current technique of testing for a long period in the hope that all operating eventualities will be met can be avoided. This pre-production phase being perhaps more correctly termed a system proving phase. Lengthy delays between completion of design and installation into production vehicles can be reduced. This is achievable solely because the software can be verified during the design phase.

6   Conclusion

This chapter has shown that the use of parallel techniques supported by appropriate hardware can provide a rigorous means of designing and implementing complete systems. It has also been shown that the transputer is an ideal means of implementing embedded controllers with hard real-time constraints. It should also be appreciated that the transputer can also be used in a number of other applications such business systems, where the aspect of easy and cheap scalability becomes very important. The critical aspect in the design of all systems is to ensure that the maximum parallelism is identified at the outset and not to be hide-bound by traditional sequential techniques. Perhaps the strongest message being "do you really need that operating system or real-time executive?".

References

[Hoare 78]   CAR   Hoare,   "Communicating   Sequential Processes", CACM Vol21 No 8, August 1978

[Hoare 85]   CAR   Hoare,   "Communicating   Sequential Processes", Prentice-Hall, 1985

[Inmos 88]   Inmos   Ltd,   "occam2   Reference   Manual", Prentice-Hall, 1988.

[Roscoe 86]   AW Roscoe and CAR Hoare, "The Laws of occam Programming",   Programming   Research   Group Monograph,   Oxford   University   Computing Laboratory, 1986.

[Welch 87]   P Welch, "Managing Hard Real-time Demands on Transputers",   in   T   Muntean   (ed)   "Parallel Programming of Transputer Based Machines", IOS Amsterdam, 1988.

Chapter 5

Construction of software for real-time computer control systems

Stuart Bennett

INTRODUCTION

The production of robust, reliable, quality software for real-time computer control applications is a difficult task which requires the application of engineering methods. During the last ten years increasing emphasis has been placed on formalising the specification, design and construction of such software, and several methodologies are now extant (see section x below). All of the methods address the problem in three distinct phases. The production of a logical or abstract model - the process of specification; the development of an implementation model for a virtual machine from the logical model - the process of design; and the construction of software for the virtual machine together with the implementation of the virtual machine on a physical system - the process of implementation.

Although there is a logical progression from abstract model, to implementation model, to implemented software, and although three separate and distinct artifacts - abstract model, implementation model, and deliverable system - are produced, the phases overlap in time. The major reason for the overlap of the phases is that complex systems as best handled by a hierarchical approach; determination of the detail of the lower levels in the hierarchy of the logical model must be based on knowledge of higher level design decisions, and similarly the lower level design decisions must be based on the higher level implementation decisions. Another way of expressing this is to say that the higher level design decisions determine the requirements for the lower levels in the system.

.1 Characteristics of real-time systems

The methodologies are based on the assumption that a real-time computer control system can be modelled best as a finite-state-machine as shown in figure 1. In this model of a real-time system the outputs are function of the inputs and the internal state but the internal state can be changed by the state of the environment and the environment can be changed by the internal state.

The characteristics of this system are:

Multiple inputs which may be:

 discrete events occurring at any time;

 continuously changing data values;

 discrete data values.

Multiple outputs which may be:

 discrete events;

 continuously changing data values

 discrete data values.

Timing - the actions have to be performed within the time scale set by the environment or synchronously with the environment. Formally the requirement can be expressed as:

 the order of computation is determined by the passage of time or by events external to the computer;

 the results of the particular calculation may depend upon the value of some

variable 'time' at the instance of execution of the calculations;
* the correct operation of the software depends on the time taken to carry out the computations

System state - the actions performed on the inputs may change according to:
* the internal state of the program;
* the state of the environment.

<u>and</u>
* the inputs may change the internal state.

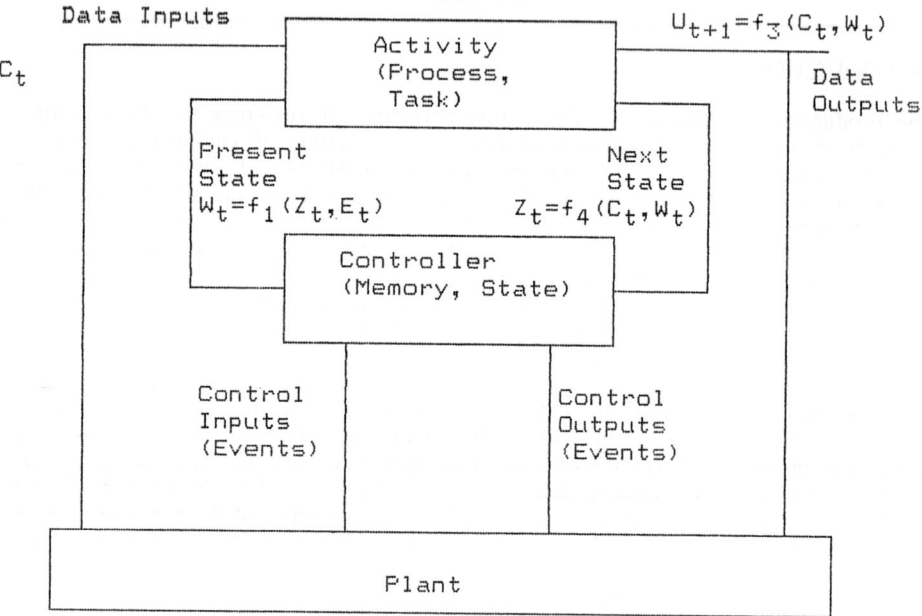

Figure 1. Finite State Machine Model

<u>1.2 Classes of real-time systems</u>

We can divide real-time computer systems into two categories:

(i)   Hard time constraint: the computation must be completed within a specified maximum time on each and every occasion.

(ii)   Soft time constraint: the system must have a mean execution time measured over a defined time interval which is lower than a specified maximum.

The first category - the hard time constraint - is obviously a much more severe constraint on the performance of the system than the second. The so called embedded systems i.e. systems in which the computer or computers form an integral part of some machine usually come into this category.

1.2.1 Hard time constraint systems

Some examples of hard time constraint systems are:

*   Control systems with the computer in the feedback loop: the control algorithm is designed for a specific sampling rate and if the computation is not carried out at this rate then the calculated control value will be wrong.

*   Computer operated alarm systems: the specification will normally require that on each and every occasion the computer responds to an alarm occurring within a specified minimum time.

*   Recording of events taking place in real time. If two events occur and the computer has failed to register the first event before the second one occurs, then only one event will be recorded. A minimum separation time between events will be specified and will form the maximum allowable response time for the real-time computer system.

1.2.2 Soft time constraints

Soft time constraint systems are typically interactive systems: an example is an automatic bank teller - the specification may require that over a 24 hour period the systems responds to a customer within an average time of, say, 30 seconds and on no occasion is the delay longer than 1 minute.

2. PROBLEMS OF REAL-TIME SOFTWARE CONSTRUCTION

Informal methods for designing and constructing real-time software have been based on design strategies involving early decisions on whether or not the system is to be implemented as a sequential program - a single task - or as an interconnected set of concurrent tasks running on a single cpu.

A task is a segment of code which the system software (for example an operating system) treats as a program unit that can be started, stopped, delayed, suspended, resumed, and interrupted.   A task is assumed to be capable of being executed concurrently, or pseudo-concurrently, with other tasks. In computer science literature the term process is used not task.

2.1 Single task

The simplest design strategy is to treat the whole of the software system as a single sequential program. The basic program structure for an embedded real-time system is then:

> *{system start-up procedures}*
> *repeat*
> *{control procedures }*
> *until forever;*
> *{system shut-down procedures}*
> *end.*

If t_c is the time taken to complete one cycle of the control loop (*repeat..until*), and t_e is the time interval for response set by the environment, the time constraint can be expressed as:

Hard constraint $t_{c(max)} < t_{e(max)}$

Soft constraint $t_{c(\text{average})} < t_{e(\text{average})}$

This approach is recommended for simple systems with a small number of inputs where the response time (t_{ei}) for each input is similar; and the time taken for the various paths through the procedures forming the control loop does not vary greatly from cycle to cycle.

As the number of inputs, actions to be performed, and outputs increases, the range of environment response times, t_{ei}, usually increases. It thus becomes more difficult to satisfy the minimum time requirement if all the actions are carried out every control cycle.   One strategy is to partition the inputs and actions according to the required environment response time which gives a system:

$$\{U_1..U_i..U_n\} = \{F_1..F_i..F_n\}\{C_1..C_i..C_n\}$$

where U_i, F_i, C_i, $i=1..n$ represent subsets of the outputs, actions and inputs respectively. The subsets are chosen such that the actions within a specified subset have to be completed within a similar response time.   The general program structure becomes:

{system start-up procedures}
repeat
if <condition_1 > then {action_1};
if <condition_i > then {action_i};
if <condition_n > then {action_n};
until forever;
{system shut-down procedures}
end.

The method used to generate the *<condition>* is implementation dependent. It is also assumed that any sharing of data between actions can be handled by the use of common memory areas.

Applying this strategy to distributed systems implies that the subsets may be implemented on separate processors.   To maintain the simplicity of the approach communication between the processors needs to be message based with each processor, as one of its actions, checking to see if a message has been received. Since there can be no synchronization between the tasks the actually message reception and storage must be handled by hardware or by a separate message processor.

2.2 Two-tasks (foreground-background)

A commonly used design approach is to partition the system into two sections, usually referred to as the foreground and background partitions.   The typically division is to place the time dependent actions in the foreground and the time independent actions in the background.   Alternatively actions with hard time constraints are placed in the foreground and those with soft constraints in the background.   The general rule for forming the partition is that the number of actions placed in the foreground partition should be minimized.

An implicit assumption is that in the system there will be a single task in each partition,   thus limiting problems of resource sharing and synchronization to resolving conflicts across the partition boundary.

The foreground - background terminology can give rise to confusion since writers concerned with non-real-time systems refer to interrupt routines, cyclic keyboard input routines, and real-time clock routines as background programs; the same usage can also be found in manuals for real-time BASIC.   In the literature on real-time systems the majority usage is that the most time critical routines are said to run in the foreground.

2.3 Multiple task

A natural extension of the foreground - background division is to partition the system into many subsets and treat each subset as a separate task. In implementation terms this is the equivalent of dividing the software into a number of separate programs. For independent subsets the software can be built from a number of independent programs each of which can be implemented using standard sequential processing techniques with the additional requirement that some of the programs will need to be synchronized to the environment.

If the subsets are not independent then in addition to any environmental timing requirements, the various programs will need to communicate with each other. Support for communication between concurrent tasks will be required.

The multi-tasking approach developed during a period when it was assumed that the implementation would be on a single processor with a real-time operating system being used to share resources between the tasks. There is, however, nothing in the approach which requires that a single processor be used.

2.4 Concurrency and synchronization

In recent years the problems of concurrency and synchronization in multi-tasking software have been studied extensively. Detailed discussions and analysis of the problems can be found in the books listed in the bibliography, a summary of the problems is given in Bennett (1988).

A problem which is fundamental to the use of concurrency is the so called mutual exclusion problem. In simplified terms it is necessary to ensure that tasks which are potentially concurrent and which share a resource of the computer, for example a common memory area, a disc file, or a printer, do not simultaneously attempt to use it. The following scenario gives an example showing how easily mutual exclusion problems can arise.

Two software modules, *bottle_in_count*, and *bottle_out_count* are used to count pulses issued from detectors which observe bottles entering and leaving a processing area. The two modules run as independent tasks. The two tasks operate on the same variable *bottle_count*. Module *bottle_in_count* increments the variable and *bottle_out_count* decrements it. The modules are programmed in a high level language and the relevant program language statements are:

> *bottle_count := bottle_count + 1; (bottle_in_count)*
> *bottle_count := bottle_count - 1; (bottle_out_count)*

At assembler code level the high level instructions become:

```
bottle_in_count                    bottle_out_count
LD A, (bottle_count)               LD A, (bottle_count)
ADD 1                              SUB 1
LD (bottle_count), A               LD (bottle_count), A
```

Now if variable *bottle_count* contains the value 10, *bottle_count_in* is running and executes the statement *LD A, (bottle_count)* then as figure 2 shows the *A* register is loaded with the value 10. If the operating system now re-schedules and *bottle_out_count* runs it will also pick up the value 10, subtract one from it and store 9 in *bottle_count* as is shown in figure 2. When execution of *bottle_in_count* resumes its environment will be restored and the *A* register will contain the value 10, one will be added and the value 11 stored in *bottle_count*. Thus the final value of *bottle_count* after adding one to it and subtracting one from it will be 11 instead of the correct value 10.

One solution to this problem is to force the operating system to treat the high level language statements as indivisible operations. A variety of techniques are available but all in principle treat the code statements needing to be protected as <u>critical sections</u> and protect the sections from interfering with each other by using semaphores.

Unfortunately the standard technique of using the critical section approach leads to problems in real-time systems with hard time constraints and alternative solutions have to be used (Bennett, 1988; Faulk and Parnas 1983). A solution which is satisfactory in many engineering applications is not to take any steps to prevent the occasional error. An assessment of the probability of an error being generated and the consequences of such an error should be made before adopting this solution.

A reg	bottle_in_count	count	bottle_out_count	A reg
?	LD A, (bottle_count)	10		
10	*context change --*	10	LD A, (bottle_count)	10
10	*forced by*	10	SUB 1	9
10	*operating system*	10	LD (bottle_count),A	9
10	ADD 1	9		9
11	LD (bottle_count),A	9		9
11		11		9

Figure 2   Effect of context change (mutual exclusion).

2.5 Virtual Machine

The concurrency and synchronization problems can be expressed in abstract terms and hence the idea of designing for a virtual machine that provides certain specified operations - <u>primitives</u> - supporting concurrency has developed. We are all familiar with the idea of a virtual machine. When we program in any high-level language we are programming a computer system which is defined by the language and its interface to a particular operating system: we are not aware of the details of the underlying computer hardware. The virtual machine is defined by the structure of the language.

This concept can be carried further and most real-time software design techniques are based on the idea of the existence of a virtual machine. The software is designed for a virtual machine. Implementation then divides into two stages: code the system for the virtual machine; implement the virtual machine on the real machine.

A virtual real-time machine must support:

Tasks: these are units which perform an action or group of actions and which can be manipulated as an entity. It is assumed that tasks can be created, started, stopped, delayed, deleted i.e. they have the attributes which would normally be associated with a <u>program</u> unit in sequential programming. No assumption is made as to the relationship between the number of tasks and the number of hardware processors;

this is left as an implementation decision.

Communication: there must be one or more methods of communication between tasks and between a task and the environment. For example methods of message passing and data sharing may be specified.

Synchronization: methods of synchronization between tasks and between a task and the environment must be provided. This may include explicit provision for the synchronization of a task to a specified standard real-time clock task.

Based on the simple concepts given above a wide range of virtual machine architectures including distributed systems can be generated. An important and interesting approach is the Rex architecture (Baler and Scallon, 1986). This architecture treats application procedures as if they were indivisible individual high level language instructions. That is an application procedure once started is guarantied to run to completion without being interrupted by another application level procedure. In this way data sharing at the application level is simplified. The penalty is that application procedures have to be short. The order in which procedures are run and the interconnection of procedures and data sets is determined by separate program modules.

The virtual machine approach has the merit of delaying implementation issues to a later stage of the design and is strongly recommended as the normally method, even if at the implementation stage it is decided to use a single program technique.

2.6 Implementation of virtual machine

There are two basic approaches to implementing a virtual machine:

(i)   map the virtual machine onto a general purpose real-time operating system;

(ii)   build the virtual machine elements in a high level language from a minimal set of primitives provided by a small system kernel.

General purpose operating systems relieve the implementor of many of the chores associated with for example memory management, task scheduling, task communication, interrupt handling. They are, however, restrictive in that they are normally constructed as a monolithic monitor and place severe limitations on the way in which a system can be implemented. For a review of this approach see Gertler and Sedlak (1983).

For simple, non-critical systems (non-critical in the sense that failure will result in inconvenience not serious loss) the combined language-operating systems provided by the so called real-time BASIC languages should be considered. Such systems can also be useful for prototyping.

The development of high level languages which support concurrency has permitted the development of systems with only a small amount of fixed operating system software - referred to as a kernel or nucleus. Additional functions can be made available as separate modules provided in a library. The user has the choice of developing specific functions for his application or using functions from a standard library.

The latter approach has the advantage of flexibility but the disadvantage of lacking any form of standardization. Suggestions have been made for specific minimum sets of primitives for real-time systems and the IEEE has issued a trial standard giving minimum sets for specific purposes, recommended interfaces to the functions, and bindings to specific languages (IEEE, 1985).

3. MASCOT

3.1 Outline

The earliest formal methodology for assisting with the development of real-time software is MASCOT. It is based on designing software for a specific virtual machine and the problem of mapping the MASCOT machine onto a real computer is considered to be a separate problem to designing and constructing the application software. The first version of MASCOT was developed by Jackson and Simpson during the period 1971-75 (Jackson and Simpson 1975). The official definition of MASCOT 1 was published in 1978 and a revised version - MASCOT 2 - was issued in 1983. Between 1983 and 1987 extensive changes to the technique were made and the official standard for MASCOT 3 was published in 1987. The discussion which follows relates to MASCOT 3.

The official handbook states that:

"MASCOT is a Modular Approach to Software Construction Operation and Test which
   incorporates:
   a means of design representation
   a method of deriving the design
   a way of constructing software so that it is consistent with the design
   a means of executing the constructed software so that the design structure remains
   visible at run time
   facilities for testing the software in terms of the design structure."
In MASCOT software is represented as:

(i)   a set of concurrent functions, and
(ii)   the flow of data between such functions.

The functions are referred to as <u>components</u>. The system consists of a set of interconnected but independent components that make no direct reference to each other. Each component has specific, user defined, characteristics that determine how it can be connected to other components.

Components are created from <u>templates</u>, that is patterns used to define the structure of the component. Two classes of templates are fundamental to MASCOT (i) <u>activity</u> (ii) <u>intercommunication data area - IDA</u>.

An activity template is used to create one or more activity components each of which is a single sequential program thread that can be independently scheduled. It is assumed that at the implementation stage each activity will be mapped onto a software task. Such a task may run on its own processor or be scheduled by a run-time system (usually referred to as the MASCOT kernel) to run on a processor shared with other activities. The activities communicate through IDAs. The IDA provides the necessary synchronization and mutual exclusion facilities.

An IDA is a passive element with the sole purpose of servicing the data communication needs of activity components. It can contain its own private data areas. It provides procedures which activities use for the transfer of data. Within an IDA, and only within an IDA, the designer has access to low level synchronization procedures and thus is not limited to using high-level operations such as monitors, message-passing, or rendezvous, provided by the implementation language but is able to use any technique appropriate to the problem. A structure containing activity components connected by means of one or more IDAs is referred to as a <u>network</u>.

3.2 Simple Example

MASCOT supports three forms of IDA: a generalized IDA; a channel; and a pool. The graphical symbols for each are shown in figure 3 .

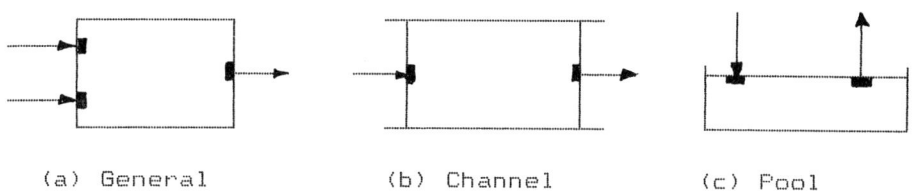

(a) General   (b) Channel   (c) Pool

Figure 3 Graphical symbols for IDAs

The channel and the pool will be familiar to users of MASCOT-2 - their behaviour is defined as follows:

channel   supports communication between producers and consumers. It can contain one or more items of information. Writing to a channel adds an item without changing items already in it. The read operation is destructive - it removes an item from the channel. A channel can become empty and also, because its capacity is finite, it can become full.

pool   is typically used to represent a table or dictionary which activities periodically consult or update. The write operation on a pool is destructive and the read operation is non-destructive.

MASCOT can be used at a simple level to provide a virtual machine supporting activities, pools and channels. A design is constructed in the form of an activity, pool, and channel network - an ACP diagram - as is shown in figure 4.

The diagram represents part of a system for the control a plant. The activity *heater_1_input* gets data from a plant interface. The data is held in a pool *heater_1_in* from where it is read by activity *heater_1_alarm* and *heater_1_con*. The required output to the plant and the alarm status are held in a pool *heater_1_status*. An activity *heater_1_report* gets data from the pool holding status information and sends it via a channel *heater_1_ch* to some other activity (not shown). Also not shown are the activities required to pass the data to the plant control. This ACP differs from a MASCOT 2 ACP since the components now contain ports and windows (shown as filled in circles and rectangles).

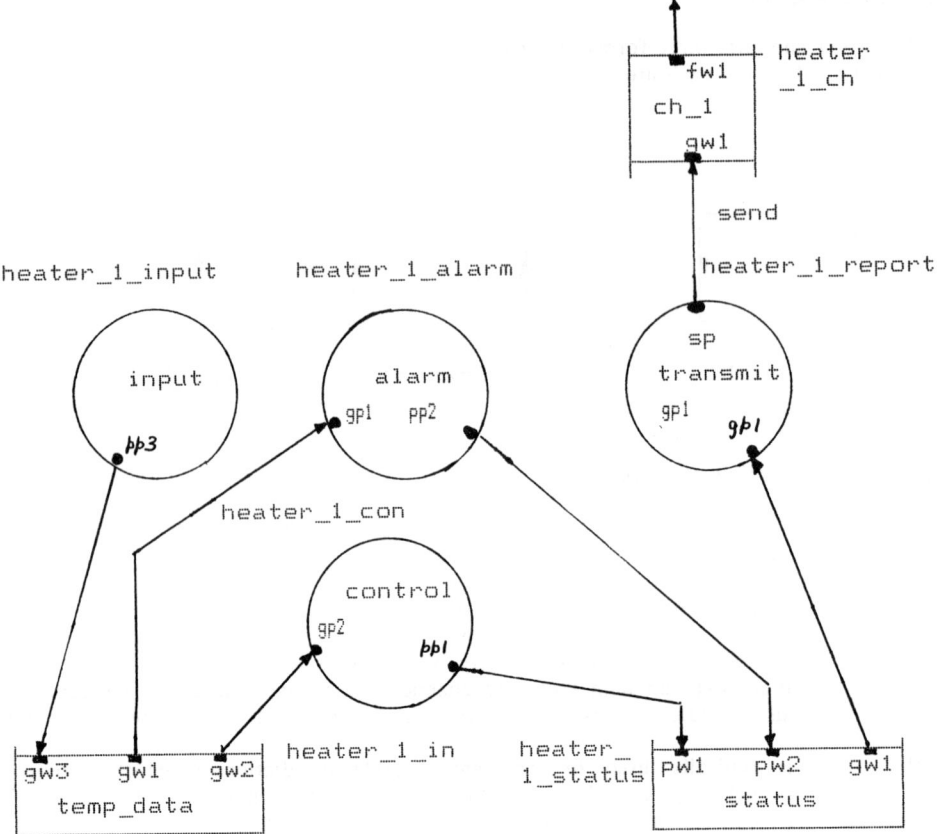

Figure 4 Example of MASCOT ACP diagram

Once the ACP diagram has been produced design of the templates for the individual components can proceed.   Many component templates will be reusable and hence only application specific ones will need to be designed.   Instances of the component are created when the network is constructed by translating the ACP diagram to textual form and entering it into the MASCOT database.

At this level a design in MASCOT may be represented either in graphical (ACP diagram) or textual form.   Both forms are equivalent and may be derived from each other.   The textual form stored in the database can be progressively updated as the design proceeds.

3.3 MASCOT Kernel

The MASCOT kernel has to provide support for the MASCOT virtual machine. In MASCOT 2 this meant supporting activities, channels and pools and structure of the support required was mandatory.   The specific schemes for synchronization, device handling, interrupts, process scheduling and priorities, are analysed and comparison with alternatives is given in Sears and Middleditch (1985).   If the language being used in the implementation supports concurrency then the implementor should consider mapping activities onto the appropriate language feature. Bugden (1985) describes a Modula 2 implementation of the MASCOT kernel.   MASCOT imposes one restriction: activities should not be created dynamically, the system network (activities, IDAs and servers) must remain invariant at run-time.   The implementor must document how the language features have been used to support the MASCOT virtual machine.

In MASCOT 3 the specific form of the kernel is not mandatory - it is a recommendation.   MASCOT 3, however, requires the virtual machine to support additional features.   For example, an activity providing direct feedback control that has a hard time constraint may require access to external data, for example in order to update controller parameters.   To meet its time constraint it must have guarantied access at all times and must not be kept waiting because another activity is accessing the data.   A simple solution to this problem but one is to allow the module to access the data directly without using the standard access procedures.   MASCOT provides for this through a construct called an access interface that must be supported by the kernel.

3.4 Summary

MASCOT 3 provides and excellent design methodology.   It is sufficiently rich in concepts to provide design flexibility but has sufficient constraints for creating safe and reliable software.   The template construct encourages the re-use of software components which contributes to increased reliability.

A major limitation of MASCOT 2 was the absence of facilities for representing hierarchical structures.   A system was represented as a two dimensional data flow network of alternate data processing and data communication elements.   Higher level elements could be utilised in developing the network but they were not retained in the database and were not recognized as design entities.   A large network could be partitioned into several arbitrary subsidiary networks the connection between adjacent networks was through the sharing of one or more communication elements.   The subsidiary network thus formed was treated as a unit for control purposes at run-time. The hierarchical structure introduced in MASCOT 3 has overcome the limitations of the previous versions.

It provides a good mix of graphical and textual notations. The incremental approach to creating software modules is of great assistance in separating design from implementation.   Even if the full project support system is not used the design techniques and notations provide a powerful free standing design technique which coupled with the use of modern languages such as Modula 2 or Ada for implementation can provide an effective means of creating real-time software.

The project support environment - the MASCOT database - provides a methodology for building the software.   It also provides the designer with some simple checks on consistency.   However the facilities are limited and at least one attempt is being made to extend the support given to the designer (Moorhouse, 1986).

A weakness of the system, but one which is true of most design methodologies, is that it has no facilities for representing or assisting with the design or implementation of error detection or error recovery.

MASCOT provides very little guidance for the developer on the difficult issues of mapping the virtual model onto a real machine or machines.   The formal methodology assumes that a design can be expanded down to the level of activities containing root and subroot modules without any consideration of how the virtual machine will be implemented.   This is unrealistic since any expansion beyond subsystem modules is likely to impinge on implementation issues.   In practice subsystem expansion will be based, at least implicitly, on assumptions about the method of implementation and will be revised in the light of implementation changes.

The MASCOT approach separates design and implementation issues but does not clearly separate design and specification.   The more recently developed methodologies very clearly attempt to distinguish between specification and design.

4. DESIGN TECHNIQUES AND TOOLS

4.1 Introduction

Several design techniques and tools have been developed specifically for real-time systems, ranging from purely specification techniques through to full development systems with or without construction tools. Some examples are:

RSL/REVS   Specification and simulation tools (Alford, 1977)

PAISLey   Specification and simulation tools (Zave, 1982)

DARTS   Design and analysis of real-time systems (Gomaa 1984)

MASCOT   Design, construction, operation and test tools

SDRTS Structured development, design and implementation system (Ward and Mellor)

SRSS   Strategies for real-time system specification (Hatley and Pirbhai).

DARTS and SRSS are similar in approach to the SDRTS method which is considered in more detail below.   The RSL/REVS method has being widely reported in general Software Engineering text books. The PAISLey technique is an important development in methods of specifying software and in software development techniques; it relies heavily on formal methods and as such is outside the scope of this Chapter. A good overview of the method is in Zave (1982).

The starting point for SDRTS (and for DARTS and SRSS) is building a software model representing the system requirements in terms of the abstract entities.   This model is called the essential model.   The second stage - design - is to derive from the essential model an implementation model.   The basic strategy involved in the design stage is based on the well known concepts of information hiding, coupling and cohesion, and interface minimisation (details of the various techniques and their advantages and disadvantages are given in most of the recent texts on Software Engineering and are not covered further here).

For real-time systems some additional rules of guidance are needed as follows:

(i)   Separate actions into groups according to whether the action is:

*   time dependent;
*   synchronized;
*   independent;

and try to minimize the size and number of modules containing time dependent actions.

Divide the time dependent actions into:

*   hard constraint;
*   soft time constraint;

and try to minimize the size and number of modules with a hard time constraint.

(iii)   Separate actions concerned with the environment from other actions.

The recommended design strategy can be expressed simply as: minimise the part of the system which falls into the category of having a <u>hard time constraint</u>.

The design stage also involves, for example, determination of the number of processors required, the memory requirements, the mapping of activities to processors and tasks within a processor.

4.2 Modelling notation and techniques

The SDRTS technique, as its name implies, is a significant extension of the structured design methodology. The notation used is an extension of standard flow diagram notation. As in standard flow diagrams, bubbles represent transformations and directed lines represent data flows. However, the notation distinguishes between different types of data flow, see figure 5.

Continuous data may be in analogue or digital form. It is represented by the double arrow head: *current_pH* and *valve_control* are continuous data flows. Data transformations of continuous data flows for example *change_pH* are assumed to operate continuously. If the data transformation is implemented digitally then the frequency with which it runs must be sufficient to approximate to continuous operation.

Discrete data may be analogue or digital although it will normally be digital. It is indicated by a single arrow head as shown on *pH_demand*. Data transformations operating on discrete data flows are assumed to be triggered by the arrival of a unit of data - a transaction.

Event data flows are shown by means of dashed lines. Events are data flows which do not have numeric content but simply indicate that an event has occurred or provide a signal or command. Thus *pH_at_desired_value* is a <u>signal</u>, and *start* and *stop* are commands. Event flows are processed by control transformations which are indicated by a bubble with a dashed outline. Control transformations can issue special event flows known as prompts and triggers. The enable/disable event flows are prompts. They are used to enable and disable data transformations. Triggers can be used to force a data transformation to run in response to a specific event or combination of events.

4.3 Modeling Conventions

The modelling method assumes that the designer will adopted certain conventions which can be summarised as:

Control transformations:	inputs -	event flows
		prompts
	outputs -	event flows
		prompts
Data transformations:	inputs -	event flows
		prompts
	outputs -	data flows
		event flows

Only control transformations may generate prompts.

Data transformations may, by generating event flows, control events outside the software system but only control transformations may control (prompt) activities within the software system.

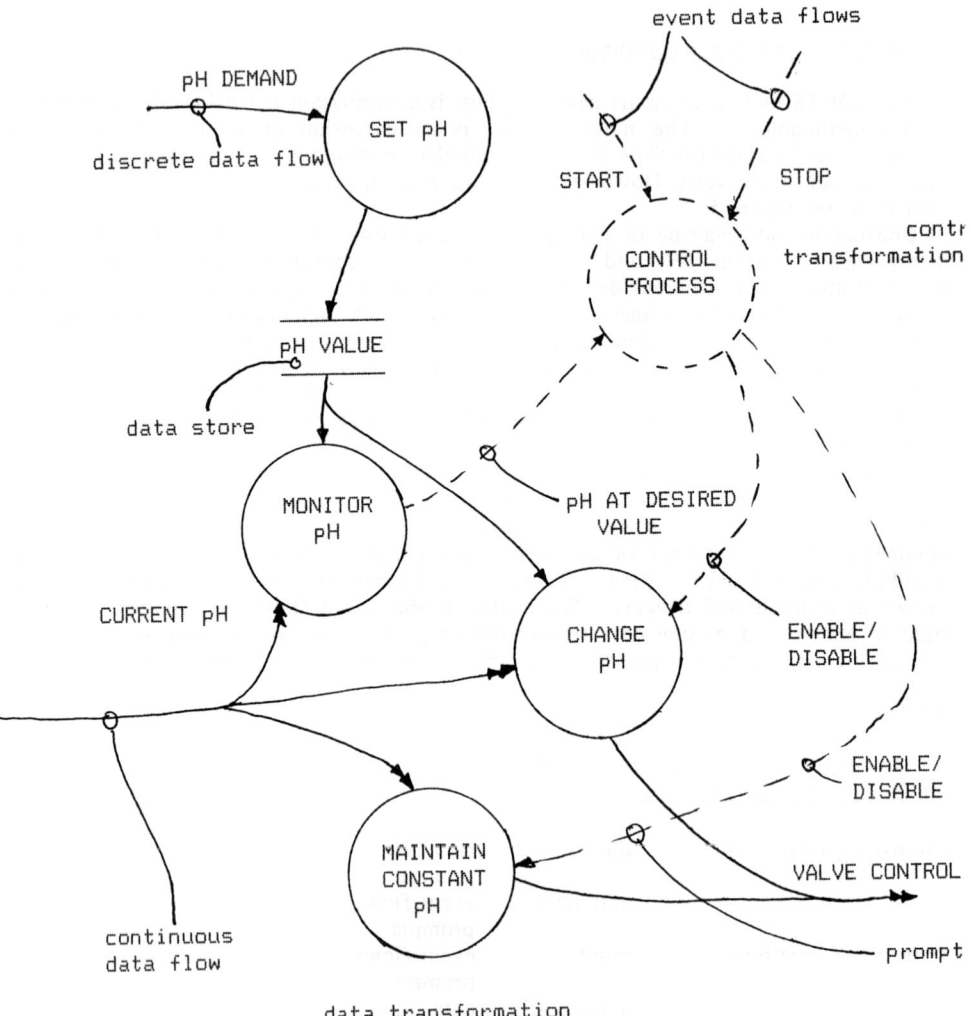

Figure 5 Example of design using SDRTS notation

4.4 Essential modelling

The essential model is created by following the procedure outlined in figure 6. The method emphasises the separation of the environment from the internal structure. The normal first stage in building the abstract model is to produce a context schema and event list to describe the environmental model.

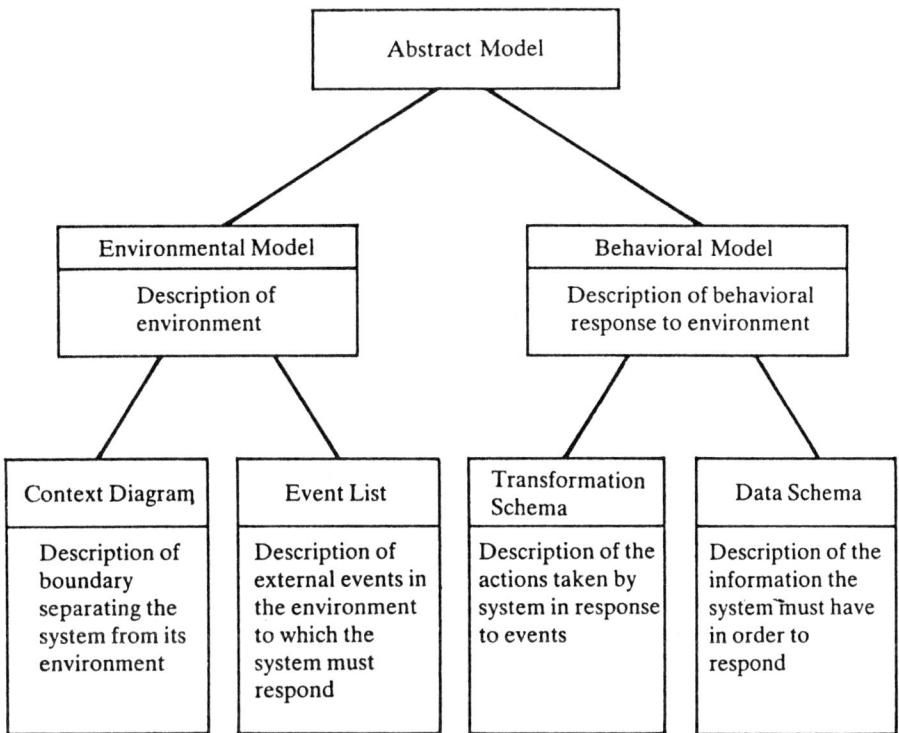

Figure 6   Outline of the abstract modelling schema

An example of a context schema is given in figure 7. The terminal units shown in rectangular boxes e.g. *plant_A10_input_interface* can be treated as virtual devices at this level rather than the actual device.

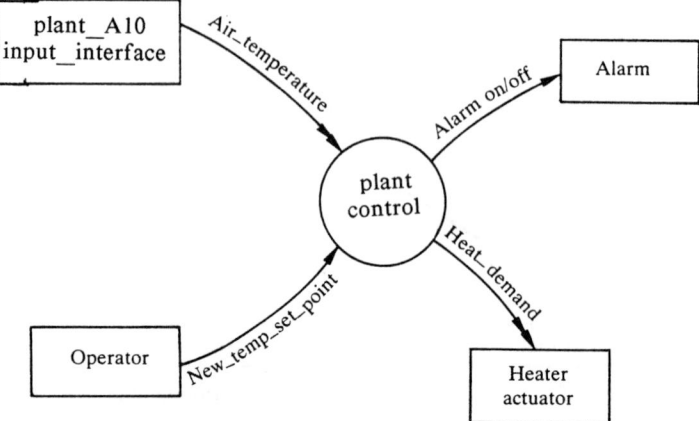

Figure 7 Example of a context schema

The modelling of an actual transducer to a virtual transducer is illustrated in figure 8. This convention fits in well with the idea of creating an 'image' of the external environment upon which the system software operates.   The 'image' has known characteristics and isolates the system from interface complications and vagaries.

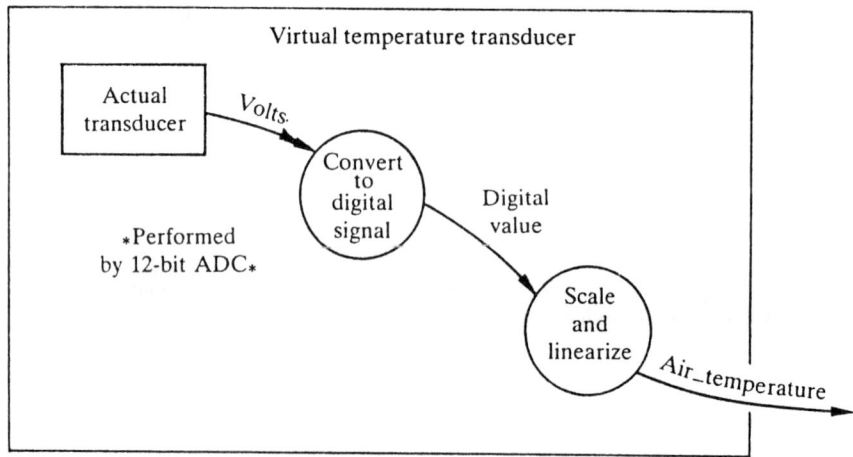

Figure 8 Modelling of interface transducer

The transformation *plant_control* is expanded into the behavioural model either by means of transformation schema or data schema: the choice depends on the nature of the problem. A possible transformation schema is shown in figure 9.

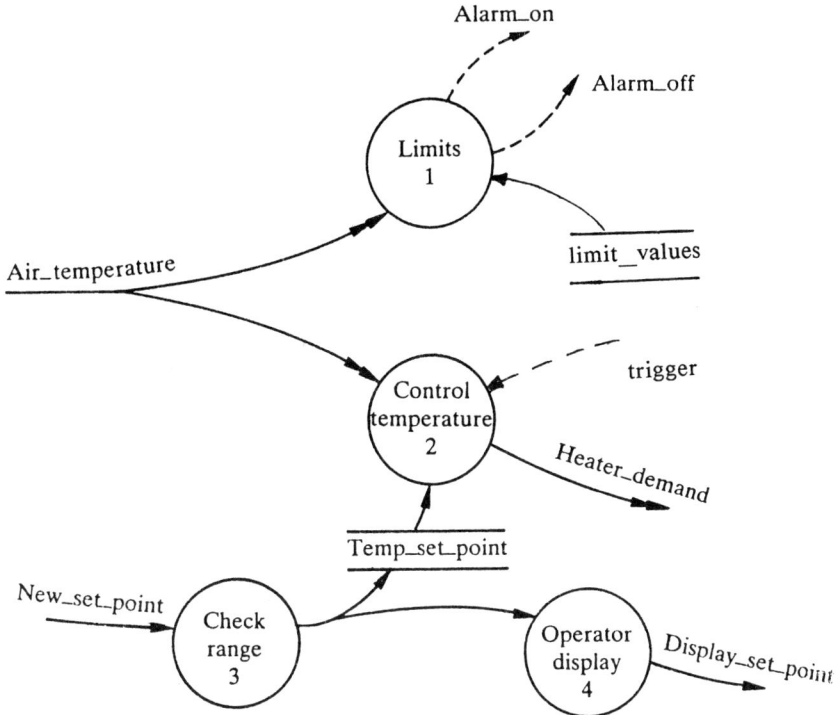

Figure 9 Transformation schema

This is not a complete system as for example there is no data flow to the data store for *limit_values*. The trigger prompt is used to indicate that *control_temperature* will act at intervals determined by the presence of a signal on trigger. Thus by firing the trigger from a clock the transformation could be specified to run at predetermined intervals.

The design procedure encourages a hierarchical approach as the elaboration of each transformation can be considered as creating a subsystem. The designer has to use her judgment to decide when to stop further elaboration. When this point is reached each transformation must be specified in some manner.

For specifying control transformations Ward and Mellor suggest the use of state transition diagrams and action tables. Their approach is based on the work of Hopcroft and Ullman Hopcroft and Ullman, 1979). An example of the notation they use is given in figure 10. The state transition technique is a powerful method and Ward and Mellor are only able to give limited coverage; more detailed explanations of the method can be found in Fairley (1985).

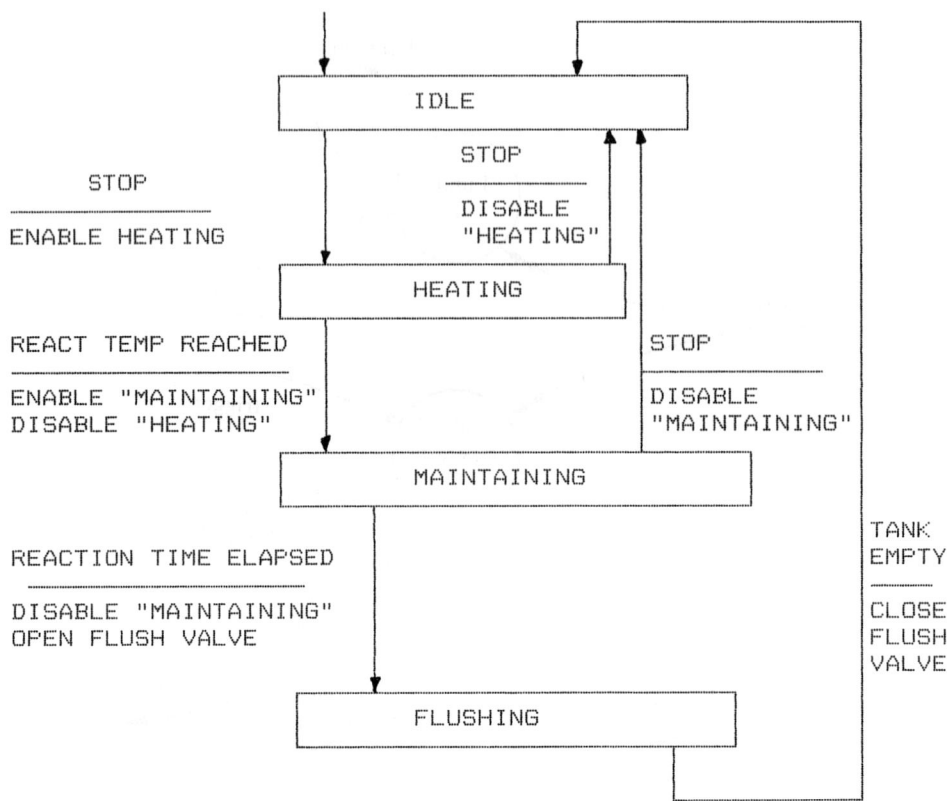

Figure 10 Example of a state transition diagram

Ward and Mellor (1986) discuss a number of methods of specifying data transformations including the standard procedural techniques of program design languages, pseudo-code and structured English. They also discuss and give examples of a non-procedural method based on the use of precondition-postcondition statements (Heniger, 1980). If the goal of producing an essential model devoid of implementation constraints is to be achieved it would seem important that specifications at this stage are expressed non-procedurally. The choice of methodology is open: any of the rapidly developing formal techniques can be used.

4.5 Checking the essential model

Ward and Mellor recommend checking the transformation schema of the model in two ways. The first is to use the rules for data flow to check for consistency. This is the equivalent of checking the syntax of a program and can be done by hand or, given the advances in graphics processing capabilities in recent years, it is now feasible to construct a graphics compiler to perform the necessary checks.

The second level of checking is to determine whether the model can be executed - can it in some sense generate outputs from a given set of inputs. The approach suggested by Ward and Mellor is based on ideas derived work on Petri nets.

The method is based on the use of tokens. The presence of a token indicates that a data flow has a value: the absence of a token indicates that it has no value. The execution is carried out by tracking the propagation of tokens through the system from some given starting point. It is assumed that provided the requisite tokens are present a data transformation will produce the appropriate output tokens. For control transformations the production of tokens is determined by execution of the state transition table specifying the transformation. The procedure can be carried out by hand, however, it is preferable to have software capable of carrying out the procedures.

At this stage the abstract modelling is complete and we are ready to move to the implementation stage.

4.6 Implementation

The first stage of implementation is to map the essential model onto the implementation model. This is the process of examining possible implementation technologies and choosing the ones which introduce minimum distortion into the mapping. Ward and Mellor illustrate what they mean by minimum distortion using as an example a satellite attitude modification system. On a modern satellite the system would be implemented as a single task on a on board microprocessor and the implementation model would thus involve no distortion as the data transformation 'modify attitude' would map to a task.

In the 1960s it would not have been possible to have an on board computer and the attitude would have been controlled from a ground station. The implementation model would thus have needed to split 'modify attitude' into a device to transmit signals to the ground placed on board the satellite and a processor on the ground. There would not be a simple one-to-one mapping between the essential and implementation models and hence distortion is introduced.

Ward and Mellor suggest following a top down approach in constructing the implementation model.

* allocate units of the essential model to processors;
* allocate units to tasks within a single processor;
* allocate units to modules within a single task.

A processor is defined as a person or machine that can carry out instructions and store data. Machines may be anything from simple analogue or digital circuits through to supercomputers.

A task is a unit of code which can be started, stopped, delayed, interrupted, suspended and resumed by the system software running on a single processor. The implementation model relevant to a given processor will consist of a network of tasks (the network may be a single task). Tasks are assumed to be concurrent.

A module is a segment of code which is treated as a unit by a task. A task is assumed to activate modules in a mutual exclusive manner.

To answer some of these questions it is necessary to elaborate the some of the time constraints given in the specification.

4.7 Major Differences between SDRTS and SRSS

The major differences between the two methodologies are in terminology and notation and a brief comparison of terminology is given below:

SRDTS   SRSS

Essential Model	Requirements Model
Implementation Model	Architecture Model
Transformation Schema	Data Flow Diagram
	Control Flow Diagram
Data Transformations	Process Model
Control Transformations	Control Model
Data Dictionary	Requirements Dictionary
	Architecture Dictionary

The two methods differ in notation in that SRSS uses separate flow diagrams to show control flows. They also differ subtly in the way they treat discrete data and control signals. In SRDTS data is represented on the transformation schema as continuous data (double arrow head) and discrete data (single arrowhead) whereas with SRSS no distinction between the two is made on the diagram. In SRDTS control transformations are activated by events which have no data values associated with them, an event occurs or does not occur, The significance is in the transition from one state to another not in the state itself. Thus turning a switch on is a different event than turning a switch off and would be modelled by two different (but mutually exclusive) event flows. In SRSS a discrete that can take on discrete values can be modelled either as a data flow or a control flow. Multi-valued discrete signals would normally be modelled as data flows and binary valued as control flows, the decision is based on the purpose for which the signal is being used.

In SRSS a notation is suggested for showing how the abstract model is being mapped onto an implementation model. The notation assists in defining the interfaces between the hardware and the software and between different software modules.

5. TIMING CONSIDERATIONS

5.1 Example 1

As an example consider a system used to provide feedback control on a plant. The actions to be performed are:

	Action	Cycle Time	Compute Time (Max)
P1	read plant inputs	t_p	t_1
P2	check alarm status	t_p	t_2
P3	compute control outputs	t_p	t_3
P4	output to actuators	t_p	t_4
P5	update operator display	t_d	t_5
P6	check operator switches	t_o	t_6
P7	output log information	t_l	t_7

The cycle time is the repeat time set by the environment: t_p is a hard constraint i.e. the plant inputs must be read, the control value calculated and sent to the actuators every t_p seconds. The values t_d, t_o and t_l represent soft constraints in that on average the actions such be performed at those intervals.

Using a single task method all the actions P1 to P7 would have to be carried out every t_p seconds which gives a condition for correct operation

$$t_p > t_1 + t_2 + t_3 + t_4 + t_5 + t_6 + t_7$$

Using a foreground - background approach actions P1, P2, P3, P4 would form the foreground partition with actions P5, P6 and P7 forming a background partition. Necessary conditions for correct operation are:

1. $$t_p > t_1 + t_2 + t_3 + t_4 + \frac{(\overline{t_5} + \overline{t_6} + \overline{t_7})}{\min\{t_d, t_o, t_l\}}$$

2. $$\min\{t_d, t_o, t_l\} > (\overline{t_5} + \overline{t_6} + \overline{t_7})$$

where $\overline{t}$ represents the average computation time not the maximum.

The above assumes that the system is run on one processor and that actions P5, P6 and P7 are run as a single task in the background and can be pre-empted by the foreground task.

If a multi-task approach is used then actions P1, P2, P3 and P4, because of their similar time scales, could be grouped as a single control task. With actions P5, P6, and P7 treated as separate tasks. Necessary conditions for correct operation then become:

1. $$t_p > t_1 + t_2 + t_3 + t_4 + \frac{\overline{t_5}}{t_d} + \frac{\overline{t_6}}{t_o} + \frac{\overline{t_7}}{t_l}$$

2. $$t_d > t_c \cdot t_d/t_p + \overline{t_5} + \overline{t_6} \frac{t_d}{t_o} + \overline{t_7} \frac{t_d}{t_l}$$

3. $$t_o > t_c \cdot t_o/t_p + \overline{t_5} \frac{t_o}{t_d} + \overline{t_6} + \overline{t_7} \cdot \frac{t_o}{t_l}$$

4. $$t_l > t_c \cdot t_l/t_p + \overline{t_5} \frac{t_l}{t_d} + \overline{t_6} \frac{t_l}{t_o} + \overline{t_7}$$

where t_c is the average time taken to carry out actions P1, P2, P3, and P4.

Using the self correcting properties of modulating feedback control the control actions can be partitioned as shown in figure 11. This partitioning is based on the assumption that if occasionally a newly computed control value is not available the disturbance to the system will be minor. On this assumption the hard time constraint is applied to the input, output and alarm actions, the control calculation itself is allowed to fall into a high priority 'on average' category.

Figure 11 illustrates another aspect of feedback control can be exploited to reduce the severity of the hard time constraint. The control action is assumed to be part of a modulating feedback control loop and to require a specific sampling rate, a simple way of coding the system is:

```
loop
{wait for timing signal}
{read inputs}
{calculate control output}
{transmit control output to plant}
end;
```

Using the above the plant inputs will be read at the fixed sample rate. However, there is no guarantee that the plant outputs will be sent out at the required sample interval since the time delay between reading the plant inputs and sending back the outputs will vary with the computational time. An improvement is obtained by changing the sequence of actions to

```
loop
{wait for timing signal}
{output control variable m(k)}
{read input variable c(k+1)}
{calculate control variable m(k+1)}
end;
```

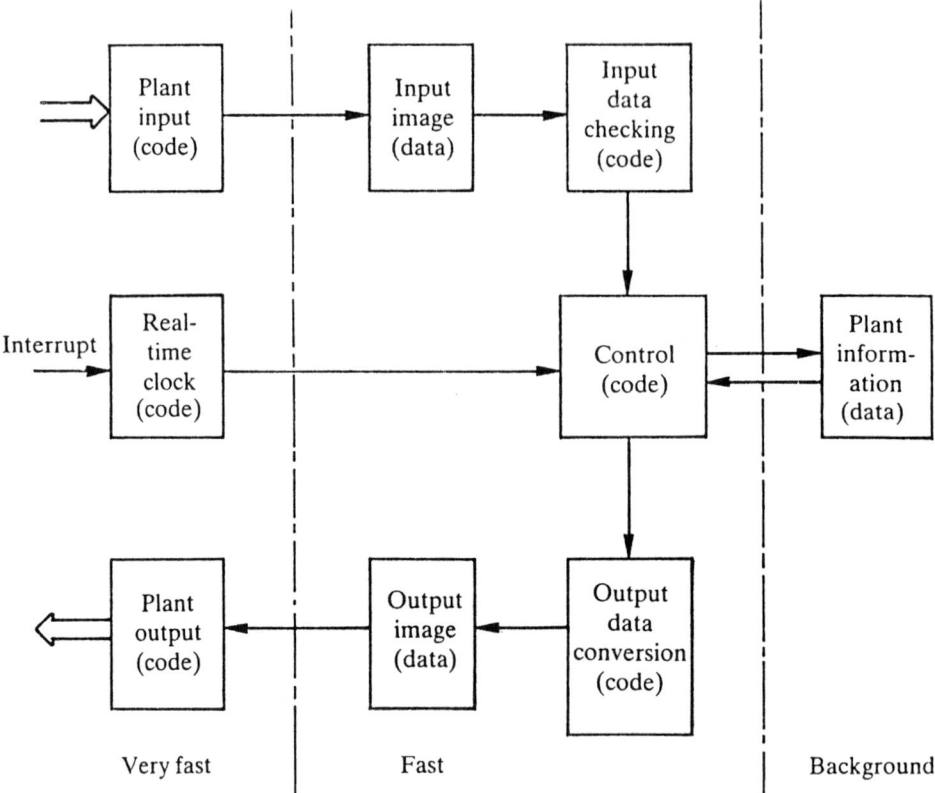

Figure 11   Separation of environment actions from main control actions.

With this sequence the variation in the time taken to calculate the control variable does not affect the rate at which it is transmitted to the plant.   The fixed delay of one sampling interval can be taken into account in designing the actual control algorithm.

Changing the order of the actions decouples the control actions from the input-output actions thus separating the environment from the internal activities.   The plant input activity creates an <u>input image</u>:   the output activity transmits the <u>output image</u> to the plant.   In order to maintain synchronization with the environment the plant input and output task must run with a hard time constraint.   The time constraint on the control task usually can be relaxed: either to the requirement that it completes at sometime within the sample interval or, since in many applications the occasional missed sample will have little effect on the plant, to a requirement that on average it completes within the sample interval.

5.2 Example of cyclic tasks

Three tasks A, B and C are required to run at 20mS, 40mS and 80mS intervals. (Corresponding to 1 tick, 2 ticks and 4 ticks, if the clock interrupt rate is set at 20 mS). If the task priority order is set as A, B and C with A as the highest priority then the processing will proceed as shown in figure 12a with the result that the tasks will be run at constant intervals.

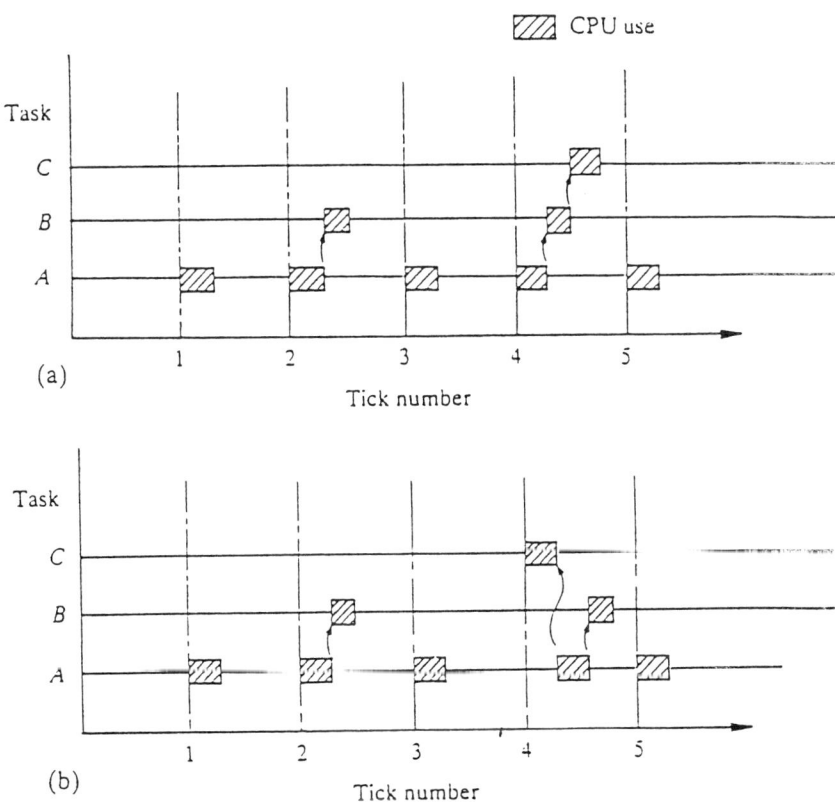

Figure 12 Task activation diagram (a) priority A, B, C (b) priority C, A, B

It should be noted that using a single CPU it is not possible to have all the tasks starting in synchronism with the clock tick. All but one of the tasks will be delayed relative to the clock tick, but the interval between successive invocations of the task will be constant.

If the priority order is now re-arranged so that it is C, A and B then the activation diagram is as shown in figure 12b and every fourth tick of the clock there will be a delay in the timing of tasks A and B. In practice there is unlikely to be any justification for choosing a priority order C, A and B rather than A, B and C. Usually the task with the highest repetition rate will have the most stringent timing requirements and hence will be assigned the highest priority.

A further problem which can arise is that a clock level task may require a longer time than the interval between clock interrupts to complete its processing (note that for overall satisfactory operation of the system such a task cannot run at a high repetition rate).

5.3 Example of timing of cyclic tasks

Assume that in the previous example task C takes 25 mS to complete, task A takes 1 mS and task B takes 6 mS. Figure 13 shows the activity diagram if task C is allowed to run to completion and task will be delayed by 11 mS every fourth invocation. It is normal to divide the cyclic tasks intro high priority tasks that are guarantied to complete within the clock interval and lower priority tasks that can be interrupted by the next clock tick.

The real-time clock handler, which acts as the dispatcher for the system and controls the activation of the clock level tasks, must be designed carefully as it is run at frequent intervals. Particular attention has to be paid to the method of selecting the tasks to be run at each clock interval. If a check of all tasks were to be carried out then the overheads involved could become significant. A method of selecting the appropriate task is given in Bennett (1988, pp. 206-207).

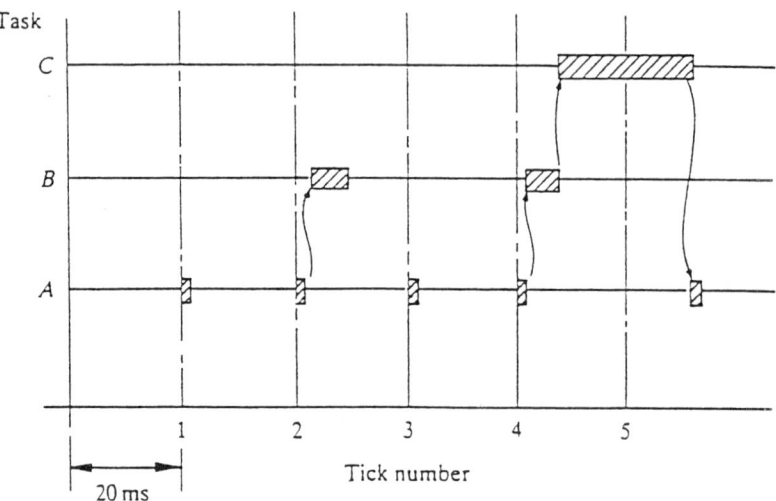

Figure 13 Task activation diagram

The virtual machine approach to design enables processes to be coded and the computation time for a process to be estimated by running on a target processor, running on a simulator, or by inspection of the code. Of course some assumption about the overheads involved in communication and task switching will have to be made as the details of these are not available until decisions on the system structure are finalised. Various performance modelling techniques can also be used to evaluate and refine designs (Vittins and Signer 1986).

6. CONCLUSIONS

It has long been recognised that designing and implementing real-time software is a significantly more difficult task than that of developing non-real-time software (see Pyle,

1979, Bennett 1988) . Two simple but important heuristic rules are thus:

(i)   partition the software into two units - one containing activities which have to be carried out in real time, the other containing non real-time activities

(ii)   minimize the number of activities in the real-time partition.

The difficulties increase if multi-tasking and inter-task communication is required, therefore a further rule is:

*   implement using a single task approach if possible.

For large, complex, real-time systems, multi-tasking and distributed systems are necessary. For such systems it is vital that decisions relating to the implementation technology are separated from the specification and design phases of development. One approach is designing for a virtual machine and is exemplified by the MASCOT methodology. Another approach is the use of abstract (essential or requirements) models, and physical (implementation or architectural) models exemplified by the more recent methodologies expounded by Ward and Mellor, and by Hatley and Pirbhai. The full use of the more recent methodologies is dependent on the existence of CASE tools and for example both Ward and Mellor and Hatley and Pirbhai are supported by the tool "Software through Pictures".

With the increased use of microprocessors in equipment and of multi-processor systems with a consequent increased concern with communications, distributed data-bases and distributed operating systems, there is a growing need for software engineers and other engineers to be familiar with techniques for developing real-time software.

7. REFERENCES AND BIBLIOGRAPHY

Alford, M.W., 'A requirements engineering methodology', *IEEE Trans. Software Engineering*, *SE-3*, 180-193 (1977).

Allworth, S.T., Zobel, R.N., *Introduction to Real-time Software Design*, Macmillan, London (1987).

Baler, T.P., Scallon, G.M., "An architecture for real-time software systems", *IEEE Software Magazine*, 3, 50-58 (1986).

Bennett, S., *Real-time Computer Control: an Introduction*, Prentice Hall, Englewood Cliffs NJ, (1988).

Bennett. S., Linkens, D.A., (editors) *Real-Time Computer Control*, Peter Peregrinus, Stevenage, (1984)

Budgen, D., 'Combining MASCOT with Modula-2 to aid the engineering of real-time systems', *Software - Practice and Experience*, 15, 767-793 (1985).

Fairley, R., *Software Engineering*, McGraw-Hill, New York, (1985).

Faulk, S.R., Parnas, D.L., "On the uses of synchronization in hard-real-time systems", *Proc.of the Real-time Systems Symposium, IEEE*, Arlington, VA. 6-8 Dec. 101-109 (1983)

Gertler, J., Sedlak, J., "Software for process control - a survey" in Glass, R.L. (editor), *Real-time Software*, Prentice Hall, Englewood Cliffs NJ, 13-44, (1983).

Glass, R.L., *Real-Time Software*, Prentice-Hall, Englewood Cliffs NJ, (1983)

Gomaa, H., 'A software design method for real-time systems' *Comm ACM*, 27 938-949 (1984).

Guth, R., *Computer Systems for Process Control*, Plenum Press, New York, (1986)

Hatley, D.J., Pirbhai, I.A., *Strategies for Real-time System Specification*, Dorset House, New York, 1987

Heniger, K.L., 'Specifying software requirements for complex systems: new techniques and their application', *IEEE Trans. Software Engineering, SE-6* 3-13 (1980)

Hopcroft, J.E., Ullman, J.D., *Introduction to Automata Theory, Languages, and Computation*, Addison-Wesley, Reading, 16-45, (1979).

IEEE, *IEEE Trial-use Standard Specifications for Microprocessor Operating Systems Interfaces*, Wiley, New York, (1985).

Jovic, F., *Process Control Systems: Principles of Design and Operation*, Kogan Page, London, (1986)

Lawrence, P.W., Mauch, K., *Real-time Microcomputer Design*, McGraw-Hill, New York, (1987)

Mellichamp, D., (editor) *Real-Time Computing with Applications to Data Acquisition and Control*, Van Nostrand, New York, (1983)

Moorhouse, T.J., "MDSE Concepts", Ferranti Computer Systems, Alvey Project Document MDSE/GEN/TN/F3.4 July (1986).

Pyle, I.C., "Methods for the design of control software", in *Software for Computer Control. Proc. Second IFAC/IFIP Symposium on Software for Computer Control*, Prague 1979, Pergammon, Oxford, (1979).

Sears, K.H., Middleditch, A.E., 'Software concurrency in real-time control systems: a software nucleus', *Software - Practice and Experience*, 15, 739-759 (1985).

Vitins, M., Signer, K., "Performance modelling of control systems", in R. Guth (editor), *Computer Systems for Process Control*, Plenum Press, New York, 141-167, (1986).

Ward, P.T., Mellor, S.J., *Structured Development for Real-Time Systems*, 3 vols. Yourdon Press, New York, (1986)

Wirth, N., "Towards a discipline of real-time programming", *Comm. ACM*, 22 577-583 (1977).

Zave, P. 'An operational approach to specification for embedded systems', *IEEE Trans. Software Engineering, SE-8* 250-269 (1982).

Chapter 6

Intelligent modelling and simulation

D. A. Linkens

1. INTRODUCTION

Interactive computing has been used for many years in Computer-Aided
Design of Control Systems (CADCS). Because of the heuristic nature of
the design process which is often based on 2D graphical representation of
mathematically manipulated functions, computer graphics have been in
common use. In this chapter, we shall consider more recent advances in
the incorporation of intelligence into the design process, attempting to
provide more readily accessible CADCS environments for a wide range of
users.

The range of functions which could be included in a CADCS environment
would involve:

1. Modelling; linear and nonlinear systems, continuous and discrete-
   time representations, model construction from components.

2. Simulation; initialization and experimentation on a model using a
   general purpose language.

3. Steady state determination, followed by linearisation.

4. Validation; determining correctness of a model abstraction of reality.

5. Linear analysis.

6. Linear design; frequency domain and time domain methodologies.

In the work described here items 1-4 are considered, while parallel
work covering all of the areas is described in the MEAD (Multi-discipli-
nary Expert aided Analysis and Design) project (Taylor et al, 1990).
In both of these projects the environment aims to provide three features
in addition to the basic design methodologies: an advanced user-interface (to expand the use of CADCS software to less expert users); database management (to rigorously track the many disparate data elements
generated during the design cycle); expert aiding (to alleviate tedium
involved in low level tasks, and provide heuristic guidance).

1.1 Intelligent Modelling and Simulation

From surveys of industrial users, it is known that simulation software is the most widely used CADCS methodology used for complex engineering system design (van den Bosch and van den Boom 1985, Araki 1985).   This has been elicited from both European and Japanese studies, and is largely due to the inherent nonlinearity encountered in practical engineering systems.   The design tools based on mathematical analysis and synthesis are only well-suited to the linear situation, and hence recourse is most commonly made to simulation which caters for both non-linear and mixed mode representations (eg continuous, digital or discrete models).

The traditional approach to simulating a dynamic system has been to satisfy a given set of technical requirements, using either a simulation language or a general purpose programming language.   Simulation was mainly performed to aid understanding of the system dynamics.   This was usually performed by a small number of people who had the expertise to develop models, write programs and run the simulation.   A typical modelling and simulation design cycle is shown in Fig 1.   A more modern approach in simulation calls for a broader perspective.   This approach is characterised by the need to satisfy the demands of both technical management and of the engineering designers, who will be working in an interactive manner using a personal workstation.   In turn, this calls for a knowledge-based environment for modelling and simulation.   The concept of the 'environment' is appealing as it supports the whole range of activities involved in a simulation study.

The Knowledge-based Environment for Modelling and Simulation (KEMS) was developed as a result of a study done at the Control Engineering Department to find an 'ideal' simulation language for simulating large systems. Several languages such as ACSL, SIMNON, PSI, etc were evaluted.   The study showed that existing simulation languages not only lack the facilities for simulating such systems but also require skilled personnel to develop and drive a simulation study.   It was also found that the improvements in hardware technology, the emergence of Artificial Intelligence (AI), and maturity in database systems and widespread use of them in recent years could play an important role in future modelling and simulation software (Linkens et al, 1988).

This chapter describes the design and implementation of a prototype KEMS.   Progress is also reported on current design for simulation and database interfaces which will provide additional facilities for model experimentation, validation, archiving and documentation.   These aspects include further AI techniques to simplify and give advice on the total methodology for personnel unskilled in the art of simulation (Rahbar et al, 1988).

The work commenced with a detailed study into a Functional Specification for an AI-augmented environment for simulation (Rahbar et al, 1987). The concepts involved in this are summarised in Fig 2.   Throughout the development of KEMS, industrial cooperation and advice has been obtained from British Gas, Newcastle.   The particular scenario employed has been that of Pressure Reduction Systems used for regulating gas pressures in pipeline networks.   A schematic diagram for such a system is shown in Fig 3.

2. FRAME-BASED ENVIRONMENT FOR MODELLING AND SIMULATION (FEMS 1)

Following an evaluation of several expert system shells we decided to construct the Frame-based Environment for Modelling and Simulation in house
(Tanyi et al, 1987). The system is based on the assumption that many
simulation users will, for the majority of the time, be working with a
limited set of components from which various models can be constructed.
The system is thus designed to make it easy to re-configure existing
models and to create new models based on an existing set of components
or submodels. The creation of models for new components is considered
to be a specialist task which will be carried out infrequently.

The robustness of this system is mainly due to an <u>object-oriented</u> knowledge representation scheme which allows complex knowledge to be expressed and organised into a single hierarchy of inheritance - the system.
This is the frame-based approach which groups knowledge into generic and
structured classes (or frames) and allows these frames to interact
through inheritance boundaries to generate a relatively complex and global model.

Components which have been implemented include pipes, valves, controllers, pumps, servomechanisms, and actuators. These can be used to construct a hierarchical system of reasonable complexity.

A system is implemented as:

system (name, structure, math model, simulation model)
structure (connectors, subsystems)
connectors = connector*
subsystems = system*
connector (NODE, Upstream subsystems, downstream subsystems)
NODE, NAME = string

Hence the hierarchical nature of a system is implicit in the definition
of structure. Details of the implementation can be found in Tanyi and
Linkens (1987), which describes how direct Prolog code is generated automatically for models comprising component frames in its repository.

The frame concept illustrated above has at least two advantages - compactness and organisation. The compactness derives from the fact that
each frame represents only a generic class of objects which can be instantiated to more specific data. The organisation is achieved through
recursive inheritance of information between closely related objects, and
the fact that each frame can be regarded as a stand-alone unit of know-
lege. An example of a frame construct is shown in Fig 4 for a process
engineering valve.

FEM1 was written as a standalone programme for demonstration purposes,
and included rudimentary forms of internal database, a user-interface, a
graphics interface, a case-study module, and a simulation advisor. Its
structure is seen in Fig 5.

3. KNOWLEDGE-BASED ENVIRONMENT FOR MODELLING AND SIMULATION (KEMS)

Having established the knowledge-representation style via FEMS1, the next
phase was the construction of good graphical interfaces and the incorpora-

tion of standard simulation languages (Fig 6).   The basic strategy has
been to use unmodified commercially available packages as much as possible and use a specially written manager to establish links between the
packages.   The prototype uses two commercial packages; EASE+ for the
user-interface and PSI as the simulator.   The overall structure of KEMS1
is shown in Fig 7.

3.1   User-Interface

Although graphics have played an important role in CADCS, it was hither-
to mainly used for plotting 2D graphs, or for enabling graphical input
of models in block diagram form.   The control engineer was thought to
'need the power' of a command-driven interface, just as the software engineer needed the cryptic details of a UNIX operating system.   With this
viewpoint, there is a danger that users will divide into two groups: expert users, and unhappy or non-users.   A graphical interface (WIMP-
based) should substantially increase the number of effective users without penalizing the expert.

EASE+ provides a graphics toolkit for handcrafting user-interfaces.
Although lacking the integrating concepts of a UIMS (User Interface Management System) it has flexibility and economy of resources, being suitable for PC-based systems.

3.2   Data-base Management

No suitable package was found for the data-base, and the basic graphical
data storage facilities of the EASE+ tools were augmented in-house
(Bennett et al, 1989).   An integrated database not only provided a
global repository system from which each component in an environment
stores and retrieves information, it also provides support tools for
browsing, documentation, version control, and back-ups.   These are essential parts of a simulation environment to ease the process of model
development, organization and maintenance.   KEMS is interfaced to a
simulation browser and a librarian program to perform these tasks.

The Librarian generates documentation entry forms for each stage of a
simulation study.   Once proper documentation is generated the archiver
stores the models, experiments, and the results (Fig 8).   Since modelling and simulation is an iterative process, several versions and alternative models of a process may be developed and a number of experiments
are usually performed on each model.   The basic role of the archiver is
to control changes to source codes, object codes, graphic pages etc.   It
stores the history of changes made to each model and allows the user to
easily revert to a prior version of a model if necessary.   It not only
documents the changes, but also documents who made each alteration, the
nature and the time of the change.   We use a commercial software package called PVCS, which provides functions for storage and retrieval of
multiple versions of a model.   In order to economise on the use of
storage space, PVCS uses the 'reverse delta technique' to store the
versions of models, experiments etc.

Ideally, a user-friendly intelligent simulation environment automatically selects the appropriate generic model from related knowledge-bases
which contain the code for user goals of a particular system.   In a
conventional simulation approach we manually define a problem to be

studied. Several versions of a model are generated, producing a large number of files with little or no documentation. After a period of time, users forget where a particular model is, who created it, and how it was developed. The browser implemented in KEMS is aimed to solve this problem. On-line documentation is provided. The user can browse through these documents associated with models and select the one which satisfies his/her requirements. Once a particular version of a model and its corresponding experiment is tagged, the browser retrieves the model automatically and loads it into KEMS, ready for inspection or execution. Figure 9 depicts the browser structure. It shows that the model PRS.MOD has four experiments. As the cursor moves over each file the description is updated. Further details are given in Rahbar et al (1989).

An important feature of modelling and simulation is the production of good documentation subsequent to satisfactory experimentation. This is done in KEMS via a post-processing module, also constructed in EASE+, and shown diagrammatically in Fig 10.

4. KNOWLEDGE ACQUISITION MODULE (KAM)

To construct models in the version of FEMS embedded in KEMS one needed to be familiar with Prolog programming. This would clearly inhibit dynamicists who wished to enter frames for new components. A knowledge acquisition module, KAM, addresses this problem. KAM defines a pseudo natural language, FKRL, which is used to construct a knowledge base of rules and frames in a simple syntax. The FKRL objects are then parsed into a form suitable for conversion into Prolog Code. KAM also incorporates a range of other utilities to which allusion has been made. These utilities reinforce the basic functions of parsing and Prolog generation and enable KAM to function as a stand-alone program. Details of KAM are given in Tanyi and Linkens (1988), and the way in which it is imbedded into the KEMS3 environment is shown in Fig 11.

The basic elements of KAM include a parser, Prolog-generator, tree-generator, query language, file-handler and in-built editor as shown in Fig 12.

The Parser

A preliminary step in describing the parser requires a definition of the FKRL language which forms the input to the parser. This is then followed by a description of the processes which constitute the parsing cycle. These involve the scanner, syntax-analyser, and error-handler.

Structure of FKRL. The syntax of FKRL frames is designed to accommodate all the desirable features of frame-based knowledge representation. These include such concepts as object hierarchies, data-abstraction, semantic relationships between objects, the distinction between conceptual and instance frames, and the assignment of values to attributes. FKRL thus consists of a hierarchy of constructs which includes FRAME, RULE, ATTRIBUTES, INSTANCES, FACETS, EQUATIONS, EXPRESSIONS, ANTECEDANTS and CONSEQUENTS.

The Syntax Analyser. This program module uses a look-ahead scheme to match groups of tokens to appropriate FKRL constructs. Successful syntax analysis results in a match between an FKRL object and a group of tokens.   Syntax analysis fails when no match is found, in which case the error-handler is again activated to display an appropriate error message in the editor.   The cursor position where syntax failure has occurred is also highlighted.   Parsing is resumed when the syntax error has been corrected.   This interactive process continues until all the FKRL text has been grouped into a list of valid syntax objects.

The Error-handler.   This program module is closely integrated with all stages of parsing.   The function of the error-handler is to assert various types of error messages into the working memory.   Each such message contains the cursor position at which the error is found.

The Code Generator

The output of the syntax analyser is a list of valid FKRL objects.   The essence of code-generation is to convert this list into Prolog structures.

The Tree Generator

The basis of the tree-generator is a recursive data structure defined as:

```
TREE     = tree(NODE,TREELIST)
TREELIST = TREE*
```

The asterisk (*) denotes a list.   This definition implies that a tree is a hierarchical structure of nodes and links.   The nodes represent the various frames described in the knowledge base, while the links represent semantic relations between frames.   It is, therefore, possible to generate a tree of arbitrary depth, depending on the complexity of the underlying knowledge base.

The Query Language

The query language is a logical extension of FKRL which facilitates interaction with the knowledge base.   Several types of query are available.   These include queries of the form:

```
SHOW AREA OF PIPE1
SHOW EQUATIONS OF VALVE
```

These are used to retrieve the values of various frame attributes. Queries of the form:

```
FIND A PIPE OF length 20
FIND A PIPE WITH length 20
```

are used to find a frame which has a prescribed attribute value.

Instances of a particular frame can be listed via queries of the form:

```
SHOW PIPES
SHOW VALVES
SHOW COMPRESSORS
```

The template describing a given frame can be displayed through queries of the form:

```
SHOW PIPE
SHOW VALVE
```

The File-handler

The file-handler implements a mixed bag of operations which enables files
to be loaded, saved, browsed and renamed.

The in-built Editor

The in-built editor is invoked during the creation of FKRL files and
during the parsing cycle whenever an error is encountered.

The integration of FEMS, KEMS and KAM into a set of tools which can be
used by either novice or expert users of simulation is illustrated in
Fig 13.

5.   CONCLUSIONS

5.1   Architecture and Implementation

The prototype environment for dynamic systems simulation has been constructed using a mixture of commercial packages and in-house software
generation.   The aim is to obtain an 'open' architecture into which new
concepts and tools can be integrated easily.   This parallels the approach of the much larger MEAD project (Taylor et al, 1990).   Whereas
MEAD uses ADA for the supervisor language, we used Modula-2 to provide
the Simulation Manager.   In both cases the manager is used to reformat
files for inter-package communication.

The KEMS hybrid toolkit runs on PC286 or PC386 systems under MSDOS,
using 'medium coupling' between software segments.   Figure 14 shows the
languages involved in the early KEMS1 environment.   The decision to use
a PC-based implementation platform was influenced by the industrial motivation to make simulation design tools available to a range of users at
widely differing sites.

5.2 Data-base Integration and Management

In agreement with the MEAD project, no commercial database package was
found to be suitable for this CADCS application.   Many features in commercial dB systems are unnecessary, and other requirements were lacking.
Instead, we chose to use the graphics data-base facilities of EASE+ as
the core format, and to add the necessary additional database support
tools, written in-house in Pascal.

A Browser was required for fast retrieval of models and experiment
frames.   In addition, a Librarian was needed for on-line documentation
and archiving.   For efficient storage and retrieval, version control
provided model data compression via the Polytron Version Control System.
The need for protection of validated modelling components is provided by
multiple security levels in the EASE+ toolkit.   Further facilities involve a consistent naming convention and encouragements in documentation
for archiving both models and experimental results.

5.3   Extensions to KEMS

The FEMS model builder produces generic code using automatic Prolog generation.   To convert this into particular simulation language code requires a specialised driver.   The first driver was for PSI (van den Bosch, 1982) which is a well-developed block-oriented simulation language.   Subsequently, a driver has been produced for ESL, which is a more recent equation-oriented language produced by the European Space Agency.   The ESL driver facilitates the use of all the main features of the language and consists of five main parts - a system definition interface, an equation solver, a submodel generator, a model generator, and an archiver (Tanyi et al, 1990).

Model validation is an important, and under-developed, aspect in the whole model development cycle.   Although KEMS supports automatic code verification, it inherently does nothing to assist in the validity of a model as some abstraction of reality.   Validation should include aspects such as conceptual model validity, data validity and operational validity.   Numerous techniques exist for these steps, and many of them rely heavily on heuristic skills.   Thus, a Validation Advisor is presently being constructed for integration into the KEMS environment (Smith et al, 1990).   It is being prototyped initially in NEXPERT, which itself has good interfacing capability with the EASE+ graphics toolkit.

The early version of FEMS included rudimentary 'help' facilities for performing simulations.   Basically, it was a summary of the user-manual. It is recognised that simulation is a skill-based discipline, with very few adequately trained practitioners in industry.   Thus, it is intended to provide an expert-advisor, similar to the Validation Advisor, which will assist the novice user in model experimentation, simulation analysis and run-time advice.   Further phases in the modelling design cycle include problem formulation and specification.   Thus, the future aim is to produce an Integrated Simulation Environment (ISE) which uses multiple cooperating Expert Systems, together with co-ordinating database management tools (Rahbar et al, 1990).   Utilising an 'open' architecture, it should be relatively simple to incorporate other features such as computer algebra, and modelling methodologies like that of Bond Graphs (Linkens, 1990), to widen access to include workers in the life sciences as well as engineering.   In addition to the hierarchical concepts incorporated in the database structure, similar principles have recently been built into the modelling infrastructure.   Such hierarchical modelling is deemed to be essential in the design and simulation of complex systems.   The embedding of further IT-related concepts into the KEMS environment will make the decision-making aspects of design for complex systems more tractable.

6.   ACKNOWLEDGEMENT

The research described in this chapter involves a team of workers including S Bennett, M T Rahbar, E Tanyi, M Smith and A Scott.   M T Rahbar acknowledges financial support via a Research Scholarship from British Gas PLC, whose collaboration is also gratefully recognised.   The last three named workers acknowledge support from SERC.

7. REFERENCES

ARAKI, M.: 'Industrial applications in Japan of CAD packages for control systems', IFAC Symp. CADCS, Lyngby, pp.71-76.

BENNETT, S., RAHBAR, M.T., LINKENS, D.A., TANYI, E., and SMITH, E. (1989): 'A Knowledge-based Environment for Modelling and Simulation (KEMS)', Proc. SCS Western Multi Conference, San Diego, Jan.

LINKENS, D.A., TANYI, E., RAHBAR, M.T., and BENNETT, S. (1988): 'Artificial Intelligence techniques applied to simulation', IEE Conf. Control '88, Oxford, UK.

LINKENS, D.A. (1990): 'Bond graphs for an improved modelling environment in the life sciences', IEE Colloquium, 'Bond Graphs in Control', April, pp.3/1-3/4.

RAHBAR, M.T., BENNETT, S., and LINKENS, D.A. (1987): 'Functional specifications for an Intelligent Simulation Environment', Proc. UKSC Conf. 'Computer Simulation', Bangor, pp.182-197.

RAHBAR, M.T., TANYI, E., BENNETT, S., and LINKENS, D.A. (1988): 'A framework for a Knowledge-based Modelling and Simulation Environment (KBMSE)', Proc. 12th IMACS World Congress, Vol.4, Paris.

RAHBAR, M.T., BENNETT, S., LINKENS, D.A., and THOMPSON, B. (1989): 'An integrated database: its role in a Knowledge-based Environment for Modelling and Simulation (KEMS)', Proc. ESC '89, Edin., Sept.

RAHBAR, M.T., BENNETT, S., and LINKENS, D.A. (1990): 'Strategies for designing a knowledge-based environment for modelling and simulation', UKSC '90, Brighton, Sept.

SMITH, M., LINKENS, D.A., and BENNETT, S. (1990): 'Model Validation for a Knowledge-based Environment for Modelling and Simulation (KEMS)', ibid.

TANYI, E., and LINKENS, D.A. (1987): 'A frame-based modelling and simulation environment', Proc. UKSC Conf. "Computer Simulation", Bangor, pp.215-219.

TANYI, E., and LINKENS, D.A. (1987): 'A frame-based expert system for dynamic systems modelling and simulation', IEE Colloq. "Expert Systems and Control".

TANYI, E., and LINKENS, D.A. (1989): 'Addition of a knowledge acquisition facility to a Knowledge-based Environment for Modelling and Simulation (KEMS)', Proc. of ESC '89, Edin., Sept.

TANYI, E., LINKENS, D.A., and BENNETT, S. (1990): 'A Prolog-based driver for the ESL simulation language', UKSC '90, Brighton, Sept.

TAYLOR, J.H., FREDERICK, D.F., RIMVALL, M.C., and SUTHERLAND, H.A. (1990): 'Computer-aided control engineering environments: architecture, user interface, data-base management, and expert aiding', Proc. IFAC World Congress, Tallinn, USSR, 13-17 August.

VAN DEN BOSCH, P.P.J. (1982): 'PSI - Interactive Simulation Program', IEEE Control System Magazine, 2, No.4, p.42.

VAN DEN BOSCH, P.P.J., and VAN DEN BOOM, A.J.W. (1985): 'Industrial applications in the Netherlands for CAD packages in control systems', IFAC Symp. CADCS, Lyngby, pp.58-61.

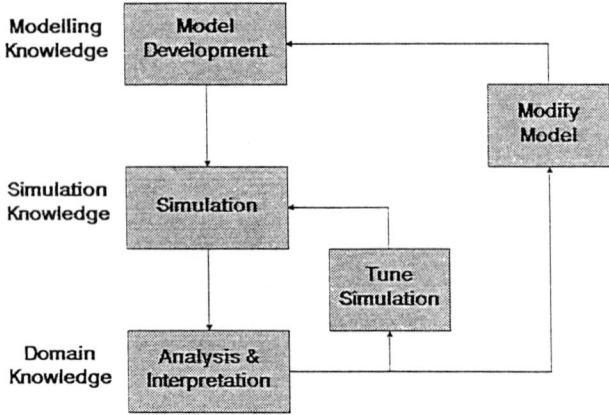

Figure 1   The modelling and simulation cycle

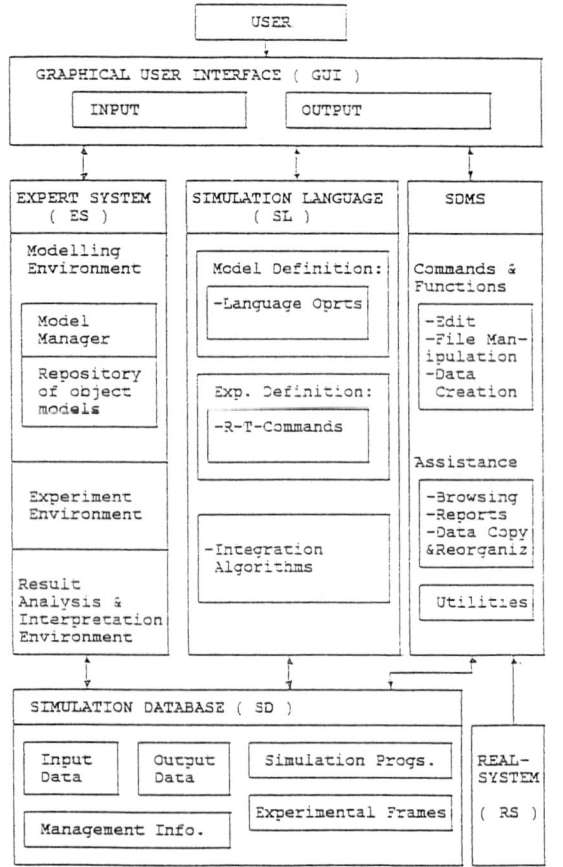

Figure 2   A Knowledge-based modelling and simulation environment

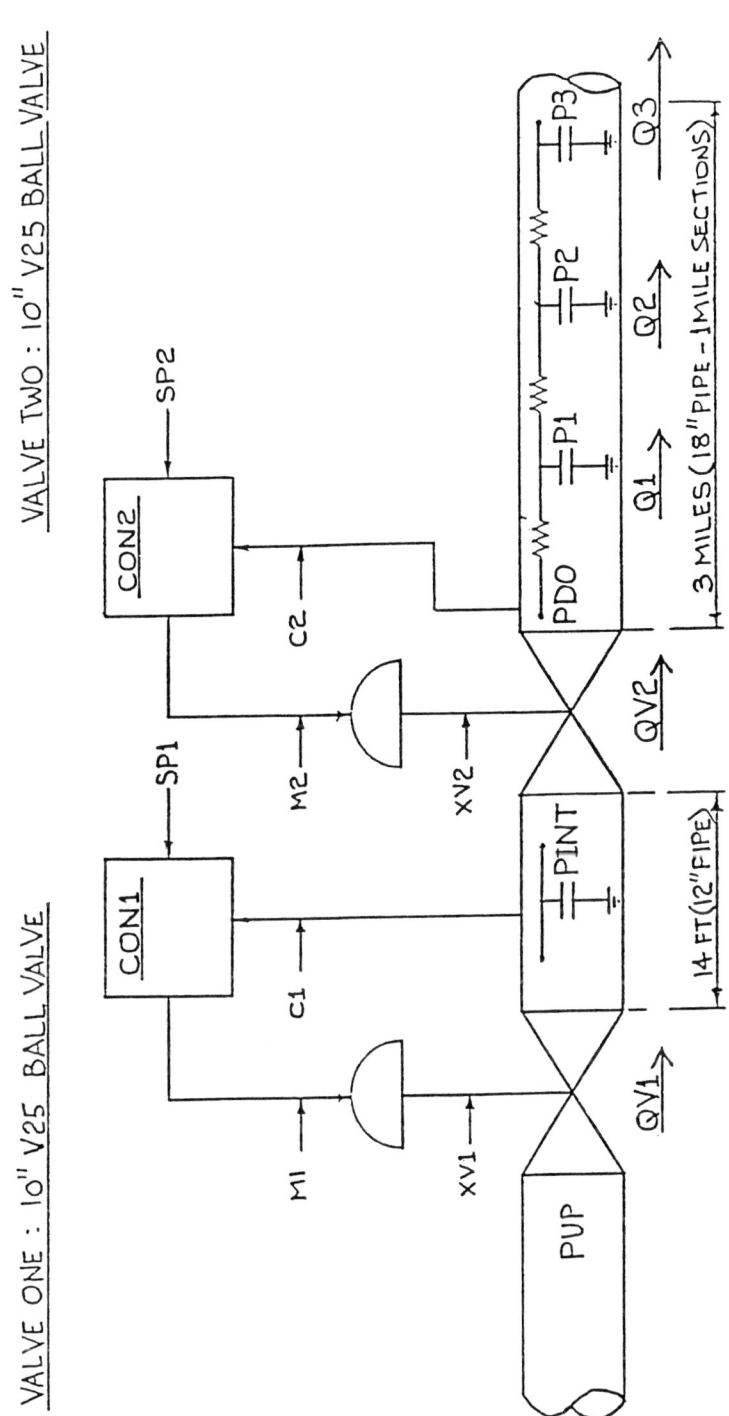

Fig 3   British Gas Pressure Reduction System

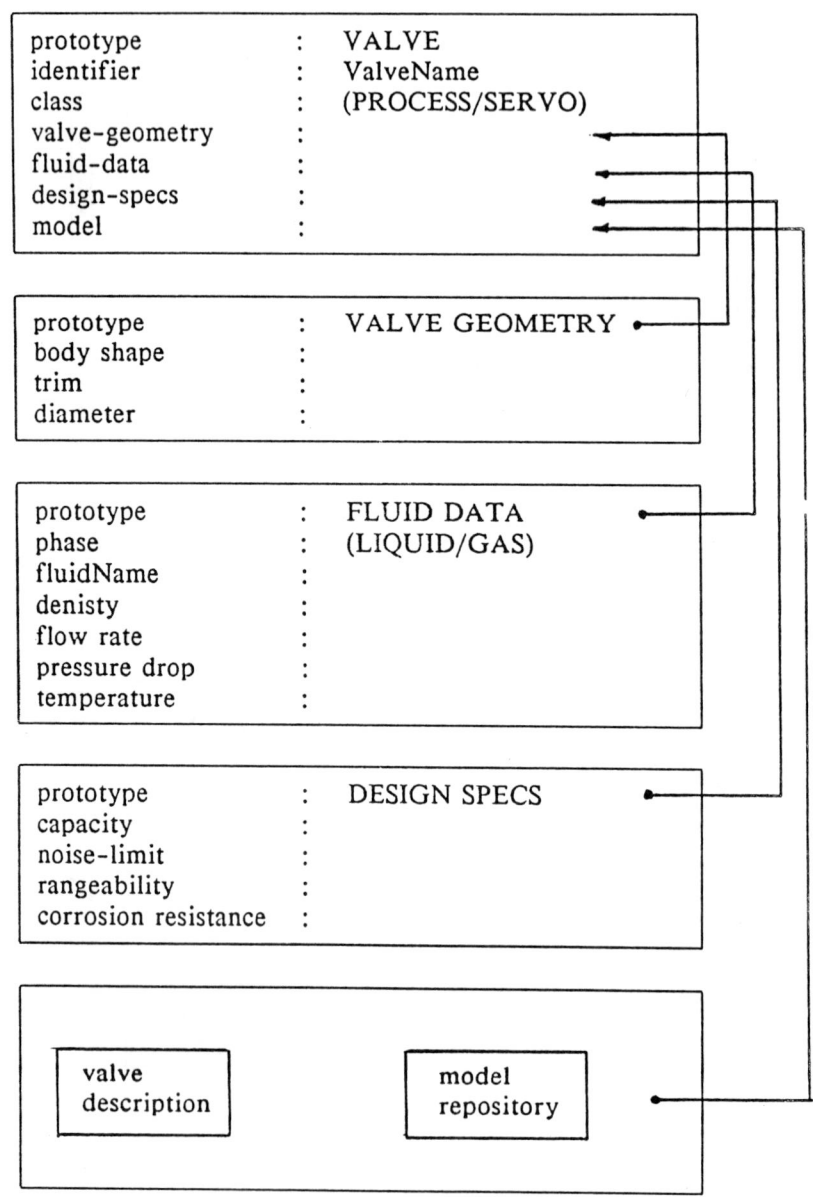

Figure 4   Frame structure for process/servomechanism
value knowledge representation

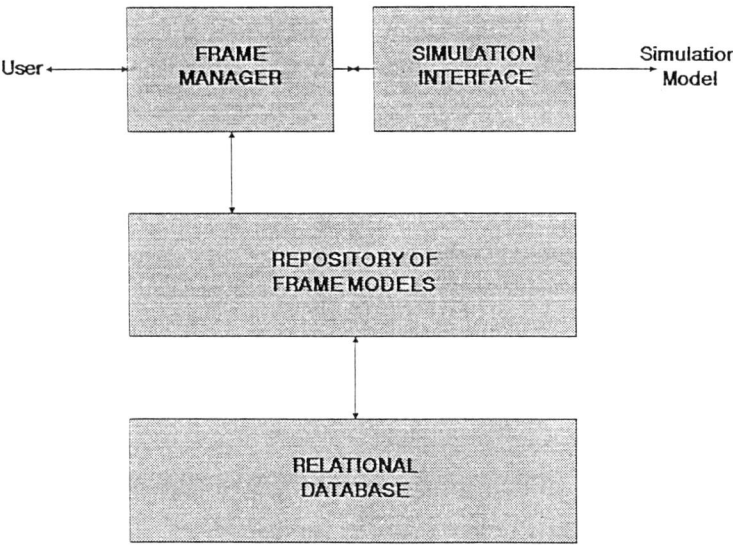

Figure 5   Structure of FEMS1 modeller

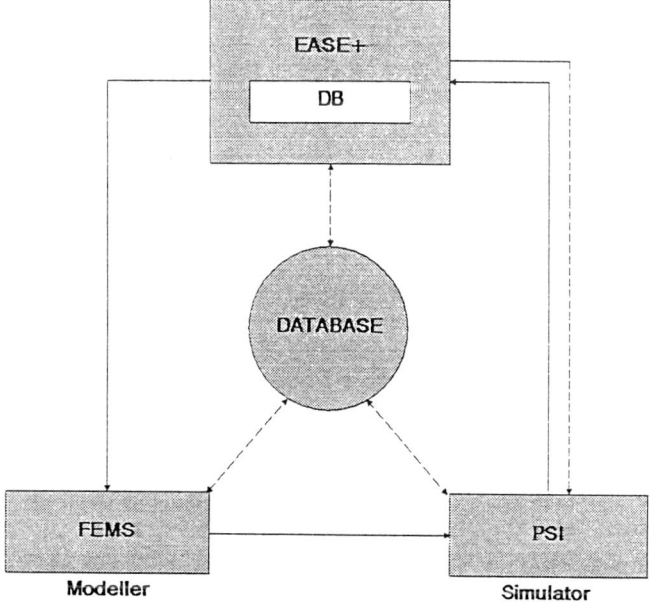

Figure 6   Structure of KEMS1 graphical environment

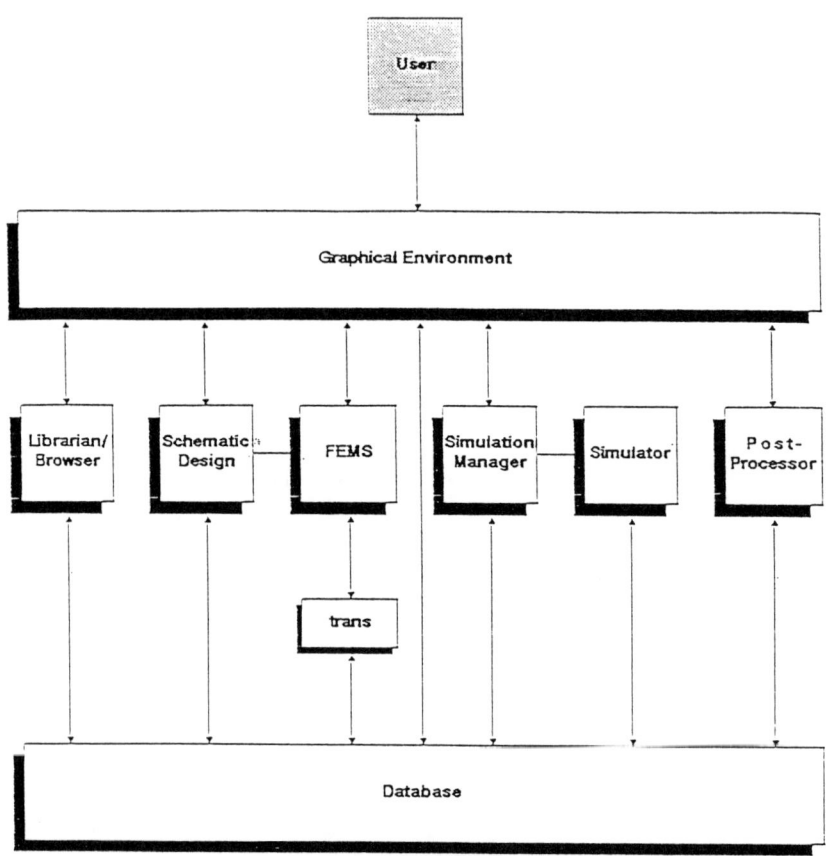

Figure 7   Schematic of KEMS1

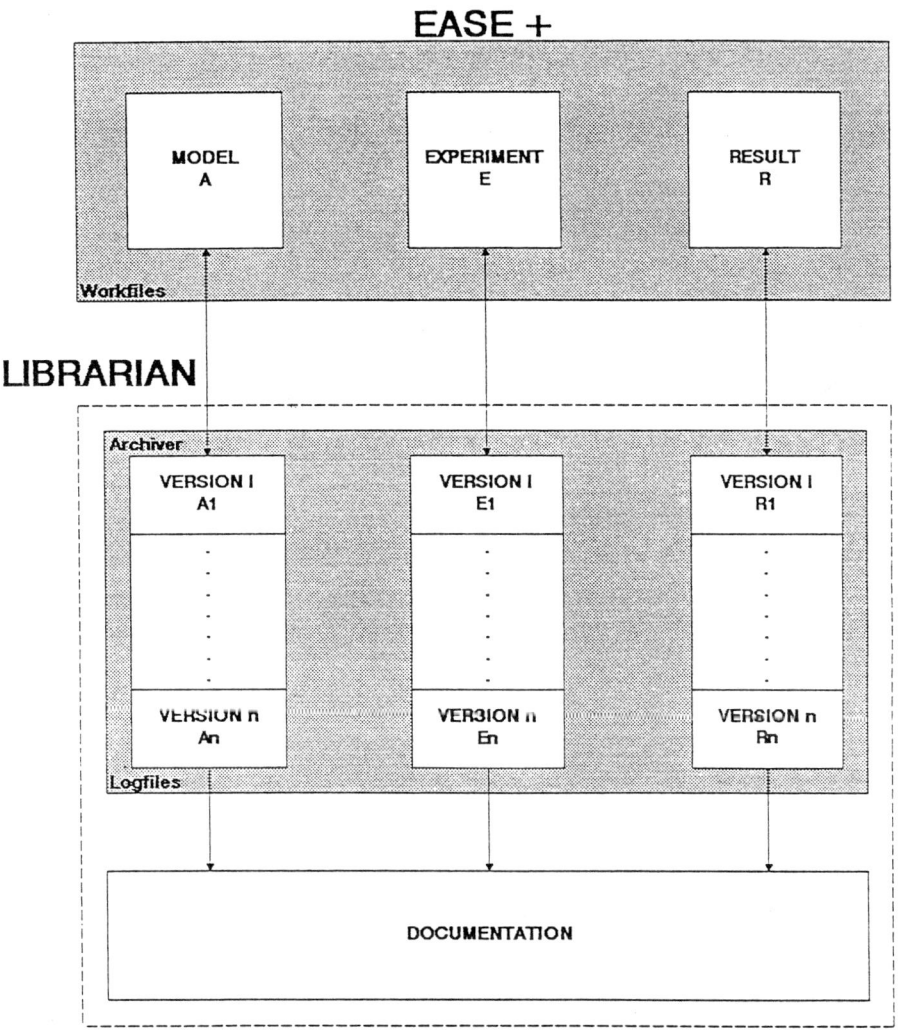

Figure 8 Interface between EASE+ and the Librarian in KEMS1

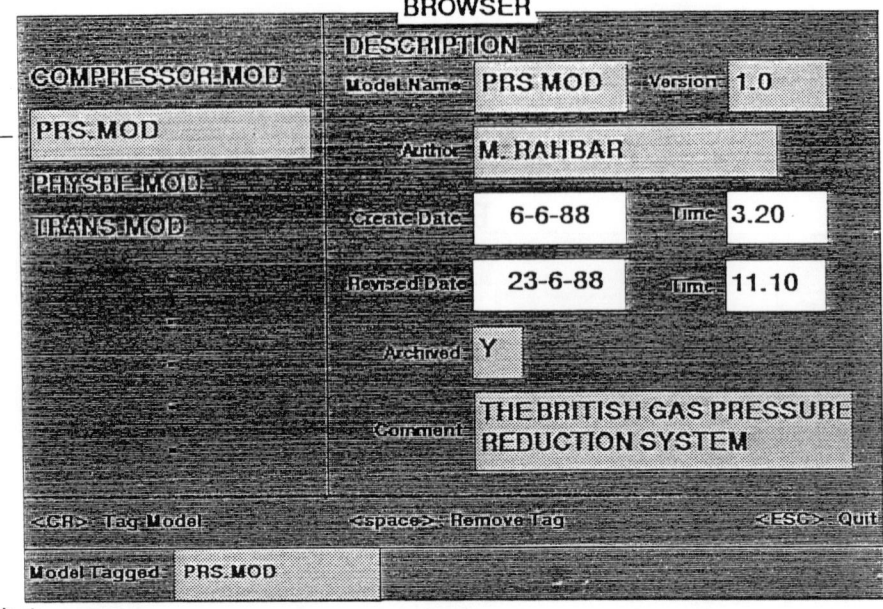

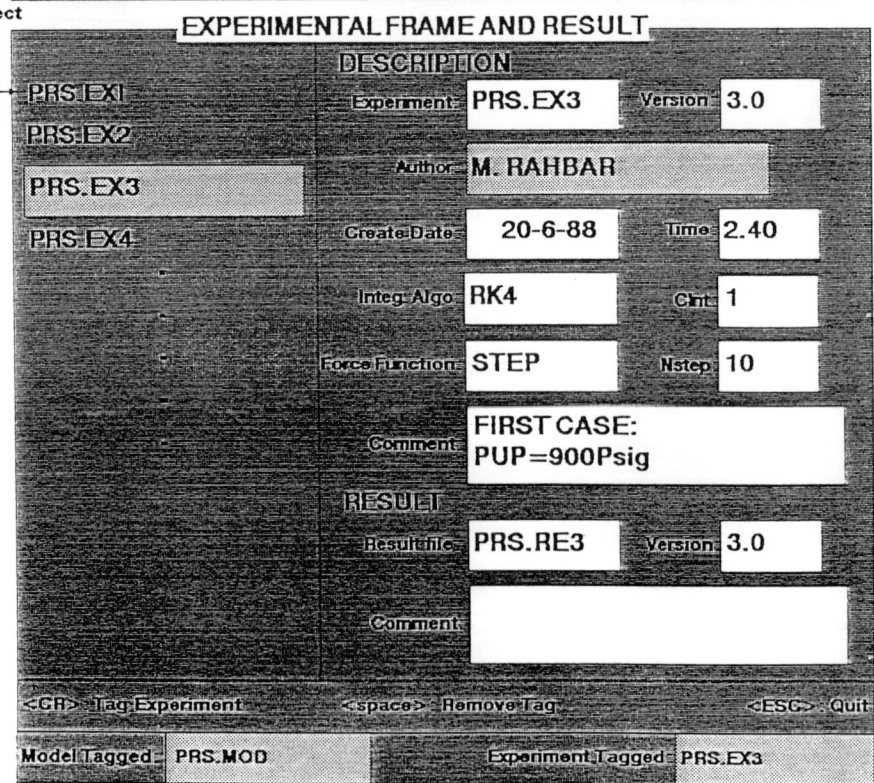

Figure 9   An example of the hierarchical browsing
structure in KEMS1

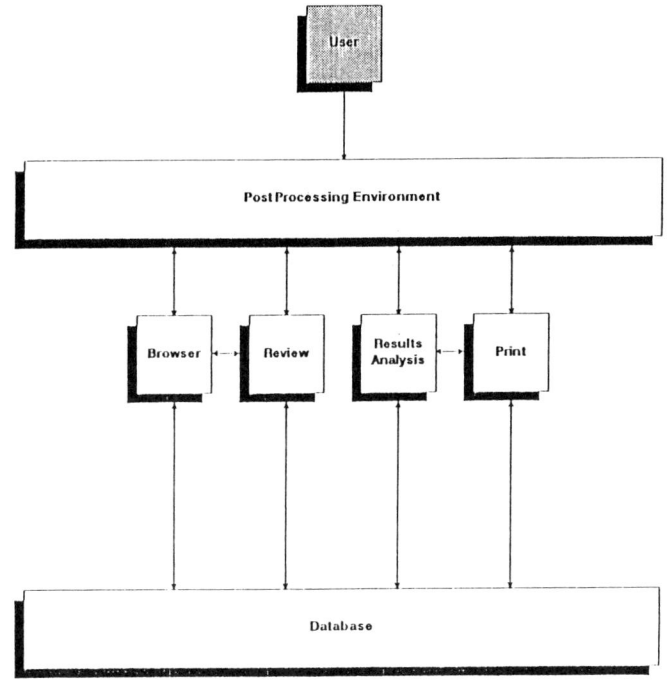

Figure 10   Schematic of post-processor in KEMS1

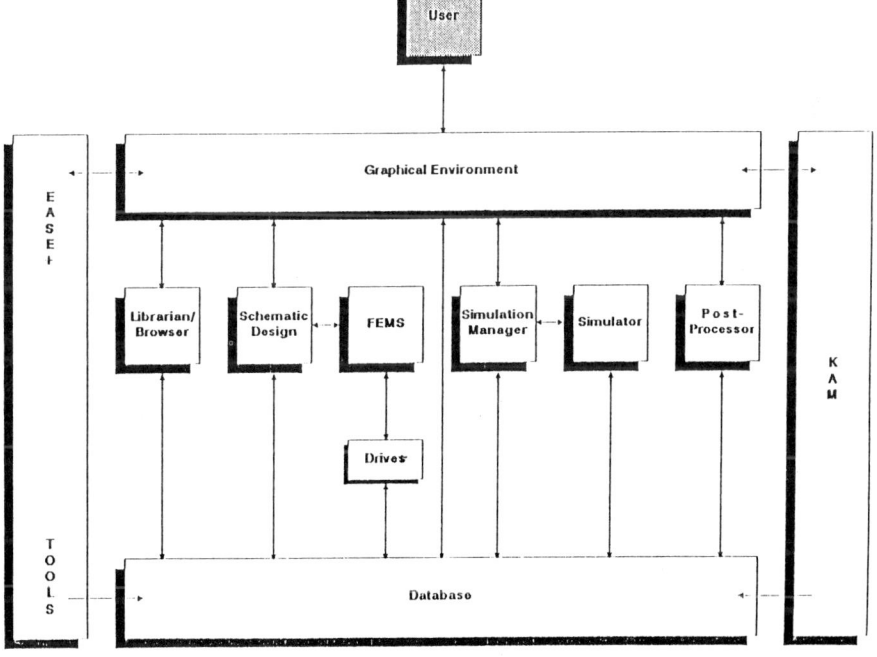

Figure 11   Schematic of KEMS3 including the Knowledge
Acquisition Module (KAM)

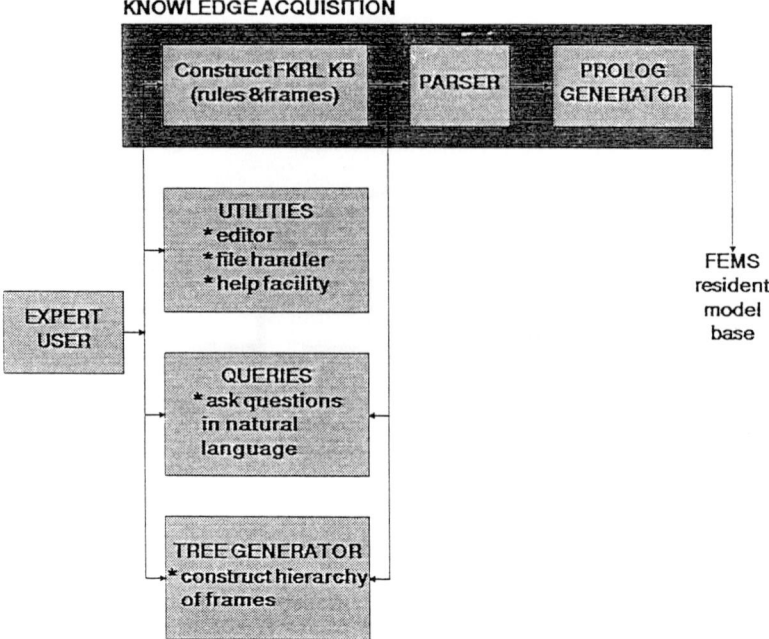

Figure 12   Structure of KAM

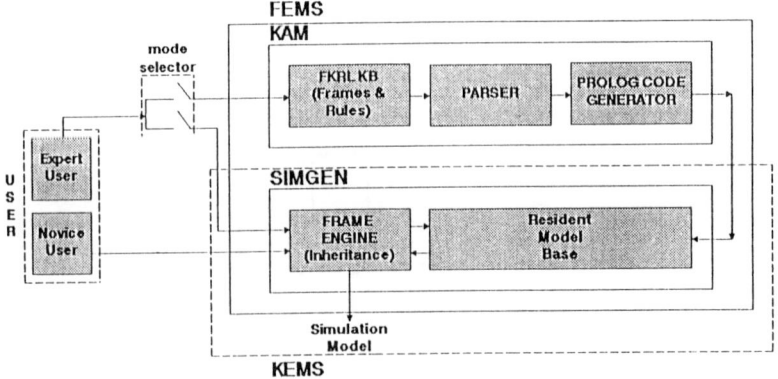

FKRL- Frame-based Knowledge Representation Language.

KAM- Knowledge Acquisition Module.

SIMGEN- Simulation Model Generator.

FEMS- Frame-based Environment for Modelling and Simulation.

KEMS- Knowleddge Environment for Modelling and simulation.

Figure 13   Integration of FEMS, KEMS and KAM for
Novice and Expert users

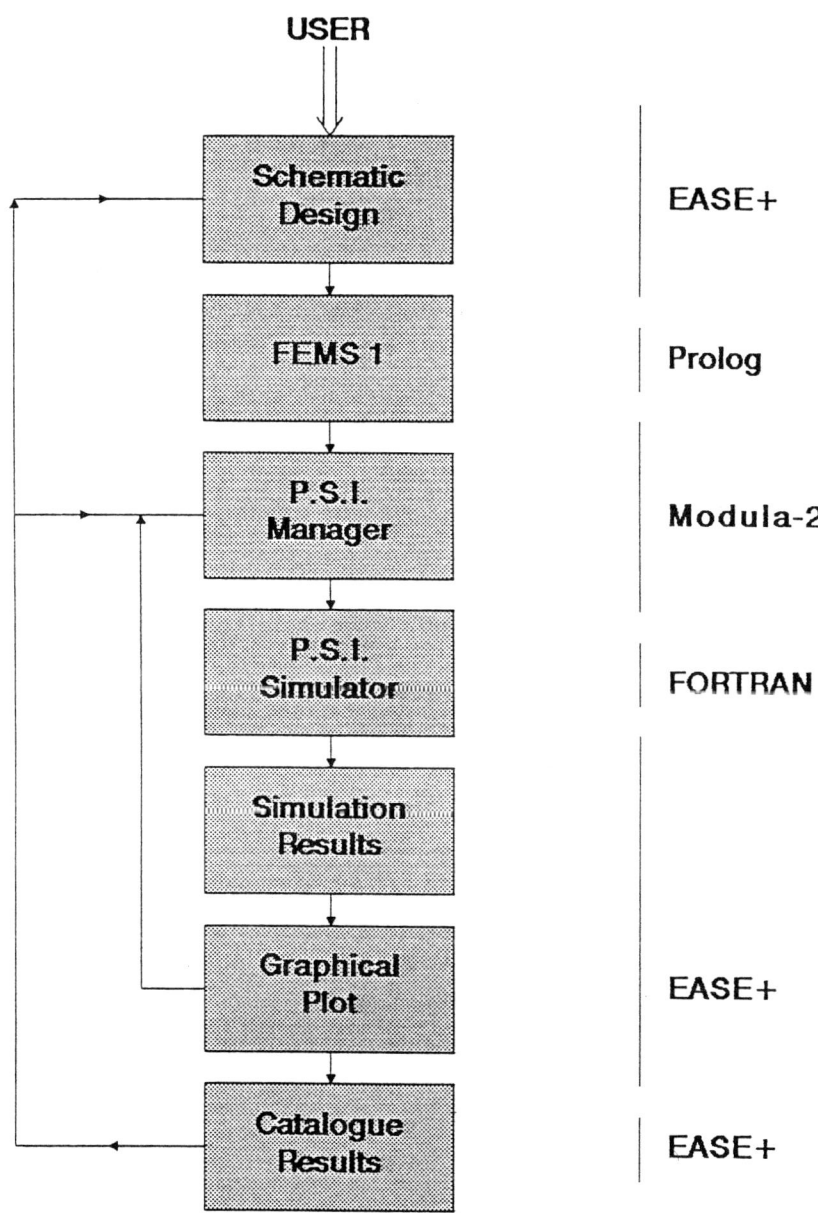

Figure 14   Languages and information flow
for the KEMS1 environment

Chapter 7

Robot control

A. S. Morris

1. Introduction

The application of robot manipulators to industrial tasks is growing at the rate of about 50% per year and therefore the industrial robot is now of great importance in the modern manufacturing scene. Robots offer the opportunity of automating manufacturing processes in a flexible way and this has far reaching consequences on the economics of automation. They have made such a great impact because the effort required to reprogram them, for instance to change the pattern of welds in a spot-welding application, requires only an adjustment to the controlling software. This is relatively simple compared with the mechanical redesign necessary when the functioning of hard-automation machinery needs changing.

An industrial robot is defined as a multi-linked mechanical system in which the motion of the links is governed by a reprogrammable controller. This can be modelled by the system shown in figure 1, where the successive links form a chain with a joint between each pair of links. Although in the general case a joint could be a screw one (having both translational and rotational motion), all joints in current industrial robots are either purely rotational or purely translational.

Each joint motion is known as a degree of freedom (DOF). For total control of the end-effector, that is, to have the ability to place it anywhere within the robot workspace and at any orientation with respect to the workpiece it is operating on, the robot must have six degrees of freedom. This configuration of six joints is the most common form of industrial robot manipulator. It is usually realised as a two-part system, a 3-DOF end-effector (tool) on the end of a 3-DOF arm.

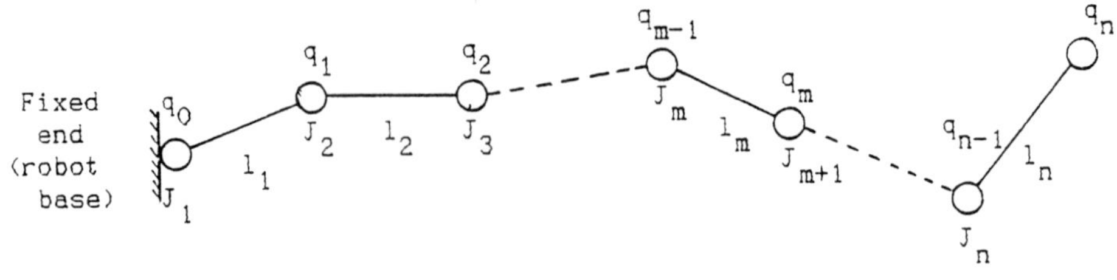

FIGURE 1 - TYPICAL CHAIN OF LINKS

Some of the problems involved in programming and controlling robots start to become apparent if figure 1 is studied more closely. The system of links comprising the robot is fixed at one end and free at the other. This is a cantilever-like structure which is naturally oscillatory. Further complication is added by the fact that the joint motions are not in general all in the same plane. This means that the geometric description of the robot is difficult for programming purposes. A more serious consequence of this, however, is that as the robot moves and its geometrical configuration changes, so the inertia forces involved in its motion change. Control of the robot is therefore made very difficult because of this time-varying nature of some of the controlled parameters.

2. Requirements and constraints for robot control

Requirements

Whatever task a robot is applied to, a fundamental requirement is the ability to place the end-effector at some defined position and orientation with respect to the target workpiece. The path that a robot follows in moving to such a defined point may be constrained or unconstrained. An unconstrained path is where there is no requirement to follow any particular route in moving from the current position to the target point. Alternatively, a constrained path is where the robot is required to follow some particular curved path through space between the two points. The latter type of path is required in surface-coating and welding applications. A constrained path can often be further complicated by the need to avoid certain obstacles which are present in the workspace.

As well as satisfying static positioning requirements, dynamic control of the robot is also often required to minimise deviations of the end-effector away from the specified path between two end points under the action of dynamic forces.

Constraints

The degree to which a robot is able to satisfy the static positioning, path tracking and dynamic control requirements depends on several factors. These factors include manipulator geometry, what the required trajectory is, what speed of robot operation is required, what computer power is available and what feedback sensors are available.

3. Geometry of manipulator arm

The position of the end effector is determined principally by the joints of the robot arm (normally three). The joints of the end-effector usually act about a fixed point in space and control only the orientation of the end-effector.

Robot arms are available with five standard types of geometry, as shown in figure 2. These differ according to the number of rotational (R) and translation (T) joints. Each geometry is given a particular name as follows:

Cartesian   - 3T
Cylindrical   - 2T, 1R
Polar   - 1T, 2R (axes at 90°)
Revolute   - 3R (also known as anthropomorphic or arm-and-elbow)
Scara   - 1T, 2R (parallel axes) (translational joint is normally pneumatic,
                          driving between two fixed positions)

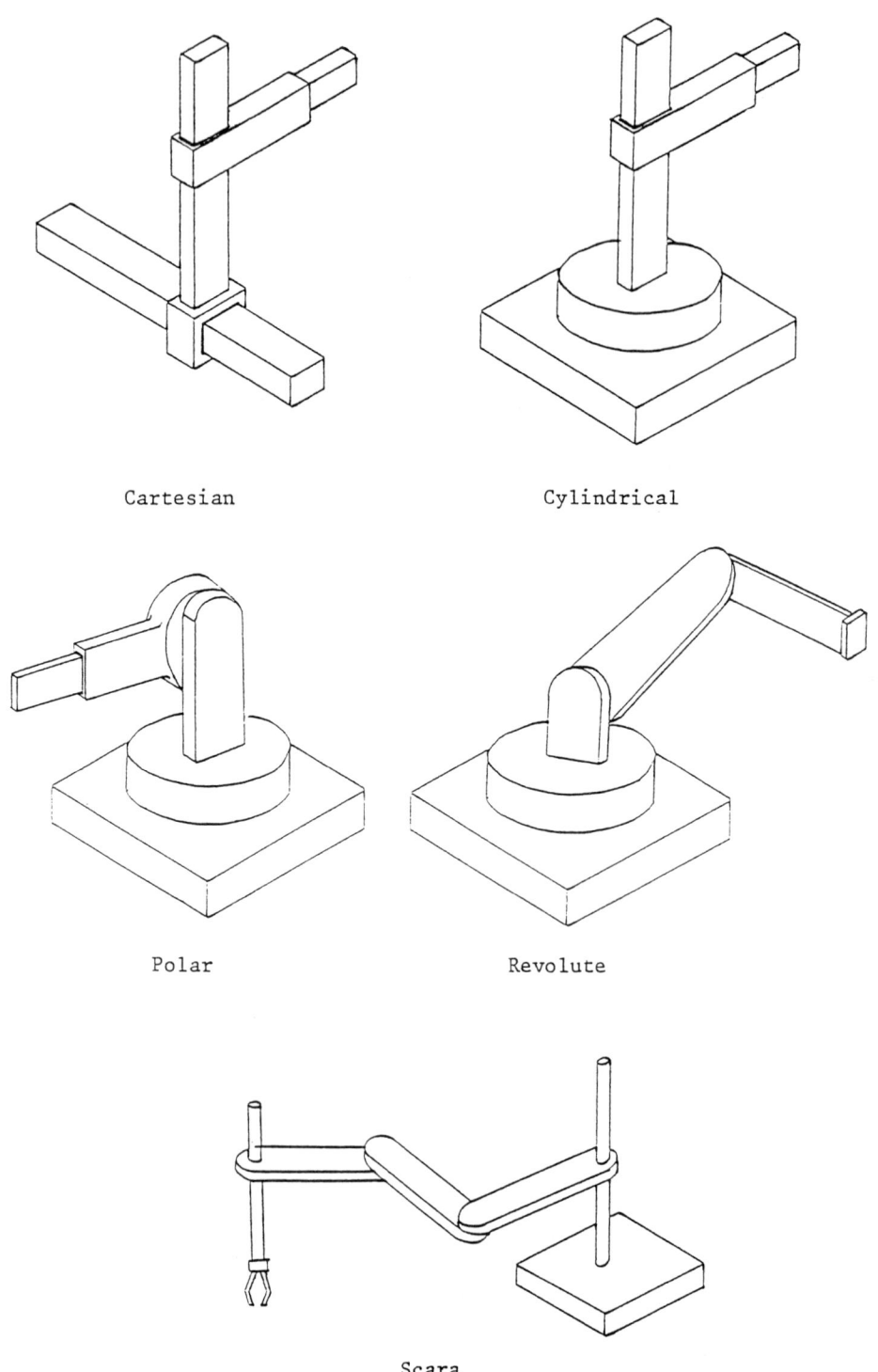

Cartesian   Cylindrical

Polar   Revolute

Scara

FIGURE 2 GEOMETRICAL ARRANGEMENTS

The accuracy with which the end-effector can be placed at a particular point in the workspace is highest for manipulators with only translational joints and decreases as the number of rotational joints increases. The programming task also becomes more difficult as the number of rotational joints increases. However, a higher number of rotational joints increases the working envelope and flexibility of the robot. The SCARA geometry (selectively compliant articulated robot arm) is a recent Japanese development which is particularly suited to assembly tasks. Compliance in the horizontal plane allows correction for small relative positioning errors between the robot and components. Choice of geometry therefore required careful consideration according to the requirements of the application.

4. Joint actuators

Joints can be actuated by hydraulic, pneumatic or electric drives. Three alternative forms of electric drive are available, dc motors, ac motors and stepper motors. The relative merits of each type of system can be summarised as follows.

dc motors	high accuracy, low maintenance, simple but low power to weight ratio.
ac motors	high accuracy, very low maintenance, simple, now competitive on cost with dc motors but still have low power to weight ratio.
stepper motors	very high accuracy, cheaper than dc/ac motors but very low power to weight ratio and can lose step for anything but very light loads due to load inertia.
hydraulic actuators	cheap, reliable, medium power to weight ratio but dynamic performance problems due to compressibility of air and normally necessary to operate them between fixed stops (hence noisy and inflexible).

To meet positioning accuracy requirements, electric motors are the clear favourite for the robot drive system, as the problems of friction and fluid leaks cause performance problems in pneumatic and hydraulic systems. However, the low power to weight ratio of electric drives precludes their use wherever the required payload of the robot is not small. Pneumatic drives are useful in 'pick and place' tasks where only simple motions are required, but the inflexibility imposed by fixed mechanical stops makes them unsuitable in many applications. Hence, for handling large loads, hydraulic drives are the only option in spite of their relatively poor accuracy.

5. Sensors

The range of sensors found in industrial robots can be conveniently classified as internal and external sensors. Manipulators having only internal sensors are generally known as first generation robots. These have no means of sensing their environment and will blindly carry out the programmed task whether it is sensible to do so or not. They have no ability to measure small errors in position, and so components to be operated on must be held in an exactly known position and orientation by means of jigs, chute systems etc. The addition of external sensors converts the robot into a second generation one and enables it to detect and correct for small positioning errors.

Internal sensors comprise those transducers which are concerned with monitoring joint motion and providing feedback information to the robot controller. This allows the controller to operate as a servomechanism and ensured that the required joint positions, as defined by the inverse kinematic transformation, are achieved. Transducers provide either position or velocity information. The usual devices used are:

Translational position - potentiometer, LVDT (linear variable differential transformer)
Rotational motion   - potentiometer, encoder (especially optical form), synchro,
                           resolver.,
Rotational velocity   - dc tachogenerator, ac tachogenerator (less common)

Achieving the defined joint positions does not necessarily mean that the required spatial position of the end-effector will be achieved, because of the presence of link-flexure and backlash in the joints. This leads to a degree of inaccuracy in end-effector positioning which can only be corrected by additional external sensors.

External sensors are those sensors which provide information about the relationship between a robot and its environment and enable small positioning errors in the end-effector to be corrected. The range of sensors in this category includes:

    range
    proximity
    touch
    force
    vision

As far as industrial applications are concerned, vision is by far the most important of these, with force sensing also being important to a lesser extent. Visions systems provide information about the identification of workpieces and their position and orientation with respect to the robot, and this information is valuable in most handling, processing and assembly tasks. Force sensing is generally used to provide information about the reaction forces between the end-effector and workpiece in assembly operations. The magnitude and direction of the reaction forces provides information about the relative orientation between the robot and workpiece and allows the appropriate correction to be carried out.

Where such external sensors are included within a robot system, provision must be made within the robot controller to handle the extra information provided.

6. Programming the robot

Three methods of programming robots are currently in use, 'lead-through' 'drive-through' and 'direct'.

In the 'lead-through' method, a human operator moves the robot end-effector through the required sequence of motions manually. The robot control computer monitors the output of position sensors on the manipulator joints whilst this is happening and builds up a time-history of positions. Subsequently, the computer recalls this stored sequence of positions from memory and the manipulator follows the taught sequence of operations. Because of the limitations of human strength in moving the robot arm about, this programming technique is clearly limited to small light robots.

The 'drive-through' method is similar to the above but involves the robot being driven through the required sequence of motions by pressing buttons on a teaching pendant, with the control computer recording a history of joint positions as before. Teaching curved trajectories and moving to exact positions by this method is very difficult.

In 'direct' programming, target points and trajectories are defined to the robot controller as a series of (x,y,z) coordinate points. Provision must be made in the controlling software to convert these spatial (x,y,z) coordinates into robot joint positions, a procedure known mathematically as the inverse kinematic transformation. The degree of difficulty in doing this is a function of the number of rotational joints in the robot. For a cartesian coordinate robot, the effort is trivial but for a revolute coordinate robot it is very complicated. Whilst direct programming poses greater difficulty than the two other alternatives, it has clear advantages safety-wise and is the only possible method if CADCAM production techniques are being considered.

The minimum provision of sensors necessary for any of these three methods of programming and control are sensors to measure the positions of the robot joints. This provision is adequate for lead-through or drive-through programming, because the human programmer applies the fine control needed to ensure that the end-effector is placed exactly at the required position. However, in direct programming, significant errors always exist in calculating the position of the end-effector in spatial (x,y,z) coordinates from joint position measurements. Such errors arise because of deviations in the link-lengths etc., of robots away from nominal values at the time of their manufacture, because of joint position transducer errors and because of link flexure, backlash etc. Therefore, the quality of control is greatly enhanced if additional, external sensors are incorporated which provide information about the absolute position of the end-effector in space and/or its position with respect to other objects in the workspace.

7. Kinematic modelling

Knowledge of the kinematic model describing its geometry is a pre-requisite for direct robot programming and control. The kinematic model describes the relationship between the robot joint positions and the spatial position of its end-effector in (x,y,z) coordinates and is associated with two mathematical transformations, the forward kinematic transformation and the inverse kinematic transformation.

The forward kinematic transformation involves the calculation of the end-effector (x,y,z) coordinates from a given set of joint positions (q_1, q_2, ... q_n).

The inverse kinematic transformation involves the calculation of the set of joint positions (q_1, q_2, ... q_n) which will cause the end effector to be at some specified (x,y,z) position in space. This is the transformation which is of principal importance for both programming and control purposes.

If a manipulator involves more than two rotational joints with non-parallel axes, writing down the kinematic relationships 'longhand' in terms of the sine and cosine relationships between successive joints is not viable. Instead, it is necessary to define the relationships in terms of a strict framework known as homogeneous transformations.

This can be demonstrated by considering the two-link manipulator shown in figure3(a). In an xyz coordinate frame with origin at A, the position of the end of the arm C with respect to A is defined by the sum of two vectors r_1 and r_2 (figure 3(b)).

$$r_1 = (l_1\cos\theta_1), (l_1\sin\theta_1), (0)$$
$$r_2 = (l_2\cos(\theta_1+\theta_2)), (l_2\sin(\theta_1+\theta_2)), (0)$$
$$r_1 + r_2 = (l_1\cos\theta_1 + l_2\cos(\theta_1+\theta_2)),(l_1\sin\theta_1 + l_2\sin(\theta_1+\theta_2)), (0)$$

This is a simple case with only two joints. Also the axes are parallel. For more than two joints, with non-parallel axes, we need an alternative form of relationship.

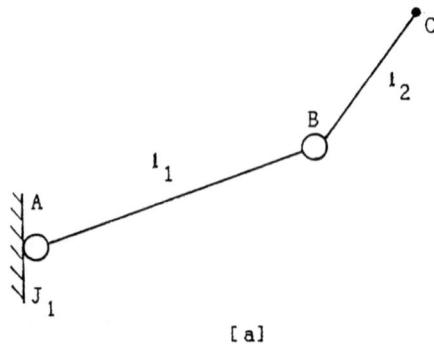

[a]

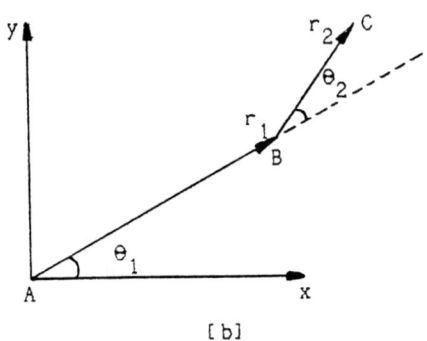

[b]

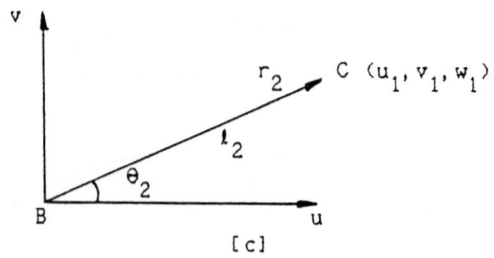

[c]

FIGURE 3

What we need to do is to be able to express the position of any link in a coordinate frame whose origin is at the activating joint for the link. Such 'link' coordinate frames can be used providing that a transformation matrix can be synthesised which relates the link coordinate frame to the reference coordinate frame, i.e. in the above example, express C in a coordinate frame with origin at B and relate this back to the reference coordinate frame at A by a transformation matrix.

Consider a coordinate frame uvw with origin at B (figure 3(c). Let the coordinates of point C in this coordinate frame be (u_1, v_1, w_1).

Then:

$$\begin{vmatrix} x_1 \\ y_1 \\ z_1 \end{vmatrix} = R \begin{vmatrix} u_1 \\ v_1 \\ w_1 \end{vmatrix} \tag{1}$$

$$u_1 = l_2\cos\theta_2 \; ; \; v_1 = l_2\sin\theta_2 \; ; \; w_1 = 0$$

We require:

$$\begin{vmatrix} x_1 \\ y_1 \\ z_1 \end{vmatrix} = \begin{vmatrix} r_{11} & r_{12} & r_{13} \\ r_{21} & r_{22} & r_{23} \\ r_{31} & r_{32} & r_{33} \end{vmatrix} \cdot \begin{vmatrix} l_2\cos\theta_2 \\ l_2\sin\theta_2 \\ 0 \end{vmatrix} \tag{2}$$

such that
$$x_1 = l_1\cos\theta_1 + l_2\cos(\theta_1+\theta_2) \tag{3}$$
$$y_1 = l_1\sin\theta_1 + l_2\sin(\theta_1+\theta_2) \tag{4}$$
$$z_1 = 0 \tag{5}$$

From (2)
$$x_1 = l_2 (r_{11} \cos\theta_2 + r_{12}\sin\theta_2) \tag{6}$$

Comparing (3) and (6), we see that whatever we choose for r_{11} or r_{12}, we cannot obtain the $(l_1\cos\theta_1)$ term without getting unwanted terms in the product (l_1l_2). Thus R cannot be expressed as a 3*3 matrix. This is because R has to describe the translation from A to B as well as the rotation of the uvw frame about the z axis with respect to the xyz frame. In fact, R has to be a 4*4 matrix to do this and equation (1) is modified to:

$$\begin{vmatrix} x_1 \\ y_1 \\ z_1 \\ 1 \end{vmatrix} = R \begin{vmatrix} u_1 \\ v_1 \\ w_1 \\ 1 \end{vmatrix} \tag{7}$$

This is known as the homogeneous coordinate representation and matrix R is known as a homogeneous transformation.

If R is chosen as
$$\begin{vmatrix} \cos\theta_1 & \sin\theta_1 & 0 & l_1\cos\theta_1 \\ \sin\theta_1 & \cos\theta_1 & 0 & l_1\sin\theta_1 \\ 0 & 0 & 1 & 0 \\ 0 & 0 & 0 & 1 \end{vmatrix}$$

it can be shown that equation (7) is satisfied.

This method of transformation between coordinate frames can be extended to any number and configuration of links, Standard homogeneous transformations exist which describe single translations or rotations between successive coordinate frames. These act as building blocks which enable any transformation matrix to be synthesised by multiplying together the appropriate standard transformations. Six such standard homogeneous transformations exist:

8. Standard homogeneous transformations

Translation by a distance a along the x axis:

$$\text{Trans}(a,0,0) = \begin{vmatrix} 1 & 0 & 0 & a \\ 0 & 1 & 0 & 0 \\ 0 & 0 & 1 & 0 \\ 0 & 0 & 0 & 1 \end{vmatrix} \tag{8}$$

Translation by a distance b along the y axis

$$\text{Trans}(0,b,0) = \begin{vmatrix} 1 & 0 & 0 & 0 \\ 0 & 1 & 0 & b \\ 0 & 0 & 1 & 0 \\ 0 & 0 & 0 & 1 \end{vmatrix} \tag{9}$$

Translation by a distance c along the z axis:

$$\text{Trans}(0,0,c) = \begin{vmatrix} 1 & 0 & 0 & 0 \\ 0 & 1 & 0 & 0 \\ 0 & 0 & 1 & c \\ 0 & 0 & 0 & 1 \end{vmatrix} \tag{10}$$

Rotations by an angle :
About x axis: $\text{Rot}(x, \theta) = \begin{vmatrix} 1 & 0 & 0 & 0 \\ 0 & \cos\theta & -\sin\theta & 0 \\ 0 & \sin\theta & \cos\theta & 0 \\ 0 & 0 & 0 & 0 \end{vmatrix} \tag{11}$

About y axis: $\text{Rot}(y,\theta) = \begin{vmatrix} \cos\theta & 0 & \sin\theta & 0 \\ 0 & 1 & 0 & 0 \\ -\sin\theta & 0 & \cos\theta & 0 \\ 0 & 0 & 0 & 1 \end{vmatrix} \tag{12}$

About z axis: $\text{Rot}(z,\theta) = \begin{vmatrix} \cos\theta & -\sin\theta & 0 & 0 \\ \sin\theta & \cos\theta & 0 & 0 \\ 0 & 0 & 1 & 0 \\ 0 & 0 & 0 & 1 \end{vmatrix} \tag{13}$

We can now see how these were used to formulate R for equation (7) earlier. Transforming between the two coordinate frames with origins at A and B involves a translation by a distance 1_1 along the x axis and a rotation by an angle θ_1 about the z axis.

Thus $R = \text{Rot}(z, \theta) . \text{Trans}(1_1,0,0)$

Using equations (8) and (13):

$$R = \begin{vmatrix} \cos\theta_1 & -\sin\theta_1 & 0 & 0 \\ \sin\theta_1 & \cos\theta_1 & 0 & 0 \\ 0 & 0 & 1 & 0 \\ 0 & 0 & 0 & 1 \end{vmatrix} \begin{vmatrix} 1 & 0 & 0 & 1_1 \\ 0 & 1 & 0 & 0 \\ 0 & 0 & 1 & 0 \\ 0 & 0 & 0 & 1 \end{vmatrix} = \begin{vmatrix} \cos\theta_1 & -\sin\theta_1 & 0 & 1_1\cos\theta_1 \\ \sin\theta_1 & \cos\theta_1 & 0 & 1_1\sin\theta_1 \\ 0 & 0 & 1 & 0 \\ 0 & 0 & 0 & 1 \end{vmatrix}$$

In a general n-link system, the coordinates of point P_m can be related to a coordinate frame with an origin at P_{m-1} by a transformation matrix A_m.

i.e. $P_m = A_m \cdot P_{m-1}$. (14)

Similarly, points P_{m-1} and P_{m-2} are related by:

$$P_{m-1} = A_{m-1} \cdot P_{m-2} \qquad (15)$$

Combining (14) and (15): $P_m = A_{m-1} \cdot A_m \cdot P_{m-2}$ (16)

Continuing in a similar fashion: $P_m = A_1 \cdot A_2 \cdot A_3 \ldots A_{m-1} \cdot A_m \cdot P_0$ (17)

P_0 is the origin of the base coordinate frame and can be expressed in homogeneous coordinates as: $P_0 = (0\ 0\ 0\ 1)^T$ (18)

It is conventional to express the matrix product which relates the end of the manipulator chain P_0 to the base coordinate frame as the quantity T_m

i.e. for an n-link manipulator, $T_n = A_1 \ A_2 \ldots A_n$ (19)

For a 6-DOF manipulator, $T_6 = A_1 \ A_2 \ A_3 \ A_4 \ A_5 \ A_6$ (20)

To apply these relationships correctly, it is important that the axes of all coordinate frames involved are defined consistently. One proven set of rules for this is the Denavit-Hartenburg system.

9. Denavit-Hartenburg manipulator representation

This establishes an orthonormal cartesian coordinate system for each link in the manipulator with the origin of each coordinate frame at the joint axes. Coordinate frame i(i = 1 ... n for an n-link system) has its origin at joint (i+1) and so the frame moves as the link moves.

For each link i, the corresponding coordinate frame i has unit vectors along its principal axes given by (x_i, y_i, z_i). An additional coordinate frame 0 is defined with its origin at the robot base (the fixed end of link 1) with unit vectors given by (x_0, y_0, z_0) along its principal axes.

Thus for an n-link manipulator, there are n+1 coordinate frames.

Every coordinate frame is defined according to three rules:

(i)   The z_{i-1} axis lies along the axis of motion of the ith joint.

(ii) The x_i axis is normal to the z_{i-1} axis and pointing away from it.

(iii) The y_i axis completes a right-handed coordinate system.

Any rotational or translational joint can be described by a set of four geometric parameters associated with its corresponding link. These four parameters are:

(a) θ_i the joint angle when turning about the z_{i-1} axis and moving from the x_{i-1} axis to the x_i axis (using the right-hand rule).

(b) d_i the distance along the z_{i-1} axis from the (i-1) coordinate frame origin to the intersection with the x_i axis.

(c) a_i the offset distance along the x_i axis from the ith coordinate frame origin to the intersection with the z_{i-1} axis, (i.e. the shortest distance between the z_{i-1} and z_i axes)

(d) α_i the offset angle when turning about the x_i axis and moving from the z_{i-1} axis to the z_i axis (using the right-hand rule).

For a rotary joint, d_i, a_i and α_i remain constant, with θ_i being the joint variable.

For a translational joint, θ_i, a_i and α_i remain constant, and d_i is the joint variable.

10. Kinematic equations of a real robot

Before going on to derive the kinematic relationships for a real robot, we need to define some rules about the manner in which coordinate frames are defined and also define some sign conventions.

A homogeneous transformation matrix relating link (i-1) to link i can be synthesised as the product of the transformation matrices representing the following successive motions:

Rotate about z_{i-1} through an angle θ_i

Translate a distance d_i along the z_{i-1} axis

Translate a distance a_i along the x_i axis

Rotate about x_i through an angle α_i

i.e. $A = Rot(z,\theta)$. Trans $(0,0,d)$. Trans $(a,0,0)$. Rot (x,α)

$$= \begin{vmatrix} \cos\theta & -\sin\theta & 0 & 0 \\ \sin\theta & \cos\theta & 0 & 0 \\ 0 & 0 & 1 & 0 \\ 0 & 0 & 0 & 1 \end{vmatrix} \begin{vmatrix} 1 & 0 & 0 & 0 \\ 0 & 1 & 0 & 0 \\ 0 & 0 & 0 & d \\ 0 & 0 & 0 & 1 \end{vmatrix} \begin{vmatrix} 1 & 0 & 0 & a \\ 0 & 1 & 0 & 0 \\ 0 & 0 & 1 & 0 \\ 0 & 0 & 0 & 1 \end{vmatrix} \begin{vmatrix} 1 & 0 & 0 & 0 \\ 0 & \cos\alpha & -\sin\alpha & 0 \\ 0 & \sin\alpha & \cos\alpha & 0 \\ 0 & 0 & 0 & 1 \end{vmatrix}$$

$$= \begin{vmatrix} \cos\theta & -\sin\theta.\cos\alpha & \sin\theta.\sin\alpha & a\cos\theta \\ \sin\theta & \cos\theta.\cos\alpha & -\cos\theta.\sin\alpha & a\sin\theta \\ 0 & \sin\alpha & \cos\alpha & d \\ 0 & 0 & 0 & 1 \end{vmatrix} \qquad (21)$$

Consider now the application of this to the six-axis Puma robot arm shown in figure 4. This is a typical mixed-application revolute coordinate industrial robot manufactured by Unimation Ltd. The six transformation matrices required to solve equation (20) can be found by substituting the parameter values for the PUMA robot into equation (21):

$$A_1 = \begin{vmatrix} \cos\theta_1 & 0 & -\sin\theta_1 & 0 \\ \sin\theta_1 & 0 & \cos\theta_1 & 0 \\ 0 & -1 & 0 & 0 \\ 0 & 0 & 0 & 1 \end{vmatrix} \quad A4 = \begin{vmatrix} \cos\theta_4 & 0 & -\sin\theta_4 & 0 \\ \sin\theta_4 & 0 & \cos\theta_4 & 0 \\ 0 & -1 & 0 & 433 \\ 0 & 0 & 0 & 1 \end{vmatrix}$$

$$A_2 = \begin{vmatrix} \cos\theta_2 & -\sin\theta_2 & 0 & 432\cos\theta_2 \\ \sin\theta_2 & \cos\theta_2 & 0 & 432\sin\theta_2 \\ 0 & 0 & 1 & 149 \\ 0 & 0 & 0 & 1 \end{vmatrix} \quad A5 = \begin{vmatrix} \cos\theta_5 & 0 & \sin\theta_5 & 0 \\ \sin\theta_5 & 0 & -\cos\theta_5 & 0 \\ 0 & 1 & 0 & 0 \\ 0 & 0 & 0 & 1 \end{vmatrix}$$

$$A_3 = \begin{vmatrix} \cos\theta_3 & 0 & \sin\theta_3 & -20.5\cos\theta_3 \\ \sin\theta_3 & 0 & -\cos\theta_3 & -20.5\sin\theta_3 \\ 0 & 1 & 0 & 0 \\ 0 & 0 & 0 & 1 \end{vmatrix} \quad A_6 = \begin{vmatrix} \cos\theta_6 & -\sin\theta_6 & 0 & 0 \\ \sin\theta_6 & \cos\theta_6 & 0 & 0 \\ 0 & 0 & 1 & 56 \\ 0 & 0 & 0 & 1 \end{vmatrix}$$

We have now established a mechanism for calculating the forward kinematic transformation which gives the position of the end effector from known joint positions. i.e., we have found a matrix T such that:

$$v = T \cdot q \qquad (22)$$

where v is the vector of (xyz) coordinates and q is the vector of joint positions.

However, this gives no information yet about the end-effector orientation which is needed on many occasions. It is inappropriate to discuss this here and the interested reader is referred to a suitable text e.g.:

Fu, K S, Gonzales, R C and Lee C S G 'Robotics: control, sensing, vision and intelligence' McGraw-Hill 1987.

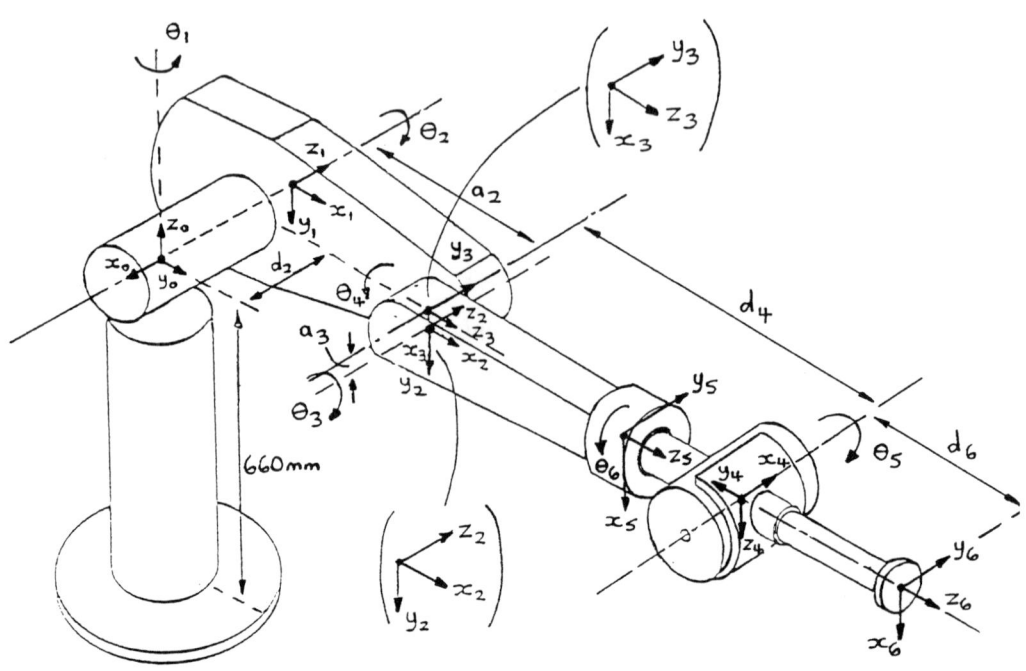

Parameters for PUMA 560 robot					
Joint	θ	α	a	d	joint range
1	+90	−90	0	0	−160 to +160
2	0	0	432mm	149mm	−225 to +45
3	+90	+90	−20.5mm	0	−45 to +225
4	0	−90	0	433mm	−110 to +170
5	0	+90	0	0	−100 to +100
6	0	0	0	56mm	−266 to +266

FIGURE 4   PUMA ROBOT

11 Inverse kinematic relationships

The inverse kinematic problem is to calculate the set of joint positions which will give the correct end-effector position specified in (xyz) coordinates, i.e. we need to find the inverse of T such that:

$$q = T^{-1} \cdot v \tag{23}$$

Extraction of the joint positions from this requires extremely lengthy mathematical manipulation which cannot be reproduced here. The full presentation can be found in:

N-Nagi, F and Siegler, A 'Engineering foundations of robotics' Prentice Hall 1987.

Comment should be made however that the matrix relationship (23) yields 12 equations in the 6 unknowns θ_1 .... θ_6. This indicates that there are multiple solutions, which can be expected since T involves sine and cosine relationships which yield alternative positive and negative values for θ. Therefore, there is no 'general case' inverse kinematic solution, and a separate solution has to be worked out for every different manipulator configuration.

12. Trajectory following and control

The mechanism for describing the required path for the robot end-effector to follow as a sequence of (x,y,z) coordinate positions and transforming this into a set of required joint trajectories has now been explained. The task of the robot controller is to apply an appropriate pattern of forces/torques to the joint actuators such that the resulting joint motions adhere to the planned trajectories.

In most current industrial robots, the control algorithm used is a simple one consisting of a supervisory computer and separate microprocessor controllers on each joint. The supervisory computer transmits demanded joint positions to each microprocessor at each sampling interval, and the microprocessors apply a simple three-term (PID) algorithm to calculate the required forces/torques which will drive the joint under their control to the demanded position, using feedback from the joint position sensors.

This simple method of control takes no account of any interaction between the joint motions. In practice, there is often a considerable amount of coupling between the individual joints because of velocity- and acceleration-related dynamic forces which occur as the end-effector moves along the demanded trajectory, causing excursions of the end-effector away from its target position/trajectory. The magnitude of these forces increases rapidly as the speed of the end-effector increases. At low speeds, these forces are small and neglecting them in this simple form of controller does not lead to large trajectory errors. However, at high robot speeds, these dynamic forces are large and neglecting them leads to large trajectory errors.

Current research is ongoing into how to design and implement control algorithms which will take account of these dynamic forces and enable accurate trajectory adhesion at speeds substantially higher than current industrial robots operate at. However, there are formidable obstacles to developing such a controller which, clearly, must include a model of the dynamic equations of motion of the arm. A major point of difficulty is that the magnitudes of the dynamic forces involved vary as the configuration of the manipulator arm changes. In consequence, the forces are time-varying. Therefore, the controller must compute the full dynamic model at each sampling interval.

Research has shown that sampling rates of the order of 60Hz are required for satisfactory control, and at least one author has suggested that a sampling rate of 300 Hz is needed for very high speed motion. The complexity of the dynamic model is such that the computational burden of computing the full dynamic model within 16 ms is beyond the capability of the sort of computers which can currently be included within robots at a realistic cost. Current research is concentrated in two main areas. Firstly, computationally simpler approximations of the dynamic model are being developed. Secondly, parallel processing techniques are being investigated for implementation using new and cheap processors that are presently becoming available which are optimised for parallel processing. The INMOS transputer is one example of this new breed of processor.

Chapter 8

3D vision for robotics

S. B. Pollard, J. Porrill, J. E. W. Mayhew and J. P. Frisby

In this chapter we describe components of the Sheffield AIVRU 3D vision system for robotics. Amongst other things, the system supports model based object recognition and location; its potential for robotics applications is illustrated by its guidance of a UMI robot arm in a pick and place task. The system comprises:

1) The recovery of a sparse depth map using edge based passive stereo triangulation.

2) The grouping, description and segmentation of edge segments to recover a 3D representation of the scene geometry in terms of straight lines and circular arcs.

3) The statistical combination of 3D descriptions for the purpose of object model creation from multiple stereo views, and the propagation of constraints for within view refinement.

4) The matching of 3D wireframe object models to 3D scene descriptions, to recover an initial estimate of their position and orientation.

1 INTRODUCTION

Edge based binocular stereo is able to provide accurate depth data provided that the camera geometry is understood. Our current stereo algorithm, PMF (Pollard et al 1985), was designed to be largely independent of the structure of the scene. It employs the assumption that the world projects with moderate disparity gradient almost everywhere. However, in common with many other stereo algorithms, the disparity/depth data produced by PMF is largely unstructured. This paper discusses some aspects of current research at the AI Vision Research Unit concerned with the extraction and combination of geometrical information from such stereo data.

Three components of a proposed, and partially completed, vision system (Porrill et al. 1987) are discussed. These are geometrical description, scene/model matching and statistical combination. Whilst not providing complete scene descriptions (topological information being most notable by its absence) these form a substantial system in themselves which has proven to be of considerable practical potential. The system has been used, for example, to combine views of a scene to incrementally model the environment and determine position in a world coordinate frame. This has obvious application to autonomous navigation. In a similar fashion a visual model description can be compiled by simply looking at an object from a sufficient number of views. Once complete, such *models* can be matched in cluttered scenes by the same matching algorithm employed in their construction. We have coupled these visual competences with a robot arm and have been successful in picking a modelled object from a cluttered scene.

2 LOW LEVEL PROCESSING

Early descriptions are currently recovered via edge based stereo triangulation. Edges are obtained from a single high frequency edge operator, we employ our own implementation of Canny's operator (1983) which also incorporates sub pixel acuity (obtained by quadratic interpolation of the peak). Edge data is transformed to a parallel camera geometry that is equivalent to the original camera arrangement.

The data structure resulting from the PMF stereo algorithm is essentially the edge segments of the [transformed] left image with matched segments appended with the computed disparity value. These are grouped into ordered strings corresponding to viewed curves by CONNECT (Pridmore et al 1985), a rule-based system which uses local topological and weak geometrical information to assign binary connections between data points. An initial grouping phase captures obvious, and notes potential, connectivities. The latter are either rejected or instantiated by subsequent application of the rulebase. On termination CONNECT produces a graph-like structure in which point strings join nodes marking junctions and line ends.

3 STEREO GEOMETRY FOR PARALLEL CAMERAS

We will use the notation (X_L, Y) for coordinates in the left image, and (X_R, Y) for coordinates of the matched point in the right image. The quantity $\Delta = X_L - X_R$ is the stereo disparity. The three dimensional space of points (X_L, X_R, Y) will be referred to as *disparity space*. (Note that this term usually refers to (X_L, Y, Δ) space). Choose the world coordinate system (x, y, z) to have its origin at the focus of the left camera and z-axis along the camera axis (this introduces an asymmetry between left and right cameras but it can be convenient to have a 'base' camera). If I is the inter-camera distance and f the common camera focal length, then points (x, y, z) in the world are related to points (X_L, X_R, Y) in disparity space by the formulae

$$X_L = \frac{fx}{z}$$

$$X_R = \frac{f(x - I)}{z}$$

$$Y = \frac{fy}{z}$$

Now suppose we have a vector $\mathbf{V} = \vec{PQ}$ joining the point P to the point Q in disparity space. We can find the associated vector $\mathbf{v}$ in the world by using the above equations to project the two points P and Q into the world to p and q and setting $\mathbf{v} = \vec{pq}$. For infinitesimal vectors (and, since the mapping projects straight lines to straight lines, for finite vectors of which only the direction and not the magnitude is of interest) this can be replaced by a linear mapping whose matrix is the Jacobian J of the stereo transformation above,

$$
\begin{bmatrix} v_x \\ v_y \\ v_z \end{bmatrix} = J(X_L, X_R, Y) \begin{bmatrix} V_{X_L} \\ V_{X_R} \\ V_Y \end{bmatrix}.
$$

The inverse transform (*world vector*) → (*disparity vector*) is accomplished by the inverse linear mapping J^{-1}. Hence, for example, if a line through the point **P** has direction **V** in disparity space then its direction in the world is given by the vector $\mathbf{v} = J(\mathbf{P})\mathbf{V}$. It must be remembered that projection into the world does not preserve distance, so that even though **V** may be a unit vector **v** will generally not be.

Care must be taken when transforming normal vectors (to planes and other surfaces). Though it is often customary to call them vectors they are in fact *covectors*, or *1–forms*. Such objects do not follow the above transformation law. A 1-form is defined by its scalar product with other vectors; for example the normal to a plane is defined by the fact that its scalar product with vectors in the plane is zero. The requirement that these scalar products be invariant under the mapping leads directly to the transformation law for 1-forms. In general, the transformation between a 1-form **N** in disparity space and **n** in the world is done according to the formulae

$$ \mathbf{n} = (J^{-1})^T \mathbf{N} \qquad \mathbf{N} = J^T \mathbf{n} $$

(where J^T is the transpose of J). The normal vector to a plane in disparity space is therefore transformed into the world by the transpose of the inverse Jacobian, and not by the Jacobian itself as ordinary vectors are. Again it should be remembered that a unit normal will not remain unit under transformations of this kind.

4 FITTING CURVES IN DISPARITY SPACE

On the projection of an image point into the world errors in its disparity produce, in general, much larger errors in depth than similar errors in its image coordinates produce in its lateral position in space. If the closeness of this point to some hypothesised structure is to be measured in the world and compared with some single threshold, then, if this threshold is to allow typical errors in depth, it will allow quite unacceptable errors in lateral position; if, conversely, it is small enough to allow only reasonable errors in lateral position, it will be far too tight for the accuracy of our depth data.

We could choose to do a simple scaling of the depth dimension in the measurement of errors, but this scaling depends on scene position. In fact a correct error measure would be both anisotropic and inhomogeneous. We adopt the more rigorous, and simplifying, approach of testing closeness of fit directly in disparity space. Here the errors in horizontal position in the two images and the error in vertical position for a matched point are all generated by the similar noise processes. A simple combination of the individual errors (dX_L, dX_R, dY) into a single Euclidean distance measure dS of the form

$$dS^2 = dX_L^2 + dX_R^2 + dY^2$$

is therefore acceptable.

The drawback to fitting in disparity space is that some structures in the world, such as circles, have a less simple description there. This problem might eventually guide the choice of higher order descriptive structures; for example, cubic splines are not invariant under projectivities, but rational splines are, and so might be preferred for least squares fitting to disparity data.

4.1 Fitting Points, Planes and Lines: Orthogonal Regression

The transformation between disparity and world space is projective, and therefore preserves lines and planes. Hence if a point string is believed to be either planar or straight we can test this hypothesis directly in disparity space.

It is relatively simple to find the best fit line or plane to a given set of points (Pearson 1901). Since the technique is generally applicable, we will not make any particular reference to disparity space, and in the rest of this section points, vectors *etc.* will be denoted by lower case letters; it should however be remembered that our application of these results *is* in disparity space.

Given N points $\mathbf{x}_i$ in space we will find the least squares best fit plane, line, or point, where the distance of $\mathbf{x}_i$ from the structure to be fitted is measured by the perpendicular distance to that structure, the residual of this best fit is the standard error measure we need. This technique is sometimes called orthogonal regression, to distinguish it from the usual linear regression, where the best fitting plane is found by minimising the sum-square error in a particular coordinate direction, which would not be appropriate here.

The best fit plane, line, and point are found simultaneously, each with an associated sum square residual ρ_{point}^2, ρ_{line}^2, ρ_{plane}^2 which is an approximately χ^2 variable on $N{-}3$, $2(N{-}2)$, $3(N{-}1)$ degrees of freedom respectively when the errors are normally distributed. If a curve contains horizontal (which are generally difficult to stereo match reliably) or unmatched segments the best fit line is projected into the left image and the squared distance in the image plane of each such point from the line added to the sum square error, which gains one degree of freedom for each such point. The maximum likelihood test for the point string to form a structure of a given type is then

$$\frac{\rho_{structure}^2}{\text{degrees of freedom}} < \text{threshold}$$

The above residuals, related by the expression $\rho_{point}^2 < \rho_{line}^2 < \rho_{plane}^2$, are examined in decreasing order of magnitude, the first to fall below threshold being taken as representative of the true description. Should all the residuals be above threshold, a default space curve tag is assigned.

4.2 Fitting Circles

After regression curves identified as planar are passed to a three point circle fitting routine. The CONNECT string is first projected onto the best fit plane down lines of sight, assigning a depth estimate to each data point. Several point triples are then selected and the residuals (measured in disparity space) associated with arcs through them computed. The description with the lowest error is considered further. If this circle's residual is below threshold it is accepted, if it is above an upper threshold the fit is abandoned, otherwise an optimal (minimal residual) arc in the best fit plane is found. If this is also supra-threshold the best fit plane becomes the primary representation.

5 GDB: THE GEOMETRICAL DESCRIPTIVE BASE

The GDB is obtained by the Geometric Descriptive Filter (GDF; see Pridmore et al 1987) a program that recursively describes and segments (if descriptions prove inadequate) CONNECT strings. The result is a 3D (and 2D where 3D descriptions are not possible) description of the scene with respect to a single image (usually the left). It consists primarily of straight line and circular arc descriptors. Where such descriptions are not possible above a threshold resolution the sections of the connect string are labeled either planar or space. An example of the geometry that can be recovered is given in figure 1 for a pseudo industrial scene typical of those amenable to characterisation in such a fashion.

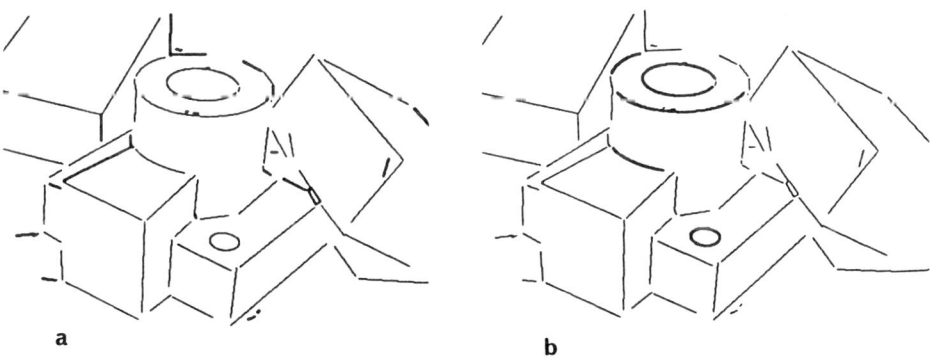

Figure 1. *In (a) both 2 and 3 dimensional descriptions, with respect to the left hand image, are shown. Primitives of the GDB that are flagged as 2D, as a result of the fact that no depth data has been recovered for them by the stereo algorithm (perhaps as a result occlusion), are displayed bold. It is important to note that these exist only as descriptions in the image plane and not as descriptions in the world. In (b) again both 2 and 3 dimensional data are shown, but on this occasion circular sections (in three dimensions and not only in the image plane) of the GDB are the ones that have been highlighted by displaying them bold.*

6 STRAIGHT LINE DESCRIPTION AND ERROR ESTIMATION

Straight line segments are represented (in an overdetermined fashion) by the triple (e_1, e_2, v_0), that is, their two end points e_1 and e_2 and the direction vector between them v_0. The centroid of a line (its midpoint $(e_1 + e_2)/2$) is denoted **c**. Where the actual physical occupancy of a line is not important it is sometimes helpful to represent it by the vector pair (p_0, v_0) where p_0 is the position of a point on the line. We extend the direction vector v_0 to an orthonormal basis (v_0, v_1, v_2) and add it to our description of the line in the GDB, this then forms an intrinsic reference frame which will be carried with the line throughout its history.

Any nearby line can be described by a position vector and a direction vector

$$\mathbf{p} = \mathbf{p}_0 + p_1 \mathbf{v}_1 + p_2 \mathbf{v}_2$$

$$\mathbf{v} = \mathbf{v}_0 + v_1 \mathbf{v}_1 + v_2 \mathbf{v}_2$$

(note that **v** is unit to first order) and we use $\mathbf{x} = (p_1, p_2, v_1, v_2)^t$ as local coordinates on the line manifold.

Other possible measurements of the position of the line are randomly distributed close to the original measurement. To describe the error in the measurement we need only describe the error distribution of the perturbation 4-vector **x**. We make the usual assumption that the measurement process is adequately described by the measurement bias (expected error)

$$E[\mathbf{x}] = \hat{\mathbf{x}}$$

and the 4×4 measurement covariance matrix s

$$S = E[(\mathbf{x}-\hat{\mathbf{x}})(\mathbf{x}-\hat{\mathbf{x}})^t] = E[\mathbf{x}\,\mathbf{x}^t] - \hat{\mathbf{x}}\hat{\mathbf{x}}^t$$

This would be the case if we were sampling **x** from a normal distribution

$$p(\mathbf{x}) = \frac{1}{(2\pi)^2 \det(s)} \exp(-\frac{1}{2}(\mathbf{x}-\hat{\mathbf{x}})^t S^{-1} (\mathbf{x}-\hat{\mathbf{x}}))$$

in this case, if the mean and variance of the distribution are small, we will say that the line measurement process is approximately normal. We assume the measurement process is not biased and set $\hat{\mathbf{x}} = 0$. This leaves the task of determining s from the nature of the measurement process.

If points are assumed to be matched without error between left and right images, and the imaging process is assumed to produce equal uncorrelated errors of variance σ^2 in the three image coordinates (X_L, X_R, Y). fitting by orthogonal regression is optimal and produces a position error in the centroid of the fitted line of variance σ^2/n and an angular error of variance $12\sigma^2/nl^2$ where l is the length of the line in disparity space and these two errors are uncorrelated (these are the errors *in disparity space*).

In terms of local line coordinates in disparity space the error covariance is thus

$$S_{\text{disp}} = \frac{\sigma^2}{n} \begin{bmatrix} I & 0 \\ 0 & \frac{12}{l^2}I \end{bmatrix}$$

where I is the 2×2 unit matrix. We must transform this result to world coordinates. The lateral position error coordinates transform by

$$p_i = \mathbf{v}_i \cdot (\mathbf{p} - \mathbf{p}_0)_{\text{world}} = \mathbf{v}_i \cdot J(\mathbf{p} - \mathbf{p}_0)_{\text{disparity}}$$

Since the Jacobian does not preserve the length of vectors the lateral direction error has an extra scalar factor

$$v_i = \mathbf{v}_i \cdot (\mathbf{v} - \mathbf{v}_0)_{\text{world}} = \frac{\mathbf{v}_i \cdot J(\mathbf{p} - \mathbf{p}_0)_{\text{disparity}}}{|J\mathbf{v}_0|}$$

We can thus calculate the error covariance of the description in the world to be

$$S = \begin{bmatrix} \Sigma & 0 \\ 0 & \frac{12}{l^2|J\mathbf{v}_0|^2}\Sigma \end{bmatrix}$$

where

$$\Sigma_{ij} = \frac{\sigma^2}{n}\mathbf{v}_i^t\, JJ^t\, \mathbf{v}_j \qquad i, j = 1, 2$$

where the base point $\mathbf{p}_0$ is taken as the projection of the disparity space centroid into the world. This covariance is adjoined to the description of the edge segment in the GDB.

The above idealisation is unrealistic for two main reasons. Firstly the stereo matching of *continuous* edges mixes the horizontal errors with the vertical errors; for edges with making angles θ with the horizontal which are close to zero depth values are highly inaccurate (when $\theta = 0$ matching is impossible). A crude way of compensating for this is to multiply J by a matrix producing an expansion factor of $1/\sin\theta$ in depth before using the above formulae. Secondly the points detected on continuous edges are not randomly scattered the edges, but wander slowly from one side to the other. This can be compensated for by replacing n by a smaller effective number of points on the line which counts these wanderings. Though crude, this model then captures most of the essential information about stereo errors.

7 SMM: THE SCENE AND MODEL MATCHER

Matches for two non-parallel line segments are sufficient to constrain all six degrees of freedom that constitute a putative transformation between a pair of scene descriptions (Faugeras *et al* 1984). Once a transformation is hypothesised, rigidity provides a powerful constraint upon other consistent matches (subject to tolerance errors). Rigidity can be exploited more cheaply (though less strongly) if expressed in terms of the consistency in a number of pairwise relationships (Grimson and Lozano-Perez 1984). Each can be stored as a range of values in look up tables, with the requirement that these ranges overlap between all pairs of consistent matches. If each pair of lines has allowable errors $|\varepsilon_1|<\alpha_1$ and $|\varepsilon_2|<\alpha_2$ on the location of their centroid and solid half angles ϕ_1 and ϕ_2 on their direction vector it is possible to derive suitable ranges for each of the chosen pairwise relationships (assuming that components add in a simple fashion). We adopt just three which are:

(i) orientation differences, given by $\theta = \cos^{-1}(v_{0_1}.v_{0_2})$; stored as the interval $[\max(\theta-\phi_1-\phi_2,0),\min(\theta+\phi_1+\phi_2,\pi)]$.

(ii) minimum separations between (extended) lines. That is $m = (c_2-c_1).u$; the component of the difference between the lines in the direction u which is normal to each. However if the lines are close to parallel it is more sensible to simply measure the perpendicular distance between the lines $m = |(c_2-c_1)-((c_2-c_1).v_{0_1})v_{0_1}|$. Stored as the interval

$$m \pm (\alpha_1+\alpha_2+|l_1|\tan\phi_1+|l_2|\tan\phi_2)$$

where l_i is the distance from c_i to the point of minimum separation on line i (which is defined to be zero if the lines are parallel).

(iii) distance to the beginning and end of each physical line with respect to the point of minimum separation and in the direction of the line. This relationship is only applicable for non-parallel lines. The vector between the points of closest approach is given by $m = ((c_2-c_1).u)u$. Adding m to c_2 gives c'_2, where lines (v_{0_1},c_1) and (v_{0_2},c'_2) are coplanar and meet at the point of closest approach on (v_{0_1},c_1). The signed distance to that point from c_1 in the direction v_{0_1} is given by $l_1 = ((v_{0_2}\times v_{0_1}).(v_{0_2}\times(c'_2-c_1)))/|v_{0_2}\times v_{0_1}|^2$. Hence the distance from p_{1_1} and p_{1_2} to that point are given by $a_1 = l_1+(c_1-p_{1_1}).v_{0_1}$ and $b_1 = l_1+(c_1-p_{1_2}).v_{0_1}$ respectively. Similarly for distances to the point of closest separation on the other line $a_2 = l_2+(c_2-p_{2_1}).v_{0_2}$ and $b_2 = l_2+(c_2-p_{2_2}).v_{0_2}$. Stored as the approximate intervals

$$a_1 \pm (\alpha_1+\alpha_2+|l_2|\tan\phi_2/\sin\theta)$$

$$b_1 \pm (\alpha_1+\alpha_2+|l_2|\tan\phi_2/\sin\theta)$$

$$a_2 \pm (\alpha_1+\alpha_2+|l_1|\tan\phi_1/\sin\theta)$$

$$b_2 \pm (\alpha_1+\alpha_2+|l_1|\tan\phi_1/\sin\theta)$$

Potential matches for each pair of descriptive elements from one scene description can be checked for geometrical consistency in the other. Rigidity implies that each of the pairwise relationships will be preserved between scene descriptions, hence any measured discrepancies must lie within a range predicted by the magnitude of allowable errors. Furthermore a pair of consistent non-parallel matches provides a powerful constraint upon the remaining matches. Hence they can be thought to represent, implicitly and weakly, a global transformation. The representation is weak because it between model and view (ω, τ) is adjoined to the state vector of the model with infinite covariance (in a mobile robot application we might use an estimate of the motion and its error given by position encoders).

For each pair of matched lines the new view of the line is adjoined to the state vector (or if a line in the model has no match in the new view an identical 'virtual' match is adjoined with infinite covariance). The constraint that they are related by the correction to the rigid motion (ω, τ) is then imposed (see Appendix). (this merges the two lines in the first case or performs the required transformation of the line and its statistics into the new frame in the second). The old version of the line is deleted from the state vector.

Figure 4 illustrates the use of the above method to optimally combine details from multiple views of the model ((a), (b) and (c)) and the impose certain obvious geometric constraints (eg. perpendicularity, intersection, parallelism, etc). The final results are shown in (d).

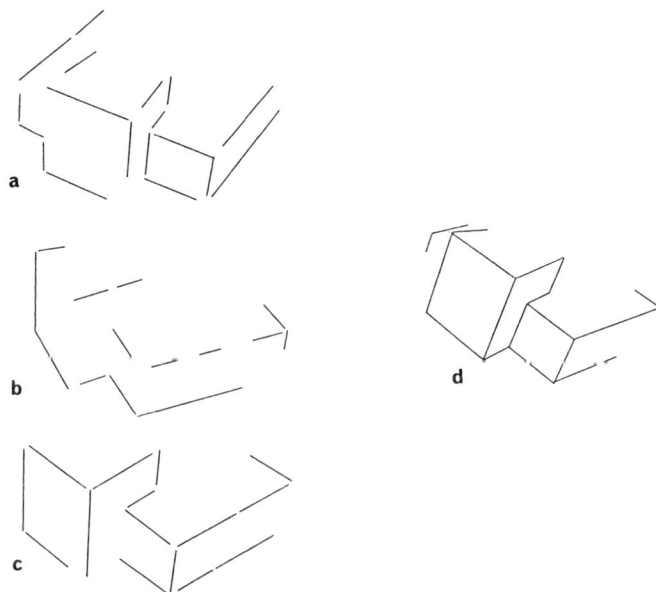

Figure 4.

9 BIN PICKING

It has been possible to link our visual system up to a UMI robot arm. Figure 5 shows the processing of a cluttered scene in the robots work space; it conists of three of the modeled test objects. The action of the robot, as it grasps an instance of the object, is shown in figure 6. Notice that the system is able to identify and accurately locate a modelled object in the cluttered scene. This information is used to compute a grasp plan for the known object (which is precompiled with respect to one corner of the object which acts as its coordinate frame).

is possible, on occasion, for matches that are not consistent with a single global transformation to satisfy the pairwise relationships. In practice such problems are not major. Furthermore if the basis of the implicit transforms is raised from a pair to a triple, quadruple or even a quintuple of matches, such inconsistencies are far less likely (additionally the margin of allowable error on each new match will be reduced).

7.1 Feature Focus

Our current approach to matching is to apply heuristics similar to those of feature focus (Bolles *et al* 1983) in order to avoid unbounded search. The strategy is to concentrate initial attention upon a number of salient features. Only matches associated with these features are subsequently entitled to *grow* hypothetical transformations. Currently processing terminates only after all focus features have been considered. The feature focus strategy adopted here differs from those considered previously as familiarity with the scene it is not assumed. As a result focus features and matching strategies are not an integral component of our scene description: they must be generated at run time.

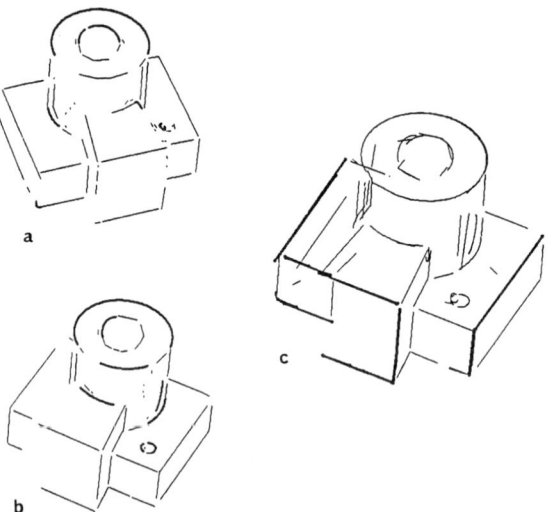

Figure 2. *(a) and (b) show GDB data extracted from two views of a test object (here obtained from stereograms produced by a version of the IBM WINSOM CSG body modeler). Each description consists of approximately 50 above-threshold GDB line primitives. The ten focus features chosen in view (a) obtained a total of 98 potential matches in view (b). The best consistent transformation included 9 matched lines. The best rigid rotation and translation (in that order) that takes view (a) to view (b) is computed by the least squares method discussed by Faugeras et al (1984) in which rotations are represented as quaternions (though for simplicity the optimal rotation is recovered before translation). In figure (c) view (a) is transformed into view (b) (the error in the computed rotation is 0.7 degrees) and matching lines are shown bold, the vast majority of the unmatched lines are not visible in both views.*

Focus features are identified in a single scene description. Currently they are chosen simply on the basis of their length, a property associated with salience. Some effort is expended to ensure that all regions of the scene are represented by chosen features, ie a feature is identified as a focus if their are not more than a certain number of longer features within a predetermined radius of it. The details of the matching algorithm are given in Pollard *et al* (1987).

An example of the performance of SMM is given in figure 2. If after matching and transformation those lines that are actually matched are replaced by their union and those that are unmatched left alone it is possible to build a more complete description of the object/scene. Furthermore descriptive primitives (such as circles) that are not currently part of the matching process itself can also be combined on the basis of their physical location. It is important to note that a circle in one scene description may be represented as a number of straight lines in the other. Once obtained this more complete scene description can be matched to yet more GDB data. This process has been repeated 8 times for the description shown in figure 3a. This description contains a large quantity of noisy data that appeared in one or other view. A cleaner model can be obtained by filtering out primitives that have never been matched (see figure 3b). In each application of the matcher statistics similar to those of the initial match were obtained. Notice that few of the occluding contours that arise from the cylinder are ever matched.

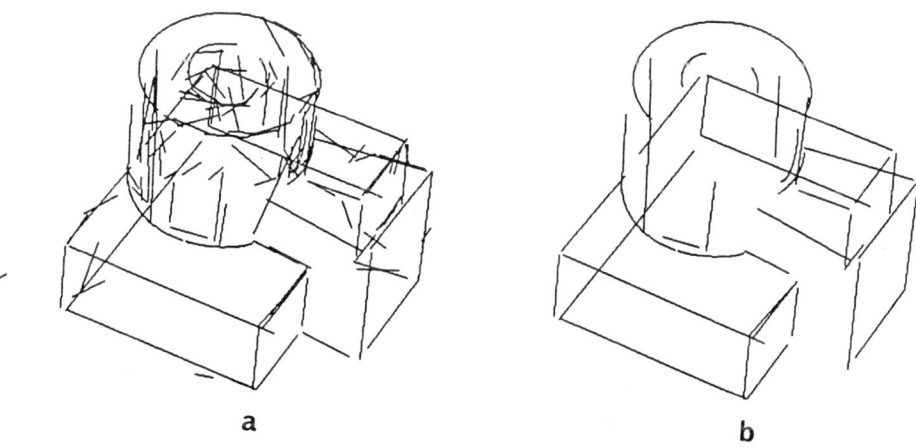

a   b

Figure 3. *(a) and (b) show noisy and clean visual models respectively.*

8 STATISTICAL COMBINATION OF MULTIPLE STEREO VIEWS

The combination and refinement of stereo data is undertaken by the GEOMSTAT modules, which use the methods of generalised (singular covariance) Gauss-Markov estimation implemented as a recursive filter. This is similar to techniques described by Durrant-Whyte (1985) and Faugeras (1986).

The basic measurement primitives returned by the AIVRU vision system are the straight edge segments and circular arcs found in the scene. The error statistics for straight lines have already been described in §6. To describe a point measurement we choose an arbitrary basis (v_0, v_1, v_2). A general perturbation of a point r_0 can then be written as

$$r = r_0 + r_0 v_0 + r_1 v_1 + r_2 v_2$$

and the point measurement is described by the structure

$$(r_0, v_0, v_1, v_2, \hat{x}, \hat{S})$$

where $\hat{x}$ and S are the mean and covariance of the perturbation vector $x = (r_0, r_1, r_2)^t$.

A plane is completely described by a point p_0 on it and its normal v_0. Again we extend the basis and describe nearby planes (p, v) by $x = (p_0, v_1, v_2)^t$ where

$$p = p_0 + p_0 v_0$$

$$v = v_0 + v_1 v_1 + v_2 v_2$$

Finally consider the case of a small rigid motion, this might represent the small motion of an object between two views. A convenient description is by a infinitesimal rotation ω and translation τ

$$p' = p + \omega \times p + \tau$$

These vectors can be expressed with respect to any basis (v_0, v_1, v_2)

$$\omega = \omega_i v_i \qquad \tau = \tau_i v_i$$

(summation convention).

In general we assume that measurement primitives in three dimensions have a convenient (but probably underdetermined or constrained) description as an object ξ_0 in $\mathbf{R}^n$. We attach a frame $B = (v_0, v_1, v_2)$ to this primitive and assume that small perturbations can be described adequately and intrinsically by a formula of the form

$$\xi = \xi_0 + F(B)x + O(|x|^2)$$

where $x \in \mathbf{R}^m$ and $F(B)$ is an $n \times m$ matrix. A measurement of the primitive is then described by the structure

$$(\xi_0, v_0, v_1, v_2, \hat{x}, S)$$

where

$$\hat{x} = E[x] \qquad S = \text{Cov}[x]$$

A composite object has a description as a list of primitives

$$\Xi = (\xi_1, \xi_2, \cdots, \xi_N)$$

with attached frames

$$B = (B_1, B_2, \cdots, B_N)$$

Any small deformation of the object can be described by a list of the perturbation vectors of each constituent relative to these frames

$$\mathbf{X} = (\mathbf{x}_1, \mathbf{x}_2, \cdots, \mathbf{x}_N)^t$$

A measurement of the composite object is completely described by the expected value $\hat{\mathbf{x}}$ and covariance $\hat{S}$ of this 'state vector'. In the case when all the constituents of the object have been independently measured the matrix $\hat{S}$ will have block diagonal form with the covariances of the individual measurements down the diagonal. In general this will not be the case since measurements, though independent in the sensor frame, will be correlated in the world through sensor calibration error. For example the error in position of an edge in a stereo scene will not in general be affected by the presence of a second edge in the scene but any stereo rig miscalibration will affect both their positions. We will show later how the required correlations in $\hat{S}$ can be set up.

8.1 Generalised Gauss-Markov Estimation Simplified

We will deal with the case where we have sufficient measurements of Ξ to determine it completely in the absence of errors, and where we can determine a good estimate Ξ_0 from a subset of these measurements. Our aim will be to calculate the optimal estimate of the state vector $\mathbf{X}$ representing the correction required.

At any stage in the calculation we can update the linearisation point Ξ_0 by making the corrections found so far, and relinearising about the new point. The new estimated correction will be $\hat{\mathbf{x}} = 0$ and the estimated covariance $\hat{S}$ will be unchanged by the re-linearisation.

Given a good estimate Ξ_0 of the set of primitives of interest we are interested in using our measurement devices to find the (assumed small) correction required, described by the state vector $\mathbf{X} \in \mathbf{R}^n$. Suppose previous measurements have told us that

$$E[\mathbf{X}] = \hat{\mathbf{x}} \qquad \text{Cov}[\mathbf{X}] = \hat{S}$$

If there are no previous measurements we can take $\hat{\mathbf{x}} = 0$ and let $\hat{S}$ be a large multiple of the unit matrix. An elegant description of the generalised (singular covariance) Gauss-Markov theory as an application of the Moore-Penrose pseudo-inverse can be found in Albert (1972). A more conventional treatment of the statistics of linear models can be found in Morrison (1976).

In order to simplify the structure of the system we have implemented our testbed programs in terms of a very simple but elegant result from Gauss-Markov theory, the optimal update rule after the imposition of a single scalar constraint. It can be shown that this is sufficient to implement any measurement or constraint equation.

Suppose we are given a single further piece of information about **x**: it satisfies an exact linear constraint

$$z + \mathbf{h}^t \mathbf{X} = 0$$

where z and **h** are known. The optimal update rule is

$$\hat{S}' = \hat{S} - \frac{(\hat{S}\mathbf{h})\,(\hat{S}\mathbf{h})^t}{\mathbf{h}^t\,\hat{S}\,\mathbf{h}}$$

$$\mathbf{k} = \frac{\hat{S}\mathbf{h}}{\mathbf{h}^t\,\hat{S}\,\mathbf{h}}$$

$$\hat{\mathbf{X}}' = \hat{\mathbf{X}} + \mathbf{k}\,(z + \mathbf{h}^t\,\mathbf{X})$$

(note that the correction is described by an 'innovation' term proportional to the error of the old estimate, this is a simple Kalman filter). The increase in residual (weighted mean square error) is

$$\varepsilon' = \varepsilon + \frac{(z + \mathbf{h}^t\,\mathbf{X})^2}{\mathbf{h}^t\,\hat{S}\,\mathbf{h}}$$

If we wanted to test the plausibility of the constraint given the previous information before imposing it then maximum likelihood test treats $\varepsilon' - \varepsilon$ as χ^2 on one degree of freedom. We can impose as many of constraints as we like as long as they are independent. The method only guarantees the satisfaction of constraints to linearised order.

8.2 Applying Geometrical Constraints

The description of the scene by the GDB is an almost totally unstructured. We propose to use simple wireframe completion heuristics to give some geometrical and topological rigidity to the description. It will include such process as edge completion, hypothesising vertices and constructing missing edges. The measurement statistics for the GDB are utilised by a module GEOMSTAT which is to act as a knowledge source for the wireframe completion module. For example if two edges are hypothesised to meet at a vertex GEOMSTAT will be asked to test whether it is plausible that the lines intersect in space given the known errors of measurement. If the vertex is accepted then GEOMSTAT can correct the data optimally so that the intersection error is reduced to zero. The systematic imposition of such constraints is necessary not only to ensure geometric integrity of the wire frame but can also greatly improve accuracy since inaccurate depth measurements will be corrected by the necessity of agreeing with more accurate lateral ones.

Suppose the GDB of a scene is the list of lines $(\lambda_0, \lambda_0', \cdots)$. We amalgamate the perturbation vectors of each line into a state vector **X** describing the whole scene with error covariance S which is block diagonal

$$\mathbf{X} = \begin{bmatrix} \mathbf{x} \\ \mathbf{x}' \\ \cdot \end{bmatrix} \qquad S = \begin{bmatrix} s & 0 & \cdot \\ 0 & s' & \cdot \\ \cdot & \cdot & \cdot \end{bmatrix}$$

Suppose the first two lines in the GDB, $\lambda_0 = (\mathbf{p}_0, \mathbf{v}_0)$ and $\lambda_0' = (\mathbf{p}_0', \mathbf{v}_0')$, are hypothesised to intersect. If this were true then their true positions $\lambda = (\mathbf{p}, \mathbf{v})$ and $\lambda' = (\mathbf{p}', \mathbf{v}')$ would satisfy the constraint

$$(\mathbf{p} - \mathbf{p}') \cdot (\mathbf{v} \times \mathbf{v}') = 0$$

using the representation for lines and assuming the corrections required are small we can linearise the above expression to

$$(\mathbf{p}_0 - \mathbf{p}_0') \cdot (\mathbf{v}_0 \times \mathbf{v}_0') + p_1 \mathbf{v}_1 \cdot (\mathbf{v}_0 \times \mathbf{v}_0') + p_2 \mathbf{v}_2 \cdot (\mathbf{v}_0 \times \mathbf{v}_0')$$
$$- p_1' \mathbf{v}_1' \cdot (\mathbf{v}_0 \times \mathbf{v}_0') - p_2' \mathbf{v}_2' \cdot (\mathbf{v}_0 \times \mathbf{v}_0') + v_1 (\mathbf{p}_0 - \mathbf{p}_0') \cdot (\mathbf{v}_1 \times \mathbf{v}_0')$$
$$+ v_2 (\mathbf{p}_0 - \mathbf{p}_0') \cdot (\mathbf{v}_2 \times \mathbf{v}_0') + v_1' (\mathbf{p}_0 - \mathbf{p}_0') \cdot (\mathbf{v}_0 \times \mathbf{v}_1') + v_2' (\mathbf{p}_0 - \mathbf{p}_0') \cdot (\mathbf{v}_0 \times \mathbf{v}_2') = 0$$

This is a linear constraint on the perturbation vector $\mathbf{X}$ of the form

$$z + \mathbf{h}^t \mathbf{x} = 0$$

where

$$z = (\mathbf{p}_0 - \mathbf{p}_0') \cdot (\mathbf{v}_0 \times \mathbf{v}_0')$$

and

$$\mathbf{h} = \begin{bmatrix} \mathbf{v}_1 \cdot (\mathbf{v}_0 \times \mathbf{v}_0') \\ \mathbf{v}_2 \cdot (\mathbf{v}_0 \times \mathbf{v}_0') \\ (\mathbf{p}_0 - \mathbf{p}_0') \cdot (\mathbf{v}_1 \times \mathbf{v}_0') \\ (\mathbf{p}_0 - \mathbf{p}_0') \cdot (\mathbf{v}_2 \times \mathbf{v}_0') \\ -\mathbf{v}_1' \cdot (\mathbf{v}_0 \times \mathbf{v}_0') \\ -\mathbf{v}_2' \cdot (\mathbf{v}_0 \times \mathbf{v}_0') \\ (\mathbf{p}_0 - \mathbf{p}_0') \cdot (\mathbf{v}_0 \times \mathbf{v}_1') \\ (\mathbf{p}_0 - \mathbf{p}_0') \cdot (\mathbf{v}_0 \times \mathbf{v}_2') \\ 0 \\ 0 \\ \cdot \end{bmatrix}$$

In the Appendix we give the formulation of other common constraints, orthogonality, parallelism, equality, as combinations of such scalar constraints.

8.3 Combining Multiple Stereo Views

Another basic application of GEOMSTAT is to the acquisition of accurate and complete wireframe models of objects or environments from multiple stereo views. Suppose we have built up a model with an associated covariance matrix from previous views, and now want to include a new view. The system uses the SMM matcher to relate the old model to the new view and calculate an approximate transformation $(R_0, \mathbf{t}_0)$ between the two. This is used to transform all the elements of the old model into the new frame. The transformation is non-optimal. The 'calibration error'

Figure 5. *Model identification is depicted (in turn) for each instance of the modeled object in a cluttered scene (the model, after transformation, is shown bold).*

Figure 6.

10 CONCLUSIONS

We have shown the current ability of our system to recover geometrical information about a scene or object from stereo data. Furthermore we have shown how such information can be combined from multiple views and statistically improved. The possible utility of the system for model acquisition and matching has been illustrated in a cluttered scene object recognition task.

11 REFERENCES

Albert, A., *Regression and the Moore-Penrose Pseudo-Inverse,* Academic Press, New York, 1972.

Ayache N, OD Faugeras, B Faverjon and G Toscani (1985) Matching depth maps obtained by passive stereo, Proc. Third Workshop on Computer Vision: Representation and Control, 197-204.

Bolles R.C, P. Horaud and M.J. Hannah (1983), 3DPO: A three dimensional part orientation system, *Proc. IJCAI 8,* Karlshrue, West Germany, 116-120.

Bowen J.B. and J.E.W. Mayhew (1986), Consistency maintenance in the REV graph environment, *Alvey Computer Vision and Image Interpretation Meeting,* University of Bristol, AIVRU Memo 20, and *Image and Vision Computing* (in press).

Burt P. and B. Julesz (1980), Modifications of the classical notion of panum's fusional area, *Perception* 9, 671-682.

Canny J.F. (1983), Finding edges and lines in images, MIT AI memo, 720, 1983.

DeKleer J. (1984), Choices without backtracking, *Proc, National Conference on Artificial Intelligence,*

Doyle J. (1979), A truth maintenance system, *Artificial Intelligence* 12, 231-272.

Durrant-Whyte H.F. (1985), Consistent integration and propagation of disparate sensor observations, *Thesis, University of Pennsylvania.*

Faugeras O.D, M. Hebert, J. Ponce and E. Pauchon (1984), Object representation, identification, and positioning from range data, *Proc. 1st Int. Symp. on Robotics Res,* J.M. Brady and R. Paul (eds), MIT Press, 425-446.

Faugeras O.D., N. Ayache and B. Faverjon (1986), Building visual maps by combining noisy stereo measurements, *IEEE Robotics conference,* San Francisco.

Grimson W.E.L. and T. Lozano-Perez (1984), Model based recognition from sparse range or tactile data, *Int. J. Robotics Res.* 3(3): 3-35.

Herman, M. (1985), Representation and incremental construction of a three-dimensional scene model, CMU-CS-85-103, Dept. of Computer Science, Carnegie-Mellon University.

Morrison, D. F. (1976) *Multivariate Statistical Methods,* McGraw-Hill.

Pearson K. (1901), On Lines and Planes of Closest Fit to Systems of Points in Space, *Phil. Mag. VI, 2,* pp 559, (1901).

Pollard S.B., J.E.W. Mayhew, and J.P. Frisby (1985), PMF: a stereo correspondence algorithm using a disparity gradient limit, *Perception,* 14, 449-470.

Pollard S.B, J. Porrill, J.E.W. Mayhew and J.P. Frisby (1985), Disparity gradient, Lipschitz continuity and computing binocular correspondences, *Proc. Third Int. Symp. on Robotics Res.*

Pollard S.B, J. Porrill, J.E.W. Mayhew and J.P. Frisby (1987), Matching geometrical descriptions in three-space, *Image and Vision Computing* Vol 5 No 2 73-78.

Porrill J., S.B. Pollard, T.P. Pridmore, J.B. Bowen, J.E.W. Mayhew, J.P. Frisby (1987) TINA: The Sheffield AIVRU vision system, submitted to IJCAI 9.

Pridmore T.P., J.E.W. Mayhew and J.P. Frisby (1985), Production rules for grouping edge-based disparity Data, *Alvey Vision Conference,* University of Sussex, and AIVRU memo 015, University of Sheffield.

Pridmore T.P., J. Porrill and J.E.W. Mayhew (1987), Segmentation and description of binocularly viewed contours, *Image and Vision Computing* Vol 5 No 2 132-138.

12 APPENDIX: GEOMETRICAL CONSTRAINTS

We give here some examples of condition on the state vector resulting from geometrical constraints on the pair of lines $(\mathbf{p}, \mathbf{v})$ and $(\mathbf{p}', \mathbf{v}')$.

1) Orthogonality:

$$\mathbf{v}\cdot\mathbf{v}' = (\mathbf{v}_0 + v_1\mathbf{v}_1 + v_2\mathbf{v}_2)\cdot(\mathbf{v}_0' + v_1'\mathbf{v}_1' + v_2'\mathbf{v}_2') = 0$$

linearises to

$$\mathbf{v}_0\cdot\mathbf{v}_0' + v_1\mathbf{v}_1\cdot\mathbf{v}_0' + v_2\mathbf{v}_2\cdot\mathbf{v}_0' + v_1'\mathbf{v}_0\cdot\mathbf{v}_1' + v_2'\mathbf{v}_0\cdot\mathbf{v}_2' = 0$$

2) Intersection:

$$(\mathbf{p} - \mathbf{p}')\cdot(\mathbf{v}\times\mathbf{v}') = 0$$

linearises to

$$(\mathbf{p}_0 - \mathbf{p}_0')\cdot(\mathbf{v}_0\times\mathbf{v}_0') + p_1\mathbf{v}_1\cdot(\mathbf{v}_0\times\mathbf{v}_0') + p_2\mathbf{v}_2\cdot(\mathbf{v}_0\times\mathbf{v}_0')$$
$$- p_1'\mathbf{v}_1'\cdot(\mathbf{v}_0\times\mathbf{v}_0') - p_2'\mathbf{v}_2'\cdot(\mathbf{v}_0\times\mathbf{v}_0') + v_1(\mathbf{p}_0 - \mathbf{p}_0')\cdot(\mathbf{v}_1\times\mathbf{v}_0')$$
$$+ v_2(\mathbf{p}_0 - \mathbf{p}_0')\cdot(\mathbf{v}_2\times\mathbf{v}_0') + v_1'(\mathbf{p}_0 - \mathbf{p}_0')\cdot(\mathbf{v}_0\times\mathbf{v}_1') + v_2'(\mathbf{p}_0 - \mathbf{p}_0')\cdot(\mathbf{v}_0\times\mathbf{v}_2') = 0$$

3) Equality:

$$\mathbf{v} = \mathbf{v}'$$

$$(\mathbf{p}' - \mathbf{p}) - (\mathbf{p}' - \mathbf{p})\cdot\hat{\mathbf{v}}'\ \hat{\mathbf{v}}' = 0 \qquad \hat{\mathbf{v}}' = \frac{\mathbf{v}}{|\mathbf{v}'|}$$

Each of these represents only two independent constraints, which can be extracted by taking the scalar product with $\mathbf{v}_1'$ and $\mathbf{v}_2'$. The result linearises to

$$(\mathbf{p}_0' - \mathbf{p}_0)\cdot\mathbf{v}_1' - p_1\mathbf{v}_1\cdot\mathbf{v}_1' - p_2\mathbf{v}_2\cdot\mathbf{v}_1' + p_1' - v_1'(\mathbf{p}_0' - \mathbf{p}_0)\cdot\mathbf{v}_0' = 0$$
$$(\mathbf{p}_0' - \mathbf{p}_0)\cdot\mathbf{v}_2' - p_1\mathbf{v}_1\cdot\mathbf{v}_2' - p_2\mathbf{v}_2\cdot\mathbf{v}_2' + p_2' - v_2'(\mathbf{p}_0' - \mathbf{p}_0)\cdot\mathbf{v}_0' = 0$$

and

$$\mathbf{v}_0\cdot\mathbf{v}_1' + v_1\mathbf{v}_1\cdot\mathbf{v}_1' + v_2\mathbf{v}_2\cdot\mathbf{v}_1' - v_1' = 0$$
$$\mathbf{v}_0\cdot\mathbf{v}_2' + v_1\mathbf{v}_1\cdot\mathbf{v}_2' + v_2\mathbf{v}_2\cdot\mathbf{v}_2' - v_2' = 0$$

(the last two constraints are sufficient to impose parallelism).

4) The two lines are connected by the small motion $(\boldsymbol{\omega}, \boldsymbol{\tau})$ if

$$(\mathbf{p}' - \mathbf{p} - \boldsymbol{\omega} \times \mathbf{p} - \mathbf{t}) - (\mathbf{p}' - \mathbf{p} - \boldsymbol{\omega} \times \mathbf{p} - \mathbf{t}) \cdot \hat{\mathbf{v}}' \; \hat{\mathbf{v}}' = 0$$

$$\hat{\mathbf{v}}' - \boldsymbol{\omega} \times \hat{\mathbf{v}} = 0$$

This linearises to

$$(\mathbf{p}_0' - \mathbf{p}_0) \cdot \mathbf{v}_1' + p_1' - p_1 \mathbf{v}_1 \cdot \mathbf{v}_1' - p_2 \mathbf{v}_2 \cdot \mathbf{v}_1' - v_1'(\mathbf{p}_0' - \mathbf{p}_0) \cdot \mathbf{v}_0'$$

$$- (\mathbf{p}_0 \times \mathbf{v}_1') \cdot \boldsymbol{\omega} - \mathbf{v}_1' \cdot \boldsymbol{\tau} = 0$$

$$(\mathbf{p}_0' - \mathbf{p}_0) \cdot \mathbf{v}_2' + p_2' - p_1 \mathbf{v}_1 \cdot \mathbf{v}_2' - p_2 \mathbf{v}_2 \cdot \mathbf{v}_2' - v_2'(\mathbf{p}_0' - \mathbf{p}_0) \cdot \mathbf{v}_0'$$

$$- (\mathbf{p}_0 \times \mathbf{v}_2') \cdot \boldsymbol{\omega} - \mathbf{v}_2' \cdot \boldsymbol{\tau} = 0$$

$$-\mathbf{v}_0 \cdot \mathbf{v}_1' + v_1' - v_1 \mathbf{v}_1 \cdot \mathbf{v}_1' - v_2 \mathbf{v}_2 \cdot \mathbf{v}_1' - (\mathbf{v}_0 \times \mathbf{v}_1') \cdot \boldsymbol{\omega} = 0$$

$$-\mathbf{v}_0 \cdot \mathbf{v}_2' + v_2' - v_1 \mathbf{v}_1 \cdot \mathbf{v}_2' - v_2 \mathbf{v}_2 \cdot \mathbf{v}_2' - (\mathbf{v}_0 \times \mathbf{v}_2') \cdot \boldsymbol{\omega} = 0$$

Chapter 9

Use of robots in manufacture

P. Taylor

1. INTRODUCTION

Manufacture typically involves the bringing together of many objects and performing various operations on them either individually or when partially assembled. If the same product is produced in large quantities over long periods of time, with perhaps minor variants such as colour, the economics of the process allow dedicated pieces of machinery, *hard automation*, to be used to give the most efficient production system. When more flexibility is required, for example if several models of car come down the same production line for welding, then some type of programmable automated system, typically using industrial robots, is likely to be beneficial. At another extreme a shoe factory has to produce many styles of shoe in lefts and rights, different sizes and sometime different width fittings. The batch size may go down to a single pair, although the overall production of the factory is still large. There are also areas of industry where specialised one-off machinery is produced. There are many difficulties involved in the introduction of robots in these last two categories, and it is currently usually more effective to use people. In order to see this clearly it is necessary to look at the capabilities of robots and the robotic systems in which they are embedded, and see how they can be used in practical applications (for more details see, for example Taylor P.M. [1990.1]). It will be seen that there are certain difficulties which need to be addressed in current research projects. It should be borne in mind that there are always overriding constraints of cost, not only in terms of equipment and running costs but in more general terms which include aspects such as quality, reliability and quickness of response to design changes.

2. THE CAPABILITIES OF A PROGRAMMABLE ROBOT

The definition given by the Robot Institute of America is 'A robot is a reprogrammable, multifunctional manipulator designed to move material, parts, tools or specialised devices through variable programmed motions for the performance of a variety of tasks'. A typical *anthropomorphic* structure is that of the Unimation PUMA robot, see figure 1, which has six revolute joints.

The key element of a robot which differentiates it from a hard automation system is its ability to be reprogrammed to carry out a different sequence of movements. In a basic robot such programming might be carried out by *teaching by guiding* where an operator manually guides the robot through the required sequence of movements which is stored in memory for recall as desired. In a more sophisticated robot it is possible to control the sequence of movements through the execution of a computer program. The program might be written in a traditional computer language such as PASCAL with libraries of procedures available to the programmer, or a special purpose robot language such as AML [Taylor R.H., 1983] or VAL [Unimation Inc, 1985] might be available. Typically, movements of the robot's gripper or *end effector* may be demanded in one of several co-ordinate systems, the most commonly used being the world co-ordinate system attached to the base of the robot. The computers associated with the robot will then perform all the co-ordinate transformations and execute the dynamic control algorithms in order to effect the desired movement. The robot's main controlling computer is likely to have several interfaces, serial and/or parallel, which may be addressed by the program and which are commonly used to interrogate signals from sensors and other equipment but which may also be used to communicate with other computers. The robot may then be part of an integrated robotic system with the robot's actions programmed to be dependent on the behaviour of other equipment and the state of the environment.

The aim of the robot is not just to wave its arm around – it is there to perform a task. Typical robot tasks are of the *pick and place* type where an object has to be moved from one point to another, usually in the shortest possible time whilst avoiding collisions. The easiest way to ensure no collisions is to define *via* points through which the end effector must pass. A different type of control is needed for such operations as welding or sewing. Here the welding torch or the robot gripper must be moved at prescribed speeds along a predefined path. This is termed *continuous path control*.

The robot will need to perform the task within a specified time. Although speed figures are usually given by robot manufacturers it can be misleading to use these when estimating the task execution time. The figures often quoted are those for maximum speed of the attachment point of the end effector. The dynamics and kinematics of most robots are highly nonlinear and so the true maximum attainable speed will depend on the operating point i.e. the current values of all the joint positions. In addition, no robot can instantaneously achieve its maximum speed when starting from any other condition. An acceleration stage is required. If small movements are made then the motion may be made up just by one acceleration stage and one deceleration stage and so the maximum attainable velocity will not be reached.

Several terms are used in defining the positioning performance of the robot. The *repeatability* is a measure of the tolerance within which the robot will return to a pre-recorded point. The *resolution* is the smallest step move which can be made at a given position (or the worst case). The *accuracy* is the error in moving to a programmed point. If a robot is programmed offline to move to a given location, say 10cm above a reference point, in practice it will not get to this point. This error arises not only because of frictional effects and discrete data errors from sensors but also because of calibration errors and errors in computing the co-ordinate transformations. These latter errors do not appear in the repeatability figure. Thus the accuracy will be worse than the repeatability and may not even be quoted.

3. COMPONENTS OF A ROBOT SYSTEM

The robot must have a mechanical structure and corresponding actuators, internal sensors and controllers to move an object around in its working volume. These are outside the scope of this paper which will assume that the robot has a satisfactory kinematic and dynamic behaviour. However, it should be borne in mind that, rather than using one fast robot having six axes of movement, it may be more economic to split the task up into a series of operations carried out in parallel by simpler, cheaper robots.

The robot must also have an end effector to hold a tool or grip a part. This end effector is usually purpose-built for the range of tasks to be undertaken. A gripping device may comprise two or more rigid or jointed fingers with the object held between them by friction, gravity and other forces applied by the fingers. However there are many other possibilities including vacuum suckers, electroadhesive plates and rollers [Monkman, 1988] as seen in figure 2, sticky surfaces and flexible fingers such as those in figure 3. A survey of robot grippers and some gripper changing mechanisms is given by Pham and Heginbotham [1986].

The objects to be worked upon have to be fed into and out of the working volume of the robot. Conveyors are typical transportation devices. Small components may be supplied in boxes and these may have to be singulated. The most elegant way to do this is often to use a vibratory bowl feeder with associated tooling (see figure 4). The bowl is twisted and shaken vertically such that individual components climb a spiral track inclined up the inside surface of the perimeter of the bowl. The end of this track is specially tooled so that only single, correctly oriented components are presented for picking up by the robot.

It is very expensive to constrain a working environment so that perfect parts are presented to a robot in the precise locations required for subsequent handling. In order that robots may be used in uncertain environments, either their operation must be insensitive to the uncertainty or sensors must provide data from which information can be extracted to reduce the uncertainty. An example of the first case is the use of a SCARA (Selective Compliant Arm for Robot Assembly) type arm, as shown in figure 5. The essential feature of this construction is the two links which move in the horzontal plane. The flexibility of the drive train and the ability of the DC motors to be back-driven allow horizontally applied external forces to move the tip of the arm even when it is powered up. Consider the case of a peg being inserted into a chamfered hole by dropping it vertically into the hole's nominal position. If this hole is misplaced, then the peg will descend and hit the chamfer rather than drop down the centre of the hole. The angle of the chamfer will cause a sideways force to be exerted on the peg which will then move in the horizontal plane towards the true centre of the hole, since it is allowed to do so through the compliant nature of the robot mechanism. Another solution to this problem is to put horizontal compliance and angular compliance into a mechanism positioned between the robot's wrist and its gripper. The operation of this remote centre compliance [Whitney and Nevins, 1979] is shown in figure 6. These approaches work well when putting pegs into chamfered holes having slightly uncertain locations. However, there are many assembly operations where such passive mechanical techniques cannot be used. In these cases sensory feedback can be used to provide the robot with the true position of the object to be handled.

The most commonly used sensors are not sophisticated vision systems, but rather simple optical and mechanical switches. Typical optical switches use a matched infra-red emitter and receiver pair. The light beam from emitter to reciver is then broken by the presence of an object or made by reflection from the object's surface. The use of infra-red reduces the effects of changes in ambient light conditions. In more extreme cases the infra-red signal is pulsed. A simple switch makes a very reliable touch sensor - better than 10^7 operations before failure being quoted for a typical microswitch.

The earliest experiments in robotic vision used Vidicon-type television cameras as the vision sensor. These have been largely replaced by CCD type cameras which are much smaller and more rugged and suitable for mounting on robot grippers. Solid state DRAM cameras have been used as a low cost alternative, but suffer from being effective over only a small range of lighting conditions. In fact good control of lighting is probably the most important factor in robot vision. Batchelor at al [1985] provide an excellent set of examples and case studies which show how a little thought at this stage can be put to good effect. Backlighting an object to give a silhouette gives a high quality outline, insensitive to ambient light and the image can be easily and reliably thresholded to give a good quality binary image. Robot applications are usually time-critical and image processing is relatively slow, so the simpler the image can be made the better.

Camera location is also important. Overhead static cameras can be used successfully to locate objects. However they cannot be used whilst the robot is between object and camera. More importantly they must be carefully and rigidly mounted in precisely known locations. This is because the image processing will give the position of the object in camera co-ordinates. This has to be converted by scaling factors and offsets to be the robot's world co-ordinates. If this transformation is incorrect or the robot is miscalibrated then the object will be picked up incorrectly.

An alternative is to mount the camera(s) on the robot gripper as seen in figure 7. A servoing technique may then be used to precisely locate the robot's gripper over the object. This is done by getting the centroid of the object in camera co-ordinates and then scaling this to move the robot until the centroid should appear in the centre of the image. If it does not then the process is repeated. If the scaling is incorrect or the camera or robot are miscalibrated then all that happens is that it takes more than one movement to achieve registration. The disadvantage of this technique is that it increases the task execution time because of the need for extra robot movements.

A single camera can also be used to obtain 3D information if used with the so-called *structured light* technnique shown in figure 8. A high intensity light source is combined with a cylindrical lens to project a plane of light. The line of light across the conveyor and object is no longer straight, the deviation being due to the height of the object.

Tactile array sensors are still in their infancy and there is not yet a light, cheap, robust tactile array sensor available which has the required sensitivity and compliance for robot assembly operations.

Other sensors commonly used are force sensors, particularly mounted at the robot's wrist, ultrasonic sensors and laser-based sensors, these last two usually as proximity sensors.

Unfortunately, as soon as array sensors are used they produce a lot of data from which a small amount of valuable information must be extracted. It is often necessary to precede this extraction by a signal conditioning phase which, for example, could be used to remove high frequency electrical noise from the signal. The most common requirements are to know where is an object and what is its orientation. Moments can be calculated to obtain these for binary images, but there is host of alternative algorithms to find these parameters, especially when grey-scale images are used.

Automated inspection is often a need associated with an automated cell. This is generally a much more difficult job than just verifying the position of an object. Consequently it generally requires state of the art computer hardware and/or special purpose electronics/optics. This usually means that it is expensive. Braggins and Hollingum (1986) give a survey of commercially available systems for both inspection and handling tasks.

4. DESIGN OF SENSORY ASSEMBLY SYSTEMS

The design of sensory assembly systems is illustrated by two such systems. The first was constructed as part of the motif application and ply separation project undertaken at Hull University a number of years ago. This workcell has now been rebuilt to act as a testbed for new research ideas on automated workcell synthesis and runtime control. The second example is of a complete garment assembly cell which is still under construction. This is much more complex and will introduce a number of important issues for workcell design.

4.1 A Single Robot System for a 'Simple' Fabric Handling Task

The garment manufacturing industry has great potential for robotic applications provided the technical and financial problems can be overcome. A collection of papers describing some of the research in this area is given in [Taylor P.M. ,1990.2]. The removal of a single ply of knitted cotton fabric from a stack (see figure 9) is a typical problem which is non–trivial for automation. Consider first the properties of the material. Knitted cotton is a limp material, it is porous, it is non–homogeneous and its mechanical properties will vary from roll to roll. The upper and lower surfaces are not identical and are such that plies tend to cling together. There will also be residual stresses within the fabric due to its manufacture and subsequent handling and cutting. As these stresses are relieved a fabric panel is likely to change in shape and in thickness, behaving in an apparently 'live' manner. The fabric itself may , of course, be of many colours and be patterned. It is partially transparent to light.

Secondly we need to consider the properties of a stack. Adjacent plies may be laid the same way up or the opposite way up, this latter case causing alternate changes in the interply forces down the stack. An ideal stack will have vertical edges and comprise whole panels of fabric. In practice, the edges will be disturbed during handling and may be discontinuous. If the cutting tool has not been sufficiently sharpened then fibres at the edge of one ply will intermingle with similar fibres from the plies above and below. Occasionally, an incomplete panel will form part of the stack. Finally, although the number of plies in the stack will be known, the height of the stack will not be known precisely enough for automation.

We can now consider how simple sensing and robotic actions can be used to tackle the above difficulties, basing the discussion on an air jet/finger ply separation device [Kemp, 1986] attached to a Unimation PUMA robot. This device is shown in operation in figure 10 where it is blowing a jet of air over, and partially through, the top ply causing it to vibrate, separate from the ply beneath and flip over the lower finger. The complete gripper must be positioned with an accuracy of a few millimetres relative to the top and edge of the stack. It will then have a single ply separation reliability of about 95%, the failures arising from the various cohesive forces.

Ignoring the 5% failures for the moment, the first sensing problem is to find the top and the edge of the stack. This is nominally only done once per stack since the position after the first and subsequent plies are removed can be calculated from the original position, assuming a perfect stack. In practice, visual and ultrasonic techniques all prove unreliable given the wide variety of fabric surfaces. The structured light approach might be feasible but is much more complex than the simple solution – a low activation force switch mounted in the underside of the lower finger as shown in figure 11. The top of the stack is found by moving the gripper vertically downwards until its change of state indicates that it has hit the top of the stack. The gripper is then drawn across the stack until the switch changes state again as it drops over the edge. A simple move of the gripper by an offset will then put the ply separation device in its correct position. In order to improve the reliability it is necessary to check the number of plies between the upper and lower fingers. The partial transparency of the material can be used very successfully. An infra–red emitter is mounted in one finger and a receiver in the other, with the light passing through any fabric in–between the fingers. The received light intensity is compared with previously taught threshold values, and a decision can be made of zero, one, or two or more plies. In the error cases the recovery action is initially to re–try the separation process. If this fails several times then the chances are that the gripper is misplaced relative to the stack and so the initialisation procedure is restarted. These sensing and recovery actions increase the reliability of single ply separation to over 99%.

This complete workcell, which included the application of a bin–picked motif to the separated fabric panel, was originally designed on an ad–hoc basis. Most of the high level computer code deals with error recovery actions rather than the actions taken when all is ideal. Unfortunately, to decide correctly which sensors to use, to implement them and to correctly specify, write and debug the computer programmes can take months of effort. The timescale involved makes such sensory systems unsuitable for small batch production of many different items.

4.2 A Multiple Robot System for Garment Assembly

Additional considerations are introduced when large multi-robot systems are built. Consider the assembly operations shown in figure 12 for a complete garment. The workcell will comprise a number of robotic modules employing techniques such as fabric ply separation, pick and place, sewing in straight and curved lines, and performing more complex folding and manipulation in three dimensions [Taylor, P.M., Wilkinson et al, 1990.2].

From an operator's point of view the inputs to the system are the stacks of fabric panels and a requirement for the production of a number of garments of a certain style and size. The outputs are the actual completed garments and information on the work in progress and problems with the operation of any subcells.

The PC-compatible computers which control the UMI-RTX robots, the sewing machinery and other handling modules, are connected in a hierarchy for downloading of software at initialisation and for error message passing and performance monitoring at runtime. The runtime control of the equipment is co-ordinated by links between adjacent subcells at the lower levels, obviating the need to send signals all the way up and then down the hierarchy and making individual subcells almost autonomous. The runtime control system must also cope with short term breakdowns in individual subcells. For example, an operator must be able to enter safely into a subcell to replenish thread on a sewing machine whilst keeping other subcells as operative as possible. A more detailed discussion of implementation strategies is found in [Taylor P.M., Wilkinson et al , 1990.1]

It has been found that the interfaces between subcells are often the most difficult part of the design. It is quite easy to devise solutions to a particular sewing problem which leave the garment subassembly in a tangle. It is rather harder to make the output of one cell such that it makes easy the input handling problem of the next. The crucial aspect of this is to determine those parts of the garment which must be handled and located accurately (usually edges and corners) and once these features are grasped then either keep hold of the feature or release it in such a way that its retrieval is simple.

This particular cell is being constructed for the assembly of two types of garment only: one style of men's Y-fronts and on style of ladies' brief. In its present state considerable reprogramming combined with a change of modules would be needed to widen the range of styles being produced.

5. SENSORY ROBOTIC ASSEMBLY: PROBLEMS AND POSSIBLE SOLUTIONS

As described above, one of the main problems preventing the extensive use of sensory systems is the difficulty in correctly designing the hardware and software so that a correctly functioning system is synthesised in a short time. It is usually not too difficult to produce an object level description of the particular assembly task. The selection of the assembly technique to be used (for example, there are several possibile ways of achieving fabric ply separation), the sensing actions to be taken and what to do with the sensory information, must all be decided upon. Following this, functionally correct controlling software must be generated. Unfortunately, many of the assembly parameters may not be well known, and in the small batch environment it is unlikely that a rigid rule-based approach will produce the optimum result.

In practice, the design of a sensory system implicitly considers such factors as the probability of the presence of the objects in the cell, their likely positional errors and the reliabilities of robots, other machines and processes. These are all probabilistic in nature. Part of the current research at Hull is based on the use of a probabilistic framework [Taylor P.M, Halleron and Song, 1990] towards a long term goal of an autonomous assembly system as shown in figure 13. The associated knowledge base will be used to generate automatically the probability vectors and matrices used in the runtime decision making processes. These vectors and matrices are automatically updated according to the runtime experiences of the cell and thus the operation automatically adjusts to varying conditions or those which are different from a priori expectations.

6. CONCLUSIONS

Robots are well established in repetitive manufacture where a limited range of products are made. Such robots generally use few, if any, sensors. Robots can be made to work successfully in less constrained environments by adding sensors into the robotic system. This gives the promise of applications in small batch manufacture and in those industries where there are inherent uncertainties in the materials and production processes. However, successful applications of sensory robotics are harder to achieve than might be realised and the synthesis and runtime control problems are still a subject of research.

REFERENCES

BATCHELOR, B.G., HILL, D.A. and HODGSON, D.C. (1985) Automated Visual Inspection, IFS (Publications), Kempston, UK.

BRAGGINS, D. and HOLLINGUM, J. (1986) The Machine Vision Sourcebook, IFS (Publications), Kempston, UK.

KEMP, D.R., TAYLOR, G.E., TAYLOR, P.M. and PUGH, A. (1986) 'A Sensory Gripper for Handling Textiles' in PHAM, D.T. and HEGINBOTHAM, W.B. (Eds), Robot Grippers, IFS (Publications), Kempston.

MONKMAN, G.J and TAYLOR, P.M. (1988) 'Electrostatic Grippers: Principles and Practice', Proc. Int. Symp. on Industrial Robots, Lausanne, Switzerland.

PHAM, D.T and HEGINBOTHAM, W.B. (Eds) (1986) Robot Grippers, IFS (Publications), Kempston, UK.

TAYLOR, P.M. (1990.1) Robotic Control, Macmillan Education Ltd, Basingstoke.

TAYLOR, P.M. (1990.2) Sensory Robots for the Handling of Limp Materials, Springer-Verlag, due for publication June/July 1990.

TAYLOR, P.M., HALLERON, I. and SONG, X.K. (1990), 'The Application of a Dynamic Error Framework to Robotic Assembly', Proc. IEEE Conf. on Robotics and Automation, Cincinnati, USA.

TAYLOR, P.M., WILKINSON, A.J., GUNNER, M.B., SAWYER, A. and GIBSON, I. (1990.1), 'Integration of a Flexible Workcell for Garment Assembly', Proc. 28th Int. MATADOR Conf.,Manchester, pp.131-136.

TAYLOR, P.M., WILKINSON, A.J., TAYLOR, G.E., GUNNER, M.B. and PALMER, G.S. (1990.2), 'Automated Fabric Handling Problems and Techniques', Proc. IEEE Conf. on Systems Engineering, Pittsburgh, USA.

TAYLOR, R.H., SUMMERS, P.D. and MEYER J.M. (1983) 'AML a Manufacturing Language', Int. J. Robotics Research, Vol 1, No 3, pp.19-41.

UNIMATION INC. (1985) Unimate Industrial Robot Programming Manual. Users' Guide to VAL II Vers 1.4B, Unimation Inc, Danbury, Connecticut, USA.

WHITNEY, D.E. and NEVINS, J.L. (1979) 'What is the Remote Center Compliance and What can it Do?', Proc. 9th Int. Symp. on Industrial Robots, Washington DC, USA, pp.135–152.

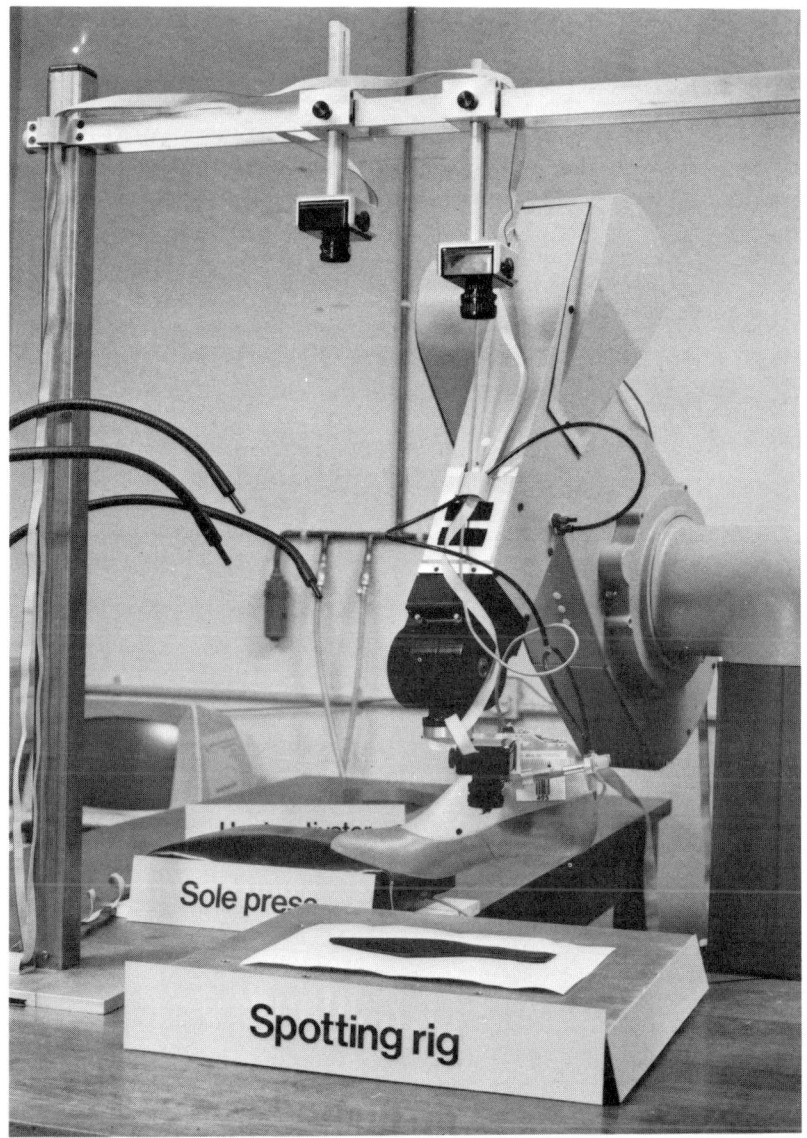

Fig.1 Unimation PUMA robot.

Fig.2 An electroadhesive end effector for fabric ply separation.

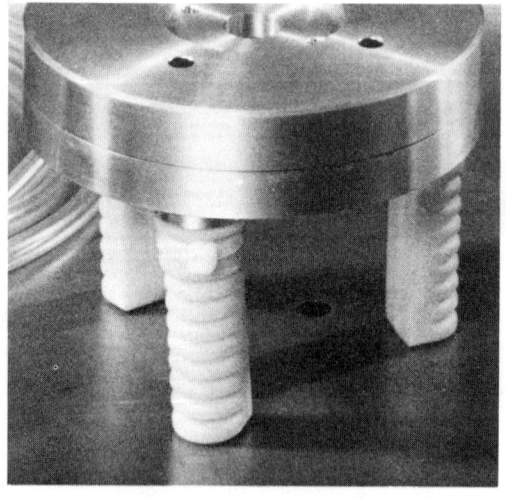

Fig.3 Air-activated flexible fingers

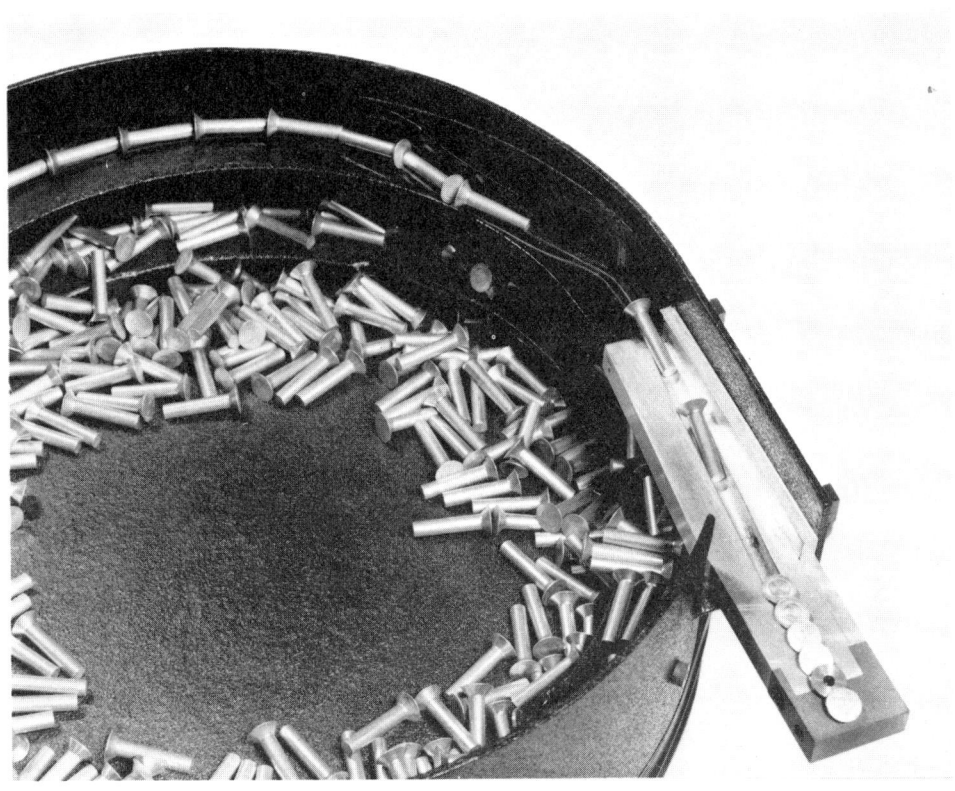

Fig.4 Vibratory bowl feeder

Fig.5 A SCARA-type robot

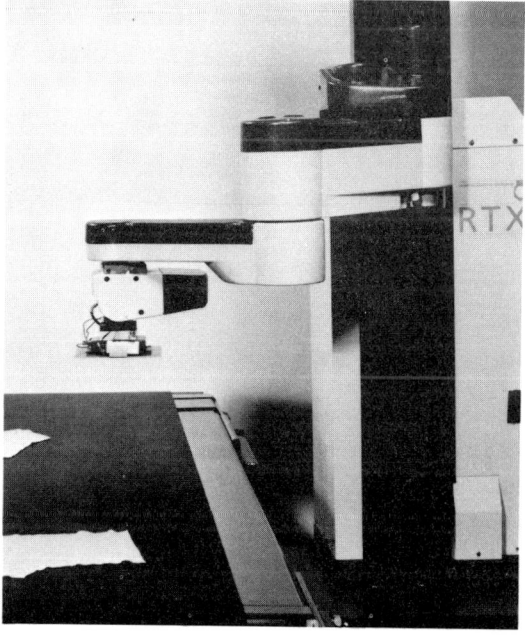

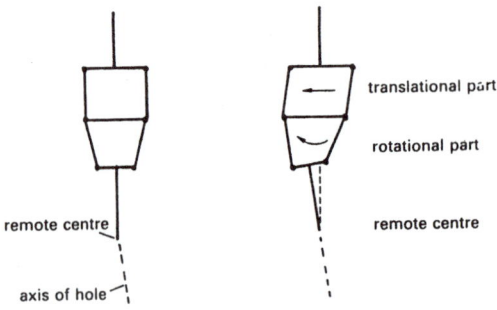

translational part

rotational part

remote centre

remote centre

axis of hole

Fig.6 Operation of a remote centre compliance

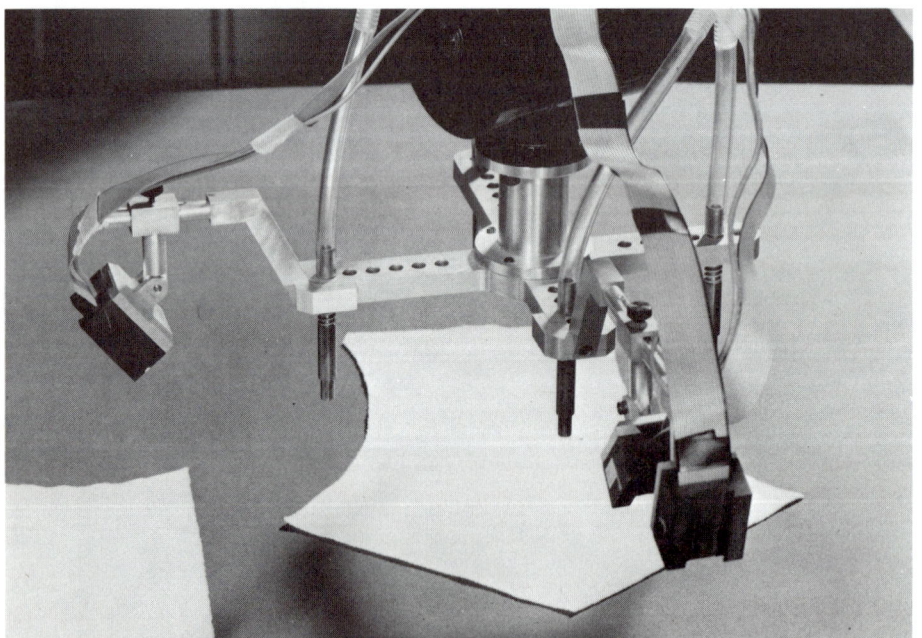

Fig.7 Gripper–mounted cameras

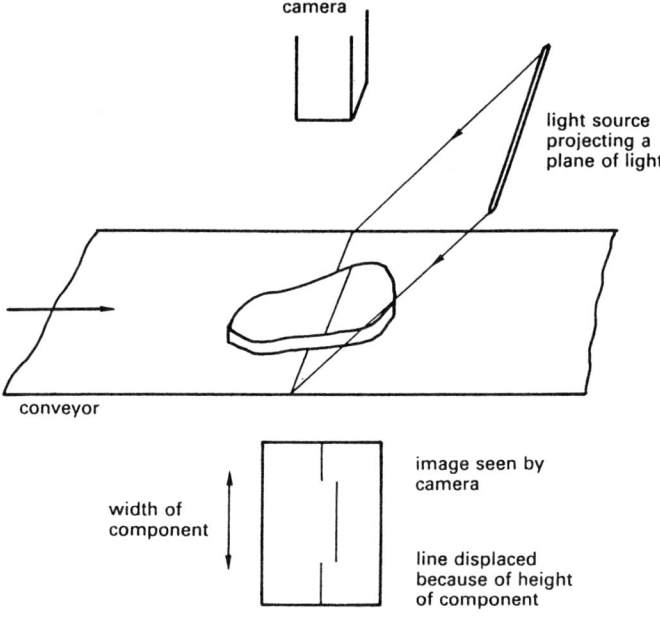

Fig.8 Structured light

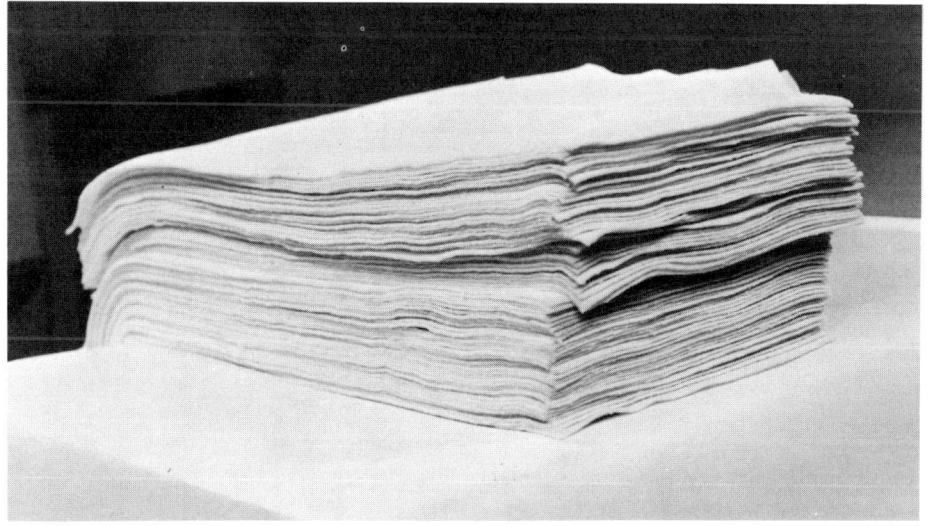

Fig.9 A stack of fabric panels

Fig.10 Air jet/finger ply separation device in operation

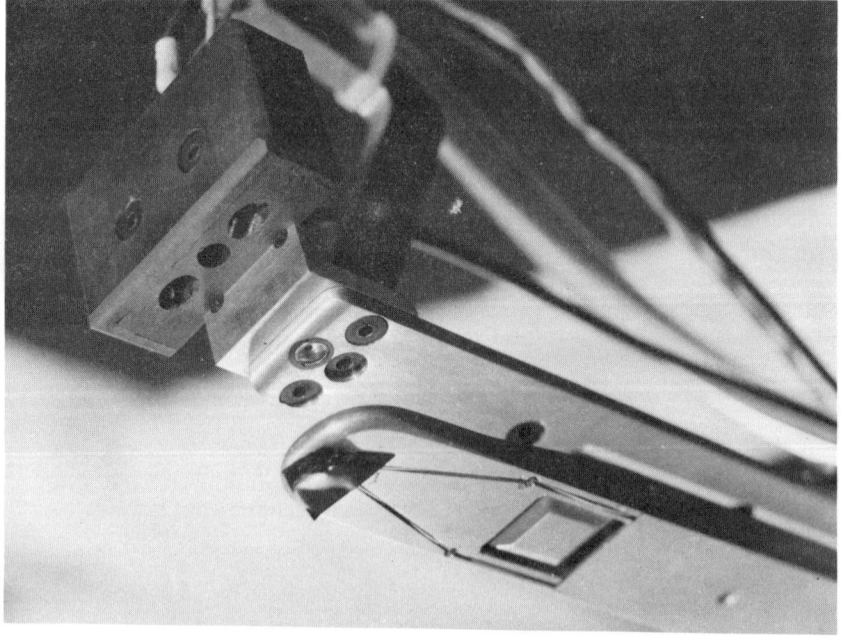

Fig.11 The separation device showing its sensors

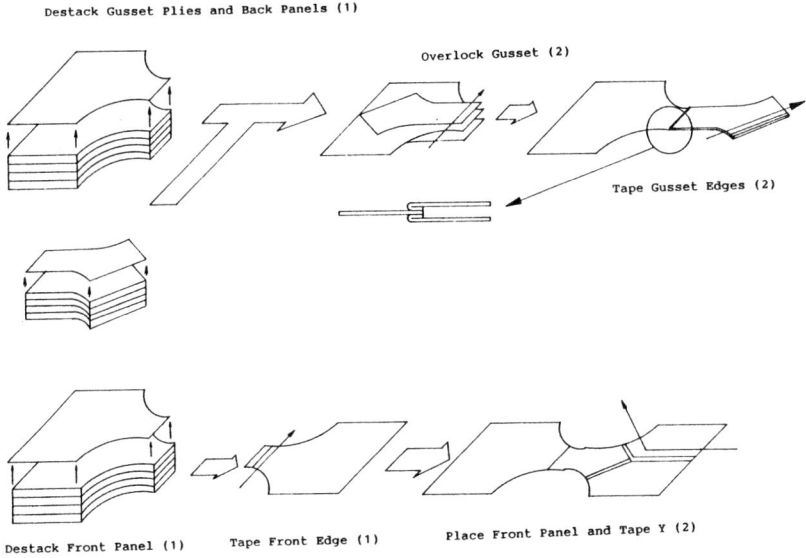

Destack Gusset Plies and Back Panels (1)

Overlock Gusset (2)

Tape Gusset Edges (2)

Destack Front Panel (1) Tape Front Edge (1) Place Front Panel and Tape Y (2)

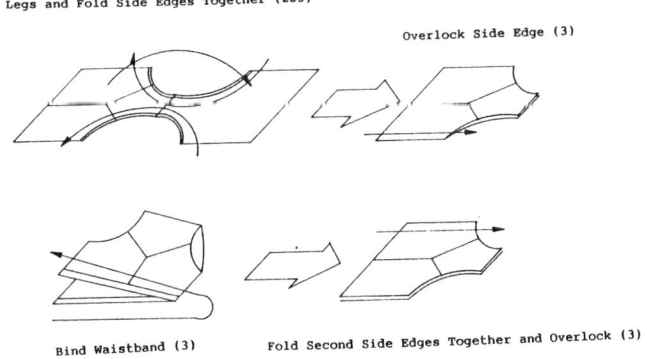

Bind Legs and Fold Side Edges Together (2&3)

Overlock Side Edge (3)

Bind Waistband (3) Fold Second Side Edges Together and Overlock (3)

Fig.12 The assembly operations for a complete garment

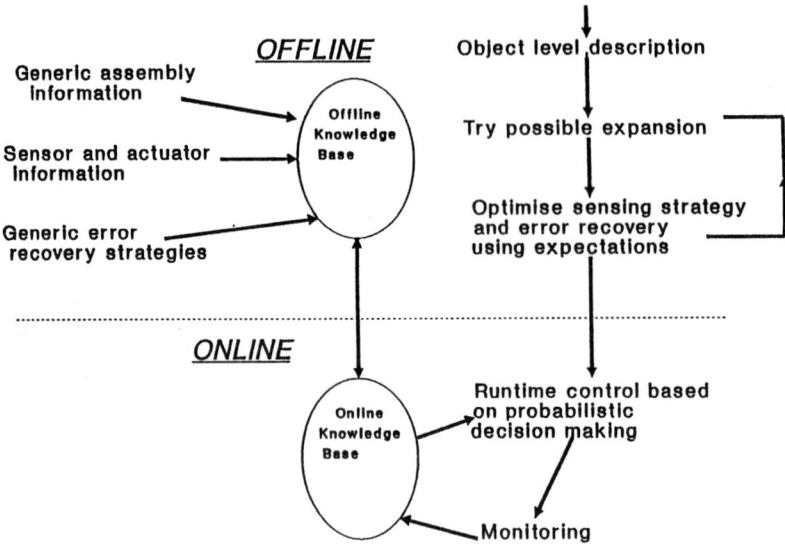

Fig.13 The structure of a possible autonomous assembly workcell

Chapter 10

Prolog programming for cognitive science

P. J. Scott

The purpose of this chapter is to provide an introduction to the programming language Prolog and to show how the declarative nature of the language can assist in cognitive science research. For the most part the chapter consists of tutorial background material on Prolog and its basic syntax, terminology and use. The focus of cognitive science research is on implementing models of psychological processes and this approach depends on how the process can be represented and how one can use this representation to solve the problem at hand.

1 WHAT IS COGNITIVE SCIENCE?

Cognitive science is an umbrella term which can be used to describe the interests of a wide range of researchers. The range includes (at least), psychologists, computer-scientists, neuro-scientists, philosophers and linguists. The one common thread which unites this diversity is an interest in computational models of cognitive processes. The general idea is that while a theory on paper is essential to the progress of the scientific understanding of some phenomenon – it is often necessary to attempt to test the theory in practice. In mechanical engineering one must take the plans off the desk at some stage and build a "bridge on paper" into a "model bridge" and then into a "full-scale bridge". Until the advent of the computer it was not possible to conceive of a psychological scientist doing a similar thing with an information processing theory. Today we are as far as ever from the possibility of building a "full scale cognitive system", but the idea of building a "model" of some cognitive system working in highly constrained circumstances on a highly constrained problem is a regular and very useful tool.

When information processing ideas began to enter into psychological science we began to frame all our questions about a cognitive phenomenon into ones which asked (i) what is the information that is involved in this task and (ii) how is it used by the information processing system? Today we typically speak of "knowledge" rather than information and treat question(i) as one relating to a choice of **representation** for that knowledge and (ii) as the **inference** that is be made over that knowledge. Typically, we also often speak of the **rule** as a simple fragment of knowledge that involves both a representation and inference bundled into one easy-to-understand chunk. The development of the programming language Prolog provided a computational tool in which all of these concepts are powerfully resident.

2 WHAT IS PROLOG?

Prolog is a major modern logic programming computer language. In fact it is now so influential that in 1981 it was adopted by the Japanese as **the** programming language for their 'Fifth Generation Project' – aimed at the creation of 'intelligent' computers. It originated in Europe and is now probably the preferred AI research language for European AI workers, though most AI researchers world-wide (particularly in the USA) use the list-processing language LISP.

Prolog is remarkably easy to read because of its declarative semantics and the basic representation methods used are easy to understand even for non-specialists in computing. It has even been claimed in that many ways it is **easier** for non-specialists to understand because computer scientists' prior training with more traditional imperative languages can interfere.

It is particularly well-suited both to :

(i) the **creation** of declarative knowledge structures - through its built-in representation of facts and rules (and through the capability of creating more sophisticated knowledge structures such as frames and scripts).

(ii) the **interrogation** of the knowledge structures in a very flexible fashion, both through its built-in search mechanism and through the capability of creating more sophisticated search algorithms.

There are many different implementations and dialects of the Prolog language. The industry standard dialect is referred to as the 'Edinburgh' syntax and the most common version in academic research appears to be the Quintus™ Prolog (of Quintus Computer Systems Incorporated, California). At Sheffield University we mainly use MacProlog™ (of Logic Programming Associates Ltd, London), a version of Prolog specifically designed for the Apple Macintosh™ which makes full use of the standard Mac microcomputer facilities, such as pull-down menus, cut and paste editing, multiple windows, excellent graphics and so on.

2.1 Some Historical Developments in Prolog and Cognitive Science

Here are a selection of interesting dates relating to the development of Prolog and the emergence of a discipline which could be called 'Cognitive Science'. The best retelling of this important story from the historical perspective is Gardner, (1985). You could select many events in the late '50s and early 60's where the influence of the ideas of information processing and the use of the computer in developing psychological theories was starting to emerge.

1956   •   Symposium on Information Theory at MIT.

               Papers by Newell & Simon, Chomsky and Miller start new era.

1962   •   McCarthy publishes LISP 1.5

1971   •   Kowalski formulates the procedural interpretation of Horn clause logic.

        •   PROLOG - PROgramming in LOGic - developed (in Fortran) by Colmerauer's group at Marseilles for natural language parsing.

1973   •   Sir James Lighthill's report critical of the potential of Artificial Intelligence. Academic funding of AI in Britain slashed.

1975   •   Warren at Edinburgh creates efficient compiler for Prolog – DEC-10 Prolog

1981   •   Japan announces a project aimed to create the 'Fifth Generation' computer by 1992. Fundamental idea is need for Knowledge Information Processing Systems. Language adopted is Prolog 1M LIPS (100-1000M LIPS for parallel machine)

        •   Clocksin & Mellish produce "Programming in Prolog" text book.

1983   •   Alvey Project set up - £350M over 5 years.

1988   •   Joint academic research councils introduce the 'Cognitive Science Initiative'.

The choice of 1956 and the MIT symposium is simply because it is one of the earliest collections of a large number of the people who were to become very influential in the later course of cognitive science research. However it was not until the advent of a powerful computer language – John McCarthy's LISt Processing language LISP – which was suited to the implementation of some of these ideas that things could really get off the ground. Lisp is a functional language with a rich and well defined mathematical basis. It handles the processing of symbols as elegantly as it does mathematics.

It was something like a decade before the idea of a programming language more directly based in logic began to appear on the scene. Researchers like Kowalski in the UK showed that it was possible to have a procedural interpretation of declarative logical statements. Alain Colmerauer and his team in France first made this work on a computer. However, again it was not until the academic work became an efficient language – with David Warren's compiler - that people could really take it seriously. Indeed the first real public access to the language was not until the early 1980's with the publication of the first popular textbook on Prolog by Bill Clocksin and Chris Mellish. Meanwhile the political scene had not been doing so well. Academic research in the UK on artificial intelligence and cognitive science topics had been dealt a severe blow by the very negative report of the Lighthill committee to an influential research funding council. Whilst UK research was struggling against severely restricted funding the rest of the world was investing great sums of money into information / knowledge based and computer oriented research. In 1981 the Japanese announced a major research project directed towards the 'fifth generation' computer. In the UK the research councils were rudely awoken and came back (after a couple of years) to announce the much more modest Alvey Project to better resource British research and most recently all the major councils have joined up to fund an (even more modest) Cognitive Science Initiative.

What was most shocking to some about the Japanese project was not so much the amount that they were investing nor the ambitiousness of their goals, but that they had chosen as the project 'core' language - the then relatively unknown and academic - Prolog. Suddenly all researchers in computing, especially those in the USA, began to take an interest in this European phenomenon.

2.2 Programming in Prolog

Most computer languages (Pascal, Fortran, Basic, C .... etc) are **imperative**. Writing a computer program in an imperative language consists of telling the computer what to do at every stage. Recently, **declarative** languages have been introduced, starting with rule-based languages such as OPS-5 and more recently **knowledge representation languages** (KRLs). The major aim behind a declarative language is the accurate and flexible representation of the underlying knowledge structures involved in the problem under consideration, rather than any attempt to specify exactly how the computer program is to solve the particular problem.

Declarative languages have several clear advantages over imperative ones:
- emphasis on the **representation** to be used. This is particularly important where we are trying to model complex knowledge structures such as those used in human cognition.
- **flexibility**. In general it is very difficult for an imperative program to answer any question other than the ones it was specifically designed for, whereas experience has shown that users always wish to tailor a particular system to their own requirements.

The problem for a declarative language is that a procedural interpretation is essential to make it *do something*. Otherwise it would just sit there - you would type in all this knowledge, but you would not be able to **query** the knowledge base in a useful way – that is, ask it some questions and get it to do some procedural work to return to you the answers. This is where Prolog comes in.

2.2.1 EXAMPLE: A simple relational Database

Question. How would you represent the relationships father, mother, male, female in your preferred conventional (procedural) language - Pascal, Fortran, Basic ...?

eg.   philip, charles and william are all male
            elizabeth is female

> philip is the father of charles
>
> charles is the father of william
>
> elizabeth is the mother of charles

In particular, how would you express knowledge about relationships such as **grandfather**? You might want to represent this knowledge as a further 'fact' as above - but clearly a better idea is to make your computer language do the work where possible! Logically you could consider 'grandfather' to **MEAN** the set of all individuals such that:

$$\forall \; (X, Z) \; \{ \; grandfather(X, Z)$$
$$if$$
$$\exists \; (Y) \; \{ \; father(X, Y) \; and \; father(Y, Z) \; \} \; \}$$

or in English:

> Forall X's and Z's we can say that X is a 'grandfather' of Z
>
>> where there exists a Y
>
>>> such that X is the 'father' of Y and Y is the 'father' of Z.

So the challenge is – how would you express this sort of knowledge computationally?

2.2.2 Why use Prolog ?

The choice of any tool for any problem requires that you fit the one to the other. So in choosing a programming language for a task such as the one above one must ensure a suitable problem & solution match. Now in general it is easier to say what a problem is not rather than what it is:

• NOT number crunching : Write a statistics program in say **Fortran**

• NOT a machine-oriented, procedural problem : Write an editor program in say **Pascal**.

But IF the **representation** of a problem **IS** the problem THEN choose Lisp or Prolog. Let us look first at **Lisp** – a Functional List-Processing Language. Now, functions act upon specific individuals to return some value. So for example you would define a function "father" to take two individuals and check their family relationship. Consider the British Royal Family as an example, where Philip and Elizabeth are the parents of Charles and so on. However the function is defined, when it was "executed" you would expect:

```
(father 'philip 'charles) to return True
(father 'philip 'elizabeth) to return False
```

So whenever either of these functions was called by Lisp the expression in the brackets would be replaced by the truth value. (Note that the first word in the parentheses is the function, and the next two words are preceded by a single quote marker to indicate that they are not variables and stand for some specific individual/value).

But, now consider the case where you want to ask :

Who is the father of charles?

or

Philip is the father of whom?

then you will require (at least) two further functions,

eg.   (gives_father_to 'charles) **to return** 'philip

(receives_father_from 'philip) **to return** 'charles

The names of these functions may not be very good but the basic idea is clear enough. The function gives_father_to means who is the father of the individual given as the argument. (NB it would not have been much more helpful to call this is_the_father_of as this could easily be the interpretation of the second function too!). The second function receives_father_from means who is the individual given as argument the child of. Unfortunately this does not solve the problem of how to find other individuals that may potentially receive the relation "father" or many other potential routes into this information.

In Prolog you could use the one **predicate** to do all of this. Prolog programs can have an elegant declarative and procedural semantics. For the above problem, this one statement could be the entire program:

```
father(philip, charles).
```

2.2.3 Logic Programming in English

Logic programming is a technique which essentially combines a declarative knowledge representation with a built-in **inference mechanism -** a method of trying to answer queries to the database of knowledge from a user. Let us return to the example from the 'Royal Family' database. The database consists of a set of facts and rules relating to the relationships between individuals in the Royal Family.

Given a **query** – is Elizabeth the **mother** of Charles? and this **database:**

---

of definitions for females and parents which are simple **facts** eg.

fact 1:   Elizabeth is **female**

fact 2:   Elizabeth is a **parent** of Charles

...

and more complex definitions with **rules** for things like motherhood eg.

rule 1:   X is the **mother** of Y **if** X is a **parent** of Y **and** X is **female**.

...

---

a logic program would take the query as its **goal** to be proved and would do its best to prove that the statement is true (ie. can be deduced from the facts and rules in the knowledge base). It would first find that there was no single **fact** in the above knowledge base which answered the question, but would still be able to come up with the answer by selecting a relevant **rule** and then trying to prove it was true.

In this case the proof for **mother** would go as follows:

(1) find a **mother** definition that might be applicable

   in this case, rule 1 with X = 'Elizabeth' and Y = 'Charles'

(2) try to solve the first condition of rule 1

   'X is a **parent** of Y' which is true (ie the fact is in the knowledge base - fact 2)

(3) try to solve the second condition

   'X is **female**.' This is also true for Y=Elizabeth   (fact 1)

Consequently the whole **goal** would succeed and the program would answer

   Yes (ie. it is 'true' ie. deducible from the knowledge base)

If it had not been able to prove the goal (ie if either condition had failed) it would reply: **No** (ie. it cannot be proved from the given knowledge base,though not necessarily false – it may be that a fact or rule had been omitted from the knowledge base!).

Before considering exactly what these would look like in Prolog we must know more about the details of the syntax of the language.

2.3 The Elementary Syntax of Prolog

Just like English - any computer language such as Prolog has a syntax which determines what it is acceptable to say and how. The essential individual elements of the Prolog language are discussed below.

Comment markers /* ... */ may contain anything. Slash-star opens the comment and star-slash closes the comment. Some Prologs support an additional comment marker such as %. This is used to indicate that Prolog is to ignore the remainder of the line after the marker. We will use the percent % comment marker more than the slash-star & star-slash combination. Anything outside of the comments is Prolog code and must obey the strict syntax of the language.

The simplest element of Prolog is the constant. The most important element of Prolog is the constant which is called an **atom**. An atom is an individual word of Prolog which contains no special characters or spaces and starts with a lower case letter a-z. After the lower-case start character the word can contain any letters a-z (or even capitals A-Z), integers 0-9, and the underscore _ character. The underscore is often used to give the impression of spaces in long words. It should be noted that you can include anything in an atom by enclosing it in single quotes, but it is usually simpler to stick to lower-case and underscores. The second most important element in Prolog is the **variable**, which follows the same rules as atoms, but must begin with a capital letter character A-Z, (or unusually, an underscore character). So the elements: fred, silly_me and 'Bird_Brain' are all **atoms**; whilst the elements: Bird, X and _fred are all **variables**.

These elements are often combined to make a third element of Prolog, the **term**. Terms are made up of predicates with some optional arguments, where the predicate is an atom that may have its arguments in brackets. If there is more than one argument they are separated by commas. Terms may have no arguments, eg **raining** could be a term used to mean "it is raining"; one argument, eg **female(elizabeth)** could mean that elizabeth is female; or any number of arguments. So the term: **owns(anne, Prolog_book)** may be used to mean that the atom **anne** is to be described as having the relationship **owns** to the atom **Prolog_book**. Indeed, predicates are sometimes called **relations** because they often represent the relations between arguments. One critical syntactic convention is that there must be no space between the predicate and the brackets which start to enclose its arguments, if any. There are a number of other elements in Prolog that are special like : strings, (anything enclosed in double quote markers eg "a string"), and integers, (any word beginning with the characters 0-9), and so on. One very important special element in Prolog that can also appear in a term is the **List**. Lists are structures which represent *sets* of individuals. The set is surrounded by square brackets with set members separated by commas. Clearly lists can contain any of the other Prolog element including other lists.

eg. [ ] is a list which represents the empty-set; [a, b, c, d] is a list with four members; while [[bread, potatoes], [milk, sugar], salt] is a list with three members, two of them also lists. So an example term which contains a list might look like this: days([mon, tues, wed, thurs, fri, sat, sun])

2.4 The Database Syntax of Prolog

Prolog programs consist of Prolog terms made up of the basic elements, that appear as either **facts** or **rules** in a **definition**, in the database.

• **Facts** are single terms that are in the database followed by a full stop.

```
person(charles).
state_of_mind(charles, happy).
days([mon, tues, wed, thurs, fri, sat, sun]).
mammal(rat).
```

These may be read as saying that it is true that charles is a 'person'. That it is true that the 'state_of_mind' of charles is happy. That it is the case that 'days' are the elements included in the list [mon ... sun]. Also that it is true that a rat is a 'mammal'.

- **Rules** are complex terms that are in the database followed by a full stop. They consist on one single term that is the head of the rule; a Prolog 'if' symbol :- and then a conjunction of one or more terms in the tail of the rule. The comma between the terms after the ':-' mean 'and'.

```
mammal(X):- warm_blooded(X), furry(X).
```

This can be read as meaning that X is a mammal **IF** X is warm blooded **AND** X is furry. This may be a good time to mention that Prolog variables are entirely local to the fact or rule in which they occur. So the three X's in the above rule refer to the same unknown individual. Whenever any one of the X's is bound to a specific value then the others automatically share that value within this rule. Outside of this rule any other uses of X are not bound to this value and are local to the clause in which they appear. There is no real concept like a 'global' variable in Prolog. If something is known to have some value it appears as a definition in the database.

- **A Definition** in Prolog is a collection of facts & rules that has the same predicate and number of arguments. Each single clause in the definition corresponds to an alternative in the definition. They can be read as representing an implicit 'or'.

```
bird(heron).
bird(eagle).
bird(X):- warm_blooded(X), lays_eggs(X).
```

This defines the relation 'bird' to be any of three things: either a bird is a heron; **or** a bird is an eagle; **or** a bird is something that is warm_blooded and lays_eggs. This is the complete definition - and is ALL that is known about the predicate relation 'bird'.

Note: the semantics of Prolog definitions. Even if you get the syntax correct, then Prolog facts and rules only "mean" what you intend them to mean. Prolog evaluates truth and falsity of queries according to the database entries alone. So if the database contains the fact `bird(rabbit)` then the semantics of this are that a `rabbit` is a `bird`. It is up to you the programmer to ensure that entries are *semantically* correct and meaningful!

2.5 Logic Programming in Prolog

The previous Royal Family example was given in English, but the syntax of Prolog is such that the English meaning is relatively transparently transformed into a Prolog language equivalent. So if we return to this example and consider some specific entries in an example database :

Prolog Code	English Interpretation
`father(philip, charles).`	**philip is the father of charles**
`father(philip, anne).`	**philip is the father of anne**
`child(X, Y) :- father(Y, X).`	**X is the child of Y if Y is the father of X**

This is a very small database regarding the relationships between three specific individuals: `philip`, `charles` and `anne`. There are two facts for the definition of `father` and one rule for the definition of `child`.

The interface with this represetetation is via a **Database Query** model which requires you to interact with the Prolog database by posing queries. In the example above you might ask similar questions to those we posed of Lisp – but here you see the complete program definition.

i) A query meaning "Is philip the father of charles?" (According to the database definition!) :

> `(?)  father(philip, charles).`

and Prolog would take this query term; match it with the database terms and return to you the value **YES**, ie it is true according to the definition of "father".

ii) On the other hand, a query like "Is philip the father of elizabeth?" would fail.

> `(?)  father(philip, elizabeth).`

NO. It must be stressed that this query will fail simply because there is no entry in the database with which it may be successfully **matched**. Prolog knows no more than this!

Similarly the semantics of queries containing logical variables is just as clear.

ii) Who is the father of charles?

> `(?)  father(X, charles).` And Prolog will reply,
> YES, it is **True**, where x = `philip`

iii) Philip is the father of whom?

> `(?)  father(philip, X).` And Prolog will reply,
> YES, it is **True**, where x = `charles`.

However, in our example database there is another entry for the father relation and with 'philip' as the first argument. So, if we ask the Prolog engine for another solution to this query it will come up with one.

> YES, it is **True**, where x = `anne`.
> `No (more) solutions.`

This behaviour is part of a mechanism called **backtracking** by which the Prolog engine may return to some point in the database where there is an alternative (as with the implicit 'or' of multiple clauses in a single definition), and try to match that alternative. Normally, backtracking works invisibly and automatically as part of Prolog's search for a successful matching solution – where it comes to a failure or 'dead-end' and has to retrace its steps to try some other clause, but you can force it to backtrack to give you more than one solution to a query.

Prolog's work becomes slightly more complex when we consider how it deals with rules. The basic mechanism employed by the Prolog theorem proving engine is to match query term with the head of the rule (the left-hand side of the "if") and then treat the tail of the rule (the right-hand side of the "if") as though it was a brand new query. So consider the query :

```
(?)   child(anne, philip).
```

Prolog will reply, YES. First it matches the query with the head of the rule, binding the variables X = anne and Y = philip. But before this match can succeed it must prove the terms after the :- if. So it treats father(Y, X) as the new query ie (?) father(philip, anne). Note that the variable names are switched around in the definition. As this new specific query is a fact then it can succeed. When the 'if' part is proved the whole match succeeds and Prolog can say YES.

So now that we are familiar with a Prolog approach to programming via representation let us look briefly at some simple examples of cognitive science work. What we are aiming to illustrate is how the Prolog implementation of these problems brings representation to the fore as the focal issue.

3 THREE ILLUSTRATIVE COGNITIVE SCIENCE PROJECTS

To show how Prolog can be used as a powerful tool in cognitive science research here is a sketch of three projects that can be easily represented in Prolog. The projects mentioned here are all in the area of research into natural language. The best detailed examination of the language processing problem from the Prolog perspective is Gazdar & Mellish (1989) and a general overview of Prolog in detailed cognitive science projects is Scott & Nicolson, *(forthcoming)*. For the three projects chosen here each is in some way more sophisiticated than the one before.

1) A pattern based conversationalist, ELIZA. This project is a parody of a natural language processor. It has no theory of language and is a useful warning about the anthropomorphism that can often cloud our view of what is a 'human like' process. The

ELIZA program can often seem much more human-like than the next two projects - but a scientific perspective she is infinitely less.

2) Representing grammar and syntax in DCG's. A parser is a grammatical theory about natural language sentence processing. A parser for a limited fragment of English is easily implemented in Prolog, indeed the langauage was originally developed for this purpose. Most modern implementations of Prolog even have a grammar rule interpreter built in.

3) Adding semantics and the world to a parser – CHAT-80. A grammatical theory alone is clearly insufficient as a theory of human language processing because we not only segment up the strings of words given to us but also use them to mean something. One view of meaning is that we should turn the grammatical structure of the parser into a logical structure that could be proven in some view of the world. CHAT-80 has a large database of world knowledge and turns input sentences into logical queries that it can have meaning by being 'run' on this database.

3.1 The ELIZA Therapist

ELIZA is a parody of a Natural Language Understander which was written by Joseph Weizenbaum in 1966. It is a program with a set of messages each of which is triggered by some input by a user. The usual scenario is that she represents a non-directive (Rogerian-type) psychotherapist.   A sample dialogue might go like this :

> USER: Men are all <u>alike</u>.
> ELIZA: **In what way**
> USER: They're always bugging us about <u>something</u> or other.
> ELIZA: **Can you think of a specific example**
> USER: Well, <u>my boyfriend made me come here</u>.
> ELIZA: **Your boyfriend made you come here**
> USER: He says <u>I'm depressed</u> much of the time.
> ELIZA: **I am sorry to hear you are depressed**
> USER: It's true. <u>I am </u>unhappy.
> ...

In fact, ELIZA is making no effort to 'understand' anything but is simply looking for key words or sequences in the user's input to deliver an appropriate conversational reply. We have underlined the probable 'trigger' words or phrases in the user's input. A Prolog model of ELIZA is relatively trivial - all that needs to be represented is a set of "patterns" that are to match with the user's input and with each store a suitably vague reply "pattern".

```
pattern([i, am | X], [why, are, you | X]).

pattern([i | X], [why, do, you, say, you | X]).

pattern (X, [tell, me, more]).
```

In this simple definition we have made heavy use of a Prolog list processing structure which could be called the list guillotine (see Scott & Nicolson, *forthcoming*). Basically, the guillotine cuts the heads of lists leaving a list tail - of undetermined length. So the first list `[i, am | X]` will match with any list beginning with the two words `i, am` binding X to a list which is the remaining words. When this x is bound the x in the second list argument is similarly bound causing the guillotine to cut it on to the three words `why, are, you`. So consider the (first only) solution to the query `(?) pattern([i, am, very, unhappy], R)`. The pattern program will reply YES. `R = [why, are, you, very, unhappy]`. If you provide a large number of such patterns and wrap this in a suitable interface you can have something which looks rather like a conversation with this program. At worst, if there is no pattern that matches your input above it ELIZA can always come back with the third fact given above : `[tell, me, more]`.

You will find that it is very easy to 'fool' any simple model like ELIZA into saying something stupid in response to you. It is actually more of a challenge to see if you can generate a plausible sounding interaction from the system! ELIZA is a poor theory because it doesn't "know" anything about conversation or language or communication of any sort! It is certainly not modelling anything that we could argue was a psychologically realisitic process. Indeed it is only because we are so good at anthropomorphism (projecting human-like values and 'understanding' onto others) that it appears to work at all!

3.2 A DCG Parser

Knowing how words can legally go together is called grammar. English speakers can readily tell you that "the man drove the car" is a legitimate sentence whilst "the car man drove the the" is not. One theory about human natural language processing starts from this perspective and seeks to represent grammatical knowledge as a set of rules in a mechanism called a parser. The specific parser discussed here is called a Definite Clause Grammar or DCG parser. It takes a sequence of words and finds appropriate syntactic categories such as 'noun', 'verb' etc for each word. Then it uses a set of rules (a grammar) to work out if words of these syntactic categories can be combined in the way that they are according to the rules of English. Its basic components therefore are a simple lexicon of nouns and verbs etc. (see below), plus a set of grammar rules. A meta-interpreter can be written which automatically converts the grammar rules shown below into something which more closely resembles the Prolog code discussed above. However the use of this rule syntax (with the rewrite arrow -->) gives unparalleled readability of the program code. So this can be regarded as 'syntactic sugar' above the Prolog level. The grammar rules should be read as 'the left-hand-side of the arrow is a grammatical component that can be rewritten as the more simple components of the right-hand-side'.

3.2.1 Lexicon

`determiner(the).`	`noun(car).`	`verb(drove).`	`adjective(red).`
`determiner(a).`	`noun(dog).`	`verb(sang).`	`adjective(very).`
`determiner(an).`	`noun(man).`	`verb(bit).`	`adjective(big).`
	`noun(house)  .`	`verb(hit)  .`	

3.2.2 Grammar Rules

	RULE		**Example**
`sentence(s(N, VP))`	`-->`	`noun_phrase(N),` `verb_phrase(VP).`	`%   the  man  drove  the` `red car`
`noun_phrase(np(D, N))`	`-->`	`determiner(D)` `noun_phrase2(N)`	`%   the car`
`noun_phrase2(np(A, N))`	`-->`	`adjective(A),` `noun_phrase2(N).`	`%   red car`
`noun_phrase2(np(N))`	`-->`	`noun(N).`	`%   car`
`verb_phrase(vp(V, N))`	`-->`	`verb(V),   noun_phrase(N).`	`%   drove the car`
`verb_phrase(vp(V))`	`-->`	`verb(V).`	`%   drove`

An input string of words is given to this grammar and what is returned is an expression which shows how these words can be assigned roles according to the rules above. This expression is derived from the argument given to the single predicate which makes up the left hand side of each rule. Using the a graphics interface capability (such as that provided by LPA MacProlog™), a parse tree such as that opposite may be derived from this expression.

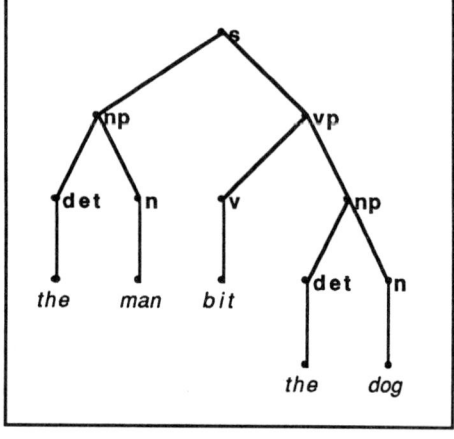

The parse tree provides a good visual idea of the linguistic decomposition of the sentence. The decomposition is driven entirely by the syntactic knowledge of the parser, ie the information in the Prolog rules given above – the syntactic roles each word can take (the lexicon) and the legitimate combinations of words (the grammar). The question a cognitive scientist must ask, as with ELIZA, is how adequate is this mechanism as an explanation of human language. That is, how much of natural human language could be coped with by this mechanism by the addition of further rules, and what aspects of language could not? In addition we must consider how this syntactic process interfaces with all of the other mechanisms involved in communication like semantics, pragmatics, language generation, conversation and so on.

3.3 The CHAT-80 Natural Language Query Database

This system is a classic example of a natural language front-end to a complex database of facts about world geography, (Warren and Pereira, 1982). The system parsed the input question (using grammar rules related to but much more sophisticated than those in the DCG above, but with some semantics built in, to produce a parse tree as shown below. This parse tree was then turned into a Prolog query using lambda calculus templates (!). This 'raw' query was then optimised by rearranging the order of its components to minimise the search time (eg. by ensuring that the component with the smallest search tree was evaluated first ...). It is not at all easy to try to give you a flavour of this much more complex program. A small selection of the facts and templates in the database is given below.

```
city(cairo, egypt, 2373 ).
country(albania, southern_europe, 41, -20, 11, 100, 2, 350,
             tirana, lek ).
verb_form(am, be, pres+fin, 1+sin ).
property(capital, feature & city, X,
                  feature & place & country, Y, capital(Y, X) ).
intrans(flow, feature & river, X, flows(X, Y),
             [slot(prep(through),  feature & place & _,  Y)]  ).
```

This range of facts includes entries which give information about: the city cairo; the country albania; the verb form 'am' which is derived from 'to be'; the properties that capital cities can have; and finally the features of the intransitive verb 'to flow' – related to flowing rivers.

The CHAT parser has extra features built into its parse rules so that rather than just build up a syntactic parse tree as it 'consumes' the words it encounters in the input sentence, it is also building up a 'logical form' which corresponds to a database meaning for the input.

To give a feel for the way that the program works here is a trace for the question :

where is the rhine ?

Parse: 90msec.

whq	*wh-question*
$VAR(1)	*unknown 1*
s	*sentence*
np	*noun phrase*
3+sin	
name(rhine)	
verb(be, active, pres+fin, [], pos)	*verb phrase*
arg	*argument*
pred	*predicate*
pp	*prep phrase*
prep(in)	*prep*
np	*noun phrase*
$VAR(2)	*unknown 2*
np_head	*head of np*
int_det($VAR(1))	*interrogative det*
[]	*no adjs*
place	*noun*

As you can see this parse output from CHAT is rather different than the DCG above in that it has logical information included with the syntactic details. It has identified the "where" form of the question as a type 'whq' and has an unusual way of noting variables $VAR(1) being the equivalent of X. So this is a 'whq' for some unknown such that there is some 'place' where the thing 'name(rhine)' is. Now this is simply interpreted more directly as a Prolog form of rule (the 'semantics' form next); and optimised slightly so that it is in a form more suited to the layout of the geography database and will answer more efficiently, (the 'Planning' form); and finally the anwer is executed and the value of the variable $VAR(1) is printed out for the user.

Semantics: 170msec.
>   answer([$VAR(1)]) :-
>   place($VAR(1))
>   & in(rhine, $VAR(1))

Planning: 160msec.   *NB change in order*
>   answer([$VAR(1)]) :-
>   in(rhine, $VAR(1))
>   & place($VAR(1))

Answer:
>   europe, netherlands, switzerland, western_europe and west_germany

4 CONCLUSION

The main aim of cognitive science research is to implement theories of human cognitive processes. Prolog is a valuable tool in this work as it provides a number of features to make the representation of the knowledge involved in the processes the focal point.

Certainly it has a number of limitations. From a logical point of view it is slightly flawed: it is not a complete First Order Logic; it is restricted to Horn Clauses; and has problems with negation; also it has a number of extra-logical facilities that can seriously worry logicians - primarily related to the procedural interpretation of its programs. From a programming perspective it can be very frustrating: declarative programming can be very difficult for traditional programmers to grasp; backtracking in particular can lead to some very odd behaviour; and it is rather difficult to go against the built-in theorem prover if you want something to work slightly differently from the way Prolog is built to. In a similar vein, the authoring environments for Prolog are still not as sophisticated as the existing Lisp environments and earlier versions can be computationally inefficient and slow.

However, on the plus side it has quite alot going for it. It is an excellent language for representing relationships – using declarative programming. It has a built-in and powerful unification theorem-prover and database matching model that most AI programmers in Lisp would have to build from scratch anyway. Its crucial strength is that while the logic may be incomplete it still bestows great advantages, the first of these being that the specification is the program – hence it is powerful rapid prototyping tool. And finally for the future it is capable of extension to parallel implementations.

In conclusion, Prolog buys cognitive science research : 1) a database programming model where the facts and rules that define relations are in a database which you access via queries. 2) A clear and logical semantics for facts, rules and inference. 3) A powerful theorem-prover which automatically does: pattern matching, unification and backtracking. Because of these features Prolog insists that representation of the problem is the primary problem – this insistence is exactly right for Cognitive Science research.

5 READINGS

5.1 Cognitive Science

1. Stillings, N. A. (et al). **Cognitive Science: an introduction**. MIT Press, 1987.
   One of the few good overview texts on Cognitive Science not just AI.

2. Gardner, H. **The mind's new science**: A history of the cognitive revolution. Basic Books, New York, 1985. *Very interesting and chatty historical perspective.*

3. Boden, M. **Artificial Intelligence & Natural Man**. OU Press, 1977 / 87.
   More of a classic than the Stillings et al, but more on AI than Cognitive Science.

5.2 Prolog

1. Clocksin, W. F. & Mellish, C. S. **Programming in Prolog**. (2nd ed). Springer-Verlag, Berlin Germany, 1986. *1st edition was the first good Prolog text. New edition not much different – they got it right first time.*

2. Sterling, L. & Shapiro, E. **The Art of Prolog**. MIT Press, 1986
   Superb style and clarity. Interesting cognitive science programs.

3. Bratko, I. **Prolog programming for artificial intelligence**. Addison-Wesley, UK, 1986. *Written from computer science viewpoint. Lots of search trees.*

5.3 The Language Projects

1. Gazdar, G. & Mellish, C. **Natural Language Processing in Prolog**. Addison Wesley, 1989.

2. Scott, P. J. & Nicolson, R. I. **Prolog Projects in Cognitive Science**. Lawrence Erlbaum, *(forthcoming)*. *Detailed Prolog projects in a variety of cognitive science areas.*

3. Weizenbaum, J. ELIZA - a computer program for the study of natural language communication between man and machine. **Communications of the ACM**, 9, 36-45, 1966. *The original ELIZA paper - a classic.*

4. Pereira, F. C. N. & Scheiber, S. M. **Prolog and Natural Language Analysis**. CLSI, Stanford, 1987. *An excellent intoduction to DCG's and CHAT. Rather hard to get hold of a rather hard to read – but well worth the effort.*

5. Warren, D. H. D. & Pereira, F. C. N. An efficient easily adaptable system for interpreting natural language queries. **American Journal of Computational Linguistics**. Volume 8, Number 3-4, 1982. *A short summary of the CHAT project.*

Chapter 11

Neurocomputing—an introduction

Robert F. Harrison

1 Introduction

Neural networks have been around for a long time, worms have them and we have them, and they work rather well. The reason, therefore, that this piece is *not* called "Neural Networks" is because our legitimate concern as IT practitioners is not with brain modelling *per se* but with the information processing and computational capabilities of brain-like networks—the neurocomputers of the title. Of course brain modelling is very important and current neural processing systems are generally modelled (to a greater or lesser extent) on the observed dynamical behaviour of the nervous system; after all why re-invent the wheel? However, from the AI viewpoint, why assume that mother nature had a monopoly on optimal information processing systems? The brain evolved in the face of many constraints other than those of simply processing signals. We shall therefore look at neural networks as non-linear dynamical systems which are capable of adjusting themselves according to their environment and experience and which can satisfy certain constraints which make them useful computational tools.

This chapter is intended to give a brief tour around a subject which, although it has only recently come to prominence, is already enormous and is growing daily. In the time and space available I shall not achieve much more than to introduce the terminology and basic ideas and hopefully motivate you, the reader, to look more deeply into this intuitively appealing, highly active branch of modern computing.

1.1 What is a neurocomputer?

Broadly speaking a neurocomputer consists of a large number of very simple processing elements called (artificial) neurons or *units*, all of which operate in parallel. The computational power of the neurocomputer lies in the way in which these units are interconnected and how these interconnections change according to experience. It is only fair to point out that, at present, general purpose neurocomputers do not exist in hardware, instead we use conventional machines to simulate them. However, the race to produce general purpose, self-modifying machines is very much on.

1.1   How does it store information?

In contrast to an ordinary computer which stores information at specific locations in its memory, stored information in a neural network is distributed throughout the network, each additional piece of information causing a small change in every interconnection. Indeed, the term *parallel distributed processing* [11] is one of the many synonyms for neurocomputing. When the network is in operation information is retrieved by providing a cue (rather than a specific address) and interpreting the activity in the network. This method of information storage and retrieval is called a *content-addressable memory* and has some highly desirable properties as we shall see.

The physical act of storage takes place as follows. The system is presented with many examples of the information (typically coded as vectors of numbers, signals *etc*). Each presentation disturbs the dynamics of the machine and, depending on these disturbances, the strengths of the connections between the artificial neurons is adjusted to meet some criterion. The comparison between neural networks and adaptive filters is clear. The latter can be considered as examples of the former. The network's long-term memory is therefore held in the spatially distributed connection strengths and its short-term memory is the time-history of the dynamic units.

1.2   What are its advantages?

Before answering this question let's compare brains and computers. Our brains, when doing arithmetical calculations are grossly inferior to, say, a pocket calculator. On the other hand, when we interpret a scene they are far superior to, say, a network of supercomputers. Computers win hands-down when memorizing arbitrary facts but for putting together facts to invent something new they hardly leave first base.

Of course there is a lesson here—use the technology appropriate to the problem. Brains are good at "soft" information processing *eg* speech and vision, therefore use computers which model the hardware of the brain for these tasks. "Hard" information processing tasks *eg* arithmetic and logic, are best served by present-day computers.

So, what are the desirable properties of neural computers?

1. They require no specific programming. In principal, when neurocomputers are realized in hardware, they will simply be self-modifying machines with an input and an output, which will learn from multiple presentations of patterns from their (data) environment.

2. They can recognize patterns easily and rapidly.

3. They are robust with regard to corrupt or incomplete data. Imagine your friend has to wear glasses. You still recognize him or her. Small changes (or even some large ones) don't affect our ability to recognize patterns, neither should they affect the computer's.

4. They are fault tolerant and resistant to damage. The death of a few thousand brain cells per day does not noticeably impair our memories. In a neurocomputer the occasional dry joint, finite word-length effect or whatever does not impair its abilities too much either.

5. They can respond correctly to previously unseen patterns. That is they are able to generalize to situations which they have not previously experienced.

1.3   Is neurocomputing a practical proposition?

Indeed it is, albeit in simulated form. Among the most famous examples are NETtalk [14]—a neural network which learns to pronounce English text and which drives a voice synthesizer, and Kohonen's "Neural Phonetic Typewriter" [17, pages 11—22] which receives spoken text and learns the phonetic structure of the language so that it can transcribe speech phonetically. Other major applications are in machine vision, medical diagnosis, natural language processing, planning, scheduling and routing, decision support *etc.*

The fact that governments, industry and commerce are preparing to invest hundreds of millions of pounds/dollars/yen in neural networks research, in the near term, may be taken as a measure of the seriousness with which this new technology is being taken.

1.4   Or is it just a flash in the pan?

Certainly not. All Turing machine programmes can be implemented as finite networks of the very simple circuitry of the McCulloch-Pitts neuron [9]. However, these machines do not exploit the full potential of neural networks since they do not learn from experience. Adaptive filters are perhaps closer to the mark.

Neural networks are in an early stage of development, they will not solve all the problems of AI, any more than the rule-based methods of the sixties and seventies did. Suffice it to say that they are simply another weapon in the artificial intelligencer's armoury.

2   Neurodynamics Simplified

We are all endowed with the archetypal neural network, the brain and its associated nervous system. In this section I am going to give a non-biologist's guide to the important features of animal brains insofar as computation goes.

The brain is made up of many components called *neurons* which effectively provide

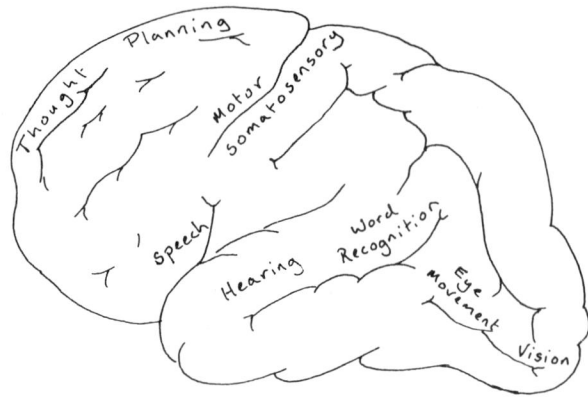

Figure 1: Schematic of the human brain showing regions of functionality

its low-level circuitry. Neurons behave rather like switches and thus have no cognitive function of their own. The basic components group naturally into *modules* which have a highly specific functionality. For example it is known that particular modules in the cerebral cortex serve to discriminate between visual fields of different orientation (differing in steps by angles of 10 deg). Finally, the modules themselves form groups called *regions* having a more general functionality still, for example speech or vision. Overall brain function results, therefore, from the co-operative interaction between the regions. Figure 1 shows a schematic of the human brain with its regions marked. Notice that regions which are in some way related to each other tend to be localized on the brain, *eg* the speech and hearing regions are close to one another. Emulating this localization is an important feature of many neural models.

In order to build a machine which emulates, or to devise an algorithm which simulates, a brain we must first look at the dynamics of the basic processing element or neuron. As mentioned, neurons behave rather like switches, they remain off until they have received sufficient excitation from their inputs. Inputs may be signals from other neurons or from nerve cells which connect to the outside world, such as the cells of the retina. Figure 2 shows a schematic of a neuron and the way in which it connects to other neurons via the *synaptic junction*.

Basically what happens is this. An electrical signal from another cell causes a chemical called a *neurotransmitter* to cross the synaptic gap (typically 20—30 nm). When enough neurotransmitter is gathered in the cell body it causes the neuron to fire, that is to emit a series of pulses. These pulses then pass along the *axon* until they reach the *synaptic nobs* which terminate the axon. The frequency of firing of the neuron is governed by the strength of the signal received and this, in turn, governs the amount of neurotransmitter passed to the next neuron. In addition to this there are different types of neurotransmitter. Broadly speaking they fall into two distinct categories, positive or *excitatory* neurotransmitters and negative or *inhibitory* neurotransmitters. A typical neuron will therefore receive both excitatory and inhibitory inputs of different strengths. These inputs are then "integrated" and an *action potential* is developed

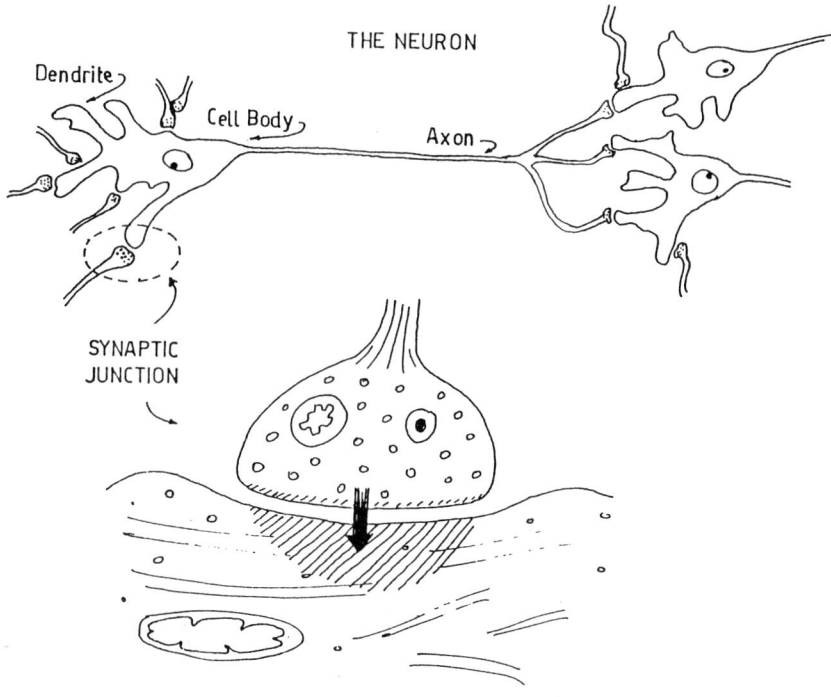

Figure 2: Schematic diagram of a neuron and a synaptic junction

causing the neuron to fire if the aggregate input exceeds some threshold.

The differing amounts of neurotransmitter entering the cell body is governed by the *synaptic strengths* at each junction. There is evidence that these connection strengths can change over time providing a mechanism for learning. The time constants involved in such changes are very long in comparison with those of the action potentials and it is said that the synaptic strengths provide long term memory (LTM) while the activity in the cells provides short term memory (STM).

2.1   The McCulloch-Pitts neuron

Based on observations of the kind made above, McCulloch and Pitts in their seminal paper [9] of 1943 proposed a highly simplified model of the neuron which nevertheless retained many of its important features. They then demonstrated that their model had interesting computational properties, that is, combinations of their *threshold logic units* could compute any logical function (don't forget that this work pre-dates digital circuitry—their neurons are entirely analogue) and proved that any Turing machine programme could be implemented using a finite network of their model neurons. To see the influence that their ideas had on the development of today's computers you need

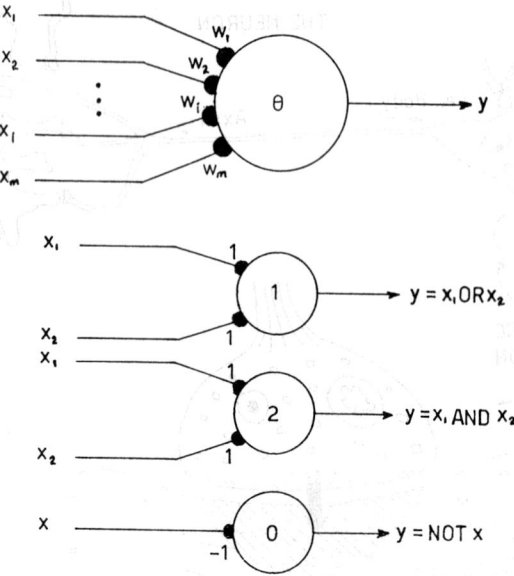

Figure 3: The McCulloch-Pitts neuron and some simple logic gates

only look to John von Neumann's memoires [15]. A diagram of the McCulloch-Pitts neuron is shown in Figure 3.

The underlying assumptions here are that the inputs to, and output from, a unit can take only the values 0 or 1. However, each input is modified or weighted by a "synaptic strength" (connection strength or weight) which may be a positive or negative real number. Clearly positive weights represent excitatory connections whilst negative weights represent inhibitory ones. The principle of operation of the threshold logic unit is this

1. form a weighted sum of the inputs, $\sum_{i=1}^{m} w_i x_i$

2. compare this net input with a threshold, θ

3. if the net input exceeds the threshold output a 1 otherwise output a 0

Figure 3 also shows how simple logic gates may be constructed using threshold logic units with appropriately chosen weights. Of course much more sophisticated circuits can be built by making the outputs of some units the inputs to some others or even feeding back to themselves. Think about how you might construct an XOR circuit using only two McCulloch-Pitts neurons.

As an analogue of the brain a network of McCulloch-Pitts neurons only goes so far. In particular it offers no mechanism for learning and is therefore inherently more suited to the "stored programme" concept which has served mainstream AI so well for thirty years. However, in 1949 Hebb [4] published a learning scheme based on biological evidence which provided a major impetus to the field of neural networks. He argued that if two interconnected neurons were active simultaneously then the connection strength between them should be increased since they both contribute to the same hypothesis. This rule has subsequently been generalized but its form still provides the basic learning mechanism today.

2.2 A general computational model

Although the ideas of McCulloch and Pitts demonstrate the interesting possibilities of neurocomputing, their model constitutes one of the simplest possible. However, as we know from the Nobel Prize winning work of Hodgkin and Huxley [5], a single neuron is a dynamic system governed by a non-linear, partial differential equation. The use of such a model for the purposes of information processing would overcomplicate matters and so we choose a happy medium—a non-linear ordinary differential equation. A structure which covers most of the salient points is given below, followed by a similarly general model for synaptic weight change.

2.2.1 STM dynamics

The short term memory of the ith unit, x_i, in our neural model is governed by the first-order, non-linear ordinary differential equation

$$
\begin{aligned}
\dot{x}_i &= f_i(x_i(t), net_i(t)) \text{ where} \\
net_i(t) &= \sum_j w_{i,j}(t) y_j(t) \text{ and} \\
y_i(t) &= g_i(x_i(t))
\end{aligned}
$$

where j ranges over all the units which connect to the ith one and $w_{i,j}$ denotes the connection strength between units i and j. For computational simplicity these equations are usually discretized to give a difference equation *ie*

$$
x_i(t+1) = x_i(t) + f_i(x_i(t), net_i(t))
$$

The functions $f_i(\bullet, \bullet)$ and $g_i(\bullet)$ are often called the *activation* and *output* functions for unit i, respectively. Figure 4 shows the form of some typical output and activation functions.

2.2.2 LTM dynamics

The long term memory of our model is governed by another first-order, non-linear ordinary differential equation

$$
\dot{w}_{i,j} = \gamma(x_i(t), d_i(t)) \times h(y_j(t), w_{i,j})
$$

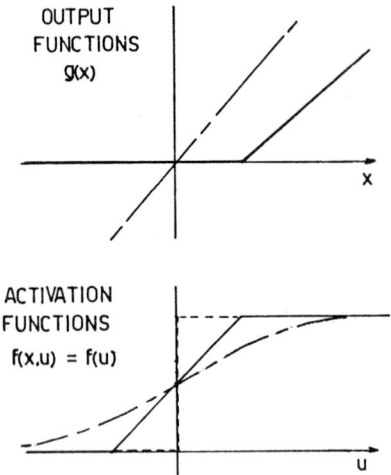

Figure 4: Typical forms of output and activation functions

or in discrete-time form

$$w_{i,j}(t+1) = w_{i,j}(t) + \gamma(x_i(t), d_i(t)) \times h(y_j(t), w_{i,j})$$

where $d_i(t)$ constitutes a kind of *teaching* input to unit i (we will look at the idea of a teacher when we consider supervised learning). In the simplest case with $\gamma(\bullet, \bullet) = g_i(\bullet)$ and $h(\bullet, \bullet)$ a linear function of its first argument, this reduces to the Hebbian rule—the change in the weights, $\Delta w_{i,j}$, is proportional to the product $y_i y_j$. Other important learning rules can be viewed as special cases of the above general form.

In addition to the units governed by the preceding dynamical equations there are two more requirements for an artificial neural system (shown in Figure 5). These are

1. a pattern of connectivity between the units

2. a (data) environment within which the system operates

The pattern of connectivity, or how the units are interconnected, is what governs how the system will behave in response to some input, how and what it can learn and how it encodes that information. Remember, the power of neural networks lies in their connections. If every unit is connected to every other one then there are N^2 interconnections for an N unit network. The relative sizes of some real neural networks are listed below.

worm	$\approx 10^3$ neurons
housefly	$\approx 10^6$ neurons
human	$\approx 10^{10}$ neurons

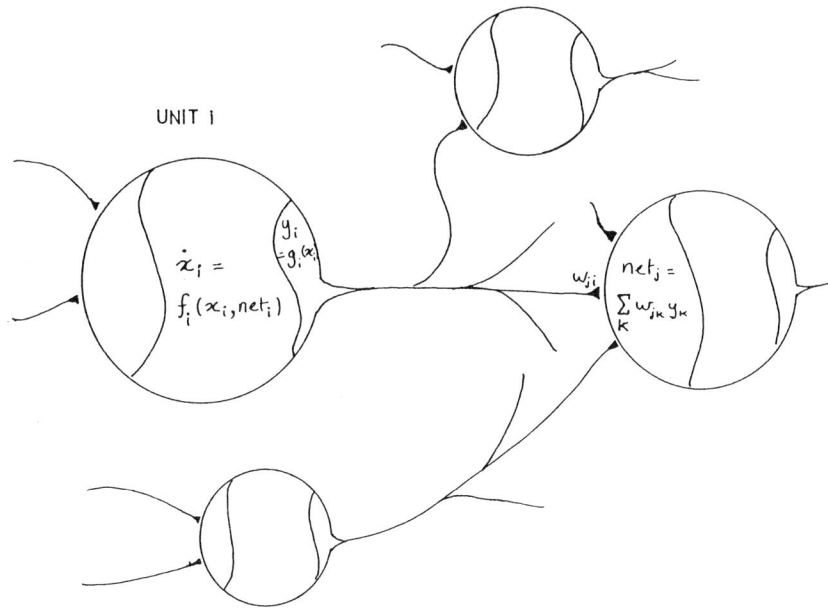

UNIT i

$$\dot{x}_i = f_i(x_i, net_i)$$

$$y_i = g_i(x_i)$$

$$net_j = \sum_k w_{jk} y_k$$

w_{ji}

Figure 5: An artificial neural system

In human beings the network is not completely interconnected, in fact each neuron connects to approximately 10^4 others giving on the order of 10^{14} interconnections. The brain is therefore made up mostly of "wire" . However, it has been estimated that about 10^{12} synapses can affect processing in every cycle, with no von Neumann bottleneck. So, even though the time constants in the brain are long ($\approx$ 5ms) compared with those in digital circuits, it is able to process information very quickly indeed. The current maximum number of units in a neural network is about the same as for the housefly.

The data environment is what is known in the field of pattern recognition as the *pattern space*. This is simply the space (set) of all vectors which are legitimate patterns for the network to operate on. What constitutes a pattern? A pattern is simply a vector of numbers or signals which in some way represents the external environment, the network's activity or its connectivity. For instance an $\nu \times \mu$ bit-map may be *coded* for by a vector of zeros and ones, of length $\nu\mu$. It doesn't matter if you stack the columns of the bit-map on top of each other or the rows side by side. Nor does it matter whether you take the rows or columns consecutively, so long as you code every bit-map in the same way. Continuous-valued quantities like temperature are often better coded as a two element binary vector with the patterns of its elements representing "low" "medium" or "high" . Clearly it is possible to represent anything in this way, however, the question of how "best" to code a particular quantity is still a research issue which we shall not consider further. Instead we shall assume that reality is available to us in coded form and is hence represented by patterns.

3   Models of Learning

In this section we shall look at some models of learning. The two categories we shall concentrate on are those of *associative learning* and of *regularity (or feature) detection*. The former is usually supposed to mean an association between patterns in the data environment and is sometimes referred to as *supervised learning* or learning with a teacher. The latter, on the other hand is often referred to as *unsupervised learning*, that is, letting the network find out something about the data for itself. However, in a broad sense both mechanisms are associative in that the second forms associations between one set of patterns (belonging to the data environment) and another—the pattern of activity in, or state of, the network.

3.1   Associative learning

In associative memory a stimulus or input pattern evokes a particular response or output pattern. Remember Pavlov's poor dogs. They were conditioned to associate the sound of a bell with the expectation of being fed. During the training phase they were repeatedly exposed to the sound of the bell as they were being fed. The association was then tested by ringing the bell alone. The result was that they salivated anyway. They had formed a conditioned response or associative memory.

The fate of these beasts illustrates a basic form of associative learning called reinforcement learning whereby an action or series of actions is associated with a crude reward or penalty. More sophisticated associative memories can be developed by using more sophisticated teaching methods. Instead of the crude reward and penalty scheme you can explain to the errant child *why* it is wrong. Similarly in artificial neural networks. It is usual to divide associative learning into three camps: reinforcement, hetero-association and auto-association. However, reinforcement and auto-association are special cases of hetero-association.

The ideal associative memory is able to learn not one but many arbitrary relationships or *mappings* between many pattern pairs. Because of the emphasis on learning these mappings, rather than the data themselves, the ideal associative memory exhibits both a robustness to poor cues and an ability to generalize to cases which have not been explicitly put to it. The robustness ensues from the geometrical structure of the system. Because the mappings are stored in dynamical structures known as *attractors*, which have distributed *domains of attraction* associated with them, this means that the key pattern does not have to be exact. Rather, it needs to be near enough to drive the state of the network into the correct domain of attraction whence the attractor takes over. Eventually the state settles down so that the network's output corresponds to the correct pattern.

3.1.1   Hetero (or cross) association

Here presentation of one pattern will evoke a different one. For instance, in animals the smell of a rose might invoke its image (or *vice versa*) or some far less obvious association. In general then the objective of hetero-association is to store the *relationship* between two patterns A and B so that, in the future, presentation of pattern A recalls pattern B from memory. During training pattern B is referred to as the *teacher* since it "tells" the network what its response should be. A number of supervised learning rules are derived by minimizing a measure of the difference between the actual response of the network and the desired response leading to equations of the form given earlier.

Clearly, because of the highly general way in which we have defined patterns, we may regard hetero-associators as pattern classifiers, given a suitably general definition of class or category. For instance the problem of medical diagnosis may be regarded as having input patterns comprising symptoms. The desired response would then be the correct classification of a disease.

3.1.2   Auto (or self) association

This mechanism is simply a special case of hetero-association where the stimulus or input pattern is associated with itself, *ie* the system is self-taught. Sometimes this is (incorrectly, I think) referred to as unsupervised learning. The objective here is to use the associative memory as a storage device so that a pattern which sufficiently resembles the stored pattern A, say, will evoke the response A. This is particularly useful for correctly retrieving a stored pattern using a degraded key *eg* in image enhancement.

3.2   Regularity detection

Regularity detection or feature extraction is an example of unsupervised learning. Here the network develops its own internal representation of the salient features or regularities of the data environment without being told which category they belong to. Neurons or sets of neurons respond to "interesting" patterns. Their response could therefore be said to "mean" something. Since there is no teacher involved, what is learnt is determined solely by the network's architecture and dynamics. Regularity discovery is usually accomplished by competitive learning, that is, the neurons or groups of neurons which respond most vigourously to a particular feature suppress the activity of the other neurons and "win" the right to update their connection strengths. This makes the active neurons more sensitive to other similar patterns and leaves the remaining neurons to code dissimilar patterns.

This mechanism may still be considered as associative learning but now features of the external environment are associated with patterns of activity inside the network. Sometimes the features which are discovered are easily interpreted, as is the case for Kohonen's "Neural Phonetic Typewriter" where short term spectra of continuous speech yield clusters of activity which correspond to the individual phonemes of the language. However, this may not always be true and the problem of calibration may prove difficult.

3.3   The stability *versus* plasticity tradeoff

In any artificial learning system there exists a basic dilemma. If the system is to adapt to its environment for ever how can we prevent knowledge which has already been learnt being overwritten by new knowledge or by spurious information? Obviously we don't wish to prevent our system from learning new things which is the case in many current neural networks. These networks go through a training phase where they learn about a particular environment. In operation, however, learning is suppressed so that the system does not continue to refine its knowledge. This is clearly not acceptable as a model of human learning since it implicitly assumes a stationary and/or finite environment.

The answer to this dilemma lies in the use of feedback mechanisms for *attentional priming*. Grossberg, in his Adaptive Resonance Theory (ART) [17, pages 77—88] has developed models for a self-regulating control structure which only permits learning when patterns are, in some sense, close enough to those already stored. Patterns which appear to the network to be novel are then given their own categories and refined only if new supporting information becomes available.

4   Architectures

It is impossible in an article of this length to discuss in any detail even the best known neural network architectures and their associated learning rules, let alone their many variants. Instead I have tried to give a suitable list of references and material for further reading. In particular the reader is referred to [17] and [8] for an overview. A list of the main architectures follows, classified according to the model of learning which best describes them.

Supervised learning systems

The major associative networks are:

- The Perceptron [10]

- The Multi-Layered Perceptron (MLP) or Back Propagation Network [12]

- The Adaline (Adaptive Linear Element) [16]

- The Madaline (Many Adalines) [17, 25—39]

- The Hopfield Net [6]

- The Boltzmann Machine [1]

Unsupervised learning systems

The major neural networks for unsupervised learning are:

- The Adaptive Resonance Theory (ART) family of architectures [17, 77—88]

- Self-Organizing Feature Maps [7]

- The competitive learning net [13]

Another well known architecture, which can be used with or without supervision, is the class known as the Cognitron or the larger-scale Neocognitron [3].

For reasons of space we will now concentrate only on the group known as the *feed-forward* networks (so called because they do not use feedback or lateral coupling in their operational phase). In the above list of supervised learning systems the first four items can all be considered as variants of the common structure shown in Figure 6. In the diagram the first (bottom) layer of units simply acts to distribute the inputs to the next layer, *ie* the units have an identity transfer function. The top layer of units is known as the output layer and the intervening layers are called *hidden* layers since they do not communicate directly with the environment.

To obtain the four feed-forward networks we may adjust the following parameters

- the number of layers

- the number of units per layer

- the form of the STM equations

- the form of the output function

- the form of the LTM equations

For instance, the Perceptron consists of a single McCulloch-Pitts neuron with many inputs and one output. Its LTM is governed by the celebrated *Perceptron convergence procedure* which says "move the weight vector towards the current pattern vector if misclassification occurs, otherwise move on to the next pattern" . The Perceptron acts as a pattern classifier and is able to distinguish between classes which are *linearly separable*, that is, they can be separated by a hyperplane in the pattern space.

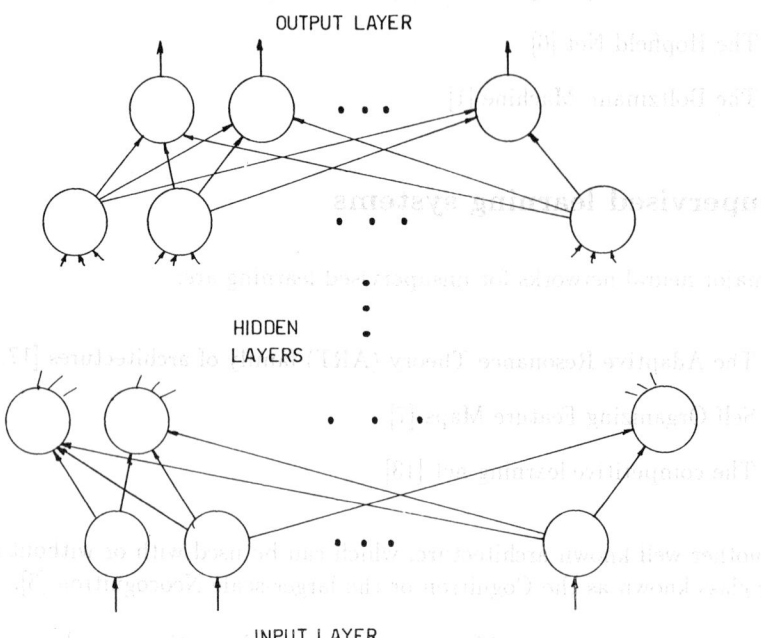

OUTPUT LAYER

HIDDEN
LAYERS

INPUT LAYER

Figure 6: General feed-forward structure

The Adaline has an identical structure to the Perceptron but has a linear relationship between the net input and the output. The learning rule employed is the so-called *Widrow-Hoff* [16] or least mean-square (LMS) rule which has proved so successful in adaptive signal processing applications. The LMS procedure compares the Adaline's response to a particular pattern with the desired response and adjusts the weight vector in order to minimize their mean-square difference. Thresholding in the Adaline takes place outside of the learning loop. Once again, the Adaline is only able to distinguish between linearly separable classes.

The restriction to linearly separable classes and some other problems regarding the complexity of network required to compute certain straightforward functions nearly killed neural network research in the early sixties. Computer scientists and AI practitioners thought that since these simple systems had problems, neural networks had little future. It took twenty years to recover from that attitude. It can be shown that in order to distinguish between pattern classes which have arbitrary boundaries (non-linear, possibly closed) it is necessary to have layers of non-linear, hidden units. It is just such a structure that the so-called Multi-Layered Perceptron and Madaline provide. However, there is a difficulty. The LTM rules are not so straightforward and have only recently been satisfactorily formulated. In the MLP the objective is still to adjust the weights to minimize the mean-square difference between the desired and actual responses. However, in the hidden layers we do not know what the desired response might be. The back-propagation rule [12] solves this *credit assignment* problem. Credit assignment in the Madaline is similarly complicated but has also been solved [17, 25—39].

The question of how many hidden layers are needed is still open. A well known result of the Russian mathematician Kolmogorov can be interpreted as saying: any arbitrary mapping between two domains can be represented by a single layer of units *with a particular functional form*. However, the functional form of the units will not in general have continuous derivatives and so does not meet the requirements of the back-propagation rule which has smooth functions. In practice, it is often found that multiple layers of hidden units can give improved results but the precise number must still be the result of trial and error.

5 Epilogue

A short tour indeed! And probably notable as much for its omissions as for anything else. As I have already mentioned, real neurocomputers are not yet with us. However, the hardware problems associated with producing self-modifying, general purpose chips are the subject of much research effort. I have deliberately shied away from these aspects since they are implementational difficulties rather than IT topics as such. Neural networks can be successfully and easily simulated on conventional machines (the bigger and faster, the better) and can be helped by using one of the many neural co-processors (heavy duty number crunchers) which are available.

Similarly, I have avoided discussion of applications. There is no sinister reason behind this, simply lack of space. Instead I have suggested some further reading, selected from a very small portion of the literature. I hope that by following up some of these suggestions you might become interested and perhaps productive in this new and exciting field.

References

[1] Ackley, D, Hinton, G and Sejnowski, T (1985) A learning algorithm for Boltzmann machines *Cognitive Science* **9**

[2] Arbib, M (1987) *Brains, Machines and Mathematics* Springer-Verlag

[3] Fukushima, K (1988) Neocognitron: A hierarchical neural network capable of visual pattern recognition *Neural Networks* **1**

[4] Hebb, D (1949) *The Organization of Behaviour* Wiley

[5] Hodgkin, A and Huxley, A (1952) A quantitative description of membrane current and its application to conduction and excitation in nerves *Jnl of Physiology* **117**

[6] Hopfield, J (1982) Neural networks and physical systems with emergent collective computational abilities *Proceedings of the National Academy of Sciences USA* **79**

[7] Kohonen, T (1989) *Self-Organization and Associative Memory* Springer-Verlag

[8] Lippmann, R (1987) An introduction to computing with neural nets *IEEE ASSP Magazine* **4**

[9] McCulloch, W and Pitts, W (1943) A logical calculus of the ideas immanent in nervous activity *Bulletin of Mathematical Biophysics* **9**

[10] Rosenblatt, F (1962) *Principles of Neurodynamics* Spartan Books

[11] Rumelhart, D, McClelland, J and the PDP Research Group (1986) *Parallel Distributed Processing* (three vols) MIT Press

[12] Rumelhart, D, Hinton, G and Williams, R (1986) Learning representations by back-propagating errors *Nature* **323**

[13] Rumelhart, D and Zipser, D (1985) Feature discovery by competitive learning *Cognitive Science* **9**

[14] Sejnowski, T and Rosenberg C (1987) Parallel networks that learn to pronounce English text *Complex Systems* **1**

[15] von Neumann, J (1958) *The Computer and the Brain* Yale University Press

[16] Widrow, B and Hoff, M (1960) Adaptive switching circuits *IRE WESCON Convention Record*

[17] Special Edition (1988) *IEEE Computer Magazine* **21**(3)

Further Reading

Aleksander, I (1989) *Neural Computing Architectures* MIT Press

Anderson, D (1988) *Neural Information Processing Systems* American Institute of Physics

Anderson, J and Rosenfeld, E (1988) *Neurocomputing—Foundations of Research* MIT Press

Cainello, E and Musso, G (1984) *Cybernetic Systems: Recognition, Learning, Self-Organization* Wiley

Denker, J (1986) *Neural Networks for Computing* American Institute of Physics

Deutsch, S (1967) *Models of the Nervous System* Wiley

Grossberg, S (1982) *Studies of Mind and Brain* Reidel

Grossberg, S (1988) *Neural Networks and Natural Intelligence* MIT Press

Hinton, G and Anderson, J (1988) *Parallel Models of Associative Memory* Lawrence Erlbaum Associates

McCulloch, W (1965) *Embodiments of Mind* MIT Press

Mead, C (1988) *Analog VLSI and Neural Systems* Addison-Wesley

Minsky, M and Papert, S (1988) *Perceptrons* MIT Press

Sampson, J (1984) *Biological Information Processing* Wiley

Wasserman, P (1989) *Neural Computing—Theory and Practice* Chapman Hall

Wasserman, P and Oetzel, R (1989) *Neural Source* Van Nostrand Reinhold

Wiener, N (1948) *Cybernetics* MIT Press

Yovits, M and Cameron, S (1960) *Self-Organizing Systems* Pergamon

Special Edition (1987) *Applied Optics* **26**(23)

Special Edition (1988) *Trans IEEE Systems, Man and Cybernetics* **13**(5)

Neural network journals

Complex Systems (1987—)

International Journal of Neural Networks (1989—)

Neural Networks (1988—)

Network (1989—)

Chapter 12

Speech recognition—possibilities and problems

P. D. Green

Introduction

This is meant to be a selective overview of research into
Automatic Speech Recognition (ASR).   It should be treated
as lecture notes rather than a polished review.   I'll
concentrate on the 'front-end'; that is the processing that
converts continuous, parametric representations of speech
events, such as frequency spectra, into discrete hypotheses
about what speech units, such as words or phones, were
present in the utterance.   There will be much less on
'back-end' lexical, syntactic and semantic processing.
Similarly, there will be no attempt to cover other aspects
of speech technology, eg coding and synthesis.   For a more
thorough text-book treatment, the reader is referred to
Holmes [1].   The place to start looking for up-to-date
papers is in the proceedings of the IEEE International
conference on Acoustics, Speech and Signal Processing
(ICASSP).   The format of this chapter is:

1. Promise and Problems of Automatic Speech
    Recognition (ASR).

2. Signal Processing for ASR.

3. Statistical Approaches to ASR.

   3a.   Dynamic Time Warping.
   3b.   Hidden Markov Modelling.
   3c.   State of the (Statistical) Art.

4. Connectionist ASR.

5. Knowledge-based Approaches to ASR.

6. Short Bibliography.

1. PROMISE AND PROBLEMS OF ASR

1.1 Promise

Interest in ASR dates back to the early 1950s. It is both a commercially attractive possibility and a scientifically interesting proposition.

There are many potential ASR application areas, for instance

> 'Hands/Eyes free' tasks
> Voice Telephone Dialling
> Automatic Dictation
> Spoken Access to Databases
> Voice Programming
> Voice Messaging
> ...

As a scientific challenge, ASR is of interest to people working in

> Signal Processing
> Pattern Analysis
> Communication Engineering
> Artificial Intelligence
> Perceptual Psychology
> Phonetics
> Linguistics
> ...

In UK academia, for instance, there are ASR research groups working in departments of Phonetics, Linguistics, Electrical Engineering, Computer Science and Applied Psychology. ASR has often been seen as a focus for interdisciplinary research, notably in the USA DARPA program, the 5th Generation programme, ESPRIT and Alvey.

ASR is **outwardly easy**: the robust performance of the human system offers a seductive existence proof.

For these reasons, ASR has been **widely researched.** However, although ASR devices have been on the market since the mid-1970s, there has been **limited commercial success.** The market for Speech Technology products was small until quite recently; the US Speech Technology market passed the $1 billion turnover mark in 1989, and the European market is said to be about 10% of this. In many cases, promising laboratory performance has not survived in real-world applications.

In **scientific terms**, there have been significant advances in each of the disciplines mentioned above, but there is no **metatheory** to link them together. For instance, there is no generally accepted methodology for making use of phonetic knowledge to improve recogniser performance.

Why has progress been so slow?

1.2 Problems

* The **apparent effortlessness** of human speech perception belies the subtlety and complexity of speech processing.

* Speech has **evolved for interpretation by a clever, flexible and powerful device.** This means that speakers can afford to be careless in their enunciation, to an extent which varies with the situation.

* **Variability, within and across speakers.** There are a host of factors effecting what is actually produced, for instance

> Dimensions of the vocal tract
> Speaker Condition (angry, tired, breathless, head-cold ..)
> Speaking Rate
> Acoustic Environment
> Dialect
> Listener (spouse, foreigner, dog..)
> ...

* **Speech is a flow rather than a succession of discrete events.** The vocal apparatus is a physical system with inertia. One sound often 'melts into' the next, with no hard boundary. Thus there is generally little evidence in the speech waveform for word boundaries. Pronunciation is markedly effected by phonetic context **(co-articulation)**, for instance

> 'did you' --> 'dija'
> 'where are you --> 'where-r-are you'

* There are often severe **Human Computer Interface problems in engineering ASR into a habitable system.** People's reaction to being mis-heard is to speak loudly, or more slowly. This will make matters worse for a dumb machine. It may not be easy to provide the feedback necessary for the user to spot errors, much less to correct them. We may have to learn new speaking styles to interact with ASR devices.

* **ASR is often funded by short-term, application driven projects rather than as fundamental research.** A solution always appears to be just over the horizon. ASR workers frequently have to promise more than they can realistically deliver in order to win contracts.

2. SIGNAL PROCESSING FOR ASR

*   Information in Speech is coded in terms of **time/frequency/energy events.**

*   Techniques used to reveal such events include:

> Filter Banks (Analogue and Digital)
> Fast Fourier Transforms
> Linear Predictive Coding
> Cepstral Analysis
> ...

*   Such techniques convert the **speech waveform** into a **parametric representation:** a sequence of **feature vectors,** typically one vector every 5 or 10 ms.

*   The traditional means of making time/frequency/energy data visible is the **Spectrogram** (see figure 1).

> x=time
> y=frequency (linear scale)
> darkness=energy.

Phoneticians have studied spectrograms intensively.   Much expert speech knowledge is inextricably tied up with this representation.   It is possible to 'read' spectrograms (see later).

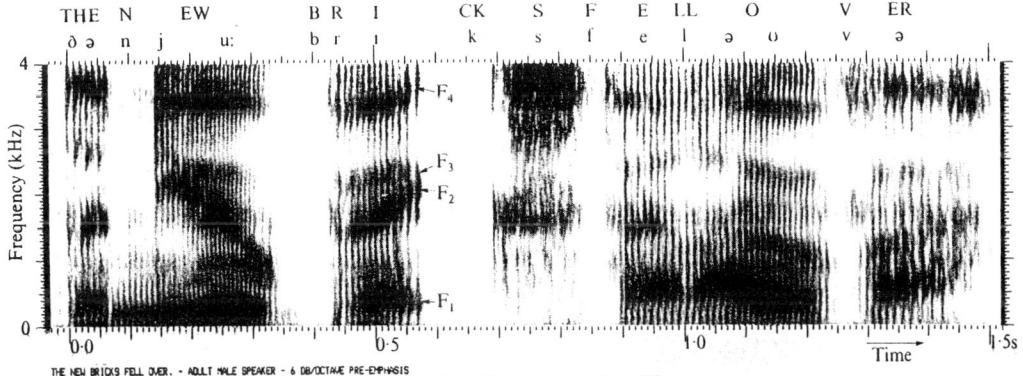

Fig. 1: **Wide-band spectrogram of an utterance 'The new bricks fell over', by an adult male speaker.   Reprinted from Holmes [1], with the author's permission.**

*   **Auditory modelling** provides a more principled alternative to conventional signal processing.   Here the idea is to produce a computational analogue of processing in the peripheral auditory system (see the next chapter).

3. STATISTICAL APPROACHES TO ASR

In direct, statistical ASR the idea is to compare the parametric representation of a new utterance with stored data about similar representations for known utterances. The simplest technique involves storing the parameter values themselves:

3.1 Dynamic Time Warping (DTW)

* This is the **basis for most recognisers currently on the market.**

* Typically, DTW recognisers are used to **classify a small vocabulary of isolated words or short phrases.**

* An initial **training phase** builds a library of stored parametric patterns for each word (**templates**).

* In **Recognition** a new word (the **'pattern'**) is compared with each template. The closest match is selected.

* Individual feature vectors (eg spectral slices) can be compared by Euclidean distance or City Block distance.

* The problem is that some sounds can be **shortened or lengthened** at will. It is therefore necessary to find the best way of stretching or squeezing the pattern to match the template, producing a **non-linear time alignment** (see figure 2).

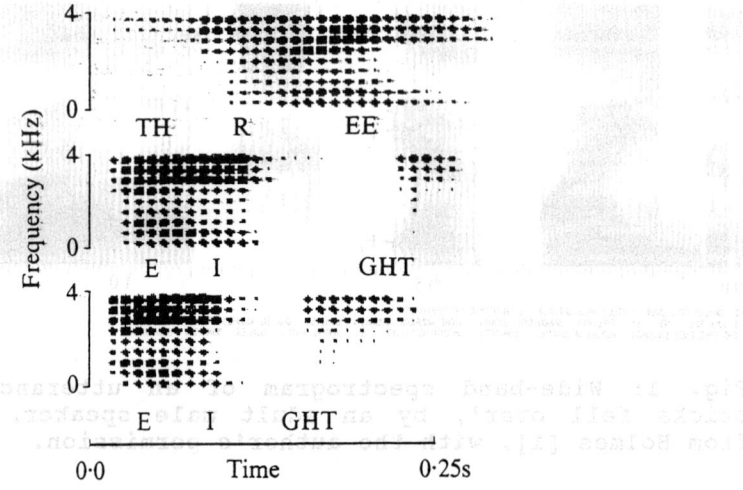

Fig 2. **Spectrogram displays of a 9-channel filter-bank analysis of one example of the word 'three' and two examples of 'eight'. It can be seen that the two eights are generally similar, except that the lower one has a much shorter gap for the [t] and a longer burst. Reprinted from Holmes [1], with the author's permission.**

* DTW finds the best time alignment, and associated score, using the **Dynamic Programming Principle** to keep computation demands down. This simply says that you only need to remember the best way of reaching a node in a search space that you have so far found (see figure 3).

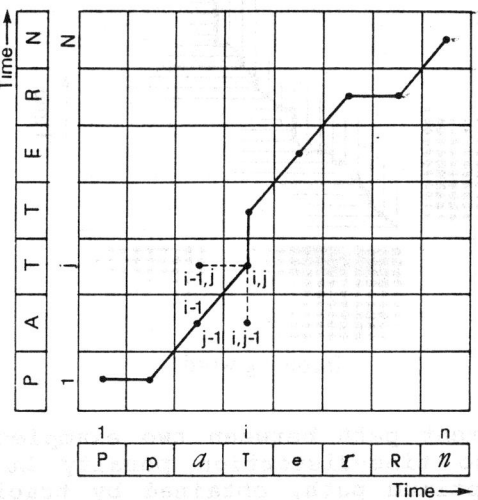

Fig 3. Illustration of a time-alignment path between two words that differ in time scale. Any point i,j can have three predecessors as shown. Reprinted from Holmes [1], with the author's permission.

* The basic DTW equation, for symmetrical time distortion routes, is

$$D(i,j) = min [D(i-1,j), D(i-1,j-1), D(i,j-1)] + d(i,j)$$

Where
     i is the frame in the input,
     j is the frame in the output,
     d(i,j) is the comparison cost of the feature vectors,
     D(i,j) is the cumulative score of the least costly path from
     (1,1) to (i,j),

This equation can be applied recursively to fill the cells in the time-time plane with their best-route cost.

* DTW is a well-investigated technique, and there are many variations, for instance

   Asymmetric routes (eg always take 1 frame from input, 0,1 or 2 from output).

   Time-scale **distortion penalties.**

   Pruning **(Beam Search):** see figure 4.

   Extension to **connected words:** see figure 5.

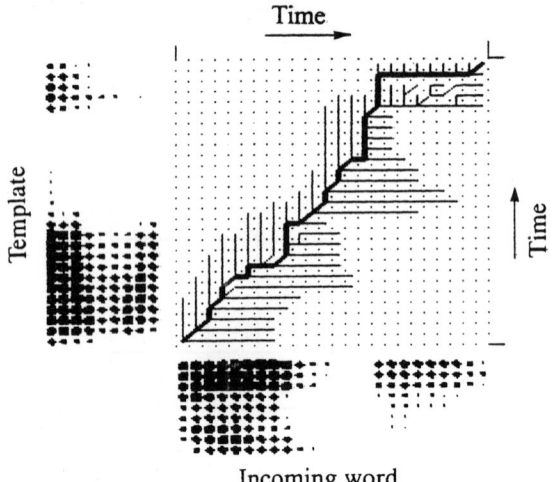

Fig 4. DP alignment path between two examples of the word 'eight', with no time-distortion penalty but with score pruning. The optimum path, obtained by tracing back from the top right-hand corner, is shown by the thick line. Reprinted from Holmes [1], with the author's permission.

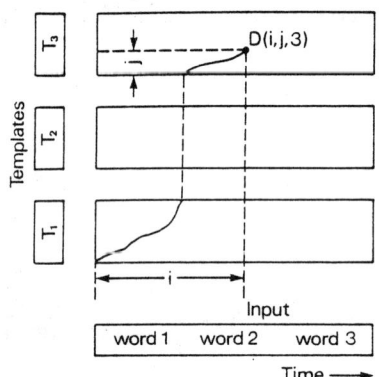

Fig. 5. Diagram indicating the best-matching path from the beginning of an utterance to the jth frame of template T_3 and the ith frame of the input. In the example shown, the point i is in the middle of the second word of the input, so the best path includes one complete template (T_1) and a part of T_3. The cumulative distance at this point is denoted by $D(i,j,3)$ or, in general, $D(i,j,k)$ for the kth template. Reprinted from Holmes [1], with the author's permission.

* DTW-based recognisers exhibit problems with

Speaker variability: they are usually speaker-dependant.

Speaking conditions.

Phonetically similar words.

Endpoint Detection.

Between-word co-articulation (for the Connected Word extension).

In general, DTW can be said to be **too simple a model of variability.**

3.2 Hidden Markov Models (HMMs)

* DTW (with time scale distortion penalties) assumes that **the same amount of variation is permitted everywhere.** In speech, some segments are more variable than others. HMMs can accommodate this.

* HMM-based recognisers are just coming on to the market. The theory is well-developed.

* The assumption is that **the sequence of observed feature vectors is the output from a statistical process (the model), whose parameters can be estimated.**

* In **HMM-based isolated word recognition**, the idea is to construct one model for each word in the vocabulary. The problem is to find **that model which is most likely to produce the sequence of observations.**

* In **HMM-based Connected Word Recognition** the problem is to find the **most likely sequence of models** to produce the observations.

3.2.1 Form of the Model (see figure 6)

* The model has a number of **states:** at any time it is in one state. The number of states is pre-chosen and is typically small (3, 5 or 7).

* The model emits a **symbol** and then moves to another state (possibly the same one). Usually most of the state transitions have probability 0.

* The chance of emitting each symbol and the chance of moving to each possible next state depends only on the current state **(the Markovian assumption).**

* What you **observe** is the symbols, not the underlying states (Hence **Hidden** Markov Model).

* **Each observed symbol is associated with a feature vector** (the space of possible feature vectors is discretised by **vector quantisation**).

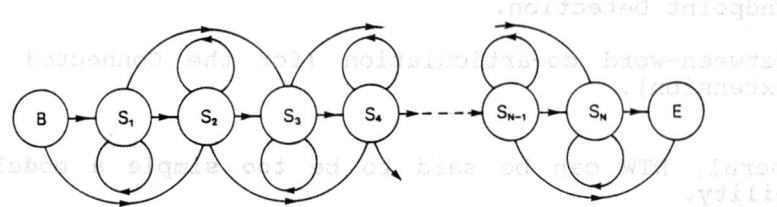

Fig 6. Permitted state transitions for a simple word model. Reprinted from Holmes [1], with the author's permission.

3.2.2 Thus an HMM is characterised by

A Set of States **{S1 S2 ..SN}**

A Set of possible output symbols **{F1 F2 .. FM}**

A Matrix specifying the probability of each symbol being emitted when the model is in each state $B = b_{ij} = p(Fj|Si)$.

A Matrix of transition probabilities between states, $A = a_{ij}$.

3.2.3 HMM Algorithms

* The Markovian assumption allows probability calculations in HMMs to be expressed recursively: for instance, if $p^+(m,j)$ is the probability of the model being in state j after having produced the first m observed feature vectors, then

$$p^+(m,j) = \{\text{Sum for i=1 to S } p^+(m-1,i) \cdot a_{ij}\} * b_{jFm}$$

,where Fm is the mth feature vector.

This relationship can be used to calculate the probability that a given sequence of observations could have been produced by a given model. In *recognition*, the best-fitting model is chosen.

* The above equation is an example of a **forward probability calculation**: it defines p(m,j) given the p(m-1,i). It is also possible to derive **backward probabilities**; we can express the probability of emitting the remaining observed vectors p⁻(m,i), given that the ith state is occupied in frame m:

$$p^-(m,i) = \{Sum \text{ for } j=1 \text{ to } S \text{ } p^-(m-1,j) \cdot a_{ij} \cdot b_{jFm+1}$$

* **Training** uses a **re-estimation** procedure: given an observed sequence of observations that the model should generate, change the parameters (**A,B**) to increase the probability of the observations. This process (**the Baum-Welch or Forward-Backward Algorithm**) is used iteratively. It is not guaranteed to give **optimum** parameter values, but it can be shown to produce **improved** values with each iteration.

* The **Viterbi Algorithm** is an alternative formulation for recognition and training. Rather than finding the overall probability of the observations, given the model (which is the sum of contributions from a large number of alternative state sequences), it finds the **most likely path** through the HMM that could have produced the observations, and the probability of that path. Viterbi processing is based on the dynamic programming principle: the summation above is replaced by an **argmax**. It is faster than the full computation: when expressed in logs, it involves only summations. The price is that the probability of the most likely path is of course only an **indication** of the total probability of the observations given the model. In practice, however, the contributions from other paths in a well-trained model are small. There is a corresponding training algorithm.

The most common technique is to use Baum-Welch in training, Viterbi in recognition.

3.2.4 Training Databases

HMMs require a good deal of training data: typically hundreds of examples of each class. Collecting and labelling the **speech corpora** required is a considerable task, especially if phonetic annotation is required. The **TIMIT** database (US) is the first large-scale example.

3.2.5 HMM Developments

HMM-based recognition is developing rapidly: here are some variations on the basic scheme:

* **Continuous HMMs**, in which the discrete set of possible output symbols is replaced by multi-variate continuous probability distributions for parameter values in each state.

* Modelling state duration probabilities. The time an HMM spends in a particular state s will be inversely proportional to the probability of the self-transition from s to s. This is a simplistic view of speech behaviour. It is possible to include explicit modelling of state durations in the HMM formalism.

* Extension to Connected Words.

* Sub-word HMMs, in which HMMs are developed for syllables, demi-syllables or phones.

3.2.6 Problems with HMMs

* The need for large speech databases.

* The need for considerable computing power (especially in training).

* The limitations of viewing speech events as a **sequence of quasi-stationary states.** Transitions are difficult to express directly.

3.2 State of the Art in Statistical ASR

Many recognition devices are on the market. They vary considerably in price, from a few hundred pounds to a few tens of thousands. By and large you get what you pay for.

The typical (claimed) performance of a DTW device might be:

95% recognition of small, well chosen vocabulary of isolated words or short phrases, in real time, after training for a single speaker.

Some machines allow vocabularies of several hundred words *(but is this what the user wants?: if the machine makes an error, have you used a word it doesn't know about?)*.

HMM-based systems have produced impressive laboratory results, and this technology is starting to appear in the market-place.

Examples:

SPHINX (Kai-Fu Lee, Carnegie-Mellon Univ:[2]): HMMs for phones and function words. Better than 95% speaker-independent word-recognition in sentences from a 1000-word fleet management domain, in a few times real time (80% without the grammar).

Integrated Speech Technology Demonstrator (CSTR Edinburgh, Marconi [3]): Cytopathology report domain. Phone-based HMMs. Training independent of application. Speaker-dependant.

IBM TANGORA [4]: Automatic Office Dictation. Word-based HMMs. Pause between words. 20,000+ word vocabulary. Speaker-dependant- 20 minutes of training speech required. Language model prunes word sequences using word trigram statistics. Runs on a beefed-up PC. Around 95% correct recognition. Said to be difficult to use.

ASR technology is now proving useful in carefully-chosen domains. Performance is still far short of human standards. There are several **'dimensions of performance'**:

    isolated words   --> read speech   -->
    conversational speech
    one speaker   --> several speakers --> all speakers
    one dialect   --> several dialects --> all dialects
    small vocabulary --> large vocabulary --> unlimited
    vocabulary
    off-line response --> real time response

The further you go in one dimension, the more you must compensate in other dimensions.

Statistical Techniques have the advantages of internal consistency and trainability, but don't attempt to **understand or reason about** the speech domain. Hence, they cannot easily handle *novel* speech problems.

4. CONNECTIONIST ASR.

ASR is a popular application area for neural nets. They can perform discriminations which are the product of a diverse, tangled set of low-level constraints, without explicit modelling of these constraints. Whereas HMM training **optimises the fit of independent models to training data,** neural net training **optimises the discrimination between classes.** For a recent review of neural nets in speech recognition, see Lippmann [5]

There have been several studies based on treating the whole of the speech data for isolated words as a static pattern. Peeling and Moore (RSRE), for instance, achieved 98% recognition of spoken digits over several speakers, using **Multi Layer Perceptrons** with a single hidden layer [6].

Kohonen and his co-workers [7] have pioneered **unsupervised learning** in nets which adapt themselves to model the topology of the training data. They have demonstrated clustering which corresponds to phonetic distinctions.

There is considerable interest in neural nets which can deal with the time-flow of speech, rather than classifying static patterns. In **Time Delay Neural Networks** [8], for instance, a time-window is swept across the utterance to provide input to a first hidden layer of units. A window across these units makes connection with a smaller number of units in a second hidden layer, which connects to output units representing the sounds to be identified. TDNNs have been used to perform reliable distinctions between, for instance, the plosives b,d and g, irrespective of time.

5. KNOWLEDGE-BASED APPROACHES TO ASR.

It is curious that while Vision and Natural Language are accepted as major topics for (Symbolic) Artificial Intelligence, the Speech and AI communities have an uneasy relationship: after an early trial marriage which failed, a later attempt at reconciliation also failed, and the fields seem as far apart as ever.

5.1 The US ARPA Speech Understanding projects (1971-76) [9]:

Aimed to recognise continuous speech from a 1000-word vocabulary, with constrained syntax and semantics.

HEARSAY (CMU): pioneered the **blackboard** model for problem-solving by co-operation between multiple, diverse Knowledge Sources (acoustic-phonetics, syntax, semantics ..).

Other ARPA-SUS systems were HARPY (CMU) and HWIM (BBN).

There were successful demonstrations, but no promise of products.

The ARPA-SUS approach was generally too 'top-heavy': poor modelling of acoustic-phonetics could not be compensated for by syntax and semantics.

5.2 'Phonetic Expert Systems' (1980-86)

There have been a number of attempts to build **'phonetic expert systems'** [eg 10, 11]. Much of the motivation for these systems came from the demonstration by Zue [12] that Spectrograms can be 'read' with high accuracy, and that this skill can be taught. Perhaps spectrogram-reading might provide a means by which experts can articulate their knowledge, in preparation for its conversion into rules.

Although there have been promising reports, no knowledge-based system has approached the recognition accuracy of the statistical approach. Why?

5.3 Problems with Knowledge-based ASR

* The knowledge-bases have often contained many arbitrary parameter values that cannot be modified automatically (ie **no training algorithm**).

* Because of the combinatorial explosion, it may not be possible to preserve **admissibility**: the guarantee that the 'best' solution will be returned.

* Acoustic-phonetic knowledge does not map easily into conventional knowledge representation formalisms.

* The problem of **inadequate representations**: how to bridge the gap between the **continuous parameter values** produced by signal processing and **discrete phonetic judgments?** Asking experts to write rules which refer to thresholds on parameter values doesn't work. Phoneticians use highly-developed skills of visual perception to organise spectrograms into meaningful **objects**: their interpretation is based on these objects, not the original numbers.

* This argument suggests an intermediate representation in the acoustic-phonetic transformation. We have called this the **'Speech Sketch'**, after Marr. Work on the Speech Sketch to 1989 is reported in [13]. For a principled acoustic-phonetics, we should attempt to model the transformations that take place in the auditory system, to build an **Auditory Speech Sketch**. This is the theme of the next chapter.

* The problem of how to **combine knowledge and statistics** is the subject of an IED-funded project at Sheffield and Leeds. Called **SYLK**, this aims to reason about syllable structures, using tests based on explicit knowledge but trained statistically, with HMMs being used to provide an initial syllable structure lattice.

6. BIBLIOGRAPHY

1 Holmes, J.N, 1988: 'Speech Synthesis and Recognition', Van Nostrand Reinhold.

2 Lee, KF et al, 1989: 'The Sphinx Speech Recognition System', proc ICASSP-89, Volume 1, p445.

3 McInnes, FR et al, 1989, 'Enhancement and Optimisation of a Speech Recognition Front-End based on Hidden Markov Models', proc EUROSPEECH 89, vol 2, p461.

4 Averbuch, A, Jelinek, F et al, 1986: 'An IBM-PC based large-vocabulary isolated-utterance speech recogniser', proc ICASSP-86, p53.

5 Lippmann, RP, 1989: 'Review of Neural Networks for Speech Recognition', Neural Computation 1,1, p38.

6 Peeling, SM and Moore, RK, 1987: 'Experiments on isolated digit recognition using the multi-layer perceptron;, Technical Report 4073, RSRE, Malvern, UK.

7 Kohonen, T et al, 1984: 'Phonotopic Maps - Insightful representation of phonological features for speech recognition', in IEEE proc 7th international conference on pattern recognition.

8 Sawai, H, Waibel, A et al, 1989, 'Spotting Japanese CV-syllables and phonemes using time-delay neural networks', proc ICASSP-89, Vol 1, p 25.

9 Klatt, DH, 1977: 'Review of the ARPA speech understanding project', JASA **62**, p1345.

10 Stern P-E et al, 1986: 'An expert system for speech spectrogram reading', ICASSP-86, p1193.

11 Zue, VW and Lamel, LF, 1986 'an expert spectrogram reader: a knowledge-based approach to speech recognition', proc ICASSP-86 p1197.

12 Zue, VW and Cole, RA, 1979, 'Experiments on spectrogram Reading', proc ICASSP-79 p116.

13 Green, PD at al, 1990, 'Bridging the Gap between Signals and Symbols in Speech Recognition', in 'Advances in speech, Hearing and Language Processing, WA Ainsworth (ed), JAI press (in press).

Chapter 13

Knowledge-based approaches to speech recognition

M. Crawford

1   INTRODUCTION

"The challenge to hearing from Marr's work is to understand sufficiently the computational problem posed by hearing. Only then will we be able to identify what representations of the acoustic signal we need and what constraints could mediate between them."

(Darwin, 1987)

The goal of this chapter is to show how the findings from psychology and physiology might be incorporated into Automatic Speech Recognition (ASR) systems, and why a representational approach to ASR is vital in order to achieve this. The problem of speech recognition in adverse conditions is given particular attention. The human auditory system is extraordinarily capable of separating the speech of a single speaker from a wide range of background sounds, not only monotonous noises such as in cars, but also the surrounding chatter at a cocktail party.

It is this author's belief that much current work in ASR would benefit from considering some of the issues raised here. The overall message is- by all means jump on the auditory bandwagon, but be prepared for it to take you on a rather different, and probably more interesting, route than that you might expect.

The first section will outline a representational approach to ASR, based on the notion of a "Speech Sketch". It is suggested here, however, that to further understand speech recognition we will have to consider the human model. The Speech Sketch approach is of particular significance as it can be readily adapted to provide the framework for an representation of speech based on auditory processing.

There is a growing interest in Auditory Models (AMs) as signal analysers for speech recognition systems. We will briefly discuss the function of the auditory periphery, and the auditory frequency scales. Auditory models are being used in particular with the aim of improving speech recognition in noise. Whilst this technique has been moderately successful, it is suggested that in order to achieve human performance of separation of speech from background sounds we need a better understanding of higher level perceptual processes. A brief overview of the constraints used by the auditory system to effect this separation is given.

We will finally report on recent work at SPLASH (SPeech Lab At SHeffield) in the Computer Science Department at Sheffield University which seeks to provide a computational model of this processing, and what this may entail for future advances in ASR.

Before we can explain some of the constraints that apply in speech perception, however, we need a basic understanding of how speech is produced.

1.1   Speech production and analysis

For an excellent, though detailed, introduction to this area, and others of relevance, see Stevens (1989). A brief overview is given in Moore (1989).

The simplest model of the speech production apparatus consists of two parts, a source, and a filter. There are two types of source in speech, leading to voiced sounds, during which the vocal cords in the larynx (glottis) vibrate and unvoiced sounds, during which they do not. The filter acts to change the observed characteristics of the source. The properties of the filter are determined by the positions of the articulators (the tongue, teeth, and lips), and the physical dimensions of the vocal tract, (the mouth and throat).

There are two principal ways in which this system can produce a "source", leading to frication and voicing. Frication occurs when air is forced through a constriction in the vocal tract. The constriction may be formed by, for example, bringing the tongue close to the teeth, in sounds like "s" and "f". We are more interested here, however, in voiced speech.

The source for "voiced" speech sounds, such as vowels is at the glottis. The glottis consists of two small muscular folds: if they are adjusted such that there is only a narrow passage between them, an air stream will cause them to vibrate. The rate at which they vibrate determines the fundamental frequency, (or F0) of the voiced sound, (e.g. if they move back and forth 100 times a second, the fundamental frequency is 100 Hz). The individual vibrations are referred to as pitch pulses. Voicing produces a series of harmonics (frequency components at integer multiples of the fundamental).

The vocal tract is often approximated to a (fairly) simple dynamic tube, with a second tube representing the nasal cavity coupled to it (see Figure 1).

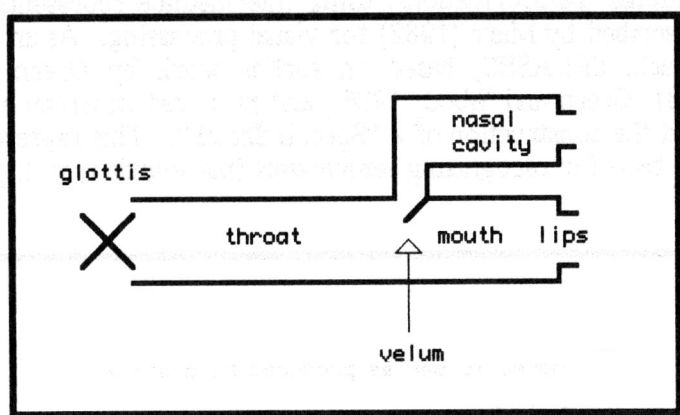

<u>Figure 1</u>:   Vocal tract as idealised tubes

The shape of the vocal tract can be altered by moving the articulators and by shutting off the nasal cavity by means of a flap called the soft palate (velum). Altering the shape of the vocal tract alters its resonant frequencies. This has the effect of "shaping" the frequency and amplitude characteristics of the output. The process is illustrated in Figure 2.

This can be seen in spectrographic representations of the signal, which are produced by the Fourier Transform. The Fourier Transform (the abbreviation FFT stands for Fourier Fast Transform) is an analysis technique which can show the major frequency components of a signal by determining the concentration of energy within a frequency range. A spectrogram produced by a fine scale, "narrow band", Fourier Transform, such as Figure 3 (upper), shows the individual harmonics present in the signal.

A coarse scale, "wide band", spectrogram (Figure 3, lower) shows the main resonant frequencies of the vocal tract during voiced speech, known as "formants", and importantly, also the periodic amplitude modulation in the signal due to each glottal pulse. The formants are referred to as F1, F2 etc., numbered from the lowest frequency upwards.   Speech sounds are traditionally thought to be characterised by the relative frequencies and movements of these formants.

2   REPRESENTATIONAL APPROACHES

Main reference: Green et al. (1990)

In this paradigm the perception of speech is seen as a sequence of representational transformations, using intermediate representations in the manner described by Marr (1982) for visual processing. As an exemplar of this approach, SPLASH2, based on earlier work by Green (Green and Grace, 1981, Green and Wood, 1986), and reviewed in Green et al. (1990), investigated the construction of a "Speech Sketch". This representation was used as the basis for recognising semivowels (the sounds r, w, l, y).

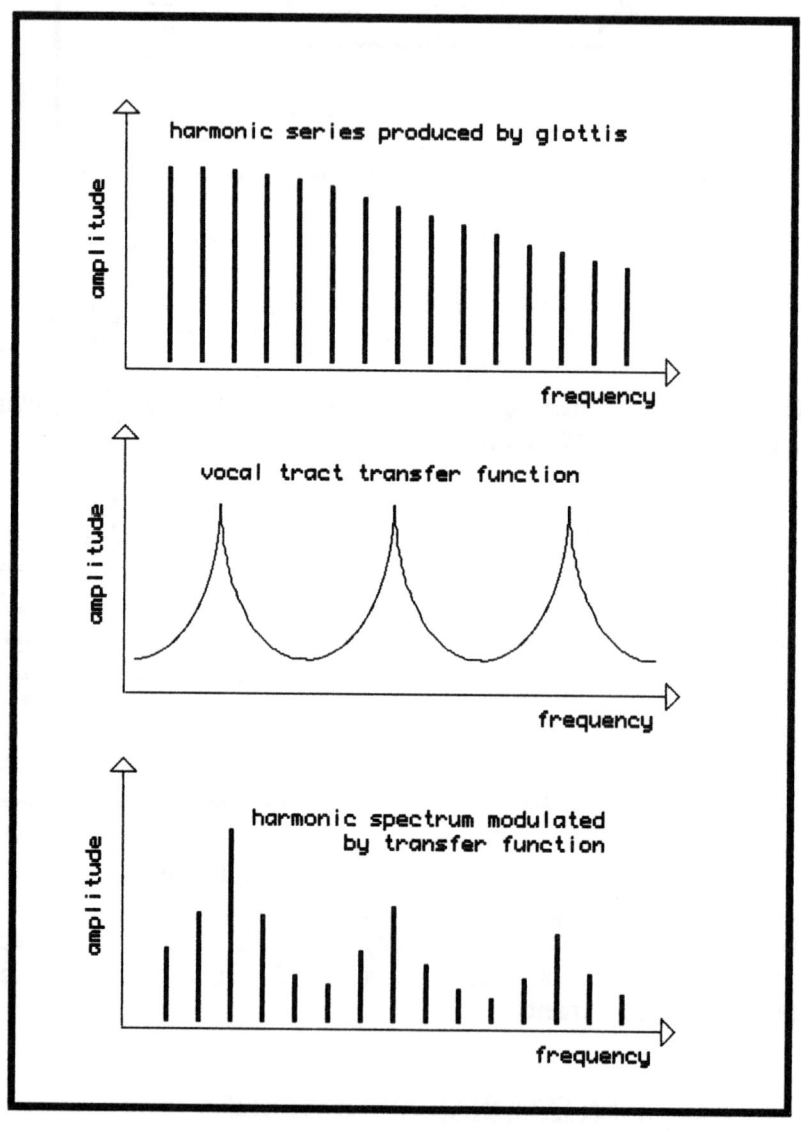

Figure 2: Modulation of harmonic source by vocal tract transfer function.

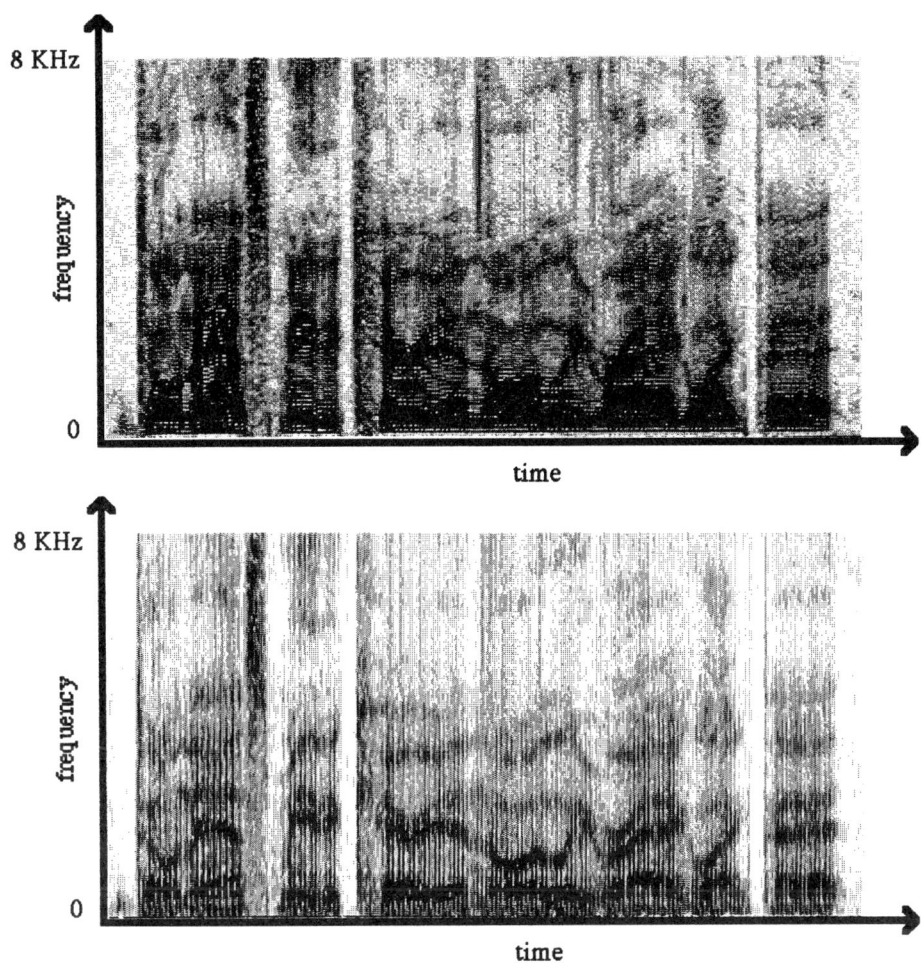

Figure 3:   Narrow band (upper) and wide band (lower)
                             spectrograms of the utterance:
                             "Don't ask me to carry an oily rag like that".

2.1   The Speech Sketch: SPLASH2

The SPLASH2 system contained only a partial implementation of the
Speech Sketch. It was restricted to finding semivowels in wholly voiced
utterances such as "Why were you away a year Roy?". It can be seen as
consisting of three parts: the builder, the matcher, and the knowledge base
(an overview is given in Figure 4).

2.1.1   The builder

input representation: speech signal
output representation: Raw Speech Sketch: a rich description of the
                               signal in which salient acoustic evidence is made
                               explicit

The builder does the signal analysis and constructs the initial
representation, the Raw Speech Sketch. It first analyses the speech signal,
and produces estimates of the formant frequencies, and an energy measure.
These are then characterised to form the highest level of this representation
which consists of objects making explicit peaks, dips and plateaux in
formants and in the energy profile.

2.1.2   The matcher and knowledge base

input representation: Raw Speech Sketch
output representation: Full Speech Sketch: as the Raw Speech Sketch,
                               but including hypotheses for the existence
                               regions of semivowels in the utterance

The semivowels tend to be characterised by particular formant
movements. Knowledge about what organisations of objects to expect was
encoded in the knowledge base in a frame-like system. The objects
produced by the builder were used by the matcher, with reference to the
knowledge base, as cues to initiate prospective matching for semivowels.
The goodness of fit of a prospective match was judged by a Gaussian
classifier.

2.2   Results and other work

Results obtained were comparable with other semivowel-spotting studies
(cf. Green et al., 1990). Good hit rates were, however, obtained at the
expense of considerable numbers of false positives, particularly for the
sound "l". This was taken as a pointer to the need to develop hypotheses
around a model of syllable structure, in order to make explicit the use of
contextual information rather than just blind spotting. This is the theme of a
new project at Sheffield and Leeds Universities called SYLK, for "Statistical
sYLlabic Knowledge".

Other work on representation-based schemes is reported by Riley (1989),
Leung and Zue (1986), and Zinovyeva (1987). One system of particular
interest, which uses representations based on line-formants derived from an
auditory mode is that of Seneff (1987). This will be discussed at greater
length after a discussion of the most relevant analyses performed by the
peripheral auditory system.

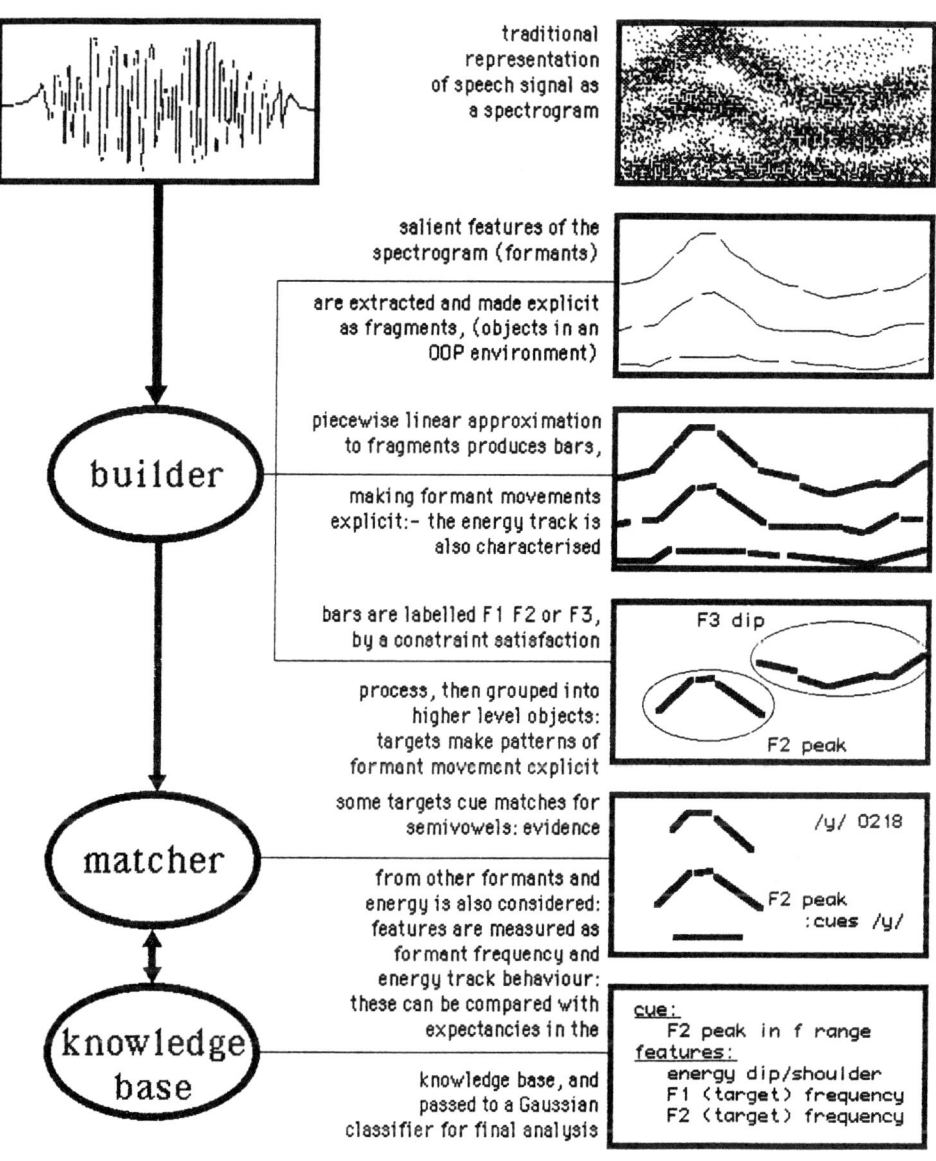

<u>Figure 4</u>:   Overview of SPLASH2

3   AUDITORY PROCESSING

Main references: Moore (1989), or Pickles (1988), Greenberg
                          (1988b,c): (Moore is of most general use)

We first address the question; "Why use auditory models?". We will then
discuss the the major characteristics of the peripheral auditory system, and
two auditory frequency scales. The auditory periphery performs a
frequency analysis similar to that of an FFT, so that the easiest way to
approximate an auditory "front end" in ASR is simply to use an auditory
scaled filterbank. Even the use of an auditory frequency scale can have a
significant effect on the representation of the signal. The use of a more
realistic model of the auditory periphery, however, has a much more
dramatic effect on the representation of speech, when compared with the
traditional spectrogram.

3.1   Why use auditory models?

As we shall see, there are many non-linearities in the hearing system,
which may also contain feedback loops. Speech production has evolved to
take account of the analysis capabilities of the auditory system (cf.Bladon,
1986). It would seem natural, therefore, that a model of perceptual analysis
might produce a representation more amenable to decoding than a
traditional Fourier Transform. Karjalainen (1987) makes the obvious (but
nonetheless worthwhile) point "The human hearing system is the best
processor to recognise speech messages; why not try to duplicate it in
technical form".

In ASR the auditory processing is therefore often treated primarily as an
alternative to the Fourier transform. Whilst it is true that the analogy holds
to some extent, it obscures much of the important processing performed by
the auditory system. For example, as noted by Møller (1982); "there is at
least one fundamental difference between the auditory spectrum analyzer
and the commonly used man-made spectrum analyzer, namely the peculiar
non-linearity of the auditory analyzer that results in changes in both the
bandwidth and centre frequency with changes in sound intensity".

3.2   Neural transduction

The transformation we are concerned with here is the following:

input representation: sound signal
output representation: neural coding in terms of nerve firings

We are not concerned here with the gross physiology of the ear. For a good introduction to both auditory physiology and psychology see Moore (1989), or Pickles (1988). Suffice to mention here that: the external ear (pinna), and the external auditory canal (meatus) tend to increase sensitivity to sounds in the region of 1 kHz, and assist sound localisation, and: the signal to nerve impulse transformation takes place within the inner ear (cochlea).

The inner ear effectively consists of approximately 30,000 hair cells arranged along a membrane (the Basilar membrane) which are finely tuned to respond to particular frequencies. These cells initiate responses in auditory nerve fibres. The frequency to which a fibre is most sensitive is known as its characteristic frequency (CF). The fibres may respond to a stimulus by "firing". The more intense the stimulus, or the nearer it is in frequency to the CF of the fibre, the more likely it is to fire.

The sensitivity of the auditory fibres to frequencies different from their CF is also of interest. The filters tend to be very finely tuned. The actual shape of the tuning curve, however, is dependent on the CF of the fibre. This may be for a number of different reasons, which include active feedback from fibres with similar CFs, and mechanical processes in the membrane along which the cells are arranged (cf. Pickles, 1988).

There are two ways in which the auditory nerve responses can be characterised, by rate, and by phase-locking, or synchrony.

3.2.1   Rate response   The transduction process is non-linear. Even when there is no stimulus auditory nerve fibres show a spontaneous rate of up to about 30 firings ("spikes") per second. (There appear to be, in fact, three populations of fibres differing in mean spontaneous rate, but this does not concern us here.) In response to a stimulus (of appropriate frequency) the rate does not increase until the intensity is sufficiently great (about 30 dB). (Again, there appear to be different populations with different thresholds.) From this threshold to about 20-30 dB above this limit the rate increases approximately linearly with stimulus level, up to a maximum of about 250 impulses per second when the discharge rate is said to be "saturated". Any further increase in stimulus intensity does not affect firing rate.

It is important to remember, however, particularly when looking at so called "neurograms" (spectrogram-like displays showing the rate responses of auditory filters cf. e.g. Greenberg, 1988b), or even when thinking of the ear as a filterbank, that, as is the case with all filters, fibres can respond to frequencies other than their centre frequency, and that the frequency to which the filter is responding can be determined. This information can be derived from the synchrony response.

3.2.2   Synchrony   Synchrony information is related to the short-term phase of a speech signal, which can be obtained from the inter-spike interval.   Even at low stimulus levels when firing rate is still at the spontaneous level, the inter-spike interval of a nerve of appropriate characteristic frequency tends to correspond to an integer multiple of the period of the stimulating tone.   Synchrony information is available for frequencies of up to about 4 - 5 kHz only.   For higher frequencies the "jitter" on cell response times is greater than the period of the stimulating tone (cf. Greenberg, 1988b).

The response of a single fibre is usually shown as a Post-Stimulus-Time Histogram (PSTH).   (The PSTH is generated by summing the discharges of a fibre with   over many presentations of a stimulus.) Figure 5 shows the output of a computer model of an auditory nerve fibre in response to the tonal stimulus shown above.   Instead of showing the number of actual firings recorded over many presentations of the same stimulus, as is the case with the PSTH, this shows the probability that the fibre would have fired at a given time.

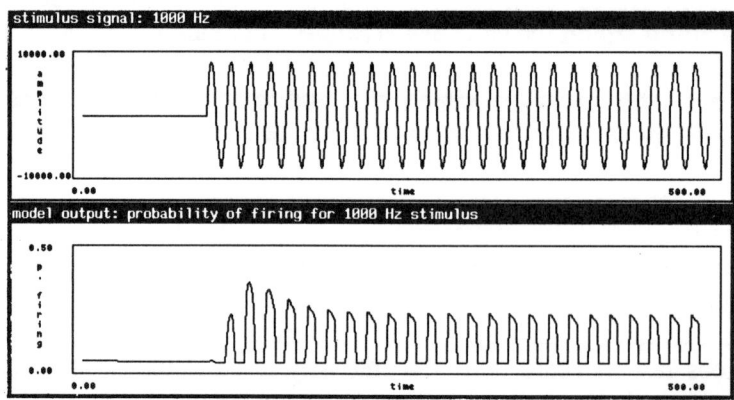

Figure 5:   Post-Stimulus-Time Histogram generated by a
                              computer model of the auditory periphery.

The relationship between the phase of the stimulus and the probability of firing can be clearly seen.   Firings are most likely to occur at the stimulus peaks.   Even though, therefore, individual fibres cannot respond at the frequency of the stimulus, there is a temporal relationship between the frequency of the stimulus and the interval between successive spikes.   The signal may be well represented by a population of fibres of similar characteristic frequency.

Phase-locking may account for the ability to perceive low intensity stimuli, when the intensity level is not above threshold for a fibre. As was mentioned earlier, even at low intensity stimulus can produce phase-locking, even when the actual response rate is not elevated. It may also be the case that the degree of phase locking increases as a function of stimulus intensity (Pickles, 1988).

It may also improve the representation of some signals, for example a vowel in noise; Sinex and Geisler (1983), compared average rate and synchrony in synthetic speech stimuli. They found that a synchrony measure could identify formant trajectories precisely, even at high noise levels.

3.2.3   Adaptation   Figure 5 also shows the effect known as "adaptation". After quickly reaching a peak, the firing rate decreases to a steady state. This has the effect in auditory representations of increasing the salience of stimulus onsets. This may be of particular importance in speech perception, as many speech sounds are characterised by abrupt onsets.

3.3   The auditory frequency scale(s)

Humans are most sensitive to (i.e. most capable of discriminating) stimuli in the range 0.1 - 4 kHz, with lower and upper limits at about 20 and 20,000 Hz. More importantly, as a consequence, the human frequency scale is not linear. There are two major scales reported in the literature, the Bark and the ERB. For a detailed account of the differences between the two scales see Moore and Glasberg, (1983)

The Bark scale is based on psychophysical studies of the "masking" effect on tone has on another. Masking is the amount by which the threshold of audibility of one sound is raised by the presence of another (the masker). This scale has received most attention, and many applications purporting to use auditory processing refer to either Bark-spaced filters, or a Hertz to Bark transformation after FFT analysis (see, for example, Blomberg et al. 1986).

For the technically minded, the ERB (Equivalent Rectangular Bandwidth) of a filter is the "the bandwidth of a rectangular filter which has the same peak transmission as that filter and which passes the same total power for a white noise input", (Moore, 1989). For our purposes, the ERB scale is important, and is becoming more popular, as it appears to reflect more accurately the frequency characteristics of the ear, particularly at lower frequencies. In particular the spectral resolution at lower frequencies is greater, reflecting the fact that the auditory system is capable of resolving the first (F1), and often second (F2), formant into harmonics. Figure 6 shows the relationship between the Bark, ERB and Hertz frequency scales

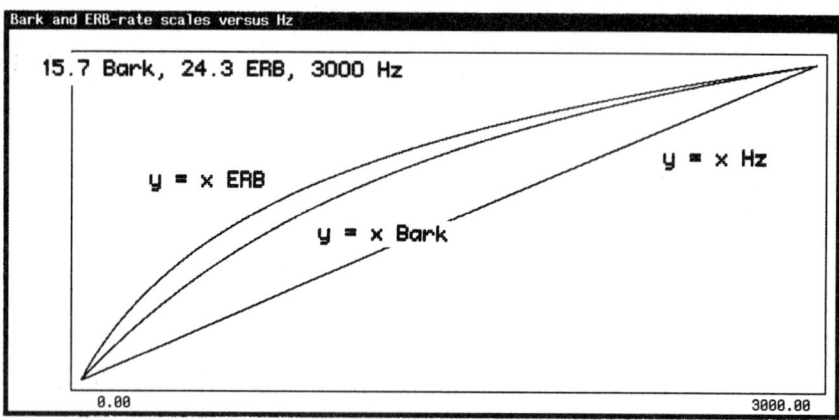

Figure 6:   Graph showing the relationship between Herz,
                             Bark and ERB frequency scales.

The differential sensitivities to different frequency ranges can be seen.
The Bark scale shows a greater sensitivity to low frequencies (below about
1500 Hz) than to higher. The ERB scale shows an even greater resolving
power in this region (as shown in Figure 7).

3.3.1   Consequences of using an auditory scale   The most important
result of ERB scaling is that F1, often F2, and occasionally F3, for high
fundamentals, is/are resolved into harmonics. This fact is rarely taken into
account in theories of speech perception although, as we shall see later, it
may be of vital importance in some aspects of auditory processing. On one
of the rare occasions when mention is made of the fact (Deterding, 1987) it
is seen as a problem to be overcome, rather than a useful source of
information to the auditory system.

3.4   Summary

The consequences of just these effects on the representation of complex
sounds such as speech in the auditory periphery are profound.
Unfortunately it is outside the scope of this chapter to cover this material
any further. However, one of the most comprehensive reviews of the
representation of speech sounds in the auditory periphery is given in the
series by Delgutte and Kiang (1984a-e). Geisler's (1988) review is,
however, rather more readable, and (obviously) more up-to-date.

4   APPLICATIONS OF AUDITORY PROCESSING

Main references: Blomberg et al. (1986) Karjalainen (1987), Seneff (1987)

The main interest here is the application of AMs to ASR, but findings from psychology and physiology have also been applied to speech coding and synthesis. The reader is referred in particular to Hermansky (1985, 1986), who describes a variation of the Linear Predictive Coding technique based on a Bark scale, and Terhardt (1987) who describes a variation of the Fourier Transform. A good review of the history of auditory modelling is given in Cooke (1989).

4.1   AMs in ASR

There are several speech recognition systems which have used, or are using, auditory-based frequency scales, or claim to analyse speech in a way similar to the peripheral auditory system. These started to appear in the early 1980's, and their arrival was one manifestation of a great upsurge in interest in the auditory periphery. Prior to this there had been few integrated models, and such as there were were generally derived by workers investigating the periphery itself.

They are based on the assumption that auditory analysis will provide a more natural, and ideally less variant, representation of speech (cf. Blomberg et al. 1986). However, hopes that invariance might be found at this peripheral level may be misplaced (cf. Geisler, 1988, Beet, 1990). Two reports (Deterding 1987, and van Alphen and Pols, 1989, cf. also Klatt, 1982, 1986) make particular note of the fact that the resolution of harmonics when using an auditory front-end is disadvantageous, since it adds to the variation of the representations produced. As we shall see later, this fact is used to great advantage by the auditory system.

4.1.1   Speech recognition in noise   As has been mentioned previously speech recognition in noise is becoming something of a forcing domain for auditory models in ASR. Representations derived from auditory preprocessing of steady state vowels and other speech speech sounds do illustrate an improvement in the ability to visually identify formants in noise.

There have been a number of studies using auditory models including synchrony information (Hunt and Lefèbvre, 1986, Ghitza, 1988, Shamma, 1988, Deng, Geisler and Greenberg, 1988, Fink and Dalsgaard, 1989). These generally show an improved recognition in noise rate when the auditory model is used when compared with a conventional signal analysis technique.

The common factor in all these models is that they use conventional techniques as the recognition module. An exception is Seneff's (1987) model.

4.1.2   Seneff's (1987) model

The model described by Seneff (1987) is of particular interest since it appears to come closer to a representation based auditory approach than any other devised so far.

The signal analysis is performed by an auditory model consisting of a bank of 40 critical-band (Bark scale) filters followed by a non-linear stage reflecting some physiological effects. The output from each channel is then analysed to give a measure of dominance of information at the CF of the channel, which corresponds to synchrony detection.

Straight-line segments, (conceptually similar to the bars in the Speech Sketch, cf. Green et al, 1990), are computed from the synchrony information. These are intended to provide a description of formant movements. A degree of speaker normalisation is achieved by subtracting F0 from the frequencies of these "line-formants" on a Bark scale. For recognition the line-formants were compared with the probability distributions from training data, with an implicit notion of a formant's movement based on the line's left and right end frequencies. The average speaker independent recognition rate was about 55%.

Whilst this approach does go some way towards making relevant information explicit, the representational scheme is very poor, and the knowledge deployed is still very much implicit. It can not, therefore, be considered as a true representational approach, although it is heading in a promising direction.

4.4   Summary and criticisms

With a few notable exceptions, the models used in ASR tend to be "engineering solutions" capturing only the gross actions of auditory processing, by for example using filterbanks based on auditory frequency scales, or converting from a linear to an auditory scale as a post- FFT process. Auditory models used in ASR have therefore often produced only a form of rate representation, usually as an alternative to the FFT spectrogram. Even more realistic models of the periphery tend simply to be used as alternative front-ends to standard recognition techniques. They are often successful, particularly in adverse conditions, since as we have seen, auditory processing does tend to emphasise features that are believed to be perceptually significant.

This approach fails to consider that there may be a mismatch between the representation produced by the auditory model and the recognition technique. It is likely to be the case that one should not simply "plug" an auditory front end onto a conventional recogniser; there should be a correspondence between the output from the signal processing stage and the recognition modules (cf. Delgutte, 1986). Generally, therefore, the recognition technique employed should be is determined by the form of representation produced, rather than the other way round.

The use of auditory models to improve recognition in noise is of particular interest. Whilst the non-linearities of the peripheral auditory system result in an improvement of the representation of speech in noise, any underlying hope that the process of speaker from noise separation may be achieved at the peripheral level may be misplaced. It ignores the fact that there are higher levels in the auditory system that decide what sounds have come from what source. In the next section we will discuss some of the constraints that the auditory system may use in order to determine what parts of the sound signal came from the same source, and how these may be modelled.

5   AUDITORY SCENE ANALYSIS

(This section owes its title to Bregman, 1984)

Main references: Bregman (1984, 1990), Cooke (1986), Darwin and Gardner (1987), Moore, (1989), Repp (1987)

It is a matter of everyday experience that speech can be perceived even in high levels of background noise. Most current speech recognition systems, on the other hand, are very sensitive to background noise. As we have already been seen, one of the goals of using models of the auditory periphery is to improve recognition in noise. In order to achieve human-like performance, however, it is likely that we will have to understand how higher level processing of the auditory system "groups" components (auditory primitives such as harmonics or formants) of a complex signal. As stated by Darwin and Gardner (1987), an understanding of the processes that separate different sound sources is "crucial in understanding the computational problem faced by hearing, and of great practical significance in constructing robust speech recognisers".

By analogy with visual processing, the auditory experience can be thought of as a "scene", (cf. Bregman, 1984, 1987), requiring a similar description process, for example in the separation of figure from ground.

As is the case in visual processing (cf. Marr 1982) there are many processes that act together to analyse the auditory scene, and many constraints that may apply. The processes which act to group sounds together are generally referred to as integrative, whilst those which give a disposition to separation are referred to as segregative. Repp (1988) gives a good overview of this area. Whilst this subject has attracted a large amount of attention in the psychoacoustic literature, it has received rather less attention in modelling (although see Scheffers, 1983, and Weintraub, 1987).

This section will explain on what bases the auditory system might separate sounds from a speaker from noise in a process known as "streaming". "A stream... is the precept of a group of successive and/or simultaneous sound elements as a whole, appearing to emanate from a single source" (Moore, 1989). There are a number of constraints that may act to assist this process.

5.1   Stream formation

Effectively we want to achieve the following transformation:

input representation: auditory primitives representing harmonics, formants etc. (not explicitly labelled)

output representation: streams: groups of auditory primitives each labelled as coming from the same source

There are a number of constraints that apply many of which loosely fall into the term "common fate". (We are not concerned here with sound localisation, which will usually also form a powerful constraint.) This is probably due to the auditory system evolving to take advantage of the fact that, generally, sounds coming from the same source share features in common. This is particularly true of speech, due to the nature of its production.

A number of constraints that might affect grouping have been proposed (cf. Repp, 1988, Moore, 1989) Some of the most relevant ones are outlined below, with appropriate experimental evidence. One way to test hypothesised grouping factors is to alter a stimulus such that a relationship between elements no longer holds. If the sounds are no longer grouped together, it is likely that the factor did affect grouping. Much interesting work in this area as been conducted by, amongst others, Darwin and his co-workers. The following sections explain constraints that may apply to grouping, and give a brief account of relevant experimental evidence.

5.1.1   Common onset/offset   As a general rule, gross features of the speech signal start and end at the same time. The onset of voicing, for

example, generally affects the whole frequency range simultaneously. (Voicing onsets in stops may be considered as two frequency limited onsets.)

Darwin (1984) synthesised stimuli in which the onset time of an individual harmonic differed from that of the remainder of the signal. The experiments showed that a tone that starts or stops at a different time from a vowel is less likely to be grouped into the vowel percept.

<u>5.1.2   Harmonicity</u>   Recall that the source in voiced speech produces a series of harmonics. We have already stated that, at low frequencies, the individual harmonics are resolved by the auditory system. Clearly, then, one possible constraint is to only group together parts of the signal which have a harmonic relationship with each other.

Darwin and Gardner (1986) mistuned harmonic components of vowels on the /I/ - /e/ continuum. The experiment showed, through a change in vowel quality, that mistuning more than about 8% resulted in the segregation of the harmonic.

<u>5.1.3   Common amplitude modulation</u> Unfortunately, the frequencies of higher formants do not have a frequency relationship to the rest of the signal. Since they are produced by the same source, however, their amplitude modulation rate should be the same as the fundamental frequency. (Recall that the source is a series of pulses, as shown in the wide-band spectrogram.) If a formant is produced by a fundamental different from that of the remainder of a vowel, it should not be grouped.

Gardner et al. (1989) used a four formant stimulus for which F1, F2 and F3 give a perception of /ru/, and F1, F3 and F4 give a perception of /li/. They found that when all the formants were on the same fundamental the percept was /ru/, but /li/ was generally heard if F2 was excited by a fundamental of sufficiently different frequency, and F2 was heard out as a separate source. Changing the fundamental of F4 did not change the /ru/ identity, but did result in F4 being streamed out.

<u>5.2   Summary and conclusions</u>

A number of constraints may apply to group together sets of auditory primitives which are labelled as having arisen from the same source. The result of grouping may be the formation of auditory streams, which correspond to objects in vision.

It is difficult to see how the constraints and processes that apply could be sensibly deployed without rich descriptions. This suggests that a representational approach is vital to ASR, or, by the time it reaches this stage perhaps, a model of speech perception. This area has received little attention in terms of computational modelling. (Cooke (1986), however, outlines proposals for progress in this area, and Williams (1989) describes a start that has been made in producing a computational environment in which models of grouping may be tested.) Current work at Sheffield, however, is aimed to redress this balance.

6   TOWARDS THE AUDITORY SPEECH SKETCH

(which, unfortunately, abbreviates to ASS)

Main references: Cooke (1986, 1990), Crawford (1990)

An aim of a representational approach to auditory speech processing might be achieve the following transformation:

input representation: sound signal
output representation: a rich description of the signal in terms of salient
                          auditory features, in which streams are also
                          made explicit

Current work at Sheffield aims, eventually, to fully model the aspects auditory processing reviewed in the previous sections. The present goal of the ASS is to provide a sufficiently rich symbolic description of a signal based on auditory analysis, by using intermediate representations, that modelling of streaming will be readily computationally tractable. This representation may then be further processed to give a representation amenable to linguistic decoding. The analysis is performed by an auditory model derived by Cooke.

6.1   Cooke's (1990) auditory model

Cooke's model currently performs the following representational transformation:

input representation: speech signal
output representation: representations of synchronous filter activity
                          which make explicit frequency and amplitude
                          variations with time

The initial analysis is performed by a model of the auditory periphery which is described in Cooke (1989). Essentially, the model consists of a bank of bandpass filters, equally spaced along the ERB scale. Each filter has a tuning curve which closely matches both physiological estimates of auditory-nerve fibre frequency selectivity and human auditory filter shapes derived by psychophysical experiments. Synchrony information is now, however, used in a similar way to that in the DOMIN model described by Blomberg et al. (1986).

Estimates of the frequency of the most prominent component in the output of each auditory filter is calculated, and filters with similar responses grouped together to form "place-groups". Place groups are aggregated over time to produce explicit time-frequency descriptions of auditory synchrony called "synchrony strands". A measure of amplitude is also calculated, and the amplitude modulation rate made explicit for each strand with respect to time. Current work investigating how onsets may be made explicit is giving promising results. A diagram showing the representations formed by the analysis is given in Figure 7.

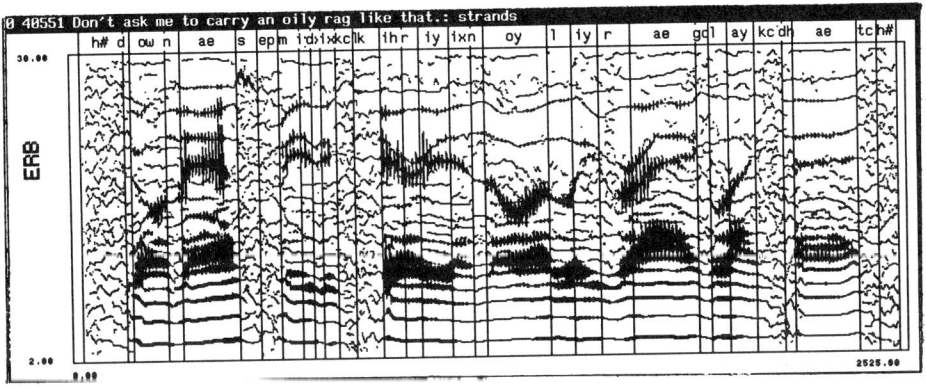

Figure 7:   Strands produced by analysis of the utterance:
                                 "Don't ask me to carry an oily rag like that".

The next stage in processing will be to use these representations as the input to a computational model of the grouping processes described in the previous section. This will produce explicit representations of streams, each consisting of the raw primitives that formed them. Hopes that separation of speech from noise seem well founded as the synchrony strand representation appears to be fairly robust even for quite low signal-to-noise ratios.

This work is aimed only at providing a rich description of the signal, and streams. This may then be subject to further processing to produce a still higher level representation which may be amenable to linguistic decoding. Parallel work is investigating how this might be used in recognition. This involves the modelling of a phenomenon known as large-scale spectral integration.

6.2   Large scale spectral integration

Research pioneered by Chistovich and Lublinskaya (1979) into the concept of the "spectral centre of gravity", has suggested that the auditory system performs a very coarse analysis of the speech signal referred to as large scale integration. This is conceptually similar to performing a very wide band FFT, and has the effect of merging formants which are within a critical distance of each other. This distance is taken to be in the region of 3.5 Bark.

3.5 Bark integration has been proposed by several authors as providing the basis for much of phoneme recognition (cf. for example Bladon, 1986; Stevens, 1989; Syrdal and Gopal, 1987). The major aim of the recent work (Crawford, 1990) has been to investigate this area using a crude computational model, based on a synchrony representation.

6.2.1   A model of large-scale auditory integration

input representation: explicit time-frequency representations of harmonics and formants belonging to one stream
output representation: explicit time-frequency representations of integrated harmonics and formants within the stream

Details of the original implementation are given in Crawford (1990). The initial transformation from signal to explicit time-frequency representations is effected by Cooke's auditory model. Since the streaming module is as yet unimplemented, the current model of integration must make the assumption that the representations produced by analysis of a single speaker in quiet conditions without streaming are equivalent to those that would be produced in a noisy environment after streaming.

The representations produced by the model are interesting. There appears to be some consistency in the representation of similar speech sounds or gestures, even between speakers. Furthermore, many major speech gestures appear to be delineated by discontinuities, as shown in Figure 8. It is proposed that integrated strands could be characterised in a manner similar to that used in SPLASH2. These higher level descriptions could then serve as the input to a linguistic classification module.

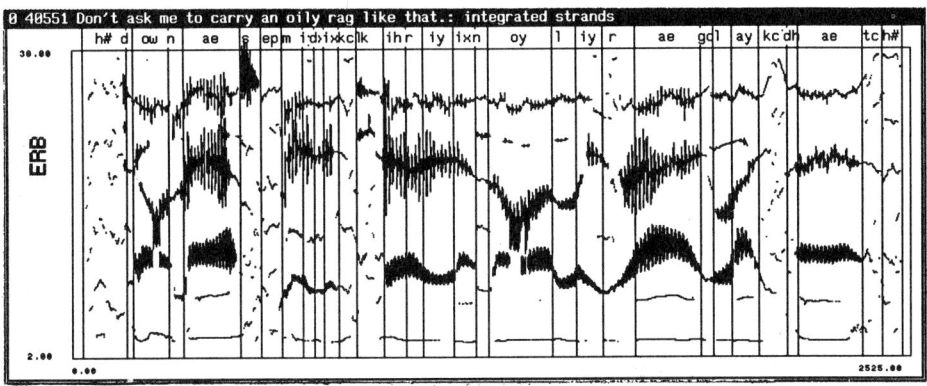

Figure 8:   Integrated strands produced by analysis of the utterance:
"Don't ask me to carry an oily rag like that".

6.3   Related work

There is ongoing work in the use of synthesis from auditory representations as a basis for validation (Cooke, 1990, cf. also Damper et al., 1987, and Hukin and Damper, 1989). The resynthesised speech is of a similar quality to the original. Interestingly, resynthesis of speech in noise appears to be more intelligible than the original. This work may have applications to speech coding.

In section 3.2 it was noted that auditory nerve fibres are tuned to particular frequencies. At levels of the auditory system beyond the periphery, neurons may also show tuning to particular rates of amplitude and frequency modulation. Recent physiological research (Schreiner and Langner 1988) has demonstrated that neurons tuned to different best amplitude modulation rates are systematically organised into neural "maps". Brown, also at the University of Sheffield, is producing a computational model of an amplitude modulation map. This will produce a novel representation of the amplitude fluctuations in speech (cf. Brown, 1989) which may provide another basis for the production of auditory primitives useful for streaming.

A question that has not been addressed so far is how should aperiodic sounds be grouped? The discussion has concentrated on voiced speech. The constraints outlined applying to voiced speech will not, as a general rule, apply to aperiodic sounds. This area will be the subject of future research.

7   SUMMARY AND CONCLUSIONS

The aim of this chapter was to shown how ASR might be informed by and benefit from an understanding speech processing by the auditory system, using speech recognition in noise as an example domain. It was suggested that in order to deploy constraints used in auditory processing, a representational approach to ASR is necessary.

An exemplar of a representational approach to speech recognition was outlined. A brief review of the major aspects of auditory processing was then given. A number of current ASR systems use auditory models as front ends, particularly to assist recognition in noise. It was suggested, however, that to achieve human-like levels of performance aspects of higher level auditory processing may have to be considered.

An overview of three constraints that appear to be used by the auditory system to group components of a periodic signal was given. An auditory model which produces a rich description of the signal was then described. The representations produced by this model will be used in a model of streaming. An approach to speech recognition based on these auditory representations using large scale spectral integration was also proposed.

8   ACKNOWLEDGEMENTS

Thanks are due to Martin Cooke, Guy Brown, Phil Green and Tony Simons for assistance with the preparation and editing of this work.

This work was supported by SERC CASE award 88501079 and by British Telecom Research Laboratories.

The sentence analysed in this chapter was train/dr2/mcem0/sa2 from the TIMIT database. Thanks are due to Dave Pallet, Lori Lamel and Maxine Eskénazi for the loan of the database.

9   REFERENCES

Beet, S. W.
(1990), "Automatic speech recognition using a reduced auditory representation and post-tolerant discrimination", Computer speech and language, 4, 1

Bladon, A.
(1986), "Phonetics for hearers"

in: McGregor G. (ed)
(1986), "Language for Hearers", Pergamon Press

Blomberg, Mats; Carlson, Rolf; Elenius, Kjell; Granström, Bjorn
(1986), "Auditory models as front ends in speech recognition systems"
in: Perkell J. S. et al. (eds)
(1986), "Invariance and variability in speech processes"

Bregman, A. S.
(1990), "Auditory scene analysis: the perceptual organization of sound",
MIT Press, Cambridge, Mass. (in preparation)
(1984), "Auditory scene analysis", Proc. 7th Int. Conference Pattern
Recognition, Montreal, pp 168-175

Brown, G. J.
(1989), "Symbolic representation of speech from the computational
modelling of higher auditory processing", Special report, Department of
computer science, University of Sheffield, December 1989

Chistovich, Ludmilla A.; Lublinskaya, Valentina V.
(1979), "The 'centre of gravity' effect in vowel spectra and critical distance
between the formants: psychoacoustical study of the perception of vowel-like
stimuli", Hearing research, 1, pp 185-195

Cooke, M. P.
(1990), "Synchrony strands: and early auditory time-frequency
representation", University of Sheffield Departmental Research Report,
March 20, 1990
(1989), "The auditory periphery: physiology, function and a computer
model", University of Sheffield Departmental Research Report, CS-89-32
(1986), "Towards an early symbolic representation of speech based on
auditory modelling", Proceedings of the institute of acoustics, Autumn
conference, Speech and hearing, Vol. 8, Part 7, pp 563-570

Crawford, M. D.
(1990), "A computational study of large scale auditory integration",
University of Sheffield Departmental Research Report, March 20, 1990

Damper, R. I. et al.
(1987), "Resynthesis and matching experiments on an auditory theory of
male/female normalisation", Proc. 11th Int. Congress Phonetic Sciences,
Tallinn, USSR, Paper Se 60.4

Darwin, C. J.
(1984), "Perceiving vowels in the presence of another sound: constraints on

formant perception", J. Acoust. Soc. Am., 76 (6), pp 1636-1647

Darwin, C. J.; Gardner, Roy B.
(1987), "Perceptual separation of speech from concurrent sounds",
    in: Schouten, M. E. H. (ed)
    (1987), "The psychophysics of speech perception", Martinus Nijhoff
(1986), "Mistuning a harmonic of a vowel: grouping and phase effects on
vowel quality", J. Acoust. Soc. Am., 79 (3), pp 838-845
(1985), "Which harmonics contribute to the estimation of first formant
frequency?", Speech Communication, 4, pp 231-235

Delgutte, Bertrand
(1986), Comments on:
    Klatt, Dennis H. (1986), "The problem of variability in speech
recognition and in models of speech perception"
    in: Perkell J. S. et al. (eds)
    (1986), "Invariance and variability in speech processes" pp 320-322

Delgutte, Bertrand; Kiang, Nelson Y. S.
(1984a), "Speech coding in the auditory nerve: I. Vowel-like sounds", J.
Acoust. Soc. Am., 75 (3), pp 866-878
(1984b), "Speech coding in the auditory nerve: II. Processing schemes for
vowel-like sounds", J. Acoust. Soc. Am., 75 (3), pp 879-886
(1984c), "Speech coding in the auditory nerve: III Voiceless fricative
consonants", J. Acoust. Soc. Am., 75 (3), pp 887-896
(1984d), "Speech coding in the auditory nerve: IV. Sounds with consonant-
like dynamic characteristics", J. Acoust. Soc. Am., 75 (3), pp 897-907
(1984e), "Speech coding in the auditory nerve: IV. Vowels in background
noise", J. Acoust. Soc. Am., 75 (3), pp 908-918
Deng, Li; Geisler, Daniel C.; Greenberg, Steven
(1988), "A composite model of the auditory periphery for the processing of
speech", Journal of phonetics, 16, pp 93-108

Deterding, D. H.
(1987), "Use of the ERB scale in peripheral auditory processing for vowel
identification", Proc. 11th Int. Congress Phonetic Sciences, Tallinn, USSR,
Paper Paper Se 23.4

Fink, F. K.; Dalsgaard, P
(1989), "Estimation of formants in noise corrupted speech using auditory
models", European conference on speech communication and technology,
Paris

Gardner, R. B.; Gaskill, Sally A.; Darwin, C. J.
(1989), "Perceptual grouping of formants with static and dynamic

differences in fundamental frequency", J. Acoust. Soc. Am., 85 (3), pp 1329-1337

Geisler, C. D.
(1988), "Representation of speech sounds in the auditory nerve", Journal of phonetics, 16, pp 19-35

Ghitza, O.
(1988), "Temporal non-place information in the auditory nerve firing patterns as a front-end for speech recognition in a noisy environment", Journal of phonetics, 16, pp 109-123

Green, P. D. et al.
(1990), "Bridging the gap between signals and symbols in speech recognition"
     in: W. A. Ainsworth (ed)
     (1990), "Speech, Hearing, and language processing"
(if this is unavailable, try:
Green et al. (1988), "Acoustic phonetic reasoning with the speech sketch- a progress report", Proc. 7th Symposium of Fed. Acoust. Soc. Europe (SPEECH '88), eds. W. A. Ainsworth and J. N. Holmes, Institute of Acoustics, pp 353-360)

Green, P. D.; Grace, P. J
(1981), "A descriptive approach to computer speech understanding", Proc. Inst. Acoust., Spring Conference, Newcastle-upon-Tyne

Green, P. D.; Wood, A. R.
(1986), "A representational approach to knowledge-based acoustic-phonetic processing in speech recognition", Proc. ICASSP-86, paper 23.4

Greenberg, S.
(1988a), "Representation of speech in the auditory periphery", Journal of phonetics, 16, p 1
(1988b), "Acoustic transduction in the auditory periphery", Journal of phonetics, 16, pp 3-17
(1988c), "The ear as a speech analyser", Journal of phonetics, 16, pp 139-150

Hamand, Hiroshi et al.
(1989), "Auditory-based filter-bank analysis as a front-end processor for speech recognition", European conference on speech communication and technology, Paris

Hermansky, Hynek; Hanson, Brian A.; Wakita, Hisashi
(1985), "Low-dimensional representation of vowels based on all-pole modelling in the psychophysical domain", Speech communication, 4, pp 181-187

Hukin, R.W.; Damper, R. I.
(1989), "Testing an auditory model by resynthesis", European conference on speech communication and technology, Paris

Hunt, Melvyn J.; Lefèbvre, Claude
(1986), "Speech recognition using a cochlear model", Proc. ICASSP-86, paper 37.7

Klatt, Dennis H.
(1986), "The problem of variability in speech recognition and in models of speech perception"
        in: Perkell J. S. et al. (eds)
        (1986), "Invariance and variability in speech processes"
(1982), "Speech processing strategies based on auditory models"
        in: Carlson, R.; Granström, B. (eds)
        (1982), "The representation of speech in the peripheral auditory system", Elsevier Biomedical press

Leung, Hong C.; Zue, Victor W,;
(1986), "Visual characterisation of speech spectrograms", Proc. IEEE ICASSP, Paper 51.1, pp 2751-2754

Marr, D.
(1982), "Vision", W. H. Freeman

Moore, B. C. J.
(1989), "An introduction to the psychology of hearing", 3rd ed., Academic Press, London

Moore, B. C. J.; Glasberg, B. R.
(1983), "Suggested formulæ for calculating auditory-filter bandwidths and excitation patterns", J. Acoust. Soc. Am., 74 (3), pp 750-753

Palmer, A. R.; Winter, I. M.; Gardner, R. B.; Darwin, C. J.
(1987), "Changes in the phonemic quality and neural representation of a vowel by alteration of the relative phase of harmonics near F1"
        in: Schouten, M. E. H. (ed)
        (1987), "The psychophysics of speech perception", Martinus Nijhoff

Repp, Bruno H.
(1988), "Integration and segregation in speech perception", Language and speech, 31 (3), pp 239-271
(1987), "The role of psychophysics in understanding speech perception"
    in: Schouten, M. E. H. (ed)
        (1987), "The psychophysics of speech perception", Martinus Nijhoff

Sachs, M. B.; Blackburn, C. C.; Young, E. D.
(1988), "Rate-place and temporal-place representations of vowels in the auditory nerve and anteroventral cochlear nucleus", Journal of phonetics, 16, pp 37-54

Schreiner, C. E.; Langner, G.
(1989), "Periodicity coding in the inferior colliculus of the cat II. Tonotopical organisation", Journal of neurophysiology, 60 (6), pp 1823-1840

Seneff, Stephanie
(1988), "A joint synchrony/mean-rate model of auditory speech processing", Journal of phonetics, 16, pp 55-76
(1987), "Vowel recognition based on 'line formants' derived from an auditory-based spectral representation", Proc. 11th Int. Congress Phonetic Sciences, Tallinn, USSR, Paper Se 95.1
(1986), "A computational model for the peripheral auditory system: application to speech recognition research", Proc. IEEE ICASSP, Paper 37.8, pp 1983-1986

Shamma, Shihab A.
(1988), "The acoustic features of speech sounds in a model of auditory processing: vowels and voiceless fricatives", Journal of phonetics, 16, pp 77-91

Stevens, K. N.
(1989), "On the quantal nature of speech", Journal of Phonetics, 17, pp 3-45

Syrdal, Ann K.; Gopal, H. S.
(1986), "A perceptual model of vowel recognition based on the auditory representation of American English vowels", J. Acoust. Soc. Am., 79 (4), pp 1086-1100

Terhardt, Ernst
(1987), "Psychophysics of audio signal processing and the role of pitch in speech"
    in: Schouten, M. E. H. (ed)
        (1987), "The psychophysics of speech perception", Martinus Nijhoff

van Alphen, Paul; Pols, Louis C. W.
(1989), "A real-time FIR -based filterbank, as the acoustic front end of a speech recogniser", European conference on speech communication and technology, Paris

Weintraub, Mitchel
(1987), "Sound separation and auditory perceptual organization"
      in: Schouten, M. E. H. (ed)
         (1987), "The psychophysics of speech perception", Martinus Nijhoff

Williams, Sheila M.
(1989), "STREAMER: A prototype tool for computational modelling of auditory grouping effects", University of Sheffield Departmental Research Report, CS-89-31

Zinovyeva, Nina;
(1987), "Spectrogram reading and expert methods for acoustic-phonetic speech signal decoding", Proc. 11th Int. Congress Phonetic Sciences, Tallinn, USSR, Paper Se 5.4

Zue, V. W.; Lamel, L. F.
(1986), "An expert spectrogram reader: knowledge based approach to speech recognition", Proc. IEEE ICASSP, pp 1193-1196

Chapter 14

Human-computer interface evaluation—
not user friendliness but design for operation

Ernest A. Edmonds

1. HOW CAN HUMAN-COMPUTER INTERFACE BE EVALUATED?

We often hear about human-computer interfaces that are 'user friendly' and, if that is an important characteristic, it is clear that our evaluations should report on that particular issue. But what does 'user friendly' mean? By analogy to the notion of being friendly between people, whatever that might mean precisely, it is not always a desirable feature. For example, I much prefer to use the gruff car mechanic who fixes my car efficiently to the very friendly but, nevertheless, inefficient one. Our important question is, then, how do we evaluate an interface in terms of what matters most, friendly or not?

A brief review of the literature on medical informatics easily demonstrates that the human-computer interface issues are quite complex. For example, when Musen et al (1) constructed a program to allow medical specialists to review cancer treatment plans represented in an expert system, they were, in effect, constructing a knowledge editor. In this work, an interface was required that enabled the specialist to work alone without a knowledge engineer and, although the use of graphics was important, the vital issue was the matching of the structure of the knowledge base with the model of cancer treatment plans as understood by physicians. Clearly, evaluating this is not a trivial task.

The most convenient method of evaluation would be to match a design against a set of guidelines that indicated generic requirements for human-computer interfaces. Unfortunately, the state of the art in applied psychology is not at the stage that makes such guidelines easy to provide. As Maguire [2] points out, advice available in the literature is quite often in conflict. For example Jones [3], Shneiderman [4] and Stewart [5] give different views on the value of non-verbal signals such as flashing characters. It may well be that, by the nature of the subject, it will always be the case that we cannot fully predict quality. Most of the guidelines that we are able to provide relate only to the presentation layer of the interface, covering issues such as text format, the use of upper and lower case and appropriate colour combinations. Thus it is known, for example, that text displayed only in upper case is less readable than text shown in the normal mixed upper and lower case format [6] but it is not known how best to provide a user with a database browsing facility. It is possible to predict some aspects of user reaction to the interface but, for the most part, only ones concerned with presentation issues. Clearly, something more is necessary.

Part of the answer is to recognise the distinctions, referred to below, of presentation, method and function. Many issues of presentation can be addressed either by drawing upon known experimental results or by conducting specific experiments in order to clarify the matter. Even here, however, it is necessary to consider the individual situation of the application. The users might employ some specific 'private' language, for example.

We know something about the methods that are provided for users, for example, menu structures with many levels can easily become confusing. However, the methods to be employed by the user often cannot be seen in a general way. Work practice and environment may have a considerable influence upon their selection. In that sense, the evaluation of the dialogue control aspects of the system must be made in the particular application context in which the system will be employed. Here the concern is with operational requirements, i.e. a failure to consider these early on can lead to very inadequate designs [7].

The functional aspects of the system can only be evaluated clearly in terms of meeting specific application requirements because the domain context determines the characteristics. Thus, no generic solutions exist and even methods are difficult to prescribe. However, it is argued that the user interface is a somewhat complex concept and, if we are to proceed further with this argument we need to address the problem of identifying just what it is that we are evaluating. So, what is the human-computer interface?

2. WHAT IS THE HUMAN-COMPUTER INTERFACE

2.1 Defining the user interface

It is tempting to identify the human-computer interface, or user interface, as that which the user sees, touches and hears. However, we cannot take such a simple view because it is insufficient to only investigate the entities with which the user interacts. For any human-computer consideration to be worthwhile we must also consider just what the user can do with the system and how they can do those things: which methods they can employ. Once we move our attention to users' methods we must look at the full environment in which they work because, almost always, their activity involves a mixture of methods, some of which are not computer based. For example, as I compose this text on a computer, I am reading a number of paper documents, I am annotating one of them with a pencil etc..

Another way of defining the interface is to say that it is everything about the system that the user is aware of including, of-course, the methods available for the operation of the computer. This view is quite satisfactory from an analytic point of view because, given any element, it is always possible to pose the appropriate question and rule it in or out of the interface. It is less helpful in design, however, because in order to take a user centred view in the design process it would be helpful to know which system components we should be concerned with, i.e. we need to be able to predict what it is that the user will be aware of.

It could be argued that the user interface that we are concerned with is, in fact, the complete system and there is some merit in this view. However, by looking at the system from a user interface point of view we find that we must model it in a rather particular way. This is the subject of the next section.

2.2 A model of the user interface

One approach to understanding the nature of the user interface has been pursued by researchers over the last decade [8]. In this view, the user interface is seen as comprising both its external objects, as in the first view, together with a software module within the system in which all the matters of direct concern to the user are represented. This approach offers the prospect of providing a specific object to evaluate and to design, but it must be recognised that there are still some research questions to be answered if such software modules are to be universally identified. In particular, there are still questions about where their boundaries should be drawn and, if there is no generic solution to that question, how in any given case such decisions might be answered. For example, the transformation of a screen image to printer format could be outside the interface and of no concern to the user unless the application was in graphic design where the user might require complete control of it, in which case it would be within the scope of the interface.

It will be helpful to briefly review the standard model of the user interface, often known as the Seeheim model [9]. In this model, the user interface software module is seen to have three layers, each dealing with different aspects of the interface, see figure 1. Naturally, this model is not universally accepted in detail, but it is certainly adequate for our purpose. For more detailed discussions see [10, 11].

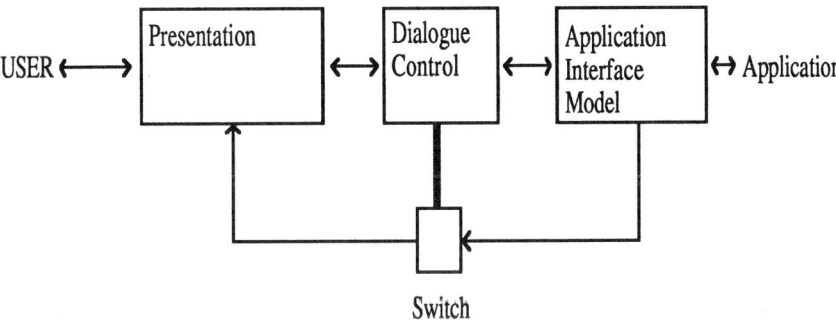

Figure 1

The first and outermost layer is known as the PRESENTATION component. This deals with one-to-one transformations between physical actions and objects, such as key depressions or lines on a screen, and internal logical descriptions of them, such as ASCII codes or screen co-ordinates. Thus, in this component, the issues dealt with are ones such as the particular font and style to be used for the characters displayed on the screen, the choice of function key or the colour of a highlighted word.

At the next level we have DIALOGUE CONTROL. This component handles the processes that the user will go through. It is here that the methods made available to the user are described. Thus, issues such as the choice of structured menus or of command language control will be dealt with in this component. In addition if menus, for example, are chosen then their specific structure will be described here. That is, the items that are included in each menu, the ways that one can move to a particular menu, whether or not one can always go directly to the top level menu etc. are specified.

Finally we have the APPLICATION INTERFACE MODEL. Here the functions of the system are represented at the most abstract level. Thus the abstract objects to be manipulated and the fundamental actions available on them are specified. If, for example, we were dealing with a patient record system for a hospital then two objects that might exist here are 'patient name' and 'patient file' and an action might be to create a file containing a given name. This does not imply, of-course, that the user would perform a single operation in order to achieve such an action. They might, for example, select a sub-menu from which the item "create" was selected before they entered the appropriate name in order to achieve this particular action.

The SWITCH is a mechanism for handling high bandwidth data that is not significant for this discussion.

We should conceive of our enterprise as one of evaluating or designing something identifiable whilst keeping in mind that we cannot guarantee in advance to have identified the complete extent of it. In evaluating the human-computer interface it will be helpful to remember the different aspects of the interface model, because they are of quite different kinds and may be seen to require different approaches. Presentation issues are reasonably well understood and many answers are generic. For example, black text on a white background is known to be the most readable. Beyond psychological results there are considerable skills in the discipline of graphic design that can be brought to bear. Dialogue control is concerned with methods and so must be less universal. It represents the operational requirements. The application interface is quite task specific and represents the functional requirements. It is interesting to note that system designers working in product development seem to find these ideas more attractive than those concerned with exploratory work, such as researchers [12]. The model of the user interface as a separate component in the system is of particular utility in the practical process of interactive system design where our question of evaluation is most critical.

3. HOW CAN HUMAN-COMPUTER INTERFACE QUALITY BE PREDICTED?

Because we are unable to fully predict human behaviour, the collection of empirical evidence, whether from interview, observation or experiment, and the production of evaluations, are vital to the interactive system design process. The possibility of predicting good or reasonable solutions must not, however, be overlooked. Thus, whilst we certainly must iterate both our description of requirements and our design solution as a result of evaluation, nevertheless the better our first attempt the smaller will be the number of iterations required.

As has been indicated above, certain results are available from generically applicable studies that can be used to predict quality. Unfortunately, these are far from complete and apply mostly just to the presentation layer. Quality, as perceived by the user, will be quite as dependent upon the application interface model and the dialogue control module as upon the presentation. That is to say, the methods that the user can employ and the functions available to them are quite as important as issues such as the screen layout. Indeed, the functionality of the system must be seen as a vital matter even when recognising that providing functions without appropriate methods is rather pointless.

At this time, prediction of quality is largely a matter of craft and a number of authors have presented rules, guidelines and checklists that help, even though they cannot fully solve the designer's problems. See for example Shneiderman [13].

Rigorous statistical methods are available for testing the conformance of an interface to well defined user performance criteria [14]. For presentation issues, in particular, we are in fact moving towards international standards. For example, very detailed work is available on the testing of the legability of visual display screens [15]. For consideration of deeper human-computer interface issues, we must consider more complex observation of users at work. One important technique here is the use of video recordings. However, it is necessary to understand the care that needs to be taken in order to obtain useful results from what is bound to be a rather labour intensive evaluation method. Laws and Barber [16] have provided a useful review of video analysis methods.

In order to ensure quality, however, we must look beyond isolated human-computer interface evaluation issues and consider the complete design and development process. Howard and Murray have presented a taxonomy of human-computer interface evaluation techniques and proposed the notion of an evaluation environment, which consists of all of the variables which can reasonably be expected to matter [17]. This is a starting point for considering the process and for keeping clearly in mind when and how evaluation fits into it. The key point of concern is to ensure that evaluation feeds into design and improves the quality of the final outcome.

4. FORMATIVE EVALUATION TOWARDS GOOD DESIGN

So far, we have discussed evaluation in terms of assessing the quality of the interface or predicting its quality given particular design decisions. It is possible, however, to see evaluation in a different light. It can be seen as an activity in design that informs the process in such a way as to lead to good solutions. This is known as formative evaluation [18]. A conventional scientific paradigm can be employed here and that is sometimes known as usability engineering [19]. In formative evaluation, however, no attempt is necessarily made to keep the evaluation process as an independent one, providing an objective assessment of what is being done. Rather, it can perhaps be more usefully seen as an intimate contributing activity tightly bound up with all the other activities in the design and development process. The evaluator is a member of the design team, not a commentator and judge of it [20].

In this view of evaluation, we are looking for methods that allow the evaluation exercises to best help the design process. We are, therefore, least interested of all in methods for assessing the quality of user interfaces within completed products, because then it is too late to change the design. Instead, we are interested in ways of increasing the feedback from empirical studies to the design and development process. It is important to understand that this feedback can cover a number of areas. Most important are:- functional requirements, operational requirements and proposed design solutions.

Perhaps the most interesting and difficult problem is the provision of appropriate feedback and the obtaining of useful guidance during the process of turning initial requirements into a solution. This is, of-course, the process of design and is clearly a mixture of art and science, using the words in the popular sense. However, good practice must involve the following of certain procedures as a norm. In the case of our particular concern, these must deal with the necessary evaluation. However, we must be clear that it is the technological result that is most important and this demands that our approach enables invention [21].

Understanding requirements, and having the opportunity for a real dialogue with users about them, might be seen as a key element in effective formative evaluation. It is in this process that we may see invention occur most naturally. In order to handle the operational requirements it may often be vital to construct prototypes because no other method might enable the end users to articulate their needs. We will come back to this point in a moment.

5. HCI EVALUATION AS DESIGN FOR OPERATION

We have seen that HCI evaluation is a feedback process in design. Because it deals with requirements as well as candidate solutions it must begin very early in the design process. A particular point must be stressed here, however, and that is that we cannot deal with functional requirements in isolation and, having agreed them, then look at the operational issues.

A model of the user interface was described above that contained three elements, presentation, dialogue control and application interface model. These elements correspond to the physical aspects of the system, the methods available to users and to the functions provided.

The distinction between functional requirements, what can be done, and operational requirements, by which methods it can be done, has quite an appeal to it from the designer's point of view, but can it be a clear distinction from a user's point of view? A moment's reflection suggests that it might not be, because, to take the earlier example, whereas we could define one function as 'create a patient file containing a given name', we could alternatively define it as 'create an empty patient file' or 'create a patient file containing name, address, date of birth and doctor's name'. What is to be seen as the functional description of a system is a matter of choice: it is itself a design decision. Thus, it is of most direct interest to the designer, rather than the user, and it is not reasonable to expect the user to firmly agree it early in the design and development process.

The first functional specification of a system may be no more than one outline view of how the system might be. As operational issues are considered that view may change. For example, the requirement to 'create a patient file containing name, address, date of birth and doctor's name' may seem perfectly reasonable, from an administrator's point of view, until one discovers that in practice some people cannot state their date of birth. Even more important is the fact that people can find it hard to articulate what they do without actually doing it [22]. Our understanding of parts of our world and the tasks that we undertake can be bound up with the operations that we perform.

HCI evaluation should be seen as a contribution to the design process that ensures the quality of the resulting system in relation to its use in practice, i.e. HCI evaluation can best be seen as design for operation. Its role begins, therefore at the very start of the design process and continues through to delivery. Its most important activities are interviews and observations in the working environment and the presentation of prototypes. These activities ensure that feedback from users and from the application situation is constantly used to inform design decisions and to adjust and correct requirement statements. That the feedback exists is more important than the provable reliability of any particular experiment or evaluation conducted.

Central to the operation of the system are the methods that the user can employ. The interviews and observations are used together to determine the constraints upon these and to initially agree with users just what they should be. Whilst an initial functional requirement specification will exist at the start of the process, the detailed specification of functions can be drawn out from this analysis and, again, agreed with the users.

Once it is possible to present prototypes for user evaluation, these decisions can be confirmed and the presentation issues can also be agreed. The nature of the prototypes can be quite tentative and incomplete whilst still yielding valuable information, largely because of the fact mentioned above that understanding through action is common [7].

It has been convincingly argued that the theory that is at the base of human-computer interaction is not abstract, but is embodied in artifacts: the interfaces themselves [23]. Thus, the role of prototypes in evaluation is more than just a mechanism for feedback. The fact that the user needs them is not a sign of inadequacy. It is correct to need them, for only in them can the requirement and design ideas be expressed in a concrete form. In this way, we can see that the interface model described above provides a framework for the construction of our design ideas. Indeed, the prototypes that we are bound to provide will then contain clear descriptions of the aspects of the design important to the user. The theory in the artifact will be clearly stated.

6. CONCLUSION

The notion of the user interface and approaches to its evaluation have been briefly discussed and, in particular, the role of evaluation in system design has been explored. The paper has not supported the notion of evaluation as a process of independent validation of user friendliness. Instead, it is suggested that evaluation should be seen as a participating activity within design and development that concerns itself particularly with the issue of the operation of the system when employed in practice. The theory that underlies the evaluation is not of a traditional scientific form, rather it is embodied in the artifact of the system itself and so cannot be dealt with in isolation from the construction of the system.

Acknowledgements

Thanks are due to Linda Candy for valuable discussions and comments on an earlier draft and to the referee who made helpful comments on the first version. The work was partly funded by the ESPRIT2 FOCUS research programme 2620.

References

1. Musen, M.A., Fagon, L.M., Combs, D.M. and Shortliffe, E.H. (1987). Use of a domain model to drive an interative knowledge-editing tool. *International Journal of Man-Machine Studies*, **26**, 105-121.

2. Maguire, M. (1982) An evaluation of published recommendations on the design of man-computer dialogues. *International Journal of Man-Machine Studies*, **16**, 3, 237-262.

3. Jones, P. F. (1978) Four principles of man-computer dialogue. *Computer Aided Design*, **10**, 3 197-202.

4. Shneiderman, B (1979) Human factors experiments in designing interactive systems. *Computer-Institute of Electrical and Electronic Engineers Computer Society*, **12**, 12, 9-19.

5. Stewart, T. F. M. (1976) Displays and the software interface. *Applied Ergonomics*, **7**, 3, 137-146.

6. Tinker, M. A. (1963) *Legibility of print* . Report: Iowa State University.

7. Edmonds, E. A., Candy, L., Slatter, P. and Lunn, S (1989) Issues in the design of expert systems for business. *Expert Systems for Information Management*, **2**, 1, 1-22.

8. Pfaff, G. E. (1985) *User Interface Management Systems* (Springer-Verlag).

9. Green, M. (1985) Report on dialogue specification tools. In [7], 9-20.

10. Edmonds, E.A. (1990). The emergence of the separable user interface. *ICL Technical Journal*. (To appear).

11. Löwgren, J. (1988). History, state and future of user interface management systems. *SIGCHI Bulletin*, **20**, 2, 32-44.

12. Rosson, M. B., Maass, S. and Kellogg, W. A. (1988) The designer as user: building requirements for design tools from design practice. *Communications of the Association for Computing Machinery*, **31**, 11, 1288-1298.

13. Shneiderman, B. (1987) *Designing the User Interface* (Addison-Wesley).

14. Bringham, F.R. (1989). Statistical methods for testing the conformance of products to user performance standards. *Behaviour & Information Technology*, **8**, 4, 279-284.

15. Östberg, 0., Shahnavaz, H. and Stenberg, R. (1989). Legibility testing of visual display screens. *Behaviour & Information Technology*, **8**, 2, 145-183.

16. Laws, J.V. and Barber, P.J. (1989). Video analysis in cognitive ergonomics: a methodological perspective. *Ergonomics*, **32**,11, 1303-1318.

17. Howard, S. and Murray, D. M. (1987) A taxonomy of evaluation techniques for HCI. *Human-Computer Interaction - INTERACT 87*, Bullinger, H. -J. and Shackel, L., editors (North- Holland), 453-459,

18. Scriven, M. (1967) The methodology of evaluation. *Perspectives of Curriculum Evaluation*, Tyler, R., Gagne, R. and Scriven, M, editors (Rand McNally), 39-83.

19. Good, M., Spine, T. M., Whiteside, J. and George, P. (1986) User-derived impact analysis as a tool for usability engineering. *Human Factors in Computing Systems - III*, Mantei, M. and Orbeton, P., editors (North- Holland), 241-246.

20. Candy, L. (1988) Computers and curriculum change: an action research perspective. *Journal of Computer-Aided Learning*, **4**, 203-213.

21. Carroll, J. M. (1989) Feeding the interface eaters. *People and Computers V*, Sutcliffe, A. and Macaulay, L., editors (Cambridge University Press), 35-48.

22. Bainbridge, L. (1981) Verbal reports as evidence of the process operator's knowledge. *Fuzzy Reasoning and its Applications*, Mamdani, E. H. and Gaines, B. R., editors (Academic Press), 343-368.

23. Carroll, J. M. and Campbell, R. L. (1989) Artifacts as psychological theories: the case of human-computer interaction. *Behaviour and Information Technology*, **8**, 4, 247-256.

Chapter 15
Hypermedia information resources: The USHIR Project

Roderick I. Nicolson and Philip Tomlinson

OVERVIEW

Hypermedia are multi-media computer-based programs within which a user can 'browse' at will, rather than being constrained to a limited number of sequential sections, as with traditional books or programs. HyperCard is the major low-cost hypermedia environment and is available on Apple Macintosh computers. Despite its excellent support for prototyping, for screen design, and for user interaction via browsing, HyperCard lacks high level authoring support in terms of program design, debugging and maintenance. Furthermore, it has little capability for answering direct questions unless the question type has been foreseen by the program designer. These limitations (added to problems of bulk and speed) severely reduce the viability of HyperCard for the construction of large scale 'information resource' types of application. This chapter describes USHIR, the University of Sheffield Information Resource, a hybrid Prolog/HyperCard environment in which HyperCard is used for prototyping, and for creation of program 'content' and as the 'foreground' information display medium; whereas the system is driven from a parallel database in Prolog. In addition to its use for answering direct queries and for handling any problem solving requirements the Prolog database is used as a 'master' for generating the HyperCard database thus providing a principled methodology for system maintenance and validation. USHIR combines both hypermedia and IKBS architectures, and so we designate it a prototype IKBH Intelligent Knowledge-Based Hypermedia) system.

Acknowledgement.

Development work on the USHIR project has been supported by the Training Agency under grant T89/23H/0186 to the University of Sheffield.

1. BACKGROUND: HYPERTEXT AND HYPERMEDIA

Hypertext is a term first coined by Nelson in the 60s to refer to *"new forms of writing appearing on computer screens, that will branch or perform at the reader's command. A hypertext is a non-sequential form of writing: only the computer display makes it practical."* In other words, a hypertext is a computer-based information resource which transcends the traditional sequential organisation of textbooks ('flat-text') to provide a variety of links (usually hierarchical) to related information. Recently, with the advent of hardware and software capable of storing and accessing hypertext materials, there has been a surge of commercial and academic interest in hypertexts, with the trend being towards the integration of text, graphics, animation and sound within a single system. The more descriptive term **hypermedia** is now used normally to refer to these multi-media hypertexts.

Hypermedia have been described in apocalyptic terms as the answer to almost any problem involving information storage or communication, including individualised, interactive films; animated archives (vision, sound, text...); general information resources; and even latter-day expert systems. Much of the literature lacks the analytical approach expected in academic circles, but a number of academic journals have now been started (such as *Hypermedia, Academic Computing, Journal of Visual Languages and Computing*) and the advantages and disadvantages of hypermedia are now becoming clearer. A full review of hypermedia is beyond the scope of this chapter — Conklin (1987) gives a clear overview of earlier systems, as do issue 31 of the *Communications of the ACM* (which presents tidied up versions of the 1987 Hypertext 1 conference) and the 1988 Special Issue of BYTE on Hypertext. The key characteristics of hypermedia systems can be summarised under five headings:

Table 1.1   Characteristics of Hypermedia Systems
•   Very flexible, easy to use, information storage system
•   Small Chunks of Information form the basic units of the system. These are usually referred to as **nodes**.
•   Navigation in the system is via user choice of one out of several **links** attached to each node.
•   Dynamic User control In addition to user control over the route, by creating, editing and linking units, users build information structures for their own purposes
•   Multi-media Hypermedia often integrate several different media such as text, vector graphics, bitmapped images, animation, videodisc, CD-ROM, digitised sound etc.

Halasz (1988) has provided a timely analysis of the limitations of early hypermedia systems, identifying seven 'issues' for hypermedia, of which five are summarised in the Table 1.2. Issue 1 is a particularly common problem for hypermedia users and has been graphically described as being 'Lost in Hyperspace'.

For the remainder of this chapter, I shall concentrate on one particular hypermedia environment, HyperCard™ on the Apple Macintosh™. While not a true hypermedia system, in that it has very limited intrinsic support for hierarchical linking between topics, it has become the *de facto* standard for low cost hypermedia by virtue of the well-engineered user interaction capabilities, and excellent support for multi-media applications.

Table 1.2   Current Problems for Hypermedia (Halasz, 1988)
Issue 1. Search and Query in a Hypermedia Network The need for more adaptive search and query facilities, especially in large, unfamiliar, heterogeneously structured databases. *"often users can describe exactly what information they are looking for, but they cannot find it in the network"*
Issue 2. Augmenting the node + link model The need for a more flexible arrangement than cards + links or stacks.
Issue 3. Dealing with changing information 'Problem of premature organisation'. Often it is difficult to restructure a system after the early design choices have been made.
Issue 4. Computation in Hypermedia networks The need for active processing with the system, especially integration of some inference capability.
Issue 5. Versioning The need for better support for software maintenance.

1.1   The Apple HyperCard™ hypermedia environment

HyperCard™ was created by Bill Atkinson of Apple as an affordable hypermedia system for everyone, and was distributed free with all new Apple Macintosh™ micros. It has the astonishing feature that even a computer novice can create attractive 'stacks' with little training, and Atkinson's dream was that this 'stackware' would become freely available to the global village of Macintosh users. An example of HyperCard's wide scope and appeal is that it is packaged with a range of stacks including an online Introduction, online Help, a 'Slide Show', 'Clip Art' (individual line drawings, each organised by a set of key words), ideas for Art, Cards, Backgrounds and Buttons, and application stacks including a Catalogue, an Expense Report, a Sales Report and an integrated Diary/Phone book. Each of these stacks can be accessed via a single card, the Home Card, by one click of the mouse (see figure 1 for a typical Home Card). A key attraction of HyperCard is that each stack can be adapted easily to a user's requirements by using the existing 'design' (the layout, the button scripts, the fields etc.) but 'customising' the 'content' (inserting one's own friends' phone numbers, one's own diary etc.). It may be seen that HyperCard™ is an intuitively appealing environment for 'browsing' (using buttons to navigate around an information source).

The basic unit of information within HyperCard™ is a 'card'. Only one card is active at any time and each card fills the original Macintosh screen (17.5 cm by 12.5 cm). A card has two 'layers', with the 'foreground' layer overlaid on the 'background' layer. Background and foreground can each contain 'buttons' (activated by clicking the mouse within them) and 'fields' (containers for text). A suite of pixel-painting tools is included which may be used to create pictures on either foreground or background. Several cards can share the same background (and its associated graphics, buttons and fields - but not the field contents) thus streamlining the construction of stacks involving a series of cards with the same design but differing content. See figure 2 for examples taken from the HyperCard™ introduction.

Figure 1.   The HyperCard™ Home Stack

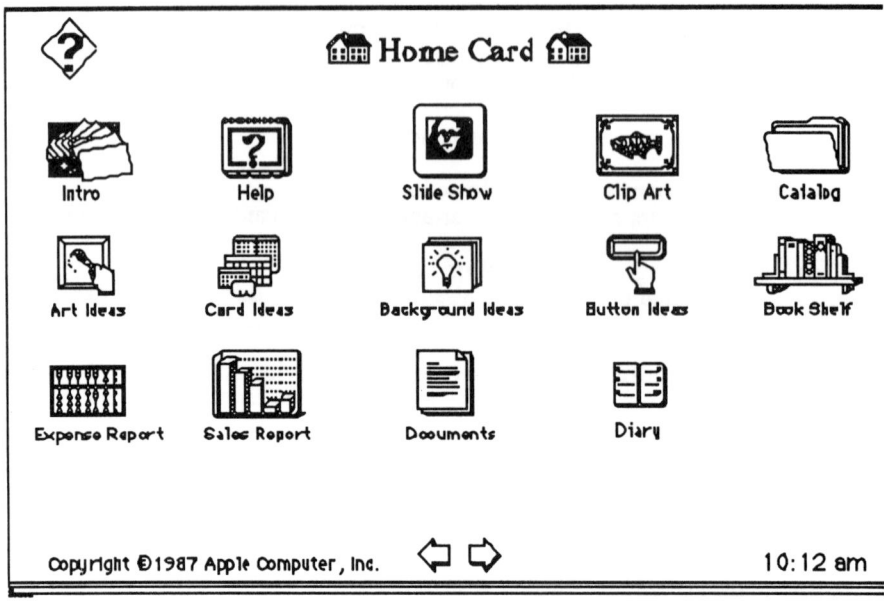

Figure 2.   Four Cards from the HyperCard™ Introduction Stack

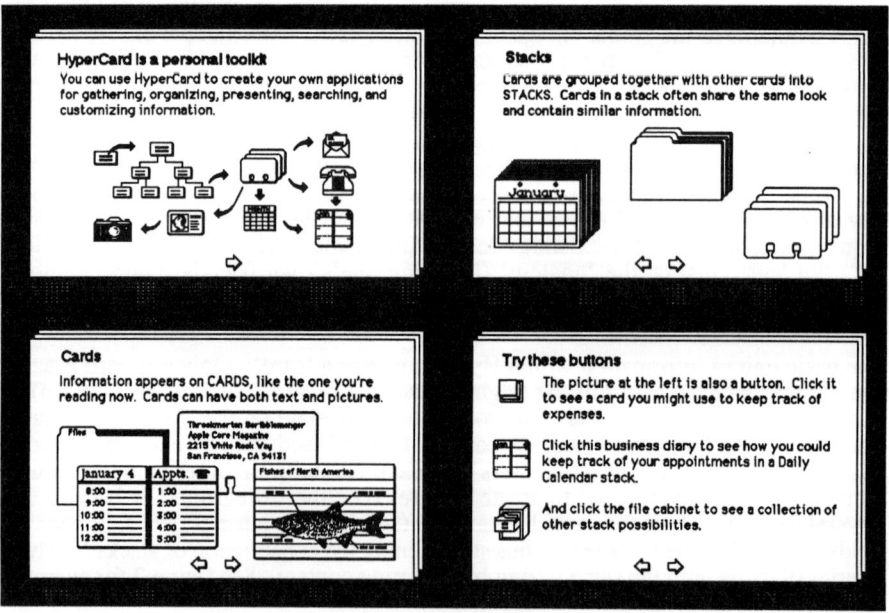

HyperCard™ was designed as an 'object-oriented' environment in which each separate entity or 'object' (ie. card button, card field, background button, background field, background, card, and stack) is essentially self-contained, and it is possible to modify each object independently of all the others. As with true object-oriented systems, objects communicate with each by means of 'messages', and each object may have a handler for any of the possible messages. For instance, when the mouse button is depressed, the message 'mouseDown' is sent to the 'target' (ie. the top object underlying the mouse pointer at the time — usually a card field or card button). If the target object has a mouseDown handler, the actions specified in the handler's script will take place. If not, the mouseDown message is passed in turn to each object in the hierarchy (to the card, then its background, then stack, the Home stack, then HyperCard) until an appropriate handler is encountered. The script of each object comprises the set of message handlers resident within that object.

HyperCard™ derives its intuitive, interactive appeal from the fact that its architecture is specialised to cope with 'events' - when the mouse button is released the message 'mouseUp' is sent ; when a card is 'opened' the message 'openCard' is sent; when the mouse pointer enters a field or button, the message 'mouseEnter' is sent to that object; and even if no event has happened in the previous unit of time (one 'tick' — a sixtieth of a second) a message (idle) is sent. There are 37 built-in system messages of this nature. A consequence of this architecture is that HyperCard™ is ideally suited to notice and to react to events.

An attraction of HyperCard™ for novice users is the ability not just to modify text and enter information, but also to create a new design - say, creating a button which links to another stack, or adding a new background field - without the need for any 'real' programming. Programmers, however, can use the HyperTalk™ language to create a 'script' for any 'object' in their stack. For instance, underlying the Help button on the Home stack (figure 1) will be a handler something like:

```
on mouseUp                  -- when the mouse button is released
  visual effect zoom open   -- a built in visual effect
  go to stack "Help"        -- this opens the Help stack
end mouseUp                 -- terminates the mouseUp message
handler
```

Many buttons will only contain a handler for the mouseUp message, but in addition to handlers for the built-in messages it is possible to write modules such as user-defined functions, as in other high level programming languages. Consequently, complex scripts can be built up and, in effect, there can be a full program contained in each button or field.

From the hypermedia viewpoint, the key feature of HyperCard™ is that it is 'extensible' — it allows 'external routines' to be created which effectively add new commands to the HyperTalk™ language. Many of these routines are available freely via electronic 'Bulletin Boards'. External routines (essentially 'resources' made of compiled code in C or Pascal) may be attached to a stack (or to HyperCard itself) and can be used to cover omissions or inefficiencies in HyperTalk™ or, more interestingly, they can be used to give access to other applications (such as Pascal and C programming languages and multimedia development tools such as a picture scanner, a sound digitiser, or a video frame grabber).

2.   THE UNIVERSITY OF SHEFFIELD HYPERMEDIA INFORMATION RESOURCE

The increasing quantity and diversity of computer-based information sources has led to an emerging need for flexible, online access. Universities are purveyors of information *par excellence* and any university able to provide an online information service to prospective applicants would have a decisive advantage over brochure-based competitors. The background to this chapter is an ongoing project to create a working demonstration system which could be used at conferences and exhibitions as a stand-alone information and publicity resource for the University. Our initial intention was to encode the current University Prospectus within HyperCard so that prospective students would be able to see at a glance what their Departments of interest offered. The system would be enhanced to include relevant pictorial information such as interactive maps of the University layout (at different scales) plus pictures of buildings etc. An additional feature would be the availability of information regarding staff and their research expertise. The resulting resource could be used by different users in different ways - a sixth former considering applying to Sheffield would be able to 'skim' the prospectus, find the relevant departments, check their requirements, look at their location and timetable; an undergraduate student could use it to plan the next year's courses or units; an industrialist looking for a consultant might be able to check quickly on the expertise available, and so on.

The rest of section 2 outlines the background relevant to our requirements analysis for the functionality of USHIR.

2.1   Types of Information Resource

As noted above, there are many different types of hypermedia application. In this chapter, as is appropriate for a chapter on Trends in IT, we shall be concentrating only on information resource hypermedia applications. It may be seen from the following attempt to provide a taxonomy of information resources that this restriction still leaves plenty of scope! Table 2 below provides an informal classification of the types of possible information resource.

Table 2. Types of Information Resource	
1. 'Lookup'	Phone Enquiries What is Rod Nicolson's phone no?
2. 'Lookup + compute'	Train timetables When does the train depart from Sheffield to Liverpool?
3. 'Database query'	Stock control program How many widgets did we sell in August 88?
4. 'Browser'	Encyclopaedia I want to find out about early Etruscan pottery ...
5. 'Expert + Database'	Information Service I want a cheap family hotel near the sea in Whitby. Who is the main manufacturer of widgets in the UK?

It is worth emphasising the difference between applications 1 and 2 above. Telephone numbers are   linked directly to the corresponding person, and so lookup is straightforward. Some train times are also straightforward — trains from Sheffield to London may be accessed directly from a timetable. However, in general, there will be no direct connection between the stations and so it will first be necessary to find a route between the stations, and then to compute the possible connection times. Route finding requires problem solving, and problem solving requires both knowledge and computation — typically beyond the scope of procedural programming. Database queries are different again. Normally a database will be organised sequentially, in terms of labelled records, and in principle the data may be accessed with considerable flexibility by means of queries constructed in a database query language tailored to the database organisation. Arbitrarily complex conjunctions of queries may be constructed, but an expert is needed to construct the query.

Application 4 is a natural for HyperCard, and there are now many HyperCard applications of this nature — many enthusiasts publicise their knowledge by creating and distributing stacks on their own specialities. The closest non-computer analogue is the encyclopaedia, or the catalogue of an art gallery, but hypermedia have significant advantages in terms of interactive browsing (advantages even over the real thing for many museums!)

Application 5 is intended to represent a large civic information service, in which an information officer gives each user a personal service, listening to their question, identifying the question type and the likely source of the answer, and then either saying the answer directly (cf. IR 1, 2, 3); or telling the user where to look for information in the library stacks (cf. IR 4). The quality of this type of service depends critically on the expertise of the information officer and the quality and quantity of information available, but a good civic information service is close to the optimal non-computer information resource, including the advantages, but not the disadvantages of the lower information resources.

2.2   HyperCard Information Resources

Probably the fullest and best-publicised HyperCard information resource in the public domain is the University of Strathclyde 'Glasgow Online' system (eg. Baird and Percival, 1989). Glasgow Online was designed as a tourist resource for the city of Glasgow, and it incorporated the major information then current about the sights, the transport, the hotels, the maps and so on, all accessible via a series of hierarchical menus. The objective of Glasgow Online was that it would be available as a stand-alone resource for use by tourists in a variety of locations, and so an early design decision was made to allow all browsing available via the mouse, with no keyboard input.

It may be seen from the above table, that Glasgow Online provides support primarily of types 1 and 4, with some support for types 2 and 5, but only where the question has been anticipated by the system designer, so that either a button has been created specially for that purpose, or the information may be deduced from the screen displays.

A detailed analysis of its strengths and weaknesses, including informal empirical assessments was undertaken. Findings to emerge were as follows:

(i)   The decision to make all interaction mouse driven allowed the development of a valuable, uniform style of interaction well-suited to undirected browsing, but less satisfactory for direct queries.

(ii)   Although laudable efforts had been made for cross-referencing and indexing, the fixed hierarchical structure inevitably made it difficult to find answers to questions which had not been anticipated at the design stage.

(iii)   The lack of explicit knowledge within HyperCard makes it impossible to use knowledge-based techniques for problem solving (eg. how do I get from A to B?)

(iv)   It seems likely that the lack of authoring support within HyperCard will make both data input and database maintenance both costly and unreliable.

2.3   User Surveys

The completed USHIR system was intended to be of use for several types of user, and so, in a further effort to inform our choice of delivery system, we conducted informal surveys of potential applicants to the University and of University staff.

These pilot surveys indicated that the functionality of a system such as Glasgow Online would be crucially incomplete, in that, though a facility for self-directed browsing was valued, a facility for direct questioning was considered to be much more important. A colleague suggested forcibly that the purpose of an information resource was to make information *accessible*, rather than buried in a find-out-yourself encyclopaedia. For him, the most crucial component of a library information centre was the human front end - the librarian who could either answer a question directly, look up the answer quickly, or tell you where to look for the answer. This view was corroborated by the results of an informal questionnaire administered to potential users. Typical questions from prospective applicants were as follows:

Where is the Students Union?
Where are the Halls of Residence?

Can I do Japanese and Psychology in the second year?
What are the requirements for UCCA entrance in Psychology?
Tell me the interests of staff in the Chemistry Department.
How do I get from {here} to the station?

Staff interests were reflected by questions such as:

What is the syllabus for Cognitive Science?
How many Pure Science students do we have in the first year?
Are there any timetable clashes between second year Psychology and Philosophy?
Who deals with research grant applications?

The insight from research on natural language interfaces (NLI) to complex databases is that a facility for just this sort of natural language query is a crucial capability, allowing arbitrarily complex queries in forms which could not possibly be foreseen by the database creator (see Schwartz, 1987, for a committed espousal of this viewpoint).

A further point to emerge from analysis from experienced users was the need for relatively painless updating of the system — there is little point in constructing a system which has fossilised even before it is complete!

2.4   Requirements Analysis for USHIR

The above considerations led to an outline requirements analysis for USHIR which is tabulated below.

Table 2.2   Outline Requirements

1.   Functionality

Browse
Answer straightforward questions adaptively
Routinely extended, maintained and adapted

2.   Type of User

Untrained
    Applicant
        What are the first year options in Pure Science
    Undergraduate
        What are the second year options for Cog. Science
    'Industrialist'
        Who is the expert on widget technology?

Expert
    Information Officer
        What's the average cost / student in Psychology...
        How many citations did Nicolson receive in 1988
    Registration Staff
        Which courses clash with Cog. Science first year?

2.5   The Need for a Hybrid IKBH environment

The twin requirements of browsing and problem solving to answer direct queries appear to rule out all existing systems! Hypermedia systems are excellent for browsing but poor for direct queries. Knowledge based systems are good for problem solving but have no browsing capability. Consequently we decided to build a prototype based on two parallel systems: a Prolog database which could be used for problem solving and for answering natural language queries; and a linked HyperCard database which supported general browsing.

3. AUTHORING COSTS IN IKBH DEVELOPMENT

Clearly undisciplined construction of a hybrid system of this nature can lead to serious problems in terms of authoring ease, system speed and, especially, system maintenance. On the other hand, use of Prolog gives access to modern authoring and database maintenance techniques which are not available in HyperCard, and so a hybrid system can, in principle, lead to significant improvements in authoring and maintenance costs. The following section provides an overview of the issues involved.

3.1 Requirements for an authoring system

Authoring a large application in a conventional programming language involves at least three stages: preparation, implementation, and maintenance. Each of these stages can be split into substages. A formal software engineering approach - see, for example, Yourdan (1975) - would argue that the preparatory stage should include four logically independent sub-stages: requirements analysis (deciding on the outline system capabilities); prototyping (constructing an implementation which fulfilled the key requirements in outline); specification (a full, declarative set of definitions for what the system should [and should not] be capable of doing); and design (a high level, complete, analysis of how the system should satisfy its specification). Following the creation of a full design, it is necessary to implement the design in the appropriate code. The formal approach to software engineering would argue that this should be a trivial process, in that all the necessary work should have been done by the design stage, with a provably correct program derivable almost automatically. For many applications, of course, this is not feasible, and much program development work - stepwise refinement, debugging, documentation etc. takes place at the implementation phase (see Partridge, 1986, for an amusing attack on the formal software engineering approach). Regardless of the approach adopted, it is valuable to distinguish between program logic (the program design) and program content (the text, graphics, screen layouts etc.). For HyperCard, any user is expected to adapt a stack by inserting his/her own content (eg. their friends' addresses for the phone stack) whereas changing the design (eg. by changing the button scripts) is only available at the 'authoring' user level. Modern authoring systems often provide good support for content creation - word processors, graphics processors etc. (see Kearsley, 1982 for an early review), and HyperCard excels in this area. The final (and often overlooked) aspect of authoring is program maintenance. This involves several aspects - dealing with any bugs, updating information (eg. lecturers' names etc. for USHIR), and adding functionality. As one might expect, enhancements to content are often straightforward, but design changes are often almost impossible.

3.2 Authoring in HyperCard: Programming for the People

One of the many impressive features of HyperCard is the beguiling ease with which even an untrained programmer can design a stack which looks professional and works fairly well - programming for the people has arrived! Even HyperTalk - the programming language underlying 'scripting' in HyperCard - appears user-friendly and straightforward. The immediate impact of HyperCard stems from the impressive quality of the screen displays and the ease with which a novice user can navigate around a stack just by use of the mouse. HyperCard is perhaps unrivalled as a browsing medium and the naturalness of user interaction stems from the 'event driven' nature of the underlying design added to the well-established Macintosh user-support environment. Furthermore, there is no doubt that content creation in HyperCard is superb - a range of user-definable fields and buttons plus good built-in painting capabilities, all within a well-integrated environment which allows smooth importing of materials from other applications and peripherals such as scanners.

Conversely, the fact that HyperCard was designed for use by beginners has tended to alienate professional programmers. The ease of prototyping invites the unwary to dive straight into stack creation with little thought as to program specification or design.

Unfortunately, the implicit design choices made initially are very hard to undo, owing to the structural rigidity arising from the stack organisation. Furthermore, small changes are often excessively tedious to implement - even with careful forethought it is often hard to avoid pasting the same change into 20 or more slightly different independent buttons! The complexity of the hierarchical structure, added to the limited program tracing capabilities, plus the difficulty of finding where routines are located, can make HyperCard debugging a very frustrating experience. Even the laudable object-oriented design of HyperTalk causes problems, in that (owing to the fact that mouse-driven events are not parameterised) it always seems necessary to circumvent the clean message passing ideals by inventing global flags to direct program flow. Program maintenance is also a problem. HyperCard does automatic saves, thus immediately replacing the tested original version with a potentially buggy 'modification'. The only answer is to copy the stack immediately before each modification, hopefully maintaining the 'best' version. Unfortunately, this type of operation appears to put an intolerable load on working memory, with the danger of creation of multiple copies, each of which is flawed in some different way! It is not that it is impossible in HyperCard to write code that is designed top-down, that is well-documented, bug-free and easily maintained, it is just that, at present there is little built-in support. Consequently, the costs of development increase quite dramatically with the size of the application.

3.3 Authoring in Prolog: Programming for the Professional

Prolog is of course the major logic programming language and its key attribute is that there is a powerful logic-based inference capability intrinsic to the interpreter. Prolog is a declarative language, and good Prolog programming style concentrates on the *representation* of the problem domain (rather than problem *solution*). Consequently, a Prolog program can often be used to solve a variety of different problems by phrasing suitable queries and relying on the built-in problem solving capability. It has excellent representational power and has been suggested as an ideal specification language. It is a superb language for relational databases, providing a uniform, declarative formalism for coding the data, natural facility for creating rules and semantic links between categories, and a powerful built-in search and inference mechanism to allow easy interrogation of a database. It is also a modern AI language, excellent for representing and reasoning about knowledge, and for allowing such techniques as heuristic reasoning, non-deterministic programming and meta-level programming. Furthermore, it is naturally adapted for the analysis of language - human and computer - and the techniques for interrogating complex Prolog databases using natural language are becoming reasonably well established (see e.g. Pereira and Shieber, 1987 and Alshawi et al, 1988).

Table 3 presents a schematic comparison of the two environments on a scale from 1 to 5 stars on various attributes. In sum, HyperCard excels for rapid prototyping - throwing together a stack which looks superb and gives a feel for how the finished product might be expected to function, but the lack of high level authoring support makes HyperCard increasingly problematic for larger applications. Prolog is almost the opposite of HyperCard in most respects. In early versions support for user interaction or content creation was negligible, as was the ability to interface with other applications. Support for authoring is excellent in terms of specification and design tools, the representational scope is very good, and a Prolog database is very much more than the sum of its individual items in that it can be interrogated automatically. Attempting to browse through a Prolog database is unrewarding — akin to studying a telephone directory — but its capability for direct question answering is excellent.

Table 3. A comparison of Authoring in HyperCard and LPA MacProlog

			HyperCard	Prolog
Scope	Representation	facts	***	*****
		text	****	**
		relations	***	*****
		pictures	****	***
		maps	***	*****
	Structure		**	*****
	Computation		***	*****
	Problem Solving		-	*****
	IKBS capability		-	*****
Author	Prototyping		*****	**
	Logic/Design		**	****
	Implementation		***	***
	Validation		*	***
	Debugging		*	****
	Tools		*	***
	Maintenance	Documentation	**	**
		Debugging	*	***
		Routine Add's	****	****
		Restructuring	*	****
		Portability	-	***
	Content	Text	****	*
		Graphics	****	**
		Screen Layout	*****	*
	Speed		*	***
	Size		*	****
User	Presentation		*****	**
	Interaction	Browse	*****	-
		Foreseen q'ns	*****	*****
		Unforeseen q'ns	-	***
		NL Input	-	****

4. THE PROTOTYPE USHIR SYSTEM

Clearly, then, there is scope for a creative synthesis of HyperCard and Prolog, with HyperCard providing the glamour and Prolog the rigour! The current USHIR prototype uses HyperCard for the initial prototyping of screen layout and for content creation. The HyperCard stacks thus created are then converted to a flat-text Prolog file, where consistency checking occurs, and the HyperCard stacks are then automatically recreated from the Prolog master. User interaction is primarily with the HyperCard front end, but direct questions are passed to the Prolog NLI and answers returned to HyperCard. Records of user interactions are stored automatically.

Maintenance is achieved via updating the Prolog database as necessary and then recreating the HyperCard stacks.

An example of the functionality of the hybrid system is shown in figure 3. This shows the HyperCard display immediately after the user has typed in the query "Show me the route from Psychology to the station". This query is passed to Prolog, which parses it into a database query "find_route('Psychology Department', 'train station')" using context-dependent pattern matching. The Prolog database includes full data about all the roads, the coordinates of al their bends, and all their junctions with other roads. The query is then solved by a bounded breadth first search, which returns a list of the verbal instructions (see the field at the top) and a list of the map coordinates for each segment of the route. These arguments are then passed back to Prolog automatically, using the MacProlog utility da_open('HyperCard'). HyperCard then displays the instructions and also shows the route graphically on the map.

Figure 3.   Knowledge-Based Problem Solving in USHIR

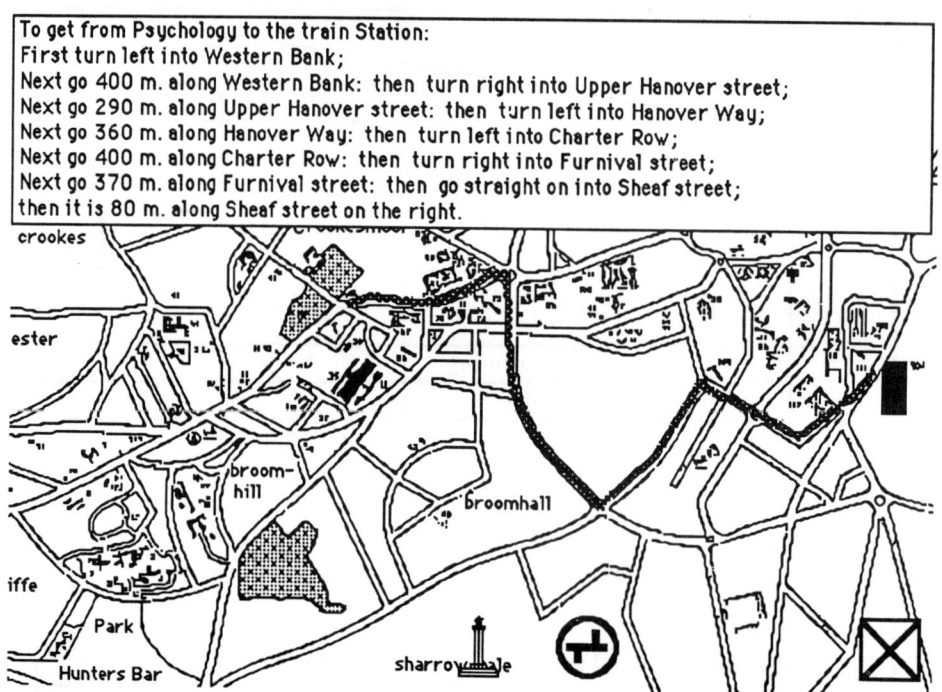

Note that the user may check the location of any road by clicking on the 'Road Junctions' icon at the bottom of the picture, and then selecting the appropriate road from a scrolling alphabetic menu. For instance, selecting "Furnival Street" would result in the display of the road which forms the dog-leg portion near the end of the route to the station.

A similar facility for locating buildings is available by clicking on the 'monument' icon to the left of the road junction icon, which will result in highlighting the building's location on the map. If more information is known about the building, the user is given the opportunity to browse further. For instance, selecting the Psychology Department will give the following picture.

Fig. 4. USHIR Browsing Capability   **Fig. 5. An USHIR Staff card**

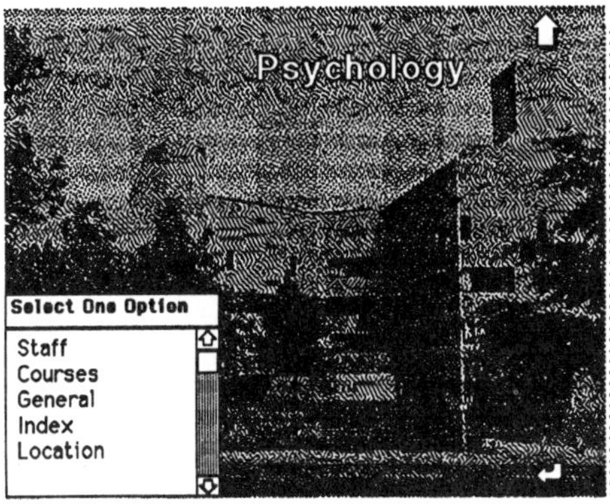

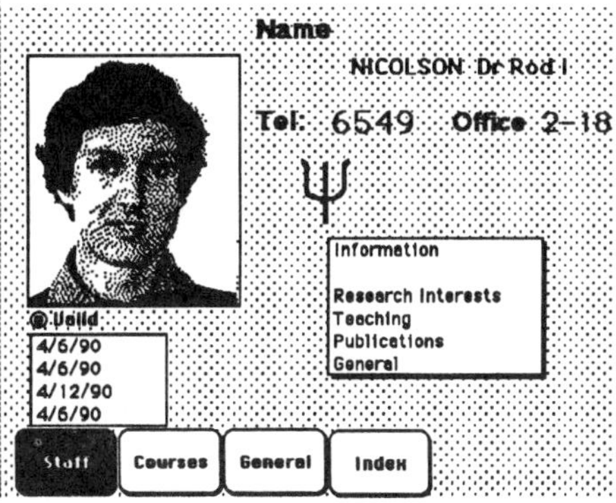

Clicking on one of the options will allow the user to select a staff member (see figure 5). Further information may be obtained by clicking on one of the information options. Note that all these HyperCard cards and stacks may be assembled automatically from flat-text files of text, pictures or sounds, with automatic index and cross-link construction. The 'sell-by' dates on the validity field on the card are used to assist database maintenance, with the dates referring to different aspects of the staff data fields (such as research interests and teaching).

Clicking on 'Courses' or later via 'Teaching' moves the user to the Course Stacks which include full information about courses and timetables. Knowledge-based problem solving capabilities are available for course information. For instance, the user may specify an arbitrary combination of course modules, and these may then be checked for validity by Prolog, and if valid, Prolog will attempt to construct a viable tiimetable, checking for any lecture clashes etc.

At the time of writing (Easter 1990), these capabilities have been demonstrated for a small subset of 8 selected departments within the University. So far, no major problems have been encountered in terms of system design, and the next phase of research involves systematic data collection for all departments within the University, together with enhanced facilities such as access to remote databases, and user evaluations. We believe that the combined IKBH features of smooth browsing together with powerful problem solving are at present unrivalled within this type of information resource, and that this approach will herald the advent of the next generation of hypermedia systems.

5. SUMMARY

1. Prolog can be interfaced with HyperCard to give a very powerful 'Intelligent Knowledge-Based Hypermedia' system.

2. It is possible to streamline the content acquisition and data input stage by systematic use of Prolog and HyperCard

3. It is likely that such a system will be more flexible and adaptable than a naked hypermedia system, thus enhancing the expected life of the system.

4. An IKBH system can significantly decrease the established hypermedia problems of:
   * Lack of Problem Solving Capability
   * 'Lost in HyperSpace'
   * 'Premature Organisation'
   * Versioning, maintenance and adaptation.

REFERENCES

Alshawi H, Carter D.M, Eijck J.Van, Moore R.C, Moran D.B, Pereira F.C.N and Smith A.C. (1988).   Research Programme in Natural Language Processing Report. SRI International, Cambridge, England.

Baird P. and Percival M. (1989). Glasgow Online: Database Development using Apple's HyperCard. In R. Macaleese (ed). *Hypertext: Theory into Practice.* Oxford, Blackwell Scientific.

Conklin, J. (1987). Hypertext: An introduction and survey, *IEEE Computer, 20*, 17-41.

Halasz F. (1988). Reflections on NoteCards: Seven issues for the next generation of hypermedia systems. *Communications of the ACM, 31, 836-852.*

Kearsley, G. (1982). Authoring Systems in computer-based education. *Communications of the ACM, 25,* 429-437.

Nicolson R. I., Scott P.J., and Gardner, P. H. (1988). The Intelligent Authoring of Computer Assisted Learning Software. *Expert Systems, 5,* 302-314.

Partridge D. (1986). *Artificial Intelligence: applications in the future of software engineering.* Ellis Horwood, Chichester.

Pereira F.C.N. and Shieber S. (1987). *Prolog and Natural Language Analysis.* CLSI Lecture Notes, 10, Chicago University Press.

Schwartz S P (1987) *Applied Natural Language Processing.* Petrocelli Books, Princeton, NJ.

Yourdan E. (1975). *Techniques of Program Structure and Design.* Prentice-Hall, Englewood Cliffs, NJ.

Chapter 16

IT and chemical structure databases

M. F. Lynch

1. INTRODUCTION

Chemistry and many of the sciences and technologies which it supports have the unique advantage, in information terms, of having the molecular structure, and particularly its expression as a structure diagram, as a tool for communication. The structure diagram is an unrivalled tool for information management - for writing on the backs of envelopes, on blackboards, for printing in textbooks and papers, and, today, for drawing and display on computer screens in order to keep track of the vast variety of known substances and the host of data associated with each [1-3].

Over 10 million substances are known, both naturally-occurring and synthetically prepared. Over 600,000 new substances are identified and recorded each year. The chemical industry and especially its pharmaceutical and agricultural sectors contribute most significantly to this growth in their continuing search for new products, drugs, pesticides, polymers and biological molecules. Information about substances is needed also by a great variety of people, including health professionals, pharmacists, transport officials, safety workers, etc.

The involvement of Information Technology in the process of chemical research and in the publication and management of the chemical knowledge base is already a mature component of the information industry. Chemical companies are heavily committed to it, and invest heavily for information access and management. In 1984, for instance, Yorke estimated that the cost of introducing a novel drug was between \$50 M and \$200 M [4]. This process involves the preparation and testing of perhaps 10,000 new substances for each product which is successfully marketed. Additionally, the pace of research, together with the requirements for satisfying regulatory measures to ensure safety, mean that the process can take between 8 and 12 years to mature, while the time remaining for which patent protection is available is limited. Any technology which enhances the probability of finding a marketable product at a reduced cost, improves the management of information in the chemical knowledge base, whether proprietary or public domain, or augments the R&D process in any way is thus immediately welcome.

These developments began 30 years ago, and were urgently required because traditional methods, based on chemical names and printed indexes, were quite inadequate for the increased demands occasioned by burgeoning R&D activities. Indeed, applications of Artificial Intelligence were being examined in this context 10 years before the name Expert System was coined and the earliest work on MYCIN published.

In general terms, no factor has had as great an influence on the speed of developments as the microcomputer. User-friendly PC software allows otherwise inexpert chemists to draw structure diagrams on a screen, store them, create chemical papers including high-quality diagrams, search for them as structures or as substructures, model their behaviour, particularly in terms of their structure and physical and biological functions - including especially their interactions with biological macromolecules - or design a synthesis which is likely to be successful. Equally, the visual display of the structures and their relations is vitally important, and in its more elaborate forms involves high resolution colour displays on screens which are more familiar in flight simulators.

Given that the topology of molecules is their most evident feature, and that a close relationship exists between the topology and the physical reality of the molecule, there are ample opportunities for the development of appropriate data structures and algorithms, often based on graph theory, which can lead to interesting or useful processes; hence, applications in chemical information systems are virtually unlimited. Some of the resultant processes are very greedy, so that there is also scope for the introduction of novel computer architectures supporting parallelism.

Today, this sector of the information industry is mature and vibrant. Centralised databases are searched from all round the globe by means of wide-band telecommunications networks. Large databases span many years, and good access methods and good in-house software systems are available for chemical industry. These are often integrated with database management systems for handling associated property or applications data. For the academic researcher in this area of information science, a special advantage is the short time which elapses between the conclusion of good research and its adoption within the industry.

2. STRUCTURE REPRESENTATIONS

We distinguish between two- and three-dimensional representations of molecules. For a great number of substances, only the 2-D structure is known. For a minority of substances, the 3-D structure has been determined or modelled. Increasingly, not only the 3-D relationships between atoms but also the overall molecular shape and a wide variety of geometrical and energetic parameters can be computed and displayed graphically (on both intramolecular and intermolecular bases). These relations are increasingly important for small, low-molecular weight substances in view of our greater understanding of their interactions with biological systems; they are absolutely essential for elucidating and understanding the functions of biological molecules such as proteins and polysaccharides. Indeed, understanding the huge biological macromolecules familiar to the molecular biologist is totally dependent on computational resources of very great magnitude, since the molecules are so large and complex and their interrelations so intricate.

With easier access to a widening range of empirical and theoretical tools, in the fine chemicals industry in particular, the blind search for molecules which evince a particular desired activity and lack undesired side effects has given way increasingly to methods of rational drug design in which IT methods are a primary consideration.

First, an overview of the state-of-the-art, with emphasis on appropriate data structures and algorithms, followed by a more detailed view of some of the areas currently under active research.

3. CLASSICAL STORAGE AND RETRIEVAL FUNCTIONS

Bread-and-butter activities in the chemical information industry and in chemical industry centre on the relatively straightforward functions of recording the structures of substances on which new information becomes available; the substances may be novel or already known. In the public domain, this is undertaken by international information services, of which Chemical Abstracts Service, a branch of the American Chemical Society, is the largest. Since 1965 it has stored records of these substances in its Chemical Substance Registry database, now totalling over 10 M records. These records are keyed to the bibliographic sources in which the substances are cited - papers, monographs, conference proceedings, patents, etc. Other major database producers include the Beilstein Institute with its Handbook, with information dating from over a century ago, now substantially in a database, and International Documentation in Chemistry, both in Germany, and Derwent Publications Ltd., specialising in patent information. The Cambridge Crystallographic Data Centre provides a database of 3-D structures, and software to search it.

Flexible software systems for chemical industry are provided commercially by organisations such as Molecular Design Ltd. in California, ORAC Ltd. at Leeds University, Hampden Data Services in Oxford, and Telesystemes-Questel of Paris.

The data structure used for 2-D substances is a graph description, a tabular compilation showing the nodes of the graph as element symbols for the atoms of the molecule, and the arcs of the graph as bonds of some order (e.g., single, double, triple); if necessary, the orientation in the plane of certain bonds can provide 2 1/2 D information. The standard representation is known as a connection table; for each non-hydrogen atom in a substance it gives the atom types (with variations such as isotopic mass), connections to other atoms, and the bond type, and may also include other details such as charge. For 3-D structures, the coordinates, derived mainly by X-ray and neutron diffraction methods (and also from molecular modelling studies), are also stored, together with cell and symmetry information for the crystal. Some variation exists in the conventions and standards for connection table representations, but software to convert them via a common format known as Standard Molecular Data exists.

In addition to structural details, other information and data, such as abstracts of the source documents, physical and chemical property values or descriptions of the synthesis of molecules, may also be stored. All of these act as keys through which the information may be retrieved. In industry, the software systems are interfaced to proprietary DBMS systems to hold data.

3.1 STRUCTURE AND SUBSTRUCTURE SEARCHES

The first kind of query to occur to a chemist is: 'Is this substance known?'. This can be answered relatively simply by searching the structure of the query against the 10 M substances, resulting in a list of the relevant citations if it is recorded in the database. The second query type, very important for chemists, since structural similarities often imply similar properties, is the substructure search: What molecules contain a given substructure? This poses much more difficult technical problems. In essence, the first query type takes advantage of the fact that regardless of how a given structure diagram is oriented on the page or screen, a unique or canonical description can be generated automatically for it, so that the search reduces to finding that record in a list. Even if the list is long, 10 M plus, there are clever ways of doing this, analogous to hash coding, so that the search is completed in a few seconds and at modest cost.

Substructure search is another matter. Like many graph-matching operations, it belongs to a class of computational problems known to be NP-complete and thus not susceptible to efficient polynomial time algorithms. The search therefore involves a two-stage process; in the first, a rapid screening scan of the entire database is undertaken on the basis of selected characteristics of query and database structures in order to eliminate the vast majority of the structures which cannot possibly contain the query. The choice of such characteristics, essentially, discriminating fragments which occur in the structures, has been the subject of much research, in Sheffield and elsewhere, during the past two decades, in order to minimise the number of candidates passing through to the second stage which is computationally much more demanding [1-3]. (There is scope here for novel architectures to reduce the costs of searching). The second stage then involves a back-tracking search comparing the query graph with each candidate structure.

3.2 SIMILARITY SEARCHING

Additionally, a novel technique has recently been found attractive by many chemists. Substructure search calls for the definition of some common structural elements; a chemist may wish instead to work on the basis of similarities; if he finds an 'interesting' substance, he may wish to see more like it. Similarity searches are now feasible by the application of automatic clustering methods, which operate on the basis of substructure characteristics like those used as screens in substructure searching, to organise databases so as to throw up those substances most like an input structure, and also to classify smaller databases so as to group together similar substances. Both methods are currently being widely adopted [5-6].

3.3 CHEMICAL REACTION SEARCHING

A related area is that of automatic analysis of records of chemical syntheses in order to identify the nature of the changes involved in the underlying reactions. Again, the solution to this problem derives from early Sheffield work [7-9]. A maximal common subgraph (MCS) algorithm compares the structures of reactant and product molecules, and identifies the unchanging parts of the molecules in order to home in on the reaction site and allow detection of the bonds broken and formed during the reaction, with a high degree of accuracy, as illustrated in Figure 1. As a result, some information services now offer facilities for searching databases of chemical reactions on the basis of the changes which the molecules undergo during a reaction, and software and databases for in-house use are available also - ORAC, REACCS and CASREACT are three examples of these.

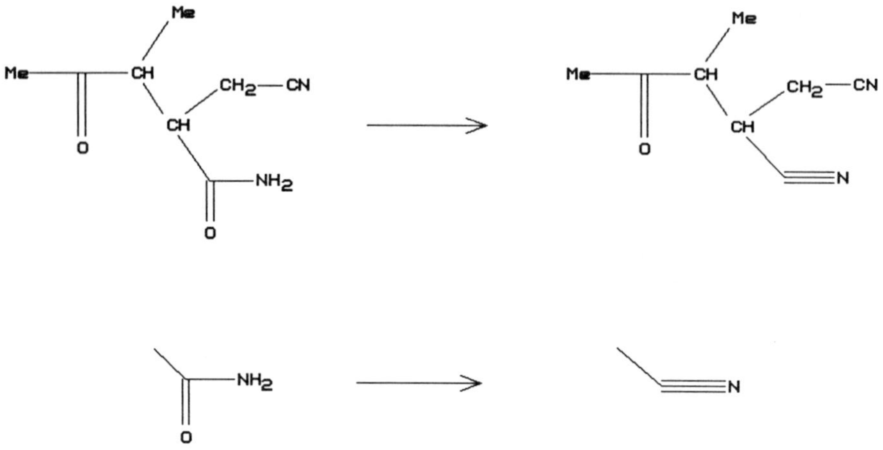

FIGURE 1. Identification of a reaction site.

Facilities such as these are most widely used in industry, both on in-house databases created in the course of research - the PC in the researcher's office is commonplace - but also on the large public service databases, which can also be accessed from these PCs. For the industrial researcher, the property sought is as much the pot of gold as the substance. Hence the widespread use of methods for relating structures and activities.

3.4 QUANTITATIVE STRUCTURE ACTIVITY RELATIONSHIPS (QSAR).

Some of these methods depend on the correlation of physicochemical properties with observed biological activities, but others use explicit structural features identifiable from the molecular graph. Among these methods, substructural analysis depends on characteristics similar to those used for screens in substructure searches; this method provides means of suggesting substances with potential activity and of identifying those features with which activity may be associated [10-11] (Carhart, Adamson). On the other hand, pattern recognition methods try to identify a classification function to distinguish between active and inactive molecules. They thus use a training set of compounds of known activity or inactivity, on the basis of which those whose activity is unknown can similarly be classified [5,12-13] (Kirschner, Stuper).

4. ARTIFICIAL INTELLIGENCE APPLICATIONS

Work on approaches based on artificial intelligence methods was started in the early 1960's by Joshua Lederberg, who conceived the idea of automating structure elucidation. This takes a number of forms, particularly the interpretation of the spectra produced under a variety of conditions by substances of unknown composition. Lederberg studied the interpretation of low resolution mass spectra of organic substances, an area of chemistry known for the demands it makes on experts. The approach to automatic structure elucidation used in the DENDRAL project, and since applied to other analytical methods, was the classic strategy in artificial intelligence - plan, generate and test. Data (in this instance, the peaks in a spectrum which derive from fragmentation of the molecule) are interpreted in terms of probable structural fragments, hypotheses are then formed on the basis of re-assembly of these substructures to form sets of candidate molecules, and these are tested to determine how closely they correspond to the original data. The project, for its time, represented a huge imaginative leap, and led to much progress in understanding the nature of such problems and strategies for Expert System design, but even after three decades of work the competence of the system is still severely limited, partly because of the complexity of the fragmentation process, and partly because of the immensity of the state space in question [14-15].

4.1 SYNTHESIS DESIGN METHODS

Computer-aided synthesis design methods (CASD), on which work also began during the 1960's, have also proved difficult. The synthesis of complex molecules is often seen as the apotheosis of the organic chemist's art. Given some target molecule, often a naturally occurring molecule with potential medicinal properties, the objective of CASD methods is to suggest to the chemist the route by which the synthesis might best be undertaken. It thus depends on automating the perceptive and cognitive functions of the expert chemist as the features of a molecule are analysed to identify routes from simpler starting substances, and the methods of combining them to form the target, possibly in a many-step sequence.

Two broad approaches to synthesis design have been studied. In the first, substructure search methods are used to identify synthetically interesting features of the target molecule, and to identify reactions from a database of standard chemical reactions which might be applied, in a retro-synthetic sense, to effect the synthesis, possibly in multiple stages [16-18]. The reactions are typically described as a language transparent to the expert chemist. Different approaches here either involve the chemist directly in the control process, or work wholly automatically. In the second and more fundamental method, a mathematical theory of constitutional chemistry is employed to predict reaction products from given starting materials, as well as retrosynthetic routes to a given target, with the possibility of more fundamental discoveries than the methods which depend on libraries of known transformations [19,20]. While the methods command much attention in industry, their application is more in the sense of the avoidance of omission rather than the expectation that they will show radically inventive syntheses.

5. 3-D CHEMICAL STRUCTURES

Chemists using 3-D databases are highly dependent on sophisticated graphics displays to reveal their intra- and inter-molecular relations, both statically and dynamically, the latter even involving head-mounted display devices from which the user can gain the experience of room-filling molecules through which he can move at will. These are needed to gain insights into the functions of molecules at atomic dimensions and over time scales as small as a few femtoseconds.

The Cambridge Structural Database is the largest single source of 3-D information on structures, with over 70,000 entries. Full coordinate as well as topological information is provided, so that recently developed methods for 3-D substructure search can now be applied. This is clearly a more demanding task than that of 2-D search, and is generally couched in terms of the distances of atoms from one another, which is of great importance in searches for pharmacophores, for instance. Pharmacophores are configurations of atoms in space which are known to be associated with certain biological properties. The implication of such searches is that topology is less important than interatomic distance, so that all such distances need to be taken into account. The 3-D structure now has to be treated as a complete graph, that is, all atom-atom distances, rather than just those pairs of atoms which are adjacent because of chemical bonding, need to be considered. Here again, a multi-stage search method is invoked, the first stage using summary characteristics of atom-atom pairs and their distances as a screening method, the second stage involving a distance search which involves computation of exact interatomic distances, with a geometric search being performed on the remaining set of candidate molecules. Thus, Figure 2 illustrates the result of a search for the adrenergic pharmacophore, comprising the carbon, nitrogen and oxygen atoms at the specified distances in the epinephrine molecule.

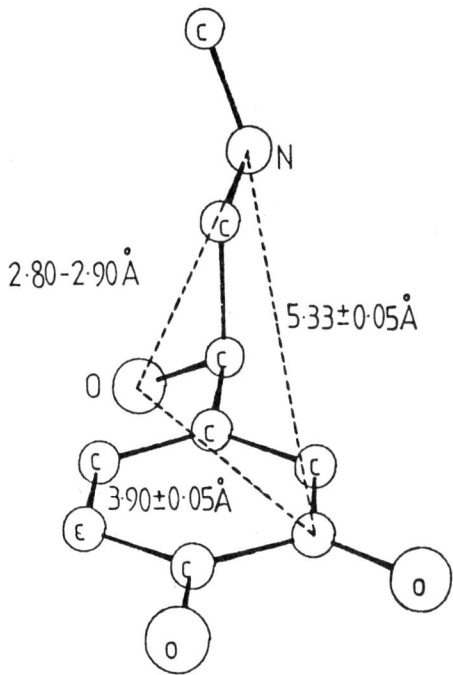

Figure 2. Identification of the adrenergic pharmacophore in the epinephrine molecule.

The second major application area of 3-D search is in the field of protein chemistry. Here, far fewer individual proteins are known in detail – some hundreds at most, within the Protein Data Bank, for instance – but their individual size is immense, often involving many hundreds of amino acid units. The focus of interest lies less in the individual atoms than in the amino acid residues and the patterns into which they fold in order to become biologically active. Despite the complexity of the molecules, a number of methods have been developed to support relatively simple searching of these protein molecules [21].

6. GENERIC CHEMICAL STRUCTURES IN PATENTS

A complex area which has engaged our attention for some years is the vexed issue of chemical patents. When companies seek to protect their intellectual property by patents, they do so not merely for single substances, but for classes of substances which include all those of interest for this purpose, and many more besides, even though the great majority of these may not have been prepared. Patents are legal rather than scientific

documents, and many countries do not examine them for
scientific accuracy; they choose to leave arguments to
their courts.

Patents contain generic chemical structures which define
families of compounds. Generic structures are descriptions
which use class-forming mechanisms, notably substituting
groups which are variable in value or in position, or both.
Combinatorial expansion can readily generate large classes
of substances. Further, these substitutions can be nested
to arbitrary degrees, so that the resulting structures can
be hugely complex. An additional level of complexity is
invoked by the description of substituent values by
intension, that is, by defining the structural features
which allowable groups may have; an instance would be an
alkyl radical with between 2 and 6 carbon atoms, however
arranged, which immediately entails a further 20 radicals
or so. In the limit there may be no constraints, so that a
valid expression is that of a radical which comprises
carbon and hydrogen atoms only. This is clearly an infinite
class, hence some of the problems. An example is shown in
Figure 3.

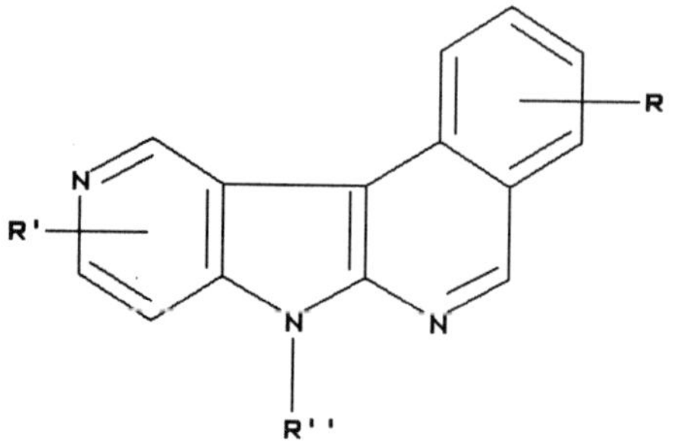

where R and R' are hydrogen, halogen,

1-4 C alkyl, 1-4 C alkoxy, or nitro.

and R'' is 1-4 C alkyl or alkenyl, or

6-12 C cycloalkyl.

Figure 3. An example generic chemical structure.

Our approach to this has been to define a language for
the expression and storage of these generic structures.
GENSAL, the language in question, has a formal basis,
similar to modern programming languages. The model is the
context-free grammar, expressible either as the Backus-Naur
form, or as syntax diagrams, which not merely provides the
means of checking whether expressions in the language are

syntactically correct, but also supports the design of algorithms and procedures both to create a fully explicit internal form of storage and to derive simpler, more readily manipulable and searchable.

Our recent work has centred on the reduced chemical graph, which mirrors the logical and structural features of even the most complex generic structures, but at a reduced level of detail. We have chosen to work with reduced graphs which conflate connected networks of carbon atoms and of hetero-atoms on the one hand, and of ring systems, also characterised by numbers and ranges of atoms, rings and other features. This intermediate representation is a powerful search medium in its own right, despite the lack of detail; it is perhaps an order of magnitude less complex than the fully explicit representation, not least by removing much of the redundancy which derives from many acyclic attachments which may be alternative to one another at some point.

The nodes of the graph are the acyclic or cyclic components; they are complemented by those characteristics which may be derived either from specific partial structures or from those which are described in intensional terms by means of the parameters, and hence they provide a common representation for retrieval. The graphs correctly describe the overall topological relations of the overall generic structure [2-25]. An example of the logical structure expressed in a generic structure, which is represented in the reduced graph, is shown in Figure 4.

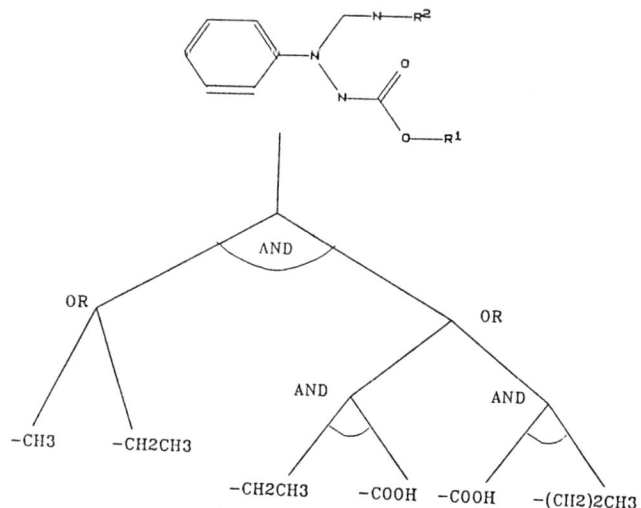

Figure 4. The logical structure of a typical generic structure

7. APPLICATIONS OF PARALLEL COMPUTER ARCHITECTURES

The scale of the computing resources needed for these tasks will be evident. Not surprisingly, there is substantial interest in improving on their cost-effectiveness and speeding them up by invoking parallelism. For the past decade, the substructure search facility known as CAS ONLINE, available for searching the 10 M structures in the Chemical Abstracts Registry System, has been searched by applying database parallelism, i.e., the database is divided over a dozen or so pairs of PDP-11 minicomputers. One machine of the pair searches the screen records, and hands the candidates which pass the screening step to the other machine, which searches the connection table record to establish whether the putative match established by the screening process holds true.

The approaches examined in Sheffield focus on several types of relatively inexpensive devices: networks or farms of communicating microprocessors, notably Transputers, and array processors. The INMOS Transputer can conveniently be used as a LEGO unit in building microprocessor farms, the configuration of which can be chosen to reflect the nature of the task and processes. In our work we have chosen to investigate linear arrays of these devices, known as farms. The AMD Distributed Array Processor (DAP) comprises a 64 x 64 2-D array of simple processing elements, each with a local 2 kbyte store. All of the processors normally act under the control of a master control unit.

Substantial economies in speed have been demonstrated by using farms of INMOS Transputers in a number of application areas. These include substructure searching of 2-D molecules and maximal subgraph identification in 3-D molecules. In the former case, database parallelism similar to that described for the CAS ONLINE is employed, and near-linear speed-up with increasing numbers of processors is experienced. In the latter case, the computationally demanding comparisons of molecular fragments necessary to identify the MCS is distributed across a number of the procesors; here, howeever, the speed-up depends on the similarities between the molecules, being greatest with the most similar pairs of molecules, and vice versa. [26]

The AMD DAP has been used to advantage both in the screening searches which form the first stage of substructure searching, where the parallelism can readily be expressed so that the screens of 4096 molecules can be compared with the query screens at one time, and in clustering substantial sets of small molecules, where sets of up to 4096 can be compared simultaneously. Parallelism clearly has much to offer here for the future, as costs of the devices fall.

8. CONCLUSION

IT offers unrivalled opportunities for the definition of data structures and algorithms for the design of a wide variety of useful applications in handling chemical structure information, opportunities which have been adopted eagerly by industrial chemists.

9. REFERENCES

1. Lipscomb, K J, Lynch, M F and Willett, P, **Chemical Structure Processing,** *in*, Williams, M, *ed.*, **Ann. Rev. Inform. Sci. Technol.**, **24**, 189-238 (1989).

2. Ash, J E, Chubb, P A, Ward, S E, Welford, S M, and Willett, P, **Communication, Storage and Retrieval of Chemical Information,** Chichester, Ellis Horwood, 1985.

3. Warr, W E, (ed.), **Chemical Structures, The International Language of Chemistry,** Berlin, Springer, 1988.

4. Yorke, B A, Pharmaceutical patent protection, *Med. Res. Rev.*, **4** (1), 25-46.

5. Willett, P. **Similarity and Clustering Methods in Chemical Information Systems,** Letchworth, Research Studies Press, 1987.

6. Willett, P, Winterman, V and Bawden, D, Implementation of nearest neighbour searching in an online chemical structure search system, *J. Chem. Inf. Comp. Sci.*, **26**, 36-41 (1986).

7. Lynch, M F and Willett, P, The automatic detection of chemical reaction sites, *J. Chem. Inf. Comp. Sci.*, **18**, 154-159 (1978).

8. McGregor, J J, and Willett, P, Use of a maximal common subgraph algorithm in the automatic identification of the ostensible bond changes occurring in chemical reactions, *J. Chem. Inf. Comp. Sci.*, **21**, 137-140 (1981).

9. Willett, P. (ed.), **Modern Approaches to Chemical Reaction Searching.** Aldershot, Gower, 1986.

10. Carhart, R E, Smith, D E and Venkataraghavan, R, Atom pairs as molecular features in S/A studies, *J. Chem. Inf. Comp. Sci.*, **25**, 64-73 (1985)

11. Adamson, G W, and Bawden D, Substructural analysis techniques for empirical structure-property correlation, *J. Chem. Inf. Comp. Sci.*, **20**, 97-100 (1980).

12. Kirschner, G L and Kowalski, B R, **The Application of Pattern Recognition to Drug Design.** New York, Academic Press, 1979.

13. Stuper, A J and Jurs, P C, ADAPT, A computer system for automated data analysis using pattern recognition techniques, *J. Chem. Inf. Comp. Sci.,* **16,** 99-105 (1976).

14. Gray, N A B, **Computer-Assisted Structure Elucidation,** New York, Wiley Interscience, 1986.

15. Gray, N A B, Artificial intelligence in chemistry, *Anal. Chim. Acta,* 210, 9-32 (1988).

16. Corey, E J, Long, A K and Rubenstein, S D, Computer-assisted analysis in organic synthesis, *Science,* **228,** 408-418 (1985).

17. Wipke, W T and Howe, W J, *eds.,* **Computer-Assisted Organic Synthesis,** ACS Symposium Series No. 61, Washington, American Chemical Society, 1977, 239 pp.

18. Johnson, A P, Computer aids to synthesis planning, *Chemistry in Britain,* **21,** 59-67 (1985).

19. Dugundji, J and Ugi, I, Algebraic model of constitutional chemistry as a basis for chemical computer programs, *Topics in Current Chemistry,* **39,** 19-64 (1973).

20. Gasteiger, J, Rose, P and Saller, H, Multidimensional explorations into chemical reactivity: the reactivity space. *J. Molec. Graphics,* **6,** 87-92 (1988).

21. Lesk, A M, Detection of 3-D patterns of atoms in chemical structures, *Commun. ACM,* **23,** 31 (1979).

22. Barnard, J M, Lynch, M F and Welford, S M, Computer storage and retrieval of generic chemical structures in patents, II, GENSAL, a formal language for the description of generic chemical structures, *J. Chem. Inf. Comp. Sci.,* **21,** 151-161 (1982).

23. Barnard, J M, *ed.,* **Computer Handling of Generic Chemical Structures,** Aldershot, Gower, 1984, 230 pp.

24. Gillet, V J, Downs, G M,, Ling, A, Lynch, M F, Venkataram, P, and Wood, J V, Computer storage and retrieval of generic chemical structures in patents, Part 8, Reduced chemical graphs and their applications in generic chemical structure retrieval, *J. Chem. Inf. Comp. Sci.,* **27,** 126-137 (1987.

25. Lynch, M F, Downs, G M, Gillet, V J, Holliday J, and Dethlefsen, W, **Generic chemical structures in patents - an evaluation of the Sheffield University Research Work,** *in*

Proceedings of the International Chemical Information Conference, Montreux, 1989, Oxford, Infonortics, pp. 161-173.

26. Lynch, M F, Rasmussen, E M, Willett, P, Manson, G A, and Wilson, G A. Chemical database processing using parallel computer hardware, *Biochem. Soc. Trans.,* **17**, 856-858 (1989).

Chapter 17

Artificial intelligence in control

R. Leitch

1. INTRODUCTION

One of the major applications of the significant change of perspective to emerge from the development of Artificial Intelligence methods is in the modelling of physical systems. This modelling activity is a prerequisite to automating many of the industrial control tasks that are currently implemented using conventional methods or indeed are only possible by direct manual control. This enlargement of the methods of system modelling offers the prospect of a significantly extended scope of automation whilst at the same time providing more robust and intelligible systems. This chapter discusses the issues underlying this 'paradigm shift' and reviews one of the most promising techniques to emerge: qualitative simulation of physical systems. Finally, a brief discussion of the potential uses of such techniques is provided.

Conventional control system design methods assume an analytic model of the process to be controlled. This involves making basic suppositions about the behaviour of the system within the anticipated range of operating conditions. Typically, linearity and time-invariance are presumed and differential calculus used to derive a differential/difference equation representation of the system. This is a crucial, and often neglected, part of the design process. Many elaborate design methods necessitate the existence of a well-posed model and proceed from there. However, for many processes, an adequate representation is difficult, if not impossible, to obtain over the complete range of operating conditions. This is certainly true of many plants found in the process industries and furthermore is also true of some so called 'well-defined' processes. In practice, even if a process is amenable to mathematical solution, the time and effort required to extract the model coupled with the shortage and expense of the necessary expertise combine to render the analytical approach non-viable. Designs based upon an ill-posed model can result in performance that is significantly different from that predicted by the theory, resulting in a loss of confidence in the system. As a consequence, a considerable theory/applications gap has developed. Although well recognised by control practitioners, this gap has largely been ignored by control theorists.

In recent years, much research has been directed at developing adaptive control methods capable of identifying, on-line, the unknown parameters of a model with assumed structure. This estimated model then forms the basis of a real-time design procedure to produce the required control action. This approach certainly extends the range of plant operation for analytic methods. However, the performance and convergence of such systems is still heavily dependent upon design assumptions of system order, inherent time delays, etc. The effect of the adaptive loop is to shift the decision making away from the design parameters of the feedback loop to the performance parameters of the adaptive loop. In current jargon, this requires knowledge of the control process (meta-knowledge) rather than knowledge about the process itself.

However, the adaptive solution is directed at processes that are difficult or ill-posed; it is knowledge about the process that is deficient. Sophisticated signal processing techniques can extend the range of acceptable performance of such systems, however, the underlying lack of knowledge about the process remains.

The human understanding of the process and its conventional mathematical description are alien and this results in a lack of an effective man-machine interface. Meaningful explanation of control decisions cannot be provided and an operator is unable to use experiential knowledge to modify the controller. In the adaptive case, this difficulty is compounded by the control 'levers' being at a further level of description removed from the feedback loop.

Based on the above comments it is tempting to conclude that many industrial processes are in fact uncontrollable. This is clearly not the case, however, as many so-called ill-posed systems are adequately, and sometimes easily, controlled using manual techniques.

1.1. Manual Methods

Manual control offers some significant advantages over conventional control methodologies, unfortunately it also has some considerable disadvantages. Paradoxically, it would now seem that the previously perceived weakness of humans is exactly what makes the human approach work. It is the intentional use of generality and vagueness that allows people to model (understand) complex processes and to infer suitable control actions. The inference procedure employed is usually symbolic in nature and is only rarely numeric. That is, the observation and interpretation of the process is made on a qualitative basis, and control decisions achieved by combining qualitative judgements. Imprecision, therefore, is a necessary part of the reasoning process. The penalty of this approach is the loss of uniqueness and optimality for a particular control scheme. However, optimality in the conventional sense is defined with respect to the assumed mathematical model. If this model is ill-posed, as previously argued, sub-optimal performance results.

A disadvantage of manual methods is that they are only applicable to processes with fairly slow response times and are liable to degradation under stress . Psychological factors, such as boredom, tiredness or lack of motivation can also lead to a deterioration in performance. There is, furthermore, a need to experiment in order to learn, consequently the control policy is in continual revision, resulting in a loss of consistency. Contrary to much of the work on Expert Systems, the rationality of human thinking (in the formal sense) can be questioned, e.g. most people experience difficulty with a simple combination of logical negatives. Furthermore, human memory is prone to forgetting and distorting stored information - as a result manual methods are volatile and retraining can be expensive in time and product. Manual methods do work, however, and in some cases work surprisingly well. The goal for Knowledge Based Control Systems is, therefore, to combine the 'vague' symbolic processing capabilities of humans with the speed, capacity and alertness of machines.

2. MODELLING A PHYSICAL SYSTEM

Traditional approaches to modelling attempt to develop as accurate a representation of reality as possible, usually for the purpose of predicting the behaviour. However, every model is necessarily an abstraction of the real world; it is precisely because it is an abstraction that it is useful. The key question is, therefore, what is the most appropriate "level of abstraction" (model) for a given task and amount of knowledge about the system being modelled. This, of course, requires a clear statement of the process of abstraction, a term which is currently used to mean different things. However, before we attempt such a clarification, consider the modelling process outlined in Figure 1.

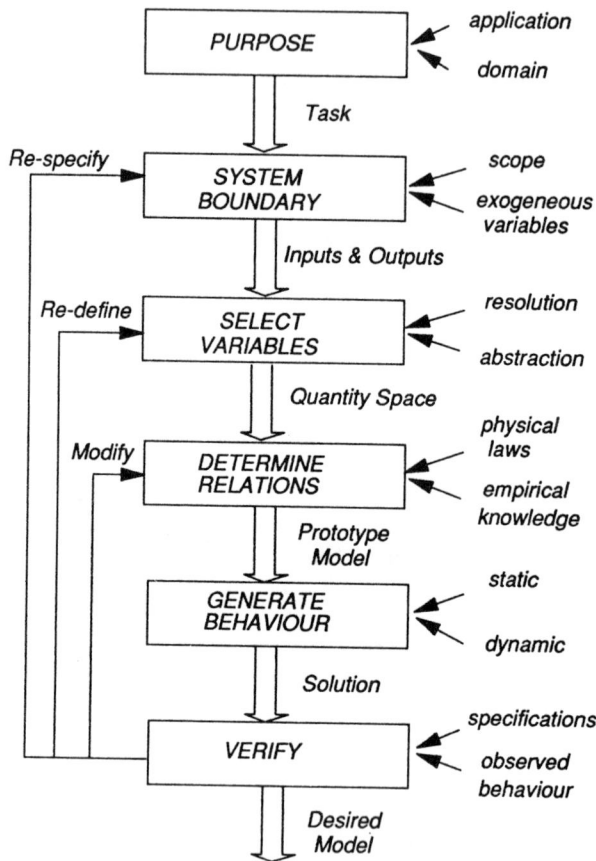

Figure 1   Steps in the Process of Modelling a Physical System

The first step is to clearly identify the specific purpose of the model; a model derived for one purpose is unlikely to be the best for other purposes. In fact, it is the development of A.I. techniques that has allowed a significant extension to the range of purposes for which models are built. For example, fault diagnosis, explanation, training, design etc., are all tasks for which qualitative models of various types have recently been built. Further, this recognition allows the prospect of multiple models, each derived for a specific purpose. The methodology for developing a range of models each suitable for one or more tasks is called *multi-faceted modelling* [Ziegler1984a].

Having established the purpose of the model the next step is to identify the set of phenomena, or attributes, of the physical system that is of interest. In modelling dynamic physical systems the observable phenomena take the form of quantities that vary as a function of time, termed *variables*, for example, velocity, voltage, force and temperature. The modeller must decide which of these variables to represent within the model and which to ignore. This is a crucial step in the modelling process and clearly limits the possible inferences that can be made. All reasoning, or in this case behaviour generation can only be about these variables; if a variable is not represented it cannot be reasoned about. Great care should be taken in selecting these variables so that they represent as wide a description space as possible. In fact, they should be "independent" to ensure that they form a canonical basis from which to generate the behaviour of the physical system. The set of variables is called the *state description*, or *states*, of the system and their value at a particular time is called the *system state*. Selecting the subset of the variables to form the system state essentially draws a boundary between the model and the (unmodelled) environment as shown in Figure 2.

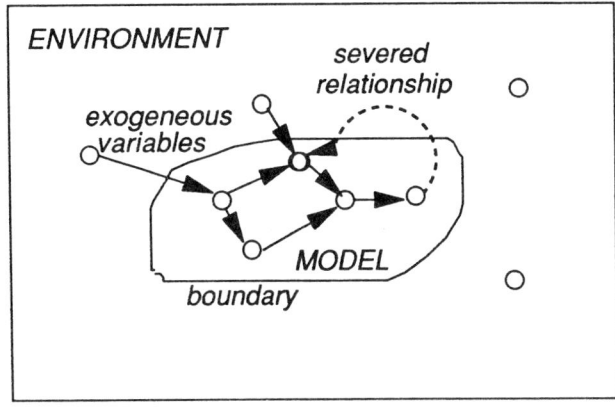

○   *variable*

—▶   *relationship*

Figure 2 Separating a Model from its Environment

The number of variables incorporated within the model determines the *resolution* or granularity of the model, and is a key design assumption. The choice is very dependent upon the task and the precision to which the specification of that task is expressed. In particular, the number of variables required to describe the behaviour of an electronic amplifier depends upon the precision to which a description of the behaviour is required, and hence the purpose of the behavioural description. Clearly, different resolutions may be required for, say, generating the time response and providing an explanation.

Having established the resolution of the model, the relationships between the variables are then determined. In this, two types of variables can be assumed: *endogenous* variables [Iwasaki1986a] where the variables are influenced by others within the model boundary and *exogenous* where variables are influenced by variables outside the model, i.e., in the environment only. In the latter case the relationships shown in Figure 2 cross the model boundary and define those variables as inputs, or primary causes. In theoretical terms, all of the variables effect each other. However, the model boundary can be interpreted as "disconnecting" these variables by neglecting their influence. Apart from the inputs that are directly effected, this formulation is particularly useful when it comes to developing a causal interpretation of the model [Iwasaki1988a].

The relationships between the endogenous variables can be determined empirically, i.e., from experience or from the application of theory in the form of physical laws. For example, the relationship between force and acceleration, as two variables, can be obtained from Newtons law of motion for rigid bodies: the time rate of change of momentum is equal to the sum of the external forces on the body. By definition, momentum is the mass times the velocity, giving that the force is equal to the mass times the time rate of change of the velocity, or acceleration, i.e. f=ma. Mass, in this expression, forms a relationship, given as a parameter, between two variables. It is important to maintain this distinction between parameters and variables, particularly for generating the dynamic behaviour of physical systems. Once the appropriate physical laws have been applied a set of equations representing the constraints or relationships between the selected variables is obtained.

It is now that the developments in Quantitative Reasoning play an important role. The first choice is to decide on the form of representation of the chosen variables. In a single observation, the observed attribute or variable takes on a particular value. To be able to determine possible changes in its value, multiple observations of the same variable must be made. This requires, however, that the individual observations of the variable, be made according to the same observation procedure must be distinguished from each other. This set of values from which the variable takes a particular instance is called the *support set*. It is exactly in the choice of the support set that recent developments in Qualitative Reasoning play an important role. In conventional modelling of dynamic physical systems the support set is taken to be the real-number line. However, in Qualitative Reasoning many other forms of support have been proposed, and is usually termed the *quantity space*. In particular, the 3-valued representation $\{+,0,-\}$ of de Kleer [Kleer1984a] did much to explore the potentiality of this weak representation of value. Many other representations for quantity have since been proposed. These range from open intervals, bounded by landmarks, as in QSIM [Kuipers1986a] to the quantity space of $\{inf,fin,negl,0\}$ used in order-of-magnitude reasoning [Raiman1986a, Weld1988a]. More recently work on fuzzy descriptors of the quantity space has been pursued [Shen1990a, Shen1990b]. The choice of support set leads to fundamentally different models with different properties [Struss1988a]. This allows the possibility of using multiple models each with different supports. Simmons [Simmons1983a] uses a quantitative and qualitative model for geological interpretation and Murthy [Murthy1988a] proposes a scheme for qualitative reasoning at multiple "resolutions". However, this use of the term resolution conflicts with the one used here. We use the term *abstraction* to represent a change in the underlying support set in the sense that as the number of different instances (cardinality) of the support set decreases a more abstract descriptor of the phenomenon results.

The choice of support for the system determines the possible relationships between the individual variables. The support set $\{+,0,-\}$ proposed by de Kleer [Kleer1984a] allows the relationships =, > and < to be used. Similarly, the support set $\{inf,fin,negl,0,-negl,-fin,-inf\}$ proposed by Raiman [Raiman1986a] allows the set of relationship to be extended to include >>, meaning very much greater than (or an order of magnitude larger than) and ~ meaning "close to". What is crucial is that the support set has at least a partial ordering between the elements of the set. The cardinality of the support set can be viewed as a "measure of abstraction in that as the cardinality decreases the number of distinctions, or amount of detail, in representing the variable decreases. In this case, we see that order-of-magnitude reasoning is less abstract than the three-valued qualitative reasoning of de Kleer. The goal of Qualitative Reasoning is, therefore to minimise the cardinality of the support set consistent with achieving the purpose of the model; or, more generally, to utilise *multiple models*, based on different supports, to achieve a given task in the most efficient and effective way. This should not be confused with the multi-faceted modelling discussed earlier. In multiple modelling the purpose, say the prediction of behaviour, stays the same whereas in multi-faceted modelling each model has a different purpose.

The set of variables, or system state, and the operators representing the relationships between the variables forms a *model* of the system. Thus a model M can be represented by an ordered pair M=(S,R), where S denotes the system state and R denotes a relation between the variables composing the system state.

Summarising, five crucial modelling assumptions have been made:

1)   Determine the purpose of the model (task definition);

2)   Select the variables to be represented (resolution);

3)   Choose an appropriate support set for the variables (abstraction);

4)   Determine the source of knowledge, i.e. theoretical or empirical, to be used (source);

5)   Select the appropriate modelling primitives (ontology);

The next step is to solve the equations, see Figure 1. That is, by assuming instances of the support set S, i.e. specific values for some of the variables, to generate the others through the use of the relations R. There are many schemes for solving equations and the major effort thus far in Qualitative Reasoning has been in generating efficient algorithms for doing this [Kuipers1986a, Williams1986a, Wiegand1989a, Davis1987a]. Such algorithms are heavily dependent upon the above four modelling assumptions. The generation of the complete state can either be at a particular instant, *static models*, or the evolution of the state (trajectory) over time, *dynamic models* [Leitch1989a]. To complete the modelling process this behaviour should be compared to the desired behaviour given by the problem specification. If it satisfies the specification a *well-posed* model is obtained. If, on the other hand, it violates the specification, the modelling process must be repeated by modifying one, or more, of the assumptions. In general, this is an iterative process of matching assumptions and verification against the specification, as indicated by the feedback loops of Figure 1. The potential and excitement within Qualitative Reasoning is that by making these assumptions explicit [Falkenhainer1988a], the modelling process itself may be automated, resulting in a significant enlargement in the effectiveness of such models.

The development of qualitative models of physical systems is currently attracting much interest from the Artificial Intelligence research community. It consists of a set of eclectic techniques designed to generate a qualitative description of the behaviour of physical systems from a description of its structure and some initial 'disturbance'. The term "qualitative" has been used in many ways and generally to mean "non- numerical" models. However, the whole field of Artificial Intelligence utilises non-numeric symbolic models. We will, therefore, use the term "qualitative modelling" to mean reasoning about systems characterised by continuously changing variables (of time) by discrete abstractions of the value of such variables. Most of the work on qualitative modelling concerns identifying appropriate 'abstractions' that allows the important distinctions, or landmarks, in the behaviour to be computed. This requires quantisation of the real-number line into a finite set of distinctions; the goal of qualitative modelling research is to identify useful discretisations for particular generic tasks.

Abstract descriptions of state make it possible to have more concise representations of behaviour. However, the generation of the behaviour from such descriptions tends not to produce a *unique* solution. This, of course, is to be expected, as the information required to produce a unique description has been eliminated in the intentional abstraction. Therefore, qualitative models produce ambiguous descriptions of behaviour. However, such ambiguous behaviour can still contain useful information for some tasks. For example, if it is required to predict whether the current state can lead to a critical or faulty condition, it may be sufficient to show that *none* of the possible behaviours leads to a critical situation. It is important to show, therefore, that the set of possible behaviours includes the 'actual' behaviour of the system. In this way, a task can be satisfied even with incomplete descriptions. Whereas in traditional methods, all of the information needs to be available, and it needs to be precisely and uniquely characterised before any inference can be made.

3. QUALITATIVE MODELLING

There exists a diverse set of motivations for people interested in the development of techniques for qualitative modelling, reflecting the various backgrounds, skills and goals of the research workers, In fact, this work is characterised by an unusually large range of contributing disciplines: mathematicians, physicists, engineers, computer scientists, economists, psychologists, cognitive scientists and philosophers, all of which are currently playing a role in developing the various theories or refining the theories to particular application domains. However, a common aspect is that the system to be modelled is somehow too *complex* for the effective or efficient utilisation of traditional approaches. The degree of complexity at which the traditional methods become suspect, of course, depends upon the task for which the model is to be used and also the characteristics of the underlying system. Such differences in motivation have led to very distinct developments of the area, confusing and contradictory terminology, and a mutual lack of understanding and appreciation of the motivation of other groups. This has resulted in significant duplication of effort and in some cases re-discovery of some basic concepts from other disciplines. However, in many cases, it is just this fresh look at old problems without any preconceptions that has generated the new approaches and insights that now form the main techniques within qualitative modelling.

The motivation for the initial work in qualitative reasoning [de Kleer1979] came from the development of an Intelligent Tutoring System for troubleshooting electronic circuits, called Sophie III. There the need was to represent 'simpler' or more abstract models of electronic circuits such that a student could obtain an understanding of the function of the device without requiring a precise description of the detailed behaviour. In this case, a detailed description in the form of a conventional mathematical model is available and reliable. However, a qualitative description should support a simpler computational mechanism than the detailed model (in practice, this has not yet been achieved) and permit a conceptual understanding of the operation to be gained without the clutter of unnecessary detail.

In other cases, however, a reliable mathematical model, usually in terms of numerical differential or difference equations, is either not available or the expense, in time and effort, of generating one is not justified for the particular application the model is to be used for. For these applications, a qualitative model may be all that can be reliably used to generate a behavioural description.

We can, therefore, identify four (non-distinct) motivations for developing qualitative models of physical systems:

(i) To provide simpler computational mechanisms than those already existing, implying that a conventional model already exists, and is well-posed, but that the computation on this model is complex and prohibitive. This is usually the motivation of people working in the domain of astronomy, for example.

(ii) To provide a description for systems where traditional methods are ineffective, either due to lack of knowledge of the system description or the development costs are prohibitive. This is often the case in the chemical or process industries, where chemical reactors, flow processes and thermal systems are more difficult to characterise than say mechanical systems of the aerospace industry or robotics.

(iii) To provide modelling paradigms that accord more closely with our "common sense" intuition of the operation of physical systems. Such descriptions do not require that the modeller, or the person utilising the model, have a knowledge of physics in order to understand the way a system behaves. This motivation is based on the premise that people interact with the physical world based on their experience and intuition and not on an understanding of the 'principles' of physical laws.

(iv) To develop modelling methods based on the principles of Knowledge Based Systems. This includes, representing the model in a declarative format such that the same description can be used for a number of different purposes or tasks, and reasoning with partial, uncertain or incomplete information. Additionally, this motivation includes the goal of providing effective explanation facilities. This aspect is, of course, vitally important for real-time applications where the need to be able to 'justify' a given decision is crucial to its acceptance and verification.

These motivations are not independent and any application domain will exhibit a mixture of these. However, the developers of the qualitative modelling techniques to be discussed usually have one of the above motivations as their primary goal.

Broadly speaking there are three main approaches to qualitative modelling, each providing its own set of representation primitives reflecting a particular ontology of the physical world, and stemming from one of the motivations of the previous section. The first of these approaches, and the most highly developed, is the Qualitative Simulation (QSIM) technique developed by [Kuipers1986a]. This is based on the so-called *constraint centred* ontology, that provides a structural description derived from an abstraction of a conventional differential equation representation. The second approach, and the earliest, utilises the identification of primitive subsystems or components of the systems. This establishes a *component-centred* ontology [de Kleer1984a]. Models are instantiated from a library of generic components and connected together through terminals. The third approach derives from the motivation to represent a "common sense" description of the world. This utilises the notion of a process acting on various parts of the system and provides a *process-centred* view of the world [Forbus 1984].

3.1. Qualitative Simulation

This approach is typified by the Qualitative Simulation (QSIM) algorithm of Ben Kuipers [Kuipers 1986a]. It has been extensively discussed and experimented with due to Kuipers' enlightened policy of distributing his software for a minimal handling charge.

3.1.1. Ontology

This approach starts from a mathematical description of the system in terms of a conventional differential equation model. As such, it makes no attempt to model "common sense" knowledge of the process. Rather, it abstracts a conventional description, derived from formal physical theories, to obtain a 'weaker' description of the system that may be more consistent with the available knowledge, but still based on formal theories. This reliance on mathematical descriptions has led some workers to discount this ontology as providing a method for qualitative (common sense) reasoning. However, if the full range of motivations discussed in the previous section is considered the constraint-based view can be seen as a technique for overcoming limitations in the conventional approach, without disregarding scientific theories.

In fact, the constraints used in QSIM can be obtained by viewing the system as a set of primitive energy storage mechanisms. Each storage mechanism represents a differential relationship between the input and output depending upon whether it has inductive storage and capacitative storage. That is, whether the through variable is proportional to the rate-of-change of the across variable (capacitative storage) or the across variable is proportional to the rate-of-change of the through variable (inductive storage). Analogues of physical systems in most domains exist in terms of these two types of storage. The structural description then comes from interconnecting these primitive energy storage devices. However, this 'pre- processing' of the differential equation is not part of the QSIM approach. The ontology adopted by QSIM is best illustrated by Figure 1 [Kuipers1986a] which clearly shows the relationships between the actual system, the conventional mathematical model and the qualitative description.

3.1.2. Quantity Space

A quantity space is the set of values that a continuous variable can take as the result of its evolution over time. In QSIM these values are termed *landmarks* and are totally ordered points on the real line. Landmarks may be either numeric or symbolic with an ordinal relationship between them. The quantity space is, therefore, an alternating sequence of points and intervals on the real line. A quantity space always includes the landmarks {inf, 0, minf} where inf and minf represent plus and minus infinity respectively. An important feature of the QSIM algorithm is that it can 'create' landmarks as the behaviour evolves (e.g. at the min or max of some variable). This significantly increases the complexity of the algorithm, but allows more distinctions on the behaviour to be generated. Forbus [Forbus1984] terms these as *temporally specific* landmarks and argues that they are only relevant to a particular behaviour, and therefore only relevant to determining properties of that behaviour, e.g. oscillations.

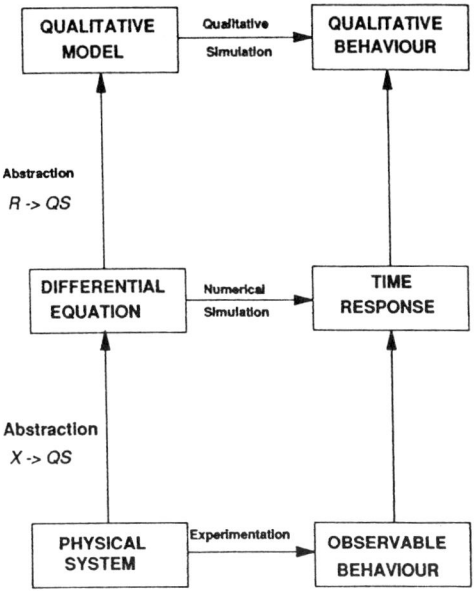

Figure 3 Qualitative Simulation as an Abstraction of a Conventional Model

At a given time the qualitative state QS of a variable V is described by the pair <qval, qdir>. The value *qval* represents the magnitude of the variable and can be a particular landmark or an interval between two landmarks, i.e.

$$QS(v, t) = < qval(v, t), qdir(v, t) >$$

where

$$qval(v, t) = l_j \qquad \text{if } v(t) = l_j \; \varepsilon \; L$$

$$qval = (l_j, l_{j+1}) \qquad \text{if } v(t) \; \varepsilon \; (l_j, l_{j+1})$$

L is the set of landmarks and (l_j, l_{j+1}) represents an open interval.

The value *qdir* represents the direction of change of v with respect to time and can take one of three values {dec, std, inc} standing for decreasing, steady or increasing respectively.

$$qdir\,(v, t) = \begin{cases} \text{inc} & \text{if } v'(t) > 0 \\ \text{std} & \text{if } v'(t) = 0 \\ \text{dec} & \text{if } v'(t) < 0 \end{cases}$$

Therefore, the qualitative state of a variable is represented by two values: a qualitative magnitude of a finite, but variable, resolution and a qualitative derivative with a fixed resolution of three elements.

3.1.2.1. Modelling Primitives

QSIM defines a variety of constraint primitives allowing ordinary differential equations to be "mapped onto" qualitative descriptions. These constraints are in three categories: arithmetic, derivative and functional.

Arithmetic constraint, at a particular time t

$$ADD\ (x,\ y,\ z)\ :\ x(t) + y(t) = z(t)$$

$$MULT\ (x,\ y,\ z)\ :\ x(t) * y(t) = z(t)$$

$$MINUS\ (x,\ y)\ :\ x(t) = -\ y(t)$$

Derivative constraint

$$DERIV\ (x,\ y)\quad :\ x'(t) = y(t)$$

Functional constraints

QSIM provides weak functional constraints between the values of the variables. This allows the partial or lack of detailed knowledge of the relationship between variables to be represented. Specifically, monotonic functional dependencies are allowed, indicating that some variable is monotonically dependent on the rate of change of another:

$$M^+(x,\ y)\ :\ y(t) = H(x(t)) \cap H'(x) > 0$$

$$M_0^+(x,\ y)\ :\ M^+(x,\ y) \cap H(0) = 0$$

$$M^-(x,\ y)\ :\ y(t) = H(x(t)) \cap H'(x) < 0$$

$$M_0^-(x,\ y)\ :\ M^-(x,\ y) \cap H(0) = 0$$

Additionally, the functional dependencies can have *correspondences* specified. A correspondence is a pair of landmarks l_1 and l_2 such that x is l_1 when y is l_2. For example, M_0^+ and M_o^- have a correspondence $<0,\ 0>$. More generally, correspondence can be used to relate a priori known values.

3.1.3. Simulation Algorithm

QSIM takes as input a set of variables (parameters in QSIM terminology), a set of constraints relating the variables, and a set of initial qualitative values for the variables. As output, QSIM produces a tree of states with each path representing a possible behaviour of the system.

The behaviour is represented by a sequence of the state of the system at a set of *distinguished time-points*. That is, those points in the quantity space where each variable takes a distinguished or critical value, e.g. an extremum or landmark. The set of distinguished time-points of a complete system is the union of the distinguished time-points of all the variables comprising the system state description. We can then define the Qualitative State for an interval $(t_i,\ t_{i61})$ where $t_i\ \varepsilon$ finite set of distinguished time-points as

$$QS\ (v,\ t_i,\ t_{i+1}) = QS\ (v,\ t)\quad t\ \varepsilon\ (t_i,\ t_{i+1})$$

The qualitative behaviour of a variable v(t) is, therefore, a sequence of qualitative states at distinguished time-points and the intervals between them.

$$QS(v,\ t_0),\ QS\ (v,\ t_0,\ t_1),\ QS\ (v,\ t_1)\ \ldots\ QS\ (v,\ t_n).$$

Time is, therefore, represented, in QSIM by an alternating sequence of points and open intervals determined by the value of *any* variable changing its qualitative state. In general, the qualitative state of the *system* is the union of the qualitative states of each variable, and represents a complete 'snapshot' or *state* of the system at a distinguished time-point. The simulation algorithm of QSIM differs substantially from conventional simulation routines. From a given set of initial conditions (states), the set of possible next state transitions are determined, by using versions of the intermediate value and mean value theorems based on the assumption of continuous and differential functions as the variables of the system. These form a set of transition 'rules' depending upon whether the system is currently at a distinguished time-point or an open interval between time-points. When transitioning from a point to an interval the set of P-transition shown in Figure 4(a) applies (taken from [Kuipers 1986a]). Similarly, when transitioning from an interval to a time- point the set of I-transitions of Figure 4(b) applies. A variable may be at either a landmark or an interval for each time-point or time-interval. The initial state is always given at a time-point corresponding to a landmark value.

From the table we can see that in some cases the next state is uniquely defined, e.g. P4 and P6: if a function is increasing (decreasing) at a time-point then it must transition into the next region depending upon the direction of change. Similarly, if a variable is between landmarks at a time-point it must continue in the same interval during the following time- point, as the variable cannot attain the endpoint of the internal instantaneously. In other cases, multiple possible next states exist, and it is not possible to discriminate between these on the basis of the propagation rules alone. For example, when a variable is decreasing during an interval there are four possible next states I5, I6, I7 and I9, corresponding to whether it hits a landmark and continues to decrease (I6) or stay steady (I5) or it continues to decrease but between landmarks (I7). The case of the variable becoming steady between landmarks (I9) is catered for by creating a new landmark which splits the open interval into two. This ability of QSIM to dynamically create new landmark values significantly extends the 'resolution' of the variable at the expense of complicating the simulation algorithm.

Once the possible next states are generated the constraints representing the relationships between the variables are applied to further restrict the set of next states. For each constraint, a set of value/derivative pairs is generated by computing the cross product of the possible next states and eliminating those pairs inconsistent with the definition of the constraint. Consistency between constraints, that share a variable, is then checked by using a Waltz filtering algorithm to further eliminate inconsistent states. Complete state descriptions are now generated from the remaining pairs and become the *successor* states i.e. the consistent state transitions. At this stage the set of next states is non-unique and may contain multiple next states from one predecessor states. This ambiguity leads to the generation of 'spurious' behaviours that do not correspond to any feasible behaviour of the actual system. Some of these behaviours can be eliminated by applying *global filters* derived from system theoretic properties of the behaviour or from other (external) sources. Common global filters include checking for no-change or divergence of a variable to infinity. Filters can also be used to check for periodic oscillation by checking for cycles of the state values.

Time Point to Interval

P1	$\langle l_j, std \rangle$	$\langle l_j, std \rangle$
P2	$\langle l_j, std \rangle$	$\langle (l_j, l_{j+1}), inc \rangle$
P3	$\langle l_j, std \rangle$	$\langle (l_{j-1}, l_j), dec \rangle$
P4	$\langle l_j, inc \rangle$	$\langle (l_j, l_{j+1}), inc \rangle$
P5	$\langle (l_j, l_{j+1}), inc \rangle$	$\langle (l_j, l_{j+1}), inc \rangle$
P6	$\langle l_j, dec \rangle$	$\langle (l_{j-1}, l_j), dec \rangle$
P7	$\langle (l_j, l_{j+1}), dec \rangle$	$\langle (l_j, l_{j+1}), dec \rangle$

Time Interval to Point

I1	$\langle l_j, std \rangle$	$\langle l_j, std \rangle$
I2	$\langle (l_j, l_{j+1}), inc \rangle$	$\langle l_{j+1}, std \rangle$
I3	$\langle (l_j, l_{j+1}), inc \rangle$	$\langle l_{j+1}, inc \rangle$
I4	$\langle (l_j, l_{j+1}), inc \rangle$	$\langle (l_j, l_{j+1}), inc \rangle$
I5	$\langle (l_j, l_{j+1}), dec \rangle$	$\langle l_j, std \rangle$
I6	$\langle (l_j, l_{j+1}), dec \rangle$	$\langle l_j, dec \rangle$
I7	$\langle (l_j, l_{j+1}), dec \rangle$	$\langle (l_j, l_{j+1}), dec \rangle$
I8	$\langle (l_j, l_{j+1}), inc \rangle$	$\langle l^*, std \rangle$
I9	$\langle (l_j, l_{j+1}), dec \rangle$	$\langle l^*, std \rangle$

Figure 4 Tables of a) P - Transitions and b) I - Transitions

A lot of work has recently been done to develop further methods of eliminating spurious behaviours. These include: applying global energy constraints i.e. that the system is assumed to be dissipative, non-intersecting constraint which utilises the uniqueness property of continuous systems, and other empirical filters based on parameter correspondences. Other methods of reducing these unwanted behaviours have been proposed. Kuipers suggests using 'temporal abstraction' to produce a model with a reduced set of variables that can be used to constrain the original description. However, the most recent interest has been in developing other representation for the quantity space that can minimise the ambiguity problem at source [Raiman1986a,Weld1988a] rather than eliminating it once it is generated. This is currently the major focus of Qualitative Simulation and will be further discussed in later sections.

The QSIM algorithm has been subjected to a number of mathematical analyses [Kuipers1986a,Struss1988a]. Kuipers has shown that although QSIM produces spurious behaviours i.e. behaviours that do not correspond to any actual behaviour of the system, it does include the 'real' behaviour. Unfortunately, for a realistic size of problem the number of spurious behaviours tends to obscure the real behaviour, making the use of 'problem specific' global filters mandatory for practical use.

4. AUTOMATION SYSTEMS

In many industrial automation applications control systems have been developed, using conventional methods, that adequately control the behaviour of the system within the desired specification. In fact, this theory has had many spectacular successes, e.g. control of space craft, and some lesser known failures, e.g. control of rotary cement kilns. These methods are based on an analytic model of the process to be controlled in terms of real-valued differential or difference equations. However, these models require a precision in representation that in many cases cannot be attained; a more complete discussion in these aspects is given in [Leitch1987a]. When precise numeric models cannot be obtained, and the rotary cement kiln is one such example, an alternative is to use KBS technology to represent the process at a 'level of abstraction' appropriate to the known information and the task in hand. Historically, Fuzzy Logic Controllers (FLC) attempted to do just that. In the terminology proposed herein Fuzzy Logic Control, or more generally rule-based, uses Fuzzy Sets to represent empirical knowledge to perform *regulatory* feedback control. In terms of the primitive tasks this can be performed as a cascade interconnection of the three tasks: interpretation, decision and execution as shown in Figure 5.

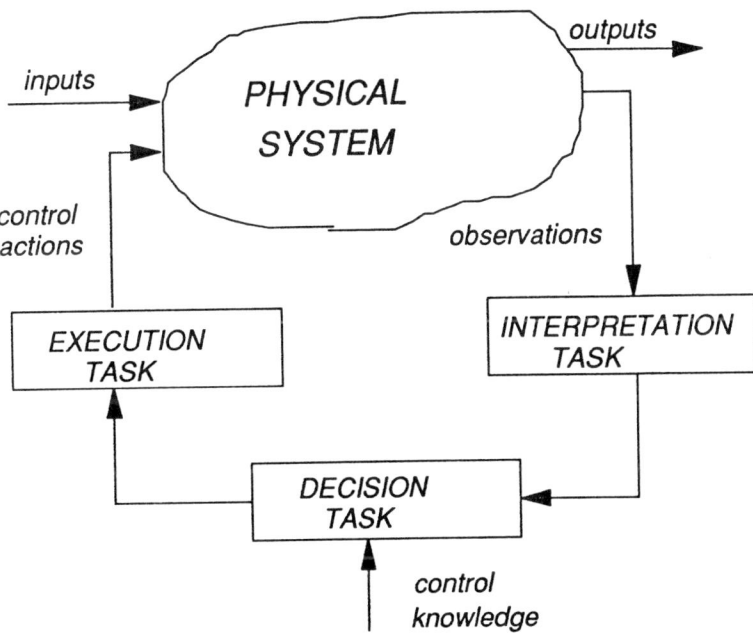

Figure 5 Regulatory Feedback Control System

This approach can be considered as having an *implicit* model of the system to be controlled, represented by its decision procedures (rule-base). It provides an efficient way to represent direct human experience in the form of a set of decision rules. An alternative approach is to have an explicit model based on ontological knowledge. In this case a *model-based control* strategy can be used to predict the next state, thereby allowing the control system to track the behaviour of the process. This approach is much more general and allows for an explicit representation of the desired performance. This is represented by the model, and the prediction task is used to generate the desired behaviour. The desired behaviour is then compared to the actual or observed behaviour. Any discrepency is used by the control system to adjust its control inputs to remove or reduce the error. This is the basic structure of an adaptive system. Such a system can be used for *servo-mechanism* control or profile following where the modelling assumptions are known to be imprecise. In terms of the primitive tasks it can be represented as a cascade interconnection of the interpretation, prediction and execution tasks as shown in Figure 6.

The above discussion reflects the conventional approach to control system design, i.e. based on numerical differential models. However, for KBS control systems, the prediction task can be achieved by using techniques from Qualitative Simulation [Kuipers1986a]. However, all Qualitative Simulation techniques suffer from an inherent ambiguity in the propagation of system states, and, as a consequence, generate spurious behaviours. Although these can be minimised through the use of different representations of value as discussed in section 2, in practice the spurious behaviors still require to be reduced. One way of overcoming this difficulty is to augment the qualitative model, based on ontological knowledge, with empirical knowledge derived from first-hand experience [Leitch1988a].

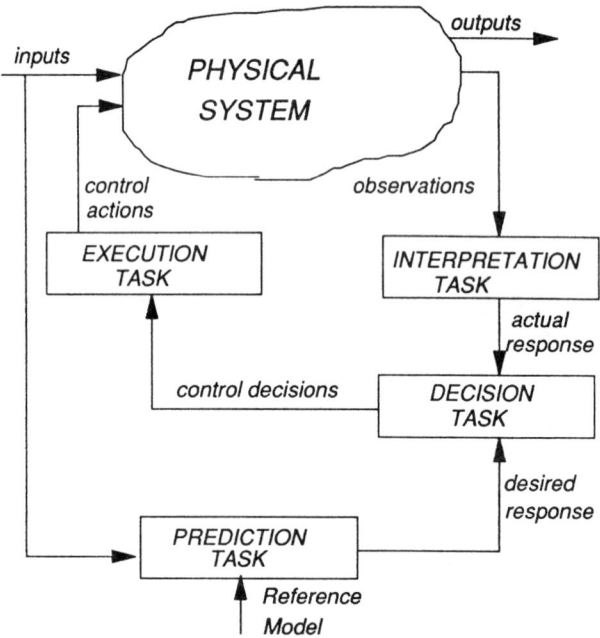

Figure 6 Model-Based Control Systems

4.1. Diagnostic Systems

Diagnostic systems have been the major focus of development for KBSs in industrial environments, and indeed represent a major motivation for this work. However, diagnostic systems can be implemented in a number of fundamentally different ways, corresponding to the choice of problem solving method, and, therefore, can be decomposed into different sets of the primitive tasks.

The technique of heuristic classification [Clancey1985], represents a general problem solving technique based on experiential knowledge. Clancey shows how a number of 'diagnostic systems' can be interpreted within this general method. Similarly, hierarchical classification, developed for medical applications by Chandrasekaren [Chandrasekaren1986] implements a diagnosis system as one of identifying a malfunction (patient case description) as a node in a fault (disease) hierarchy. In this case the fault hierarchy is obtained from pre-compiled knowledge. Such *classification* problem solving methods can be represented in terms of the primitive tasks of interpretation, decision and execution, as shown in Figure 7.

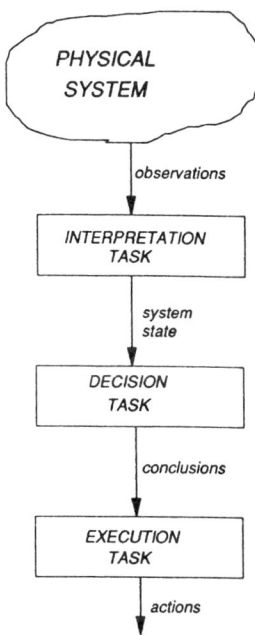

Figure 7   Classification Based Diagnostic Systems

An alternative approach to diagnostic systems, and one that is currently receiving much attention, is *model-based* diagnosis. In this case, an explicit model of the system (to be diagnosed) is represented and used to generate predictions of the state which are matched against the current observed state until there is no discrepancy, or, at least, the discrepancy is minimised. In which case the model generating that matching behaviour represents the fault model and the cause of the malfunction can be deduced. This model-based approach can be viewed as being constructed from three elements. The first, and most crucial, takes possible faults, called fault candidates and evaluates the effect on the system state. This is called *candidate evaluation* or verification and produces an estimate or prediction of the current state. This step clearly corresponds to a Prediction task of the proposed cassification. Secondly, the predicted state is 'matched' against the observed state to determine whether the asserted fault candidate produces a similar state description. This process is called *state matching* and directly corresponds to the Decision task. Finally, a 'task' is required to relate discrepancies in the matching process to possible fault candidates. This is called *candidate generation* and, in a purely 'autonomous' diagnostic system, using explicit models based on physical laws, corresponds to the Identification primitive task. The interconnection of these primitive tasks within the model-based reasoning structure is shown in Figure 8.

The essential difference between general model-based reasoning and classification-based reasoning, is that the former utilises an explicit model that maps system inputs into outputs in a way similar to the operation of the actual physical system. As such these models can support a causal interpretation [Iwasaki1988]. In model-based diagnostic systems the model is used to 'predict' symptoms resulting from hypothesised faults. On the other hand, classification-based diagnostic systems provide mappings from symptoms to fault causes and are fundamentally *acausal*, that is in spite of the term 'causal model' being used for such representations. These systems actually map observed outputs into (possible) inputs, and cannot, therefore be used in a synchronous mode and must, therefore, have all the information available prior to the start of the diagnosis. Model-Based diagnosis, can continuously compare the evolution of the predicted state with the observed state. This aspect is crucial to the development of diagnostic systems for continuous dynamic systems.

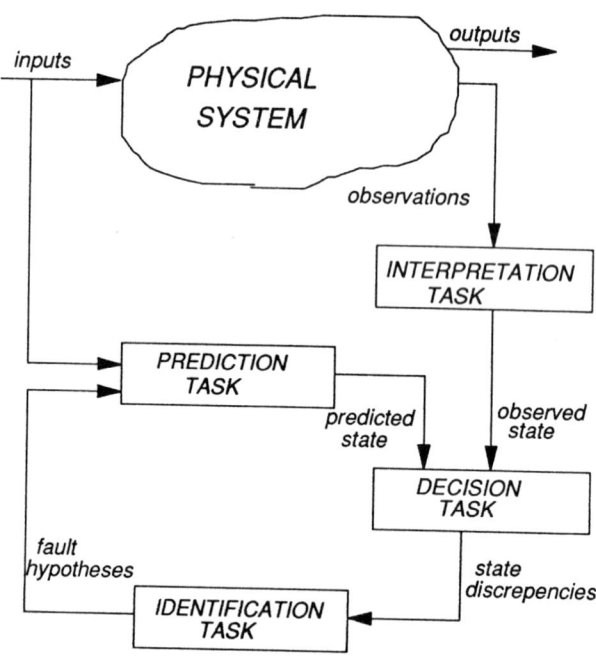

Figure 8   Model-Based Diagnostic Systems

5. CONCLUSION

The most significant impact that Artificial Intelligence methods have on the domain of Industrial Control Systems is a fundamental re-appraisal of the techniques used for modelling a physical system. Specifically, the purpose of the model must be clearly understood and used to choose the most appropriate representation. The use of more abstract representations, than real numbers, is currently being explored under the name Qualitative Modelling. This currently represents a set of eclectic techniques to derive a qualitative description of the behaviour from a structural model. Qualitative Simulation is the most advanced of these techniques and is beginning to find application in control applications. The most important aspect here is the development of model-based reasoning for diagnostic and control applications. This allows the benefits of a formal description of the system through the representation of physical laws together with the use of Artificial Intelligence methods to cope with the inherent uncertainty and incompleteness found in practical industrial problems.

References

Davis1987a.
E. Davis, "Order of Magnitude Reasoning in Qualitative Differential Equations," Tech. Rep. 312, New York University, 1987.

Forbus1984a.
K.D. Forbus, "Qualitative Process Theory," *Artificial Intelligence*, vol. 24, no. 1, pp. 85-168, North-Holland/Elsevier, Amsterdam, 1984.

Iwasaki1986a.
Y. Iwasaki and H.A. Simon, "Causality in Device Behaviour," *Artificial Intelligence*, vol. 29, pp. 33-61, North-Holland/Elsevier, Amsterdam, 1986.

Iwasaki1988a.
Y. Iwasaki, "Causal Ordering in a Mixed Structure," in *Proceedings of the Seventh National Conference on Artificial Intelligence (AAAI-88)*, vol. 1, pp. 313-318, Saint Paul, Minnesota, U.S.A., 1988.

Kleer1984a.
J. de Kleer and J.S. Brown, "A Qualitative Physics Based on Confluences," *Artificial Intelligence*, vol. 24, no. 1, pp. 1-83, North-Holland/Elsevier, Amsterdam, 1984.

Kuipers1986a.
B. Kuipers, "Qualitative Simulation," *Artificial Intelligence*, vol. 29, pp. 289-338, North-Holland/Elsevier, Amsterdam, 1986.

Kuipers1987a.
B. Kuipers, "Abstraction by Time-Scale in Qualitative Simulation," in *Proceedings of the Sixth National Conference on Artificial Intelligence (AAAI-87)*, vol. 2, pp. 621-625, Seattle, Washington, U.S.A., 1987.

Leitch1988a.
R. Leitch and A. Stefanini, "QUIC: a development environment for Knowledge Based Systems in industrial automation," in *Proceedings of Fifth Annual ESPRIT Conference (ESPRIT 88)*, ed. Commission of the European Communities, vol. 1, pp. 674-696, North-Holland, Amsterdam, 1988.

Leitch1987a.
R.R. Leitch, "The Modelling of Complex Dynamic Systems," *IEE Proceedings*, vol. 134/D, no. 3, pp. 245-250, 1987.

Leitch1989a.
R.R. Leitch and M.E. Wiegand, "Temporal Issues in Qualitative Reasoning," in *Proceedings of 5. Osterreichische Artificial-Intelligence-Tagung*, ed. K. Leidlmair, Informatik-Fachberichte 208, pp. 1-13, Springer-Verlag, Berlin, 1989.

Murthy1988a.
S.S. Murthy, "Qualitative Reasoning at Multiple Resolutions," in *Proceedings of the second Qualitative Physics Workshop*, ed. F. Gardin, IBM Paris Scientific Centre, Paris, France, 1988.

Raiman1986a.
O. Raiman, "Order of Magnitude Reasoning," in *Proceedings of the Fifth National Conference on Artificial Intelligence (AAAI-86)*, vol. 1, pp. 100-104, Philadelphia, U.S.A., 1986.

Shen1990a.
Q. Shen and R.R. Leitch, "A Semi-Quantitative Extension to Qualitative Simulation," in *to appear in Proceedings of Special Conference on Second Generation Expert Systems (AVIGNON 90)*, Avignon, 1990.

Shen1990b.
Q. Shen and R.R. Leitch, "Integrating Common-Sense Reasoning and Qualitative Simulation by the Use of Fuzzy Sets," in *to appear in Proceedings of the fourth Qualitative Physics Workshop*, Lugano, 1990.

Simmons1983a.
R.G. Simmons, "The Use of Qualitative and Quantitative Simulations," in *Proceedings of the National Conference on Artificial Intelligence (AAAI-83)*, pp. 364-368, 1983.

Struss1988a.
P. Struss, "Mathematical Aspects of Qualitative Reasoning," *International Journal of Artificial Intelligence in Engineering*, vol. 3, no. 3, pp. 156-169, July 1988.

Weld1988a.
D.S. Weld, "Comparative Analysis," *Artificial Intelligence*, vol. 36, pp. 333-373, North-Holland/Elsevier, Amsterdam, 1988.

Wiegand1989a.
M.E. Wiegand and R.R. Leitch, "A "Predictive Engine" for the Qualitative Simulation of Continuous Dynamic Systems," in *Proceedings of the third Qualitative Physics Workshop*, ed. P. Hayes, Stanford University, Ca., U.S.A., 1989.

Wiegand1989b.
M.E. Wiegand and R.R. Leitch, "A "Predictive Engine" for the Qualitative Simulation of Dynamic Systems," in *Artificial Intelligence in Manufacturing: Proceedings of the fourth International Conference on the Applications of Artificial Intelligence in Engineering, Cambridge, U.K., July 1989*, ed. G. Rzevski, pp. 141-150, Computational Mechanics Publications, Southampton and Springer-Verlag, Berlin, 1989.

Williams1986a.
B.C. Williams, "Doing Time: Putting Qualitative Reasoning on Firmer Ground,"

in *Proceedings of the Fifth National Conference on Artificial Intelligence (AAAI-86)*, vol. 1, pp. 105-112, Philadelphia, U.S.A., 1986.

Zadeh1973a.

L.A. Zadeh, "Outline of a New Approach to the Analysis of Complex Systems and Decision Processes," *IEEE Transactions on Systems, Man, and Cybernetics*, vol. 3, no. 1, pp. 28-44, January 1973.

Ziegler1984a.

B. Ziegler, *Multi-facetted Modelling and Discrete-Event Simulation*, Academic Press, 1984.

Index